The Insider's Guide to
MANCHESTER UNITED

CANDID PROFILES OF EVERY RED DEVIL FROM ROWLEY TO ROONEY

JOHN DOHERTY
WITH IVAN PONTING

EMPIRE
PUBLICATIONS

EMPIRE PUBLICATIONS
1 NEWTON STREET, MANCHESTER M1 1HW
copyright John Doherty & Ivan Ponting 2005

ISBN 1 901 746 41 0

Layout and cover design: Ashley Shaw
The cover includes the name of every player to have appeared for Manchester United in debut order since the war. Those names in bold are featured in John Doherty's all-time United XI (page 350).
Photographs: Colorsport

ACKNOWLEDGEMENTS

FROM JOHN DOHERTY: my wife Barbara, my children and my grandchildren; Paddy Crerand for his generous foreword.

FROM IVAN PONTING: Pat, Rosie and Joe Ponting; designer Ashley Shaw for his imagination and endless patience; the indefatigable Andy Cowie of Colorsport; Frank Wilson, who also supplied photographs; Cliff Butler, 'The Oracle'; and Barbara Doherty, who taught me the full glory of Elephants' Feet.

CONTENTS

INTRODUCTION

I was up to my neck in lovely warm water, being splashed unmercifully by two of my grandchildren, when the idea for this book popped into my head.

Those who know me best will testify to the fact that I have never been short of opinions on football in general, and Manchester United in particular. That's been true, I have to confess, since my treasured days as a Busby Babe back in the 1950s, when I was fortunate enough to win a League Championship medal with the greatest club in the world.

For all that, I had never contemplated committing my thoughts to paper until one gloriously sunny afternoon in a Portugal pool. Before taking the plunge with James and Ben, I had been reading a book about Jimmy Murphy, which I had imagined would be an ideal holiday diversion for an old feller like me who had grown up enjoying the inspirational guidance and friendship of Matt Busby's fierce, passionate but essentially warm-hearted lieutenant.

But as I turned the pages, I was appalled. That's not right, I thought, and neither is that; and as for that, it's utter rubbish! Not being known for my ability to suffer in silence, I held forth at some considerable length until they were well and truly fed up with it. In the end one of the boys called my bluff. 'Grandad, why don't you write a book, and tell the story of United the way it should be told? Then we might get a bit of peace.'

Next my wife, Barbara, took up the cudgels: 'Everybody says you're a decent judge and people seem to respect what you say, so why don't you put your money where your mouth is? Do

THE MATT BUSBY WAY. The Boss passes on his expertise to a group of young players in the mid 1950s. That's me on the left, with Albert Scanlon, Colin Webster, Tony Hawksworth, Paddy Kennedy and Alex Dawson all listening attentively.

what your grandsons tell you and write your own book!'

Probably just to shut them up, I said: 'All right, when I get home I'll do something about it.' Eventually I got round to mentioning it to Ivan Ponting, a writer I'd known for longer than either of us cared to remember, and after putting our heads together we came up with *An Insider's Guide to Manchester United*.

After kicking around various ideas, we decided to tell the story through my impressions of all the players and managers who have served the club since the war because, after all, they are the people who have been the heart and soul of the remarkable institution that means so much to so many millions of people around the globe.

In all due modesty, I think I'm as well placed as anybody to do justice to the task which I set myself that afternoon in the pool at Villamoura. As a little boy in short trousers I watched Matt Busby's first great team in the late 1940s, I signed for the club in 1950 and I have remained in close touch with it ever since.

I've been closely involved with the Manchester United Former Players Association since it was formed 20-odd years ago – I've been chairman for the last five – and I must have watched many hundreds of games at Old Trafford, as well as quite a few at Maine Road, where United played for several years after the war because their own ground had been bombed. So there's been no lack of continuity, and on that basis I feel just as qualified to offer opinions on Wayne Rooney and Ruud van Nistelrooy as I am on John Carey and Charlie Mitten.

In my examination of the 350 footballers and eight managers between these covers, I have not set out to be cruel, or clever, or sarcastic. I might point out that if so-and-so was a player then I can plait sawdust, or maybe offer the observation that somebody else has not won a bowl of soup. Believe me, though, no personal slight is intended. Obviously when I give opinions, some are favourable and some aren't, but the keyword is honesty. At the end of the day, when I put my head on the pillow every night, I'll sleep well, safe in the knowledge that I haven't intentionally slated or belittled someone just for the sake of it.

I have loved football for

ARM IN ARM: I viewed it as a privilege to know Sir Matt for most of my life, to be part of his glorious young team in the 1950s, and to be his friend.

as long as I can remember. It's the most beautiful of all games and, most of the time over the last 60 years, United have been a good, exciting, attacking side who have played it in the right way. Of course, there have been occasional periods when they have left a lot to be desired, but that happens to every club and is all part of the rich tapestry of history.

The Manchester United story has been an unusually compelling one, partly for overwhelmingly tragic reasons. The Red Devils always enjoyed sufficient stature to go down as a great club served by magnificent players, but the Munich disaster of 1958 pushed them into another dimension. The memory of what befell the Busby Babes on that slushy German runway has passed into folklore; the memory of it will never die and we all have to live with it, some being far closer to it than the rest of us.

Although my playing career finished early because of injury, directly and indirectly Manchester United continued to have a huge say in my life. The mere fact that I was a Busby Babe opened doors, certainly in business, and I've always felt it was better to have been an Old Trafford 'has-been' than a 'never-was'. The more I've gone through life, the more I've realised my wonderful good fortune in being a part, however tiny, of the Manchester United story. Indeed, merely being involved with the Former Players Association, raising money for charity and maintaining contact with lifelong friends, has been a rare and precious privilege.

Having reflected on so much that is positive, I feel I must register briefly my concern for the game that I love, which is changing at a bewildering rate of knots. Of course it was wrong in the old days, when clubs treated players like serfs and directors ruled footballers' lives like tinpot dictators. But it's equally outrageous that top players in the 21st century are holding the game to ransom with their astronomical wage demands. Sadly, I can see more and more clubs going down the pan. Most of

IN MY ELEMENT: It was a joy to be part of the Manchester United side that lifted the League title in 1955/56. Back row, left to right: Eddie Colman, Ray Wood, Mark Jones, Bill Foulkes, David Pegg, Duncan Edwards. Front row: Johnny Berry, myself, Roger Byrne, Tommy Taylor, Dennis Viollet. Insets: Ian Greaves, Billy Whelan, Freddie Goodwin, Jeff Whitefoot, Jackie Blanchflower.

them can't afford what they're paying now and the situation is worsening season by season. I'm afraid that oblivion is beckoning for the majority unless there is a revolution in the prevailing attitude. I'm not holding my breath.

Thank God, though, there remain things that money can't buy. For a variety of reasons I wasn't part of the Munich tragedy, yet I've been involved with Manchester United for more than half a century and have experienced untold pleasure through the incomparable game of football; I've been blessed with a wonderful wife, three super kids and a collection of lovely grandchildren. What more can one man ask out of life?

John Doherty,
September 2005.

FOREWORD

Picture by Frank Wilson

Football is a wonderful game of opinions, but it's a fact that some of those opinions are more informed and entertaining than others. John Doherty's happen to be of the incisive variety, invariably honest, often witty and always delivered with his love of the subject utterly apparent.

He's been a Manchester United man for more than half a century, he's a brilliant raconteur with a fantastic memory, and I can't think of anyone better qualified to talk about the hundreds of players to represent the club since the war. Not everyone will agree with every word – that wouldn't do at all! – but it is obvious that he speaks with profound common-sense, and from the heart.

The first time I saw John was in April 1956, when he was playing for United against Celtic at Parkhead in a benefit match for the Leonard Cheshire Foundation, which does so much to help disabled people. I was just a young lad on the Celtic books at that time, and it was a thrill to see the newly-crowned English champions at close quarters.

In fact, United were already my favourite English team because of their great captain, John Carey, who meant a lot to me because of my Irish family background. It helped, too, that one of my other heroes – Jimmy Delaney, who spent his prime with Celtic – operated on United's right wing. As a kid I had listened on somebody else's radio to the 1948 FA Cup Final, in which Matt Busby's first terrific side came from behind to win, and it had made a lasting impression.

It was a long time later, though, that I got to know John well, particularly during the years that we have been involved together in the Manchester United Former Players Association. Quickly I came to realise that he's one of the most interesting men you could imagine keeping company with. At dinners, everyone wants to sit by him because he's such great fun, a born storyteller who seems to know everything about everybody.

When you stop playing, what you miss most is the banter and the relationships with team-mates, but the Association has brought all that back for us. Usually our meetings last ten minutes, then we spend three hours talking about the latest United match, passing opinions on players, managers, everything under the sun. John is at the centre of all that, the leader in all the fun and games, and it would be difficult to imagine the Association without him.

Certainly he is a tremendous judge of a footballer. Although a little while after his retirement as a player – sadly premature because of the knee injuries which plagued him even before he won a title medal on merit in 1956 – he did spend some time scouting professionally, I'm surprised that he never stayed in the game. Sometimes such valuable individuals are lost to football, and it's a crying shame. Perhaps it's because some people might think that a character as strong-minded and knowledgeable as John might be a threat to their own positions; it's hard to fathom.

His views in *The Insider's Guide To Manchester United* are often colourful, but never malicious, and I'd say the readers were in for a treat. Many youngsters don't appreciate all that's gone before to make up the history of their club, and I'd say that John's reflections offer much-needed education and enlightenment. I recommend both the book and, more importantly, the man.

Paddy Crerand,
September 2005.

INDEX OF PLAYERS

IN DEBUT ORDER - ALL STATISTICS CORRECT TO END OF JULY **2005**

1. BERT WHALLEY

BORN	ASHTON-UNDER-LYNE, LANCS 6TH AUGUST 1912
DIED	MUNICH 6TH FEBRUARY 1958
POSITION	WING-HALF OR CENTRAL DEFENDER
JOINED UNITED	MAY 1934 FROM STALYBRIDGE CELTIC
UNITED DEBUT	DONCASTER ROVERS (H) DIV. 2 - 30/11/1935
UNITED FAREWELL	BLACKBURN ROVERS (H) DIV. 1 - 19/04/1947
RETIRED	MAY 1947 UNITED COACHING STAFF

BERT WHALLEY		
COMP.	APPS	GLS
LEAGUE	33	0
FAC	6	0
TOTAL	39	0

What a lovely man. It was a pleasure to have known Bert and I don't think I've ever heard a single soul say a wrong word about him. I first met him in 1949 when I was playing for Manchester Boys and he invited me down to United to start my life at Old Trafford. It is a memory that I still treasure.

He had barely played after the war, having lost what would have been his best years to the conflict, like so many of his generation. But it was clear that he had been a useful performer in his time, a stylish central defender who was comfortable on the ball and invariably had time to move it on without panicking.

He wasn't big for a centre-half, standing perhaps two inches under 6ft, and certainly he didn't go around kicking people, but he carried authority because he had a certain presence about him.

Most of his football was played for United in unofficial wartime competitions, in which he also guested for Oldham, Bolton and Liverpool. When peace resumed he was in his mid-thirties and played only three first-team games before becoming skipper of the reserves. In the end he had to hang up his boots because of an eye injury, and Matt recruited him to the coaching staff.

The hierarchy when I arrived was Matt Busby at the top, with Jimmy Murphy and Bert doing most of the coaching and sharing an office until Bert died at Munich.

He was terrific to all the young players, always ready with a kind word to lift our spirits. A Methodist lay-preacher, he was a quiet man, in contrast to Jimmy, who was more fire-and-brimstone in his approach, likely to singe the hair on the back of your neck.

Some people didn't like Jimmy's methods and they would moan to their mates about it, even though

IRON HAND, VELVET GLOVE: Jimmy Murphy (left) and Bert Whalley, two terrific men who inspired a generation of young Red Devils.

they knew he was rollocking them for all the right reasons, to make them into better players.

Meanwhile Bert offered a buffer zone where we could recover our equilibrium after feeling the Murphy wrath, although he was nobody's fool and people couldn't take advantage of his good nature.

Jeff Whitefoot and I used to play head tennis against him and Murphy, but we could never win because Jimmy used to have his own method of counting and we were never allowed to keep score. When we protested Jimmy would scorch the air and make the perceived injustice seem even worse, while Bert would just disarm us with a gentle smile. That was a perfect illustration of the difference between them but, looking back, I loved them both.

BORN	SOUTH ELMSALL, YORKSHIRE 12TH NOVEMBER 1912
DIED	1980
POSITION	WINGER
JOINED UNITED	JANUARY 1937 FROM WOLVERHAMPTON W.
UNITED DEBUT	SHEFFIELD WEDNESDAY (A) DIV. 1 - 23/01/1937
UNITED FAREWELL	BLACKPOOL (A) DIV. 1 - 19/10/1946
LEFT UNITED FOR	BOLTON WANDERERS JANUARY 1947

BILLY WRIGGLESWORTH		
COMP.	APPS	GLS
LEAGUE	30	8
FAC	7	2
TOTAL	37	10

2. BILLY WRIGGLESWORTH

OTHER CLUBS:
CHESTERFIELD 32/3-34/5 (34, 6);
WOLVERHAMPTON W. 34/5-36/7 (50, 21);
BOLTON W. 46/7-47/8 (13, 1);
SOUTHAMPTON 47/8 (12, 4); READING 48/9 (5, 0).

I remember Billy Wrigglesworth vividly, even though I was only a kid when I watched him playing regularly for United at Maine Road, our headquarters for a few years after the war because Old Trafford had been devastated by Hitler's bombs.

He was a tiny little fellow, maybe about 5ft 4ins, with two good feet and he could go past a defender on either side. Billy was as quick as lightning, he could do tricks for fun and would turn somersaults when he scored a goal. All in all he was a marvellous entertainer, just what the crowds wanted to see.

Sadly, his career was gutted by the war. He was only 24 when he signed for United and two years later he was packed off to do his bit for his country in the forces. When he returned, therefore, he was past his best.

Billy was a bit of a rum character, often trying to take the mickey out of full-backs, perhaps nipping past them and then tapping them on the shoulder. As you mature in the game, you realise that sort of treatment is not very nice. It's always wrong to make fun of your fellow professionals.

Certainly Billy cannot be classed among United's all-time greats, and he was never enough of a team man to be new manager Matt Busby's type of player, but in terms of impressing a young lad in love with football, he was a delight.

3. JOHNNY CAREY

HONOURS:
29 REPUBLIC OF IRELAND CAPS 1937-53.
7 NORTHERN IRELAND CAPS 1946-49.
FOOTBALLER OF THE YEAR 1949.

MANAGER:
BLACKBURN ROVERS 1953-58;
EVERTON 1958-61; LEYTON ORIENT 1961-63;
NOTTINGHAM FOREST 1963-68; BLACKBURN ROVERS 1969-71.

JOHNNY CAREY		
COMP.	APPS	GLS
LEAGUE	306	17
FAC	38	1
OTHERS	2	0
TOTAL	346	18

BORN	DUBLIN 23RD FEBRUARY 1919
DIED	MACCLESFIELD 22ND AUGUST 1995
POSITION	FULL-BACK OR WING-HALF
JOINED UNITED	NOVEMBER 1936 FROM ST. JAMES' GATE, DUBLIN
UNITED DEBUT	SOUTHAMPTON (H) DIV. 2 - 25/09/1937
UNITED HONOURS	DIV. 1 1951/2 DIV. 2 PROMOTION 1937/8 FA CUP 1947/8
UNITED FAREWELL	MIDDLESBROUGH (A) DIV. 1 - 25/04/1953
LEFT UNITED FOR	BLACKBURN ROVERS AUGUST 1953 - MANAGER

John Carey was an amazing footballer, in his own way something of a genius. That's a strong word, not one I would apply to many individuals, but in his case it is appropriate.

He was as fine an all-rounder as any who ever lived, playing whole games for United in ten different positions, including goalkeeper. For example, in only my third appearance, at Chelsea just before Christmas 1952 – an occasion which remains crystal clear in my mind because I scored my first two senior goals that afternoon – regular 'keeper Jack Crompton fractured his cheekbone in a collision with the Pensioners' centre-forward Roy Bentley. With no substitutes allowed in those days, John went in goal and still we won the game.

'He had no pace at all, yet no matter where he turned out, speed was never an issue, his pure ability and shrewdness getting him through every time.'

Even more astonishingly, at Sunderland a couple of months later, Crompton was taken ill shortly before kick-off, so Carey spent the whole 90 minutes between the posts and we drew 2-2.

John was blessed with superb touch with both feet, he was magnificent in the air, and he could chest a ball with almost as much assurance as Manchester City's Roy Paul. Against that, amazingly enough, he had no pace at all, yet no matter where he turned out, speed was never an issue, his pure ability and shrewdness getting him through every time. Indeed, the older he got, the more clever he showed himself to be, always endeavouring to remain goal side of the ball so that he wouldn't be exposed.

His most settled niche was at right-back, and he helped to win the FA Cup in that role in 1948, yet when United lifted the championship four years later he had switched to right-half. Not many people are blessed with so much talent that they

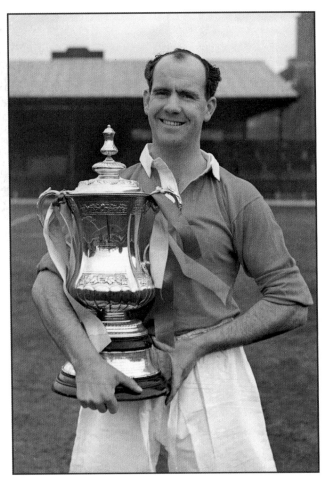

THAT'S MY BABY: Johnny Carey nurses the FA Cup, which he helped to lift in a contest of breathtaking splendour at Wembley in 1948.

can move forward in the team like that; the natural progession is to move back, so this was an unbelievable achievement by the skipper.

In the Coronation Cup in 1953 he played at centre-half, and there were plenty of neutral observers who reckoned he proved himself the best centre-half in Britain. What our regular stopper Allenby Chilton, a fine and vastly underrated stopper, thought about that, I can only guess. But the situation illustrated graphically that having Carey was like having an extra half a dozen players on the staff.

He was known as 'Gentleman John' but in some ways that was a load of rubbish. He pulled more shirts and took more people by putting his foot in than anybody, but he was discreet about it. I remember him saying to me: 'Son, you don't jump up to head a ball face on. You jump up sideways and you protect yourself with your elbow.' Of course, he wasn't doing it to hurt people, merely to look after himself.

John was a genuinely nice man, a quiet character who smoked his pipe and saw football as his job, going to work at Old Trafford as routinely as other men might go to their office.

He was a wise old sage, too. After my senior debut against Middlesbrough, I was in a hurry to get away when a fan asked me to sign a programme. I said: 'Can't stop, got a bus to catch.' On the Monday Carey drew me to one side at training and said he'd seen me refuse to sign. I mentioned my bus but he replied: 'Son, there'll come a time when nobody asks you for your autograph, so sign 'em all while you've got the chance.' That was sound advice. He knew that the supporters are the people who pay your wages, and that you should offer them courtesy.

What was John's best position? I don't think he had one. He could play brilliantly wherever the manager wanted to put him, and his stature in the game was demonstrated by his selection to captain the Rest of Europe against Great Britain shortly after the war. If you are picking the best ever Manchester United side, there has got to be a place for John Carey.

4. JACK ROWLEY

OTHER HONOURS:
6 ENGLAND CAPS 1948-52.

OTHER CLUBS:
BOURNEMOUTH 36/7-37/8 (22, 12);
PLYMOUTH ARGYLE 54/5-56/7 (56, 14).

MANAGER:
PLYMOUTH ARGYLE 1955-60;
OLDHAM ATHLETIC 1960-63;
AJAX OF AMSTERDAM 1963-64; WREXHAM 1966-67;
BRADFORD PARK AVENUE 1967-68; OLDHAM ATHLETIC 1968-69.

JACK ROWLEY		
COMP.	APPS	GLS
LEAGUE	380	182
FAC	42	26
OTHERS	2	3
TOTAL	424	211

BORN	WOLVERHAMPTON 7TH OCTOBER 1920
DIED	SHAW, LANCS 27TH JUNE 1998
POSITION	CENTRE-FORWARD OR WINGER
JOINED UNITED	OCTOBER 1937 FROM BOURNEMOUTH, £3,000
UNITED DEBUT	SHEFFIELD WED. (H) DIV 2 - 23/10/1937
UNITED HONOURS	DIV. 1 1951/2 DIV. 2 PROMOTION 1937/8 FA CUP 1947/8
UNITED FAREWELL	MANCHESTER CITY (A) FAC - 29/01/1955
LEFT UNITED FOR	PLYMOUTH A. - FEB. 1955 PLAYER/MANAGER

Jack Rowley was a fantastic goal-scorer, averaging one strike every two games over his 18-year career at Old Trafford. He won six England caps and played in four different positions for his country, taking every forward berth except outside-right.

I simply cannot believe that he wasn't worth more caps. True, he faced competition from the wonderful Tommy Lawton immediately after the war, and then there was Stan Mortensen and Nat Lofthouse, but that doesn't explain it for me. More telling, I'd say, is that United never had any of their directors on the FA Council which selected the team in those days.

Jack upset a few people in his time; he wasn't the most tactful of characters and he didn't suffer fools at all, let alone

gladly. No one would have called him popular around the club and I suppose you could say he had a bit of a nasty streak in him – but he could play.

He had two great feet, and I mean great for any footballer, not just an old-fashioned centre-forward. His left foot was like a hammer and his right was very nearly as powerful, but his touch was subtle as well. For a spearhead he wasn't the biggest

WHAT THE SMART YOUNG FOOTBALLER WAS WEARING IN THE EARLY 1950s. Kitted out in Manchester United club sweaters are, left to right, back row: Stan Pearson, Johnny Berry, Gordon Clayton, Eddie Lewis, Jeff Whitefoot, David Pegg, Jackie Blanchflower, Tommy McNulty, Middle row: coach Jimmy Murphy, reserve team trainer Bill Inglis, John Aston, Jack Crompton, Mark Jones, unknown, Tommy Hamilton, Bryce Fulton, John Downie, Paddy Kennedy, physiotherapist Ted Dalton, trainer Tom Curry. Front row: Jack Rowley, Tommy Taylor, Allenby Chilton, Colin Webster, Noel McFarlane, Frank Mooney, Albert Scanlon, Billy Whelan, Henry Cockburn, Don Gibson, coach Bert Whalley.

of men, measuring a mere 5ft 9ins, but he was as strong as an ox, he was hard as nails and ruthless with it, and he never stopped scoring goals.

That made Jack special, and although you would never say he was Matt Busby's cup of tea as a person, being rather too rough and ready, Matt pandered to him because he knew he was vital to the team.

As a 15-year-old new boy at United when he was in his pomp, I considered myself lucky to have a decent relationship with Rowley. Training in the close season was at the university grounds at Fallowfield, so I used to get the number 50 bus; one morning I saw him coming along in his car and I was shocked when he pulled up, told me to jump in, and offered me a regular lift. It was mind-boggling to be treated so kindly by the great Jack Rowley, who had a reputation as an unpleasant beggar, to say the least. Undoubtedly he was a strange character, but I can only speak of him as I found him.

Jack, who began and ended his United days as an outside-left, scored four against Swansea Town in only his second match for the club and didn't stop banging them in for the better part of the next two decades.

When you look at the silly money that is paid for strikers now, he wasn't a bad acquisition for £3,000 from Bournemouth, was he? Modern critics will tell you that it was easier to score goals in his day, but my reply is that people who make those remarks have never played. Take it from me, goals have never been easy to score, and it must be remembered that Jack lost six years of his pomp to the war. What his record would have been had he not been interrupted, heaven only knows.

5. STAN PEARSON

OTHER HONOURS:
8 ENGLAND CAPS 1948-52.

OTHER CLUBS:
BURY 53/4-57/8 (122, 56);
CHESTER 57/8-58/9 (57, 16).

MANAGER:
CHESTER 1957-61.

STAN PEARSON		
COMP.	APPS	GLS
LEAGUE	315	128
FAC	30	21
OTHERS	1	0
TOTAL	346	149

BORN	SALFORD 11TH JANUARY 1919
DIED	ALDERLEY EDGE, CHESHIRE 17TH FEBRUARY 1997
POSITION	INSIDE-FORWARD
JOINED UNITED	DECEMBER 1935 FROM JUNIOR FOOTBALL
UNITED DEBUT	CHESTERFIELD (A) DIV. 2 - 13/11/1937
UNITED HONOURS	DIV. 1 1951/2 DIV. 2 PROMOTION 1937/8 FA CUP 1947/8
UNITED FAREWELL	ASTON VILLA (H) DIV. 1 - 24/10/1953
LEFT UNITED FOR	BURY FEBRUARY 1954

Stan Pearson was a fabulous footballer and an absolutely smashing man who got on with everybody, a gentle fellow who wouldn't hurt a mouse. He wouldn't hurt the ball, either, invariably passing it into the net, something he did over and over and over again. Indeed, for a player whose approach was in no way physical, I'll bet he scored more times from inside the six-yard box than anyone who has ever walked on to a pitch, and he wasn't even the team's main marksman.

Stan played as an inside-forward, lying much deeper than Jack Rowley, and he created even more goals than he scored. It is beyond me why he didn't win plenty more than his eight England caps. I know there were some excellent performers knocking around, but Raich Carter, arguably the pick of them, didn't last long after the war and Stan was the equal of anybody else.

'If only he'd had the aggressive streak of, say, Paul Scholes, there's no telling how good Stan might have been.'

He didn't have great pace but seemed to stroll gracefully through his games. He scored a lot of goals with his head and with both feet, his control and passing was neat and tidy and he had marvellous awareness of the ever-changing picture around him.

If only he'd had the aggressive streak of, say, Paul Scholes, there's no telling how good Stan might have been. He would have been awesome, a world-beater. Not that opponents were able to take advantage of his lovely nature, because he was that good a player that he didn't give them the chance, and if ever there was a problem, then the likes of Allenby Chilton, Henry Cockburn or Johnny Morris, who could all kick a bit, would look after him.

After leaving United he scored plenty more goals for Bury, then became boss of Chester, but really Stan was too nice for the rat-race of football management. He can be described fairly as one of the most loved individuals I have known in a lifetime in the English game. It was an honour to have played with him and a supreme honour to have known him well. That Stan Pearson, he was really something.

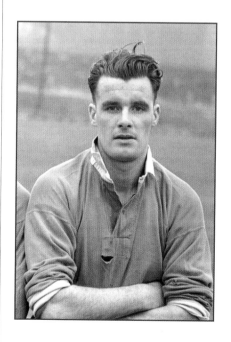

BORN	BATLEY, YORKSHIRE 7TH FEBRUARY 1915
DIED	1975
POSITION	CENTRE-FORWARD
JOINED UNITED	FEBRUARY 1938 FROM NEWCASTLE UTD - £6,500
UNITED DEBUT	BARNSLEY (A) DIV. 2 - 02/02/1938
UNITED HONOURS	DIV. 2 PROMOTION 1937/8
UNITED FAREWELL	PRESTON N.E. (A) FAC - 30/01/1946
LEFT UNITED FOR	BLACKBURN ROVERS MARCH 1946

JACK SMITH		
COMP.	APPS	GLS
LEAGUE	37	14
FAC	5	1
TOTAL	42	15

6. JACK SMITH

OTHER CLUBS:

HUDDERSFIELD TOWN 32/3-34/5 (45, 24);
NEWCASTLE UNITED 34/5-37/8 (104, 69);
BLACKBURN ROVERS 46/7 (30, 12);
PORT VALE 46/7-47/8 (29, 10).

It's amazing the things you remember as a kid. What stands out for me about big Jack Smith was his long, black, wavy hair – at least it was long by the standards of the day.

As a player, he was decent in the air and a bit of a bustler, but it's fair to say that he wasn't a great favourite with the United fans because he seemed to miss more chances than he converted. That said, his record for the team wasn't bad, and later he did even better with Huddersfield and Newcastle.

Jack's main achievement was helping to gain promotion from the Second Division after arriving halfway through 1937/38, but then his gathering impetus would have been shattered by the outbreak of war.

After that, maybe, he didn't fit the requirements of the new manager, Matt Busby, and Jack Rowley, his main rival for the centre-forward berth, was on his way to becoming an established star. Hardly an easy situation.

BORN	TREALAW, GLAMORGAN 21ST SEPTEMBER 1911
DIED	TONYPANDY, GLAMORGAN, 4TH OCTOBER 1980
POSITION	WING-HALF
JOINED UNITED	JUNE 1938 FROM SWANSEA TOWN
UNITED DEBUT	ASTON VILLA (A) DIV. 1 - 05/11/1938
UNITED FAREWELL	NEWCASTLE UTD. (A) DIV. 1 - 22/04/1950
LEFT UNITED FOR	OLDHAM A. - JUNE 1951 PLAYER/COACH

JACK WARNER		
COMP.	APPS	GLS
LEAGUE	105	1
FAC	13	1
OTHERS	1	0
TOTAL	119	2

7. JACK WARNER

OTHER HONOURS:
2 WALES CAPS 1937-39.

OTHER CLUBS:
SWANSEA TOWN 33/4-37/8 (132, 8);
OLDHAM ATHLETIC 51/2 (34, 2);
ROCHDALE 52/3 (21, 0).

MANAGER:
ROCHDALE 1952-53

Welshman Jack Warner was a fiery character, bloody hell he was! I played once alongside him for the reserves and he rollocked everybody so thoroughly that I thought he would blister the paint on the stands.

Like many old footballers, he was in the game primarily for himself, but if you're looking after yourself and playing well, then invariably you're doing a good job for those around you.

There's no doubt that Jack could play. He was an abrasive tackler, but he could pass the ball, too, and certainly from what I saw of him as a veteran, he must have been pretty fine in his pre-war prime. Then the hostilities broke out when he was in his late twenties and his progress was cruelly curtailed.

Even then, he didn't give up the fight, retaining a regular place at right-half in 1946/47 and also starting the 1948 FA Cup campaign before losing his place to Johnny Anderson. Then he bounced back with 25 appearances in 1949/50, when he played his last game for United at the age of 39 before becoming a bookmaker in Stretford.

8. JOHNNY HANLON

OTHER CLUBS:
Bury 48/9-49/50 (31, 1).

JOHNNY HANLON		
COMP.	APPS	GLS
LEAGUE	64	20
FAC	6	2
TOTAL	70	22

BORN	MANCHESTER 12TH OCTOBER 1917
DIED	MANCHESTER, JANUARY 2002
POSITION	CENTRE-FORWARD
JOINED UNITED	NOVEMBER 1934 FROM JUNIOR FOOTBALL
UNITED DEBUT	HUDDERSFIELD TOWN (H) DIV. 1 - 26/11/1938
UNITED FAREWELL	ASTON VILLA (H) DIV. 1 - 25/09/1948
LEFT UNITED FOR	BURY - OCTOBER 1948

A nippy customer who could play anywhere across the forward line, Johnny Hanlon was best known as a central marksman. He was only tiny yet, as I recall, his brother Billy was a giant of a man, and a useful centre-forward in local football.

Much was expected of Johnny in his youth, and he was starting to make his name before the war. Then he spent time in a prisoner-of-war camp and didn't seem the strongest of men when he returned, though he wasn't a spent force, making 27 League appearances in 1946/47.

He was adept at linking the play, joining in with the likes of Pearson, Rowley, Delaney and Mitten, and he didn't look out of place. He was a sharp finisher, too, and had the all-round class which would have made him a Busby type of player.

But as he was 31 in 1948 and surrounded by top-quality rivals for a place, it was unlikely that he was going to develop his career at Old Trafford, so he moved on to Bury.

Later, I'm told, Johnny proved a dream to play alongside at non-League Altrincham, helping and teaching the younger lads, and it was a pity, perhaps, that he didn't stay in the game as a coach.

BORN	S. HYLTON, CO. DURHAM 16TH SEPTEMBER 1918
DIED	16TH JUNE 1996
POSITION	CENTRE-HALF
JOINED UNITED	NOVEMBER 1938 FROM LIVERPOOL (AMATEUR)
UNITED DEBUT	CHARLTON ATHLETIC (A) DIV. 1 - 02/09/1939
UNITED HONOURS	DIV. 1 1951/2 FA CUP 1947/8
UNITED FAREWELL	WOLVERHAMPTON W. (H) DIV. 1 - 23/02/1955
LEFT UNITED FOR	GRIMSBY TOWN MAR. 1955 - PLAYER/MANAGER

ALLENBY CHILTON		
COMP.	APPS	GLS
LEAGUE	353	3
FAC	37	0
OTHERS	2	0
TOTAL	392	3

9. ALLENBY CHILTON

OTHER HONOURS:
2 ENGLAND CAPS 1950-51
OTHER CLUBS:
GRIMSBY TOWN 54/5-56/7 (63, 0).
MANAGER:
GRIMSBY TOWN 1955-59;
HARTLEPOOLS UNITED 1962-63.

What a character! Allenby didn't give a monkey's about anybody so long as he was all right. They say he was a leader of the United players, and some credit him, rather than manager Matt Busby or captain John Carey, with the half-time team talk which led to the fightback from 2-1 down to win the 1948 FA Cup Final against Blackpool.

Well, it might have happened that way, but knowing Chilly it would have been because he was worried about his win bonus. He was desperate to win at all costs, and woe betide any team-mates who weren't doing their jobs. He'd rollock 'em and bollock 'em, and undoubtedly he had a knack of getting footballers going.

Allenby was always moaning, I never knew him not to. Everything was too expensive for him, the coal, the milk, the bread. It was a different world then – can you imagine today's players being worried about the price of coal? I never knew him even have a car, he walked to the ground every morning from home – I think he lived in Ryecroft Road – then walked back after training with his chum Jimmy Delaney.

Allenby was a big, ungainly, muck-and-nettles centre-half who I believe was worth far more than his couple of caps for England, and I wouldn't have thought many forwards would have enjoyed lining up against him. His aim in life was to sort out his opponents and to stop them doing what they wanted to do. He was dominant in the air, he was better on the ball than most people believed, and he was as courageous as they come, always ready to hurl himself into places where angels fear to tread. Then, having imposed his will and won the ball, he would help it on to one of the lads who could really play. The club has known plenty of top defenders down the years, but it's difficult to think of a more effective out-and-out stopper than Allenby Chilton.

I could never say, hand on heart, that he had the sort of personality that endeared itself to the manager, but Matt Busby understood his worth and knew that he would always do a damned good job for Manchester United. Despite his forbidding aspects, Allenby was viewed favourably by most of the

players, who knew he was honest to the core and would always give 100 per cent, yet there were times when he made us suffer.

As a youngster I was unfortunate to find myself with him one night in Scarborough, where we had gone for a week's special training in the middle of winter. We stayed at the Grand Hotel and the lads were going out in the evening, but Allenby ordered me to stay in with him. It turned out that my job was to go and fetch his drinks from the bar, and to pay for them! But that was Big Chilly and somehow, strange as it may seem now, I never resented him for it and always felt a certain warmth towards him.

You have to bear in mind that men like him had fought in a war. He made his debut at Charlton on the Saturday before the conflict commenced and the next thing he knew he was in the Army, fighting for his life, eventually being injured in battle at Caen. So he, and others like him, were entitled to have a different outlook on life to my generation. They had done things and faced things that we never had to, which set them apart. He wasn't afraid of anybody, certainly not anyone he might meet on the football field, or of Matt Busby. Why should he be? He had fought the same war that Matt had fought and now they were working for the same employer.

People lose track and don't appreciate that it was a terrible time in history that these men had just lived through. That put football in perspective, and though the game was life and death to Chilly in terms of his livelihood, he understood its true importance.

THE GLORIOUS 48-ERS SHOW OFF THE FA CUP. Left to right, back row: Matt Busby (manager), John Anderson, Jack Warner, Allenby Chilton, Jack Crompton, Henry Cockburn, John Aston, Tom Curry (trainer). Front row: Jimmy Delaney, Johnny Morris, John Carey, Jack Rowley, Stan Pearson, Charlie Mitten.

BORN	MANCHESTER
	18TH DECEMBER 1921
POSITION	GOALKEEPER
JOINED UNITED	JUNE 1944 FROM
	MANCHESTER CITY (AMATEUR)
UNITED DEBUT	ACCRINGTON ST. (A)
	FAC - 05/01/1946
UNITED HONOURS	DIV. 1 1951/2
	FA CUP 1947/8
UNITED FAREWELL	HUDDERSFIELD TOWN (H)
	DIV. 1 - 22/10/1955
LEFT UNITED FOR	LUTON TOWN
	OCT. 1956 - TRAINER

JACK CROMPTON		
COMP.	APPS	GLS
LEAGUE	191	0
FAC	20	0
OTHERS	1	0
TOTAL	212	0

10. JACK CROMPTON

MANAGER:
LUTON TOWN 1962;
BARROW 1971-72;
MANCHESTER UNITED (CARETAKER) 1981

No one can deny the marvellous contribution that Jack Crompton made to Manchester United down the decades, both as a long-serving goalkeeper who helped to disappoint Stanley Matthews and company as Blackpool were beaten in that fabulously entertaining 1948 FA Cup Final, and then as a trainer and coach under several managers.

One of the old guard who rose through the ranks of the local nursery club, Goslings, the quietly-spoken Crompo is a lovely character, truly one of life's gentlemen. Also he is one of the sprightliest eightysomethings I have ever met, and while it might sound ridiculous, he seems to have barely changed since his playing days.

Jack was always a fitness fanatic who wouldn't think twice about putting in a rigorous training session with the rest of us, then adjourning to a gymnasium for extra work before setting off on a long-distance hike through the hills, just for the joy of it.

United had plenty of 'keepers on their books in the immediate post-war years and Jack, who forged a reputation as a serial saver of penalties, was the pick of them. There was nothing showy about him, but generally he was efficient and reliable; certainly he must have satisfied the manager, who selected him for more than a double-century of appearances.

That said, if I'm totally honest, I don't think he was the equal of Reg Allen, the man who replaced him. It's a matter of opinion, but I think the point is made by the fact that United were runners-up in a succession of title races with Jack in the side, but they finished as champions when Reg took over in 1951/52.

'There was nothing showy about him... the manager selecting him for more than a double-century of appearances.'

Equally I don't think Crompo was ever going to challenge Frank Swift of Manchester City for the England jersey. Indeed, Frank might have succeeded Jack at Old Trafford after surprisingly retiring from his Maine Road position in September 1949.

The rumour was that he had left City early so that he could work for his pal, Matt Busby, but that the Blues scuppered that little scheme by retaining Big Swifty's registration for another six years.

As for Jack, after finishing as a player in 1956 he became Luton's trainer, then returned to Old Trafford to help Jimmy Murphy pick up the pieces in the wake of Munich.

He was an integral part of the club's backroom staff throughout the glorious 1960s, then after taking several different jobs, including coaching for Bobby Charlton at Preston, he came back to his beloved United yet again, ending up in charge of the first team on a summer tour of the Far East.

Crompo was a wonderful servant to Manchester United and remains one of my favourite men.

11. JACK ROACH

JACK ROACH		
COMP.	APPS	GLS
FAC	2	0
TOTAL	2	0

BORN	MANCHESTER
POSITION	FULL-BACK
JOINED UNITED	OCTOBER 1941
	FROM LOCAL FOOTBALL
UNITED DEBUT	ACCRINGTON ST. (A) FAC - 05/01/1946
UNITED FAREWELL	ACCRINGTON ST (H) FAC - 09/01/1946
RETIRED	MAY 1947

Jack Roach was yet another graduate from the phenomenally successful production line of Goslings, the team named after its founder, local fishmonger Abe Gosling.

A solid left-back who played 45 times for United during the war but was never granted an official League outing, Jack faced Accrington in both FA Cup meetings in 1945/46 before losing his place to the classier Joe Walton. It's fascinating to recall now that cup ties were settled on a home-and-away aggregate basis in that first post-war season, in an attempt to raise extra revenue.

BORN	ASHTON-UNDER-LYNE, LANCS 14TH SEPTEMBER 1923
DIED	MOSSLEY, LANCS 2ND FEBRUARY 2004
POSITION	WING-HALF
JOINED UNITED	SEPTEMBER 1943 FROM GOSLINGS
UNITED DEBUT	ACCRINGTON ST. (A) FAC - 05/01/1946
UNITED HONOURS	DIV. 1 1951/2 FA CUP 1947/8
UNITED FAREWELL	WOLVERHAMPTON W. (A) DIV. 1 - 02/10/1954
LEFT UNITED FOR	BURY - OCTOBER 1954

HENRY COCKBURN		
COMP.	APPS	GLS
LEAGUE	243	4
FAC	32	0
TOTAL	275	4

12. HENRY COCKBURN

OTHER HONOURS:
13 ENGLAND CAPS 1946-51.
OTHER CLUBS:
BURY 54/5-55/6 (35, 0).

Henry Cockburn never paused for breath and how he played, with the amount of talking he did, I could never quite fathom. What made it all the more mysterious was that most of the talking was shouting and screaming, nothing thoughtful or measured about it at all. But he was an absolute darling of a man, and he never changed throughout his life.

He was a pleasure to play with because, if it had been possible to give more than 100 per cent, then Henry would have done. He never stopped running, never stopped probing, never stopped tackling and, of course, never stopped yammering away at the top of his voice.

He and Allenby Chilton were like Morecambe and Wise or Little and Large, a giant of a central defender and a tiny left-half who made up a wonderful double act, ceaselessly moaning at each other, battling away like cat and dog.

'Henry had a reputation not unlike Nobby Stiles in later years. Everybody was afraid of him because he was such an abrasive little beggar on the pitch.'

Henry had a reputation not unlike Nobby Stiles in later years. Everybody was afraid of him because he was such an abrasive little beggar on the pitch.

He played left-half off his right foot and earned more than a dozen caps, starting as England's first choice straight after the war, forming a decent half-back line with Billy Wright and Neil Franklin.

He did well and it was surprising when he lost his place although, hand on heart, I couldn't say he was better than Portsmouth's Jimmy Dickinson, who eventually enjoyed a lengthy run in the international team.

Henry was essentially a defensive operator, similar to Nobby but not quite as accomplished, not so assured in his distribution. Despite his lack of inches he was competitive in the air, but there was one thing he couldn't do – he was the worst thrower of the ball I have ever seen, simply couldn't take a throw-in to save his life.

Overall, he wasn't bad, Henry, and he'll be remembered forever as a character and a half.

13. BILL BAINBRIDGE

OTHER CLUBS:
BURY 46/7 (2, 1);
TRANMERE ROVERS 48/9-53/4 (168, 63).

BILL BAINBRIDGE		
COMP.	APPS	GLS
FAC	1	1
TOTAL	1	1

BORN	GATESHEAD 9TH MARCH 1922
POSITION	INSIDE-FORWARD
JOINED UNITED	DECEMBER 1944 FROM ASHINGTON
UNITED DEBUT & FAREWELL	ACCRINGTON ST. (H) FAC - 09/01/1946
LEFT UNITED FOR	BURY - MAY 1946

Bill was a hard-running attacker who went on to serve Tranmere Rovers with distinction, but his game lacked the refinement for the top level. Still, he scored on his sole senior outing for United before yielding the number-ten shirt to the versatile John Carey, who was yet to settle at right-back.

14. JOE WALTON

OTHER CLUBS:
PRESTON NORTH END 47/8-60/1 (401, 4);
ACCRINGTON STANLEY 60/1 (18, 0).

JOE WALTON		
COMP.	APPS	GLS
LEAGUE	21	0
FAC	2	0
TOTAL	23	0

BORN	MANCHESTER 5TH JUNE 1925
POSITION	FULL-BACK
JOINED UNITED	APRIL 1940 FROM JUNIOR FOOTBALL
UNITED DEBUT	PRESTON N.E. (H) FAC - 26/01/1946
UNITED FAREWELL	PORTSMOUTH (H) DIV. 1 - 25/12/1947
LEFT UNITED FOR	PRESTON N.E. MARCH 1948 - £10,000

Joe Walton was a quick, stylish, ball-playing full-back who appeared to have every chance of making the grade at Old Trafford. Certainly the United coaching staff were confident about his chances, but he didn't really make the expected impact in terms of appearances and then right out of the blue he was transferred to Preston.

It was an unusual deal because Joe was only 22 years old, largely unproven at First Division level, and yet he changed hands for £10,000, the biggest fee ever paid for a full-back at that time.

It seemed like an absolute fortune, but there was no doubting the Walton credentials. He was comfortable on the ball, he could join in with passing movements and he was a decent tackler, so it was no surprise when he went on to do a magnificent job for Preston, playing more than 400 games over the next dozen years.

Had he stayed at United, Joe might have claimed a first-team berth on either defensive flank. Though John Carey and John Aston were still at their peak at the time of his departure, and there were several youngsters around for cover, openings occurred in the seasons ahead, and undoubtedly Walton possessed more natural ability than most who have filled the right-back slot.

BORN	BEDLINGTON, NORTHUMBERLAND 27TH APRIL 1921
DIED	DECEMBER 1999
POSITION	WING-HALF OR FULL-BACK
JOINED UNITED	JANUARY 1946 FROM BLYTH SPARTANS
UNITED DEBUT	GRIMSBY TOWN (H) DIV. 1 - 31/08/1946
UNITED FAREWELL	SUNDERLAND (H) DIV. 1 - 20/10/1951
LEFT UNITED FOR	LINCOLN CITY - JULY 1952

BILLY McGLEN		
COMP.	APPS	GLS
LEAGUE	110	2
FAC	12	0
TOTAL	122	2

15. BILLY McGLEN

OTHER CLUBS:
LINCOLN CITY 52/3 (13, 0);
OLDHAM 52/3-55/6 (68, 3).

I wouldn't have thought Billy McGlen was Matt Busby's type of player. He was a rough, tough north-easterner who gave the impression that he would kick his own grandmother if she wouldn't give him the ball, though that was misleading because he was a delightful fellow with a heart of gold.

Billy was an extremely effective defender, whether playing left-back or left-half, and though he offered very little class, when he pulled on the shirt he was ready to die in the team's cause. He could be particularly influential in man-marking a star inside-forward, and if he rarely took the eye himself, often he made sure that his quarry didn't, either.

In the end I suppose the competition from more talented individuals at Old Trafford proved too hot for Billy, but he could leave with his head held high.

BORN	CLELAND, LANARKSHIRE 3RD SPETEMBER 1914
DIED	CLELAND, LANARKSHIRE 26TH SEPTEMBER 1989
POSITION	WINGER
JOINED UNITED	FEBRUARY 1946 FROM CELTIC FOR £4,000
UNITED DEBUT	GRIMSBY TOWN (H) DIV. 1 - 31/08/1946
UNITED HONOURS	FA CUP 1947/8
UNITED FAREWELL	CHELSEA (A) DIV. 1 - 11/11/1950
LEFT UNITED FOR	ABERDEEN NOVEMBER 1950 - £3,500

JIMMY DELANEY		
COMP.	APPS	GLS
LEAGUE	164	25
FAC	19	3
OTHERS	1	0
TOTAL	184	28

16. JIMMY DELANEY

OTHER HONOURS:
13 SCOTLAND CAPS 1936-48.

OTHER CLUBS:
CELTIC 34/5-45/6 (143, 68);
ABERDEEN 50/1-51/2 (31, 8);
FALKIRK 51/2-53/4;
DERRY CITY, NORTHERN IRELAND, 53/4-54/5;
CORK ATHLETIC, REPUBLIC OF IRELAND, 55/6.

Like Eric Cantona many years later, Jimmy Delaney was the catalyst who turned Manchester United from a very useful side into a great one.

He gave Matt Busby's post-war team much-needed width on the right, but equally as important, he brought with him oceans of experience and knowledge. After all, he had spent a decade as a pretty regular member of his country's side at a time when there were a lot of talented Scotsmen about, and he had starred as Celtic had lifted two League titles and the Scottish Cup. Beyond a shadow of a doubt, Delaney was a match-winner and one hell of a performer.

Jimmy was a flyer with speed to burn. He would knock the ball past his full-back, leave him for dead and cross it beautifully. He'd do it over and over again, enough to drive defenders mad because it didn't give them a chance to play.

Also, he was tall and strong for a winger, and had spent some of his Celtic days at centre-forward, so he was quite happy to cut inside and go for goal. They used to call him the penalty king, not because he used to take the spot-kicks but because he was very good at falling down in the box. Oh, there's nothing new in this game!

Jimmy was brilliant for United in his thirties, so it's quite frightening to contemplate what he must have been like in his pomp north of the border, yet it could be said that Matt brought him back from the brink of the scrapheap when he signed him for £4,000 in February 1946.

He was christened 'Old Brittle Bones' following a sequence of injuries, he was reaching the veteran stage and most of the pundits reckoned the United manager was taking a huge gamble. Well, Matt was never averse to a wager, but he can't have had many produce such spectacularly successful results as his punt on Delaney.

Pound for pound at £4,000 I would think Jimmy represented Matt Busby's most rewarding excursion into the transfer market, and when you consider that he took only a £500 loss when he sold him nearly five years later, it really wasn't too bad a deal, was it?

THE DANCING FEET OF JIMMY DELANEY: as experienced by a prostrate Bradford Park Avenue defender during an FA Cup replay in 1949.

BORN	RANGOON, BURMA 17TH JANUARY 1921
DIED	STOCKPORT 2ND JANUARY 2002
POSITION	WINGER
JOINED UNITED	AUGUST 1936 FROM STRATHALLAN HAWTHORN
UNITED DEBUT	GRIMSBY TOWN (H) DIV. 1 - 31/08/1946
UNITED HONOURS	FA CUP 1947/8
UNITED FAREWELL	FULHAM (H) DIV. 1 - 29/04/1950
LEFT UNITED FOR	SANTA FE, COLOMBIA MAY 1950

CHARLIE MITTEN		
COMP.	APPS	GLS
LEAGUE	142	50
FAC	19	11
OTHERS	1	0
TOTAL	162	61

17. CHARLIE MITTEN

OTHER CLUBS:
SANTA FE, COLOMBIA, 50/1;
FULHAM 51/2-55/6 (154, 32);
MANSFIELD TOWN 55/6-57/8 (100, 25).

MANAGER:
MANSFIELD TOWN 1956-58;
NEWCASTLE UNITED 1958-61.

Charlie Mitten was an entertainer supreme, and here's a perfect example of why. I'll remember it until the day I die.

On a Wednesday afternoon in the spring of 1950 United met Aston Villa at Old Trafford and trounced them 7-0. Charlie scored four times, a header and a hat-trick of penalties, but that's only the ordinary half of a story which I might believe was apocryphal if we didn't have the trusty verification of Messrs Chilton, Pearson and Cockburn.

The first penalty struck the left-hand stanchion, so did the second, but as he stood over the ball to take the third, Villa 'keeper Joe Rutherford thought he'd try to put the taker off. So he strode forward and queried: 'Where's this one going, Charlie?' Back came the deadpan reply: 'Same place' and a moment later, unerringly and without batting an eyelid, Charlie duly obliged. For pure panache it couldn't be bettered, and it was typical of the man.

Playing on United's left flank, Charlie offered a nice contrast with Jimmy Delaney on the right. Whereas Delaney was as brave as could be, and stunningly direct, Mitten wasn't.

But Charlie could drop a shoulder to produce tricks which weren't in the Scot's repertoire and, even more significantly, he possessed a left foot which could thread cotton through the eye of a needle. He could have done the most intricate crochet work the world has ever seen with that foot. It was so gentle and tender when he was caressing crosses on to the heads of Rowley and Pearson that he might have been dealing with a little baby, but the explosion which issued from it when he chose to shoot was utterly dramatic.

He was a fantastic player who somehow never won an England cap, being unlucky that he played in the era of the marvellous Tom Finney and even more unfortunate, perhaps, that Jimmy Mullen played for Wolves, who had a representative on the FA Council.

Of course, it all went wrong for Charlie when he was lured by the equivalent of a king's ransom to sign for Santa Fe of Colombia when that country was outside FIFA. When that dream ended in disillusionment and he returned to England – having spurned Alfredo di Stefano's invitation to join him at Real Madrid – he found himself banned and transfer-listed by United.

Yet for all that, I believe that if Matt Busby had been asked to name his best ever United team, then Charlie would have been his outside-left, with George Best on the right.

Why didn't the manager put up a greater fight to get him back? Those were different times, when authority was harder to question, and I would guess also that Matt didn't relish having a player put one over on him in the first place. But I'm sure that, in his heart, he would have loved to welcome Charlie back to the fold.

Whatever happened to him Charlie was an outrageous, audacious character with his finger in every pie known to man, and he never changed.

18. JOHN ASTON SNR

OTHER HONOURS:
17 ENGLAND CAPS 1948-50.

JOHN ASTON SNR.		
COMP.	APPS	GLS
LEAGUE	253	29
FAC	29	1
OTHERS	2	0
TOTAL	284	30

BORN	MANCHESTER 3RD SEPTEMBER 1921
DIED	MANCHESTER 31ST JULY 2003
POSITION	FULL-BACK
JOINED UNITED	JANUARY 1938 FROM MUJACS
UNITED DEBUT	CHELSEA (H) DIV. 1 - 18/09/1946
UNITED HONOURS	DIV. 1 1951/2 FA CUP 1947/8
UNITED FAREWELL	SHEFFIELD UTD. (A) DIV. 1 - 24/04/1954
RETIRED	1955
	UNITED COACHING STAFF

John earned his prominence, and collected all his England caps, as a full-back, but he was playing centre-forward when I made my debut alongside him.

It's amazing that when United won the title in 1951/52, at the beginning of April, John was playing centre-forward, Jack Rowley was at outside-left and Roger Byrne was at left-back. But for the last six games of the season, Matt switched things around, moving Roger to the left wing, Jack to lead the attack and Big Asto to left-back.

How many managers have made three such radical changes, kept the same 11 players and yet still lifted the title? It seems barely believable, but it happened. I suppose there's got to be a bit of luck involved, but it didn't half help that Matt Busby had assembled a squad of men with such comprehensive all-round capabilities.

In John's case, he had already shown he could play at full-back, centre-forward, inside-forward and wing-half without ever letting United down, so Matt knew all about his amazing versatility.

John Aston was a wonderful clubman, a good lad and a fine player. He had no pace, but he was neat and tidy in possession, he was exceedingly brave and he was blessed with a big bum,

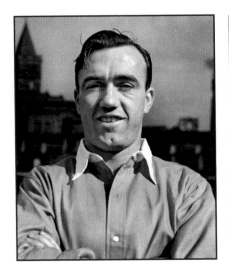

which made it difficult to get past him as a full-back. When he was playing at the back with John Carey, there wasn't another pair to compare with them.

That said, as an inside-right, I loved it when John was at centre-forward next to me. He was brilliant in the air, he scored his share of goals, he was superb at holding the ball and shielding it from opponents while the rest of us ran into position, and he was totally unselfish.

That outlook did him great credit, but it didn't help him on the international scene. After winning his England place at full-back in the autumn of 1948, he played 15 consecutive games and acquitted himself really well, eventually losing his place solely because he had been shifted to centre-forward by his club. Typically, he never complained, just got on with his job and did whatever the manager asked him to do.

As far as Matt was concerned, Big Asto was a marvellous man to have around. He could fill in practically anywhere and the team wouldn't suffer, though that's not always the best thing for the player's own prospects.

It was a shame that John's career finished early because of TB, and I remember visiting him in a sanatorium when he was recovering, after which I was lucky enough to play in his benefit game in 1956.

Anything Big Asto got, he deserved. As a man, he was extremely well-liked, and as a footballer he was universally admired and respected.

Later he continued working for the club as a coach, then finished up as chief scout. Manchester United have had few more worthy and loyal servants.

BORN	RADCLIFFE, LANCS 27TH SEPTEMBER 1923
POSITION	INSIDE-FORWARD
JOINED UNITED	AUGUST 1939 FROM MUJACS
UNITED DEBUT	SUNDERLAND (H) DIV. 1 - 26/10/1946
UNITED HONOURS	FA CUP 1947/8
UNITED FAREWELL	BRADFORD P.A. (H) FAC - 29/01/1949
LEFT UNITED FOR	DERBY COUNTY MARCH 1949 - £24,500

JOHNNY MORRIS		
COMP.	APPS	GLS
LEAGUE	83	32
FAC	9	3
OTHERS	1	0
TOTAL	93	35

19. JOHNNY MORRIS

OTHER HONOURS:
3 ENGLAND CAPS 1949.

OTHER CLUBS:
DERBY COUNTY 48/9-52/3 (130, 44);
LEICESTER CITY 52/3-57/8 (206, 33).

Johnny Morris . . . now he was my favourite. He was a sensational footballer, and for those not fortunate enough to have seen him play, it's not a bad description to call him the Paul Scholes of his day.

Johnny was the baby of that fabulous post-war forward line – I just love to say the names: Delaney, Morris, Rowley, Pearson and Mitten – and he could do virtually anything.

He was majestic with his right peg and more than useful with his left; he wasn't very big but he was wonderful in the air; he scored loads of goals and created even more for others; he was quick and he was intelligent; he put his foot in, he could be a nasty so-and-so and he was fazed by nobody . . . I could go on indefinitely.

As a kid I saw him play for United against Burnley at Maine Road on New Year's Day 1948. It was a filthy, muddy day, rain bucketing, and I simply couldn't believe his energy. There wasn't a square inch of that gluepot of a pitch he didn't cover and though Rowley scored three and Mitten grabbed two in a 5-0 win, Morris was the man who took my eye.

One of his stock balls was the raking crossfield pass from the inside-right channel to Charlie on the left wing and he offered a lovely delivery service to his own winger, Jimmy Delaney, too, while linking up beautifully with Rowley and Pearson.

Unfortunately a situation arose between Matt Busby and John that had to be sorted out and, certainly at this distance, it seems criminal that the only way of doing so was John's departure at the age of 25, having played not quite three full seasons of League football.

Of course, there would have been more if it hadn't been for the war. Still, when he left Old Trafford to join Derby County for a British record transfer fee of £24,500 he had a footballing lifetime ahead of him and it's shocking to me that he received only three England caps.

I just wish I'd have seen the people around at the time who were better than him, because they must have been quite something. Of course, in reality, there weren't any. I don't care how many big-name inside-forwards England could call on, they weren't better than John.

I know that Matt had his problems with him, and eventually let him leave Old Trafford on a point of principle. John was a fiery, spiky character, a forthright sort of fellow who always said his piece. Once he had settled on his point of view he was immovable, so I suppose that, having experienced diferences, there was never a hope in hell of John and Matt getting together. Neither of them were going to perform somersaults.

Sadly, he was never replaced adequately. In fact, that would have been impossible because his sort of talent was utterly irreplaceable.

I love him to pieces, not only as a player but as a person. We were at Leicester together and we've been good friends for a long, long time, but that is not what shaped my opinion of his ability.

Don't take it from me, take it from Stan Pearson, John's fellow inside-forward, a top performer in his own right and a seasoned judge of a player. Stan maintained that Morris was technically the best footballer he ever saw. Enough said!

BORN	DORMANSTOWN, YORKSHIRE 13TH AUGUST 1921
DIED	2003
POSITION	CENTRE-FORWARD
JOINED UNITED	MAY 1946 FROM LUTON TOWN (AMATEUR)
UNITED DEBUT	SUNDERLAND (H) DIV. 1 - 26/10/1946
UNITED FAREWELL	NEWCASTLE UTD (A) DIV. 1 - 30/04/1949
LEFT UNITED FOR	HUDDERSFIELD TOWN JUNE 1949 - £16,000

RONNIE BURKE		
COMP.	APPS	GLS
LEAGUE	28	16
FAC	6	6
OTHERS	1	1
TOTAL	35	23

20. RONNIE BURKE

OTHER CLUBS:
HUDDERSFIELD TOWN 49/50-51/2 (27, 6);
ROTHERHAM UNITED 52/3-54/5 (73, 56);
EXETER CITY 55/6-56/7 (42, 14).

Ronnie Burke was a big, willing, muscular Yorkshireman with an impressive scoring record who probably deserved more recognition than he got.

He didn't make his United debut until he was 25 – yet another example of a career being severely restricted by the war – but then he made the most of his limited opportunities as the spearhead of a brilliant attack.

Ronnie won plenty of aerial duels, which set up a lot of chances for Morris and Pearson, and he was ready to chase and battle forever. If Rowley was injured, or if Matt wanted to deploy Jack on the left wing, which he did quite often in 1946/47, Ronnie was the ideal man to play through the middle.

True, essentially he was an understudy and he didn't have Jack's class, but then, few centre-forwards did.

Ronnie Burke could be proud of what he achieved with United, and he went on to score goals everywhere he went. Had he been granted the luxury of an uninterrupted career, his final goal tally would have been a formidable one.

BORN	MIDDLESBROUGH 3RD MARCH 1920
DIED	SEPTEMBER 1990
POSITION	GOALKEEPER
JOINED UNITED	MAY 1946 FROM JUNIOR FOOTBALL
UNITED DEBUT	ASTON VILLA (A) DIV. 1 - 02/11/1946
UNITED FAREWELL	BLACKBURN R. (A) DIV. 1 - 14/12/1946
RETIRED	MAY 1947

CLIFF COLLINSON		
COMP.	APPS	GLS
LEAGUE	7	0
TOTAL	7	0

21. CLIFF COLLINSON

Goalkeeper Cliff Collinson was a burly Teessider who made a favourable impression when he entered First Division football for the first time as a deputy for Jack Crompton. That afternoon at Villa Park he kept a clean sheet and retained his place for the next six games, but then Jack returned and Cliff slipped out of the reckoning for good. After that I didn't see him again until the formation of the Former Players Association, which he supported enthusiastically for the rest of his life.

22. HARRY WORRALL

HARRY WORRALL		
COMP.	APPS	GLS
LEAGUE	6	0
TOTAL	6	0

BORN	NORTHWICH, CHESHIRE 19TH NOVEMBER 1918
POSITION	FULL-BACK
JOINED UNITED	OCTOBER 1937 FROM WINSFORD UNITED
UNITED DEBUT	WOLVERHAMPTON W. (A) DIV. 1 - 30/11/1946
UNITED FAREWELL	EVERTON (H) DIV. 1 - 22/11/1947
LEFT UNITED FOR	SWINDON TOWN JUNE 1948 - £1,000

The outbreak of war dictated that poor Harry Worrall waited nine years after signing from non-League Winsford before making his first senior appearance. A former inside-forward who was converted to left-back, he was a decent footballer but couldn't overcome the brisk competition for places at Manchester United – certainly there was no way he was going to unseat John Aston – and soon he was sold to Swindon, for whom he never enjoyed a League outing.

23. TED BUCKLE

TED BUCKLE		
COMP.	APPS	GLS
LEAGUE	20	6
FAC	4	1
TOTAL	24	7

BORN	SOUTHWARK, LONDON 28TH OCTOBER 1924
DIED	MANCHESTER 14TH JUNE 1990
POSITION	WINGER
JOINED UNITED	OCTOBER 1945 FROM FORCES FOOTBALL
UNITED DEBUT	CHARLTON ATHLETIC (A) DIV. 1 - 04/01/1947
UNITED FAREWELL	SUNDERLAND (H) DIV. 1 - 01/10/1949
LEFT UNITED FOR	EVERTON - NOV. 1949

OTHER CLUBS:
EVERTON 49/50-54/5 (97, 31);
EXETER CITY 55/6-56/7 (65, 12).

Ted was a bit of a dasher with a marvellous left peg, and he knew the way to goal. His United record of nearly one strike every three games is excellent for a winger and it suggests that he was unlucky not to be given an extended run in the team.

But then you consider that he was up against the flying machine Jimmy Delaney on one flank and the conjuror Charlie Mitten on the other, and the scale of the challenge facing mere mortals during that era becomes clear.

Ted had to cope with the same situation as Ronnie Burke and plenty of other decent players, which illustrates the fabulous standards set by Matt's first great team.

Eventually he proved himself with Everton, where he enjoyed the best form of his career.

BORN	BROADHURST, CHESHIRE 17TH JUNE 1915
POSITION	GOALKEEPER
JOINED UNITED	JANUARY 1947 FROM BOLTON W. (PART-EXCHANGE FOR WRIGGLESWORTH)
UNITED DEBUT	NOTTINGHAM FOREST (H) FAC - 25/01/1947
UNITED FAREWELL	DERBY CO. (A) DIV. 1 - 15/03/1947
RETIRED	JUNE 1948

BILL FIELDING		
COMP.	APPS	GLS
LEAGUE	6	0
FAC	1	0
TOTAL	7	0

24. BILL FIELDING

OTHER CLUBS:
CARDIFF CITY 36/7-38/9 (50, 0)

Bill Fielding, God bless him, is still coming to most of the social events staged by our Former Players Association when he was not too far short of his 90th birthday.

Before arriving in Manchester, Bill had done well as a goalkeeper with Cardiff and Bolton, with whom he won a wartime cup medal in 1944/45, then he joined United in the deal which saw Billy Wrigglesworth move to Burnden Park.

He couldn't have enjoyed his League debut too much, conceding six to Arsenal at Highbury, but Matt persevered with him for another five games before Jack Crompton resumed first-team duties. By then Bill was in his thirties and he retired the following year.

BORN	NORTHWICH, CHESHIRE 3RD JULY 1921
POSITION	WINGER
JOINED UNITED	JUNE 1947 FROM WITTON ALBION
UNITED DEBUT	PRESTON N.E. (A) DIV. 1- 27/09/1947
UNITED FAREWELL	STOKE CITY (H) DIV. 1 - 04/10/1947
LEFT UNITED FOR	PORT VALE APRIL 1948 - £1,000

JOE DALE		
COMP.	APPS	GLS
LEAGUE	2	0
TOTAL	2	0

25. JOE DALE

OTHER CLUBS:
PORT VALE 47/8-48/9 (9, 1).

Joe Dale was a skilful outside-right who joined United from Witton Albion, bringing with him a sparkling reputation gained at the lower level. Unfortunately, but understandably, he failed to make the massive leap from non-League to the First Division.

In fairness, Joe was asked to fill the boots of the great Jimmy Delaney at a time when the side was enduring a spell of dismal results, a forbidding task for anyone, let alone a 26-year-old with no professional experience. After leaving Old Trafford he didn't settle with Port Vale, but returned to Witton, whom he helped to win the Cheshire League title in 1948/49.

26. KEN PEGG

OTHER CLUBS:
TORQUAY UNITED 49/50 (2, 0);
YORK CITY 50/1 (1, 0).

KEN PEGG		
COMP.	APPS	GLS
LEAGUE	2	0
TOTAL	2	0

BORN	SALFORD, LANCS 4TH JANUARY 1926
DIED	MANCHESTER 25TH AUGUST 1999
POSITION	GOALKEEPER
JOINED UNITED	MAY 1945 FROM JUNIOR FOOTBALL
UNITED DEBUT	DERBY COUNTY (A) DIV. 1 - 15/11/1947
UNITED FAREWELL	EVERTON (H) DIV. 1 - 22/11/1947
LEFT UNITED FOR	TORQUAY UNITED AUGUST 1949

Ken Pegg was yet another goalkeeper whose United career was spent striving unavailingly to escape from the considerable shadow cast by Jack Crompton.

He played competently enough in his two League games, both of which ended in draws, but then he slipped out of the reckoning and headed for the West Country.

Later Ken became a match-day steward at Old Trafford and was a keen member of the Manchester United Former Players' Association until his death.

27. JOHN ANDERSON

OTHER CLUBS:
NOTTINGHAM FOREST 49/50-50/1 (40, 1).

JOHN ANDERSON		
COMP.	APPS	GLS
LEAGUE	33	1
FAC	6	1
OTHERS	1	0
TOTAL	40	2

BORN	SALFORD 11TH OCTOBER 1921
POSITION	WING-HALF
JOINED UNITED	OCTOBER 1937 FROM JUNIOR FOOTBALL
UNITED DEBUT	MIDDLESBROUGH (H) DIV. 1 - 20/12/1947
UNITED HONOURS	FA CUP 1947/8
UNITED FAREWELL	PORTSMOUTH (H) DIV. 1 - 07/05/1949
LEFT UNITED FOR	NOTTINGHAM FOREST OCT. 1949 - £9,000

It looked as though John Anderson's Manchester United career was passing him by, his progress having been hampered cruelly by the war. But halfway though 1947/48 and at the ripe age of 26, he sprang from the obscurity of the reserves, then retained his place on merit and finished the season as a Wembley goal-scoring hero as United beat Blackpool to win one of the best FA Cup Finals of all time.

His opportunity arrived unexpectedly. John was standing at Leeds railway station, on his way to Newcastle for a Central League game, when he heard a loudspeaker announcement ordering him back to Manchester. John Carey had fallen ill and Anderson was needed to play at right-half for the first team against Middlesbrough – and just for good measure he had to mark the England star Wilf Mannion.

John rose to the occasion magnificently and was rewarded with a regular berth at the expense of the ageing Jack Warner, missing only one game on the way to the final.

In all honesty, John was a journeyman wing-half, a win-it-and-give-it grafter rather than a thoroughbred, not that there's anything wrong with that. Every team needs players who can win the ball, keep it and use it sensibly. Artists such as the Famous Five forward line could not have weaved their magic without artisans like John to provide them with possession in the first place.

However, he didn't last long with United after his great day at Wembley, moving on to Nottingham Forest, then coaching and training at Peterborough before they joined the Football League.

Still, despite his road being somewhat rocky in the early part of his career, he forged a good life in the game and tasted the type of glory that most players can only dream about.

No one could have deserved it more than John, a cracking fellow who remains a familiar face at Former Players Association events well into his eighties.

BORN	ST. HELENS 25TH DECEMBER 1920
DIED	SALFORD JANUARY 1995
POSITION	HALF-BACK
JOINED UNITED	1935 FROM JUNIOR FOOTBALL
UNITED DEBUT	CHARLTON ATH. (A) DIV. 1 - 03/01/1948
UNITED FAREWELL	ASTON VILLA (A) DIV. 1 - 15/10/1949
LEFT UNITED FOR	BRADFORD P.A. FEB. 1951

28. SAMMY LYNN

OTHER CLUBS:
BRADFORD P.A. 50/1-52/3 (73, 0).

SAMMY LYNN		
COMP.	APPS	GLS
LEAGUE	13	0
TOTAL	13	0

Sammy Lynn was an unusual footballer and a darling of a man. He had tremendous ability; in fact, for a central defender he was such a beautiful passer that it barely seemed true. He reminded me of Neil Franklin, who played for Stoke and England, and it was pure pleasure to watch him.

Sadly, Sammy never won a regular long-term place because he didn't possess an ounce of nastiness. He wasn't interested in kicking people, like most stoppers of his era, he just wanted to play.

Mainly he turned out at centre-half for the reserves, enjoying his longest senior run in the autumn of 1949 when Allenby Chilton, whose approach was exactly the opposite of Sammy's, was having some sort of row with Matt Busby over re-signing.

To me, as a young man in the club when Sammy was a mature player, he was a smashing character. He was kind and approachable, everybody liked him, and he enjoyed his easy-going life to the full.

Sammy would have been on perhaps a tenner a week, which doesn't sound much now, but people get confused with the passing of years. At the time I had uncles who were time-served engineers, bringing up families on £6 for a five-and-a-half day week. Compared to that, pulling in a tenner for a couple of hours on the training pitch every morning didn't seem too bad!

On another tack, Sammy was a St Helens lad and there's a story that he went to Matt, advising him to sign a young goal-keeper who was doing well for St Helens Town, name of Bert Trautmann.

Rightly or wrongly, Matt decided that it might be too soon

after the war to be recruiting a German ex-prisoner of war, and Bert joined Manchester City, with whom he became as fine a goalkeeper as there has ever been. I believe that if United had signed him then, round about 1949, they'd have won the Boat Race, let alone the League Championship – and they'd have had lovely Sammy Lynn to thank.

29. BERRY BROWN

OTHER CLUBS:
DONCASTER ROVERS 48/9 (4, 0);
HARTLEPOOL UNITED 51/2-55/6 (126, 0).

BERRY BROWN		
COMP.	APPS	GLS
LEAGUE	4	0
TOTAL	4	0

BORN	WEST HARTLEPOOL 6TH SEPTEMBER 1927
POSITION	GOALKEEPER
JOINED UNITED	MAY 1946 FROM JUNIOR FOOTBALL
UNITED DEBUT	SHEFFIELD UTD. (A) DIV. 1 - 31/01/1948
UNITED FAREWELL	BLACKPOOL (H) DIV. 1 - 01/09/1948
LEFT UNITED FOR	DONCASTER ROVERS JANUARY 1949

Berry Brown was a lanky lad from the north-east who made a promising start to his brief stint between United's posts when he saved a penalty on his debut against Sheffield United at Bramall Lane, and he can be proud of preserving clean sheets in half of his four League outings for the club.

But in the end he fared no better than Cliff Collinson, Bill Fielding or Ken Pegg when it came to usurping Jack Crompton's jersey on a regular basis, and he was allowed to leave, eventually enjoying his best time back in his home town of Hartlepool during the first half of the 1950s.

30. TOMMY LOWRIE

OTHER CLUBS:
ABERDEEN 50/1-51/2 (29, 1);
OLDHAM ATHLETIC 52/3-54/5 (79, 5).

TOMMY LOWRIE		
COMP.	APPS	GLS
LEAGUE	13	0
FAC	1	0
TOTAL	14	0

BORN	GLASGOW 14TH JANUARY 1928
POSITION	WING-HALF
JOINED UNITED	AUGUST 1947 FROM TROON ATHLETIC
UNITED DEBUT	MANCHESTER CITY (H) DIV. 1 - 07/04/1948
UNITED FAREWELL	OLDHAM ATHLETIC (H) FAC - 06/01/1951
LEFT UNITED FOR	ABERDEEN - MARCH 1951

Tommy Lowrie was Sammy Lynn's big pal and they had a great time together, loving the horses and the dogs and playing a bit of golf. When he first came down from Scotland, Matt and Jimmy Murphy had high hopes for him, and he had a good little start as a wing-half, energetic, hard-working and not a bad passer.

But then, the story goes, he played against Sunderland and ran into Len Shackleton at his most provocative. Apparently Shackleton had the ball in the corner, and he played wall-passes against the flagpole, beckoning Tommy to try and get it off him.

That made Tommy look helpless and it can only have played havoc with his confidence, a piece of behaviour that was totally unnecessary. As much as I admired Shackleton's exceptional talent as an inside-forward, it is always absolutely wrong to take the micky out of a fellow professional, and there can be no excuse for it.

Tommy didn't play another League game for United and while it wasn't the end of his career, he never regained his earlier impetus.

31. JOHNNY BALL

BORN	WIGAN 13TH MARCH 1925
POSITION	FULL-BACK
JOINED UNITED	FEBRUARY 1948 FROM WIGAN ATHLETIC
UNITED DEBUT	EVERTON (A) DIV. 1 - 10/04/1948
UNITED FAREWELL	FULHAM (H) DIV. 1 - 29/04/1950
LEFT UNITED FOR	BOLTON W. - SEPT. 1950 PART-EXCHANGE FOR HARRY MCSHANE

JOHNNY BALL		
COMP.	APPS	GLS
LEAGUE	22	0
FAC	1	0
TOTAL	23	0

OTHER CLUBS:
BOLTON WANDERERS 50/1-57/8 (200, 2).

Johnny Ball was a more-than-useful performer, as he proved after leaving Old Trafford by compiling a double-century of appearances for Bolton in their First Division heyday, facing Blackpool in the 1953 FA Cup Final and winning Football League and England 'B' honours. But his problem as a Manchester United full-back was being stuck in the pecking order behind Messrs Carey and Aston, two of the very best there have ever been.

Johnny was quick and strong, pretty good at passing and intercepting, and an outstanding exponent of the sliding tackle, one of the footballing arts which has practically disappeared from the modern game.

These days defenders are encouraged to stay on their feet more, and it should be remembered, too, that the quality of pitches has changed dramatically. Back in the 1950s they were little better than mud patches from October through to March, and that encouraged the slide.

32. LAURIE CASSIDY

BORN	MANCHESTER 10TH MARCH 1923
POSITION	CENTRE-FORWARD
JOINED UNITED	JANUARY 1947 FROM JUNIOR FOOTBALL
UNITED DEBUT	EVERTON (A) DIV. 1 - 10/04/1948
UNITED FAREWELL	MANCHESTER CITY (A) DIV. 1 - 15/09/1951
LEFT UNITED FOR	OLDHAM ATHLETIC JULY 1956

LAURIE CASSIDY		
COMP.	APPS	GLS
LEAGUE	4	0
TOTAL	4	0

OTHER CLUBS:
OLDHAM ATHLETIC 56/7 (4, 1).

A cursory glance at Laurie Cassidy's record suggests that he made scant contribution to the Manchester United cause – but nothing could be further from the truth.

In fact, he became a famous headmaster in Manchester, he was manager of Manchester Schoolboys, he was involved with England Schoolboys, and he was instrumental in the rise to prominence of Old Trafford stars such as Nobby Stiles and Brian Kidd. So although he didn't play many games or score many goals, Laurie played a hugely significant part in the history of United. You could say that his first love was teaching, and in that role his impact was indelible.

For my money, Laurie Cassidy is as big a name as Jack Rowley, but for totally different reasons.

33. JOHN DOWNIE

OTHER CLUBS:
BRADFORD PARK AVENUE 46/7-48/9 (86, 33);
LUTON TOWN 53/4 (26, 12);
HULL CITY 54/5 (27, 5);
MANSFIELD TOWN 58/9 (18, 4);
DARLINGTON 59/60 (15, 2).

JOHN DOWNIE		
COMP.	APPS	GLS
LEAGUE	110	35
FAC	5	1
OTHERS	1	1
TOTAL	116	37

BORN	LANARK 19TH JULY 1925
POSITION	INSIDE-FORWARD
JOINED UNITED	MARCH 1949 FROM BRADFORD P.A. - £18,000
UNITED DEBUT	CHARLTON ATH. (A) DIV. 1 - 05/03/1949
UNITED HONOURS	DIV. 1 1951/2
UNITED FAREWELL	LIVERPOOL (H) DIV. 1 - 20/04/1953
LEFT UNITED FOR	LUTON TOWN AUGUST 1953 - £10,000

John Downie was asked to accomplish mission impossible, that of replacing Johnny Morris, who had joined Derby County after experiencing a difference of opinion with the manager.

'He is a smashing fellow ... it's just a crying shame that he never realised what an exceptional player he had it in him to be.'

The great shame was that nobody ever saw the best of John, who had fantastic footballing talent and every opportunity in the world to make the most of it. The only reason I can advance for his comparative lack of fulfilment – and we must remember that he wasn't a flop, by any stretch of the imagination – is that the stage on which he was asked to play was just a little too grand for him.

In practice matches, John was virtually unstoppable: he'd get the ball, he'd go past two or three people and smash it into the back of the net, time and time again. But on a Saturday afternoon, after going past his markers he'd be looking for someone to pass to instead of shooting for goal. It was as though he didn't want, or couldn't handle, the responsibility when it really mattered.

It was easy to see why Matt identified Downie as the man to follow Morris. He had pace, he had two fine feet, he was splendid with his head, there wasn't very much that John didn't have, and he had showcased all that ability with several fabulous displays in Manchester for Bradford Park Avenue, notably against City.

But when he pulled on the Manchester United shirt, we didn't see quite the same player. I always had the feeling that he was a bit over-awed, that he didn't quite believe that he should be there.

That said, John averaged a goal every three games for United when he wasn't the main striker, and he earned a Championship medal, so any criticism I make is only comparative to the intimidating standards expected at this club.

I lined up with John in the reserves, where his talent made him a pleasure to play with, and then he was dropped to give me a chance in the first team. I always got on wonderfully well with him; he is a smashing fellow and we never had a cross word. It's just a crying shame that he never realised what an exceptional player he had it in him to be.

BORN	SALFORD 18TH NOVEMBER 1931
DIED	SOUTH AFRICA
POSITION	INSIDE-FORWARD
JOINED UNITED	MAY 1946 FROM JUNIOR FOOTBALL
UNITED DEBUT	WEST BROM. ALBION (H) DIV. 1 - 27/08/1949
UNITED FAREWELL	HUDDERSFIELD TN. (H) DIV. 1 - 03/11/1951
LEFT UNITED FOR	WOLVERHAMPTON W. MARCH 1952 - £10,000

BRIAN BIRCH		
COMP.	APPS	GLS
LEAGUE	11	4
FAC	4	1
TOTAL	15	5

34. BRIAN BIRCH

OTHER CLUBS:
WOLVERHAMPTON WANDERERS 51/2 (3, 1); LINCOLN CITY 52/3-54/5 (56, 15); BARROW 56/7-58/9 (60, 27); EXETER CITY 58/9-59/60 (19, 1); OLDHAM ATHLETIC 59/60-60/1 (35, 10); ROCHDALE 60/1-61/2 (11, 0).

Brian Birch was another tremendous talent, and unlike John Downie, he did not lack confidence in his own ability. In fact, it's fair to say that Birchy believed he was God's gift to the human race.

He was all left peg and he had immense natural talent, full of tricks, though he was never the strongest of lads. Maybe a good comparison would be Tommy Harmer of Tottenham or West Bromwich Albion's David Burnside, both fantastically skilful inside-forwards who flourished in the 1950s without ever quite touching the heights their ability appeared to warrant. Not that Birchy ever achieved as much as either of them, it must be said.

Brian had a magical little spell for United midway through the 1950/51 season, but he never sustained it and went to Wolves for £10,000, a lot of money at the time. He failed to make the grade under Stan Cullis, though, and he left Molineux when he was only 21, going on to see out his career in the lower divisions. For a player with such gifts to fall away as dramatically as that, there must have been a serious problem – and I believe it was between his ears.

I'll always remember an incident in the dressing room when he swaggered in wearing his England Youth blazer, mouthing off insufferably to Allenby Chilton and John Aston, two of the old school. That proved a grave error, as Chilly and Asto grabbed hold of him and hurled him head-first into the big bath, blazer and all. If ever a boy had delusions of grandeur it was Brian Birch.

35. TOMMY BOGAN

OTHER CLUBS:
CELTIC 45/6-48/9 (34, 5);
PRESTON NORTH END 48/9 (11, 0);
ABERDEEN 50/1-51/2 (4, 1);
SOUTHAMPTON 51/2-52/3 (8, 2);
BLACKBURN ROVERS 53/4 (1, 0).

TOMMY BOGAN		
COMP.	APPS	GLS
LEAGUE	29	7
FAC	4	0
TOTAL	33	7

BORN	GLASGOW 18TH MAY 1920
DIED	23RD SEPTEMBER 1993
POSITION	FORWARD
JOINED UNITED	AUGUST 1949 FROM PRESTON N.E.
UNITED DEBUT	CHARLTON ATH. (H) DIV. 1 - 08/10/1949
UNITED FAREWELL	MIDDLESBROUGH (H) DIV. 1 - 03/02/1951
LEFT UNITED FOR	ABERDEEN - MARCH 1951

Tommy Bogan's greatest claim to fame was that he was carried off after one minute of his only game for Scotland. He chased a long ball down the middle, ran into big Frank Swift and that was the end of his international career. Poor Tommy didn't even get a cap for his trouble, because it was an unofficial wartime game.

Sadly he never really came off at United either, despite having decent talent. Tommy could surprise defenders with a sudden burst of speed, he was a clean striker of the ball and he could play out wide or in the middle.

Yet he never really settled anywhere, never became established, and he was a far better player than his patchy record suggests. He was 29 when he came to United, and Matt must have been hoping that he could recapture the sparkle of his Celtic days, but it never happened.

I remember Tommy mainly as a super fellow who was an excellent golfer and was full of stories about the old days.

36. SONNY FEEHAN

OTHER CLUBS:
WATERFORD 44/5-48/9;
NORTHAMPTON TOWN 50/1-51/2 (39, 0);
BRENTFORD 54/5-58/9 (30, 0).

SAMMY FEEHAN		
COMP.	APPS	GLS
LEAGUE	12	0
FAC	2	0
TOTAL	14	0

BORN	DUBLIN 17TH SEPTEMBER 1926
DIED	1995
POSITION	GOALKEEPER
JOINED UNITED	NOVEMBER 1949 FROM WATERFORD, R.O.I.
UNITED DEBUT	HUDDERSFIELD (H) DIV. 1 - 05/11/1949
UNITED FAREWELL	BIRMINGHAM CITY (H) DIV. 1 - 07/04/1950
LEFT UNITED FOR	NORTHAMPTON TOWN AUGUST 1950 - £525

Sonny Feehan, or Ignatius to use his given name, represented another attempt by Matt and Jimmy to provide goalkeeping competition for Jack Crompton.

He was granted more senior chances than most of his predecessors because Jack suffered a broken wrist, but he lacked consistency. Sonny was tall and extremely agile but his performances varied from very good to very bad, and that was not the recipe to make the grade in our First Division.

It can't have been easy to step up from Irish football and life can be very brutal for a young goalkeeper, as he discovered, but he had his moments of glory, notably a brilliant display when United beat Portsmouth, the reigning League champions, in an FA Cup tie at Fratton Park.

BORN	HEBBURN, CO. DURHAM 11TH JUNE 1931
DIED	BEXHILL, SUSSEX 7TH JULY 2002
POSITION	GOALKEEPER
JOINED UNITED	DECEMBER 1949 FROM DARLINGTON - £5,000
UNITED DEBUT	NEWCASTLE UTD. (H) DIV. 1 - 03/12/1949
UNITED HONOURS	DIV. 1 1955/6, 1956/7
UNITED FAREWELL	WOLVERHAMPTON W. (A) DIV. 1 - 04/10/1958
LEFT UNITED FOR	HUDDERSFIELD TOWN DECEMBER 1958 - £1,500

RAY WOOD		
COMP.	APPS	GLS
LEAGUE	178	0
FAC	15	0
EUROPE	12	0
OTHERS	3	0
TOTAL	208	0

37. RAY WOOD

OTHER HONOURS:
3 ENGLAND CAPS 1954-56.

OTHER CLUBS:
DARLINGTON 49/50 (12, 0);
HUDDERSFIELD TOWN 58/9-64/5 (207, 0);
BRADFORD CITY 65/6 (32, 0);
BARNSLEY 66/7-67/8 (30, 0).

MANAGER:
LOS ANGELES WOLVES, USA, 1968; CYRPUS NATIONAL TEAM 1969-72;
APOEL, CYPRUS, 1972-73; TRIKKALA, GREECE, 1973; SALYMIA, KUWAIT, 1973-74;
KENYA CLUB AND NATIONAL TEAMS 1974-78; UNITED ARAB EMIRATES CLUBS 1978-82.

Ray's introduction to Manchester United was both dramatic and unusual, being pitched into first-team action as an 18-year-old goalkeeper only days after his arrival from Darlington.

Because of an injury crisis he played against Newcastle in a 1-1 draw, and then he didn't get another outing in the senior side for several years. It was an odd situation, as during that time he was given a chance as a centre-forward in the 'A' team and scored a few goals. He could move like lightning, being a professional sprinter in the summers back in the north-east, and he capitalised on that.

While all this was going on, Matt Busby signed Reg Allen and United won the title, Jack Crompton was still around and there were some promising youngsters knocking about. So Ray's prospects did not seem to be that bright, but then suddenly he came back with a bang, making the most of a few opportunities in 1952/53 and claiming a regular place in the following season.

Now he won some England caps, helped to lift two League titles and played in the 1957 FA Cup Final, retaining his place until United signed Harry Gregg in the following December.

First and foremost, Woodie was a magnificent shot-stopper, thanks to outstanding agility and those very quick feet. However, he was never the soundest judge of a cross and dear old Tom Curry, the trainer who lost his life at Munich, used to say: 'If there was a barrelful of hay going across, you couldn't be sure that Ray would grab a handful.' To be fair, he was only talking about the occasional game, but I could see where Tom was coming from.

I thought Ray's finest hour was when United met Borussia Dortmund in our first European Cup campaign. It was a miserable, freezing Rhineland night and the Germans threw everything at Ray, but he dealt with the lot and we had him to thank for securing the goalless draw which saw us win the tie on aggregate.

Maybe the turning point in Ray's career was suffering a shattered cheekbone early in that '57 final, when Peter McParland of Aston Villa clattered into him and he finished the game as a passenger on the wing.

Probably that incident dented his confidence, his form dipped in the early months of 1957/58 and Matt turned to Harry Gregg.

Ray, who went on to become a globetrotting coach, was a dear pal of mine. When he first came down to Manchester from Hebburn as an 18-year-old in 1949 he stayed with my mum and I, and we never lost that link. Most people, though, might recall him as being the fastest 'keeper in the country, despite smoking like a chimney.

Where would Ray Wood stand in the roll-call of United's leading goalies? Behind Harry Gregg, Peter Schmeichel and Reg Allen, for sure; but having made those exceptions, he was one of the best.

BORN	STOCKPORT 28TH APRIL 1926
POSITION	GOALKEEPER
JOINED UNITED	MAY 1949 FROM LOCAL FOOTBALL
UNITED DEBUT	CHELSEA (H) DIV. 1 - 14/01/1950
UNITED FAREWELL	PORTSMOUTH (H) FAC - 11/02/1950
LEFT UNITED FOR	ACCRINGTON STANLEY NOVEMBER 1950

JOE LANCASTER		
COMP.	APPS	GLS
LEAGUE	2	0
FAC	2	0
TOTAL	4	0

38. JOE LANCASTER

OTHER CLUBS:
ACCRINGTON STANLEY 50/1 (1, 0).

As a goalkeeper, if you produce two clean sheets and share in three wins and a draw in your only four appearances for Manchester United, you might be entitled to wonder why you weren't offer further opportunities.

But after that cluster of outings early in 1950, Joe Lancaster was discarded by Matt Busby, overshadowed by the likes of Reg Allen, Jack Crompton and Ray Wood.

It must have seemed like a rollercoaster fantasy to Joe, who was plucked from the amateur ranks in May 1949, then made his big-time entrance as a 23-year-old just seven months later, and departed to Accrington by the end of that year. Soon after that he was back in non-League territory with Northwich Victoria.

BORN	SALFORD 27TH MAY 1930
DIED	WORSLEY, LANCS 1970
POSITION	INSIDE-FORWARD
JOINED UNITED	MARCH 1948 FROM JUNIOR FOOTBALL
UNITED DEBUT	SUNDERLAND (A) DIV. 1 - 18/02/1950
UNITED FAREWELL	STOKE CITY (H) DIV. 1 - 11/10/1952
LEFT UNITED FOR	STOCKPORT COUNTY FEBRUARY 1953

FRANK CLEMPSON		
COMP.	APPS	GLS
LEAGUE	15	2
TOTAL	15	2

39. FRANK CLEMPSON

OTHER CLUBS:
STOCKPORT COUNTY 52/3-58/9 (246, 35);
CHESTER 59/60-60/1 (67, 8).

Frank Clempson was an inside-forward with bags of ability, a schemer who always looked happy with the ball, and at one time it seemed as though he might make the grade with United.

It didn't quite happen and he joined Stockport County right out of the blue, the move coming about so fast that it surprised everybody.

Frank was a really nice lad, one of the Salford group that also included Brian Birch and Tommy McNulty, and he deserved the decent career that he enjoyed subsequently at Stockport, and then under Stan Pearson at Chester. After that he went on to become player-boss of Hyde United, where I helped him for a season in which he won the Cheshire Senior Cup.

Frank, who kept a fish-and-chip shop just off the East Lancs Road at Worsley Mains, died tragically young.

40. TOMMY McNULTY

OTHER CLUBS:

LIVERPOOL 53/4-57/8 (36, 0).

TOMMY McNULTY		
COMP.	APPS	GLS
LEAGUE	57	0
FAC	2	0
OTHERS	1	0
TOTAL	60	0

BORN	SALFORD 30TH DECEMBER 1929
DIED	SALFORD 1979
POSITION	FULL-BACK
JOINED UNITED	MAY 1945 FROM JUNIOR FOOTBALL
UNITED DEBUT	PORTSMOUTH (H) DIV. 1 - 15/04/1950
UNITED HONOURS	DIV. 1 1951/2.
UNITED FAREWELL	MIDDLESBROUGH (A) DIV. 1 - 16/09/1953
LEFT UNITED FOR	LIVERPOOL FEBRUARY 1954 - £7,000

Tommy McNulty won a title medal in 1951/52, when he was only 22. He was quick as a whippet at right-back, with a rather unusual upright running style, and he looked a fair bet to become a long-term fixture at Old Trafford. But then all of a sudden there was a personal problem, nothing to do with football, and Matt Busby got rid of him.

Tommy went to Liverpool, where he made an excellent start in a poor team which was relegated from the First Division at the end of his first season at Anfield.

He was still young and it seemed that he might prove an able successor to the long-serving Ray Lambert, but then he lost the number-two shirt to John Molyneux, his appearances became fewer and in 1958 he disappeared from the scene.

Later on Tommy tasted some success in business, running a tobacconists shop in Fitzwarren Street, Salford, before dying prematurely of a brain tumour.

41. JEFF WHITEFOOT

OTHER CLUBS:

GRIMSBY TOWN 57/8 (27, 5);
NOTTINGHAM FOREST 58/9-67/8 (255, 5).

JEFF WHITEFOOT		
COMP.	APPS	GLS
LEAGUE	93	0
FAC	2	0
TOTAL	95	0

BORN	CHEADLE, CHESHIRE 31ST DECEMBER 1933
POSITION	WING-HALF
JOINED UNITED	JULY 1949 FROM JUNIOR FOOTBALL
UNITED DEBUT	PORTSMOUTH (H) DIV. 1 - 15/04/1950
UNITED HONOURS	DIV. 1 1955/6
UNITED FAREWELL	BRISTOL ROVERS (A) FAC - 07/01/1956
LEFT UNITED FOR	GRIMSBY TOWN NOV. 1957 - £11,500

Ah, Jeff Whitefoot. I thought the world of him when we were playing together and I think the world of him now. In my opinion, he was as fine a wing-half as has played for Manchester United since the war, but then I am terribly, terribly biased where he is concerned.

That personal interest declared, I can say honestly that I have never seen a footballer with better feet than Jeff, and that includes all the great stars who have lit up Old Trafford down the years.

He was an absolutely tremendous passer of the ball, a play-maker who read the game beautifully, an ability that did not diminish throughout the 1960s when he adorned several fine Nottingham Forest sides, first under Billy Walker, with whom he won the FA Cup in 1959, then Andy Beattie, and finally his

former United team-mate, John Carey.

Whitefoot could tackle, too, and he wasn't bad in the air for such a little fellow. To sum it up, he had the lot, he was pretty well the complete wing-half, and he deserved some England caps to go with the under-23 honours he received in 1953/54.

So if Jeff was that splendid a footballer, why did he lose his place to Eddie Colman, and then leave Old Trafford when there was so much still in front of that wonderful young team? I believe it boils down to a difference of opinion with Matt Busby, and Jeff was neither the first nor the last top performer to pack his bags because of that. The mere fact that Eddie was coming along was no reason in itself for Jeff to depart. There's always room at any leading club for two players of that calibre.

A lot of people were surprised that Jeff didn't return to United after the Munich disaster, and some say he was asked but that he refused. Only he knows the answer to that. All I know is that it's a great pity he didn't come back, because he would have been a fantastic addition to the team. Certainly he would have been welcomed, both because of what he could do on the field and because he was such a popular lad, a lovely, warm character. Whatever else, Jeff remains the youngest man ever to play senior football for United, at 16 years and 105 days, no matter how many people might reckon it was Duncan Edwards.

Born	Marylebone, London 3rd May 1919
Died	Ealing, London 1976
Position	Goalkeeper
Joined United	June 1950 from QPR for £11,000
United Debut	Fulham (H) Div. 1 - 19/08/1950
United Honours	Div. 1 1951/2
United Farewell	Wolverhampton W. (A) Div. 1 - 04/10/1952
Retired	June 1953

Reg Allen		
Comp.	Apps	Gls
League	75	0
FAC	5	0
Total	80	0

42. REG ALLEN

Other clubs:
Queen's Park Rangers 38/9-49/50 (183, 0).

I've not seen a better goalkeeper than Reg Allen anywhere since the war, and it's a tragedy that his devastating health problems halted his career so soon after he had played a colossal role in United's League title triumph of 1951/52.

Reg was superb in every aspect of his craft. He was a wonderful shot-stopper, he collected crosses like he was shelling peas and he knew when to leave his line and when to stay put. He cut a formidably dominant figure between the posts, and his presence created confidence right through the defence.

But poor Reg fought in the war, then spent a long time in a prisoner-of-war camp, where he must have suffered unimaginably, and it left a terrible mark on him. As a result of his horrific experiences, he fell ill and it cost him what was left of his playing days.

He arrived at Old Trafford in 1950 after United had finished as Championship runners-up for three years and then dropped to fourth place. In his first season Matt Busby's team climbed back up to second, then in his next they finally took the title, and I am convinced that he made the crucial difference.

Now that might sound harsh on Jack Crompton, who was a tidy operator, but Jack would be the first to admit that Reg Allen was an exceptional performer when Matt bought him for £11,000, a fortune for a goalkeeper at that time.

The sad thing is that Reg wasn't a young man even when he came. He was 20 when war broke out, he went on to play nearly 200 League games for Queen's Park Rangers in the lower divisions and when he finally fetched up at Old Trafford he was already 31.

After winning the League, he went away with United on their summer tour of America, where he became distressingly ill. When he returned home he appeared to make some steps towards recovery, but he played only twice during the following autumn before he was hospitalised.

In his last game, at Molineux in October, the Wolves winger Johnny Hancocks hit a hopeful effort from about 60 yards and Reg just stood by the post and watched it roll in. Matt brought him out of goal and put him on the right wing for the rest of the match.

With all that talent, why did he remain so long with Queen's Park Rangers? It seems a bit of a mystery now, but English football was full of marvellous goalkeepers in the post-war years, a vivid contrast to modern times. I'm sure that if the likes of Reg was lurking in the Third Division today, he would be snapped up immediately.

What happened to him was a tremendous shame. He was a bit of a spiky character but he was well liked at the club, and off the field he fitted in well enough. More importantly, everything he did on the park was top-notch, and this much is sure: Reg Allen never received a fraction of the credit he deserved during his playing days, and an honoured place in the annals of Manchester United is long overdue.

BORN	GREENOCK, RENFREWSHIRE 21ST OCTOBER 1924
DIED	1989
POSITION	WING-HALF
JOINED UNITED	AUGUST 1950 FROM PHILADELPHIA NATIONALS
UNITED DEBUT	FULHAM (H) DIV. 1 - 19/08/1950
UNITED FAREWELL	LIVERPOOL (A) DIV. 1 - 23/08/1950
LEFT UNITED FOR	WATERFORD, ROI. JULY 1953 PLAYER/MANAGER

EDDIE McILVENNY		
COMP.	APPS	GLS
LEAGUE	2	0
TOTAL	2	0

43. EDDIE McILVENNY

OTHER HONOURS:
UNITED STATES OF AMERICA CAPS.

OTHER CLUBS:
MORTON 46/7;
WREXHAM 46/7-47/8 (7, 1);
PHILADELPHIA NATIONALS 48-50;
WATERFORD 53/4.

Eddie McIlvenny was simply not good enough for Manchester United, but he possessed a unique claim to fame which could never be taken away from him. When England stunned the sporting world by somehow contriving to lose 1-0 to the United States during the 1950 World Cup Finals, Eddie was the skipper of that giant-slaying American combination.

But why Matt Busby brought him back to Old Trafford and started the next season with him at right-half, heaven only knows. Eddie might or might not have been worth a place in the lower divisions, but with United he was way out of his class.

BORN	MANCHESTER 12TH MAY 1929
POSITION	WING-HALF
JOINED UNITED	NOVEMBER 1946 FROM JUNIOR FOOTBALL
UNITED DEBUT	BOLTON W. (A) DIV. 1 - 26/08/1950
UNITED HONOURS	DIV. 1 1951/2
UNITED FAREWELL	CHELSEA (H) DIV. 1 - 30/04/1955
LEFT UNITED FOR	SHEFFIELD WED JUNE 1955 - £8,000

DON GIBSON		
COMP.	APPS	GLS
LEAGUE	108	0
FAC	6	0
OTHERS	1	0
TOTAL	115	0

44. DON GIBSON

OTHER CLUBS:
SHEFFIELD WEDNESDAY 55/6-59/60 (80, 2);
LEYTON ORIENT 60/1 (8, 0).

To Don Gibson, who was Matt Busby's son-in-law, fell the task of taking over from Eddie McIlvenny after the United States captain had been found wanting at First Division level.

Don was a decent, steady, straight-up-and-down wing-half who cemented his berth in the team for most of that season, then made enough appearances in the early part of 1951/52 to earn a title medal before being replaced by John Carey in a tactical reshuffle.

Pretty soon after that Don was overtaken by a wave of young performers who were far more talented than he, the likes of Jeff Whitefoot, Jackie Blanchflower and Eddie Colman, and it came as no surprise eventually when he was allowed to leave for Sheffield Wednesday.

Later on, being still married to Sheena Busby at the time, probably he was as responsible as anyone for Albert Quixall departing Hillsborough for Old Trafford, as he would have been in a position to report to Matt on Albert's form.

Don and I were good pals when we were at United together, and I was a groomsman at his wedding.

45. HARRY McSHANE

OTHER CLUBS:
BLACKBURN ROVERS 37/8 (2, 0);
HUDDERSFIELD TOWN 46/7 (15, 1);
BOLTON WANDERERS 47/8-50/1 (93, 6);
OLDHAM ATHLETIC 53/4-54/5 (41, 5).

HARRY McSHANE		
COMP.	APPS	GLS
LEAGUE	56	8
FAC	1	0
TOTAL	57	8

BORN	HOLYTOWN, LANARKSHIRE 8TH APRIL 1920
POSITION	WINGER
JOINED UNITED	SEPTEMBER 1950 FROM BOLTON W. PART-EX. FOR JOHN BALL
UNITED DEBUT	ASTON VILLA (H) DIV. 1 - 13/09/1950
UNITED FAREWELL	ASTON VILLA (H) DIV. 1 - 24/10/1953
LEFT UNITED FOR	OLDHAM ATHLETIC FEB. 1954 - £750

Harry McShane was horribly unlucky not to pocket a title medal in 1951/52 when he played a dozen games early in the season, but then suffered a knee injury and never regained his place. You needed 14 appearances, one third of the total, to get a gong in those days, and the League was not prone to making exceptions for sentimental reasons.

He was a little flyer and there was no doubt that he could play. He had two good feet, could operate on either wing and while he didn't relish the rough stuff as much as, say, Johnny Berry, his successor, he was an extremely useful man to have at the club.

Harry did well for United in the brief interlude between two generations of outstanding wingers. When he arrived Charlie Mitten had just departed and Jimmy Delaney was about to go, while Berry would soon be purchased and David Pegg was on the brink of emerging. He might have made an even greater impact, but I had this theory that, maybe like Tommy Bogan, he felt he knew more than the manager, which wouldn't have gone down too well with Matt.

Later on he worked for United as their public-address announcer and then as a scout. A thoroughly nice man, Harry was one of the founder members of our Former Players' Association and he is the father of the actor Ian McShane, best known as TV's *Lovejoy*.

BORN	MANCHESTER 29TH JANUARY 1928
DIED	1994
POSITION	FULL-BACK
JOINED UNITED	JUNE 1944 FROM JUNIOR FOOTBALL
UNITED DEBUT	SHEFFIELD WED. (H) DIV. 1 - 07/10/1950
UNITED HONOURS	DIV. 1 1951/2
UNITED FAREWELL	CARDIFF CITY (H) DIV. 1 - 03/04/1954
LEFT UNITED FOR	BURY JUNE 1954

46. BILLY REDMAN

BILLY REDMAN		
COMP.	APPS	GLS
LEAGUE	36	0
FAC	2	0
TOTAL	38	0

OTHER CLUBS:
BURY 54/5-55/6 (37, 1).

Billy was a draughtsman and never a full-time professional footballer, which must have held him back. It's got to be a hindrance if you're not training with your team-mates every day and giving the game your undivided attention.

Still, he played the first 18 games of United's 1951/52 title-winning campaign at left-back, before being replaced by Roger Byrne. That was more than enough to earn him his medal, which he thoroughly deserved.

Billy was a very promising player, skilful with both feet and he was very composed. In fact, I'm sure the world could have collapsed around him and he would have just gone on doing his normal thing. He was absolutely unflappable, a bit like David Sadler in later years.

Had he been a full-timer like the rest of us, I'm sure that he could have been looking at a highly successful future in the game because Matt Busby and Jimmy Murphy both rated him extremely highly. As it was he trained only on Tuesday and Thursday nights, and perhaps tended to be something of an afterthought when the team was being planned.

Billy forged a successful career in business, though, so who's to say he made the wrong choice?

BORN	LONG VALLEY, YORKSHIRE 15TH JUNE 1933
DIED	MUNICH 6TH FEBRUARY 1958
POSITION	CENTRE-HALF
JOINED UNITED	JUNE 1948 FROM JUNIOR FOOTBALL
UNITED DEBUT	SHEFFIELD WED. (H) DIV. 1 - 07/10/1950
UNITED HONOURS	DIV. 1 1955/6. 1956/7
UNITED FAREWELL	RED STAR BELGRADE (A) EC - 05/02/1958

47. MARK JONES

MARK JONES		
COMP.	APPS	GLS
LEAGUE	103	1
FAC	7	0
EUROPE	10	0
OTHERS	1	0
TOTAL	121	1

Mark Jones was a gem. You're privileged in life to meet people like him, and he meant so much to me that I named my eldest son after him. He had a wonderful outlook on life, understanding fully how very lucky we all were to be earning our livings by playing the game.

Plenty of his relations and friends back in Yorkshire had gone down the mines, so he thought that being paid for kicking a football was like winning the pools every day of the week – and he was right, wasn't he? Big Mark was essentially a simple man, in the best possible meaning of that description. He loved nothing better than smoking his pipe, looking after his pigeons and walking his dog in the countryside. He was a traditional family man, who had been going out with the girl that he married since he was 11 years old.

His giant stature, his strength and his courage made him a natural in the old-fashioned centre-half role, as defined at Old Trafford by Allenby Chilton before him. He was a bit raw to start with, maybe, but he was majestic in the air and there was never any doubt that he was going to make the grade, right from the days when he played for the same England Schoolboys side as Dennis Viollet, Jeff Whitefoot and Cliff Birkett. They all joined United together, along with Jackie Blanchflower from Belfast, so it wasn't a bad intake that year!

One vivid memory of Mark is of going for a drink after we had beaten Borussia Dortmund in the European Cup. We were all in the bar together when a fellow started punching Ray Wood; Mark put his glass down, strolled over and smacked the offender on the chin, then picked up his pint again as if nothing had happened. It wasn't that he was given to violence – quite the opposite, in fact – but just that he would never stand for bullying and knew how to look after a pal.

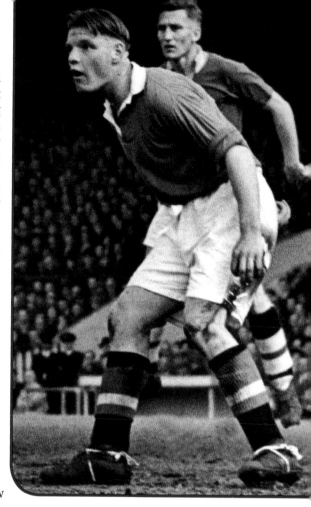

GENTLE OFF THE FIELD, FEARSOME ON IT: big Mark Jones polices Chelsea and England centre-forward Roy Bentley.

'Plenty of his relations and friends had gone down the mines, so he thought that being paid for kicking a football was like winning the pools every day of the week – and he was right, wasn't he?'

Of course, the great unanswered question about Mark Jones is a taxing one: would he or Jackie Blanchflower have become United's regular centre-half in the long term? They were both magnificent players, but with vastly contrasting styles – Mark with his awesome power and Jackie with his far more stylish approach. Though Mark was in possession of the number-five shirt at the time of Munich, having taken it back after Jackie had enjoyed a decent run, it would have been a very tight call.

Certainly, had he been spared on that dreadful day, Mark would have had a terrific chance of collecting some caps in the years that followed. He was as good, if not better, than Peter Swan and Maurice Norman, the men who succeeded Billy Wright at centre-half for England.

BORN	HAYDOCK, LANCASHIRE 17TH SEPTEMBER 1933
DIED	JANUARY 1997
POSITION	WINGER
JOINED UNITED	1949 FROM JUNIOR FOOTBALL
UNITED DEBUT	NEWCASTLE UTD. (H) DIV. 1 - 02/12/1950
UNITED FAREWELL	BIRMINGHAM CITY (A) FAC - 24/02/1951
LEFT UNITED FOR	SOUTHPORT - JUNE 1956

CLIFF BIRKETT		
COMP.	APPS	GLS
LEAGUE	9	2
FAC	4	0
TOTAL	13	2

48. CLIFF BIRKETT

OTHER CLUBS:
SOUTHPORT 56/7 (14, 4).

Those who hailed Cliff Birkett as something of a boyhood prodigy did not share my opinion, but I never thought that he had sufficient knowhow to play in the top grade.

He was blessed with ample speed and strength, which stood him in good stead when he was facing schoolboys, and he scored a few goals at that level, but he would never have lasted against experienced professionals. Quite simply, they would have kicked bits out of him and he wouldn't have had the tricks, the cuteness, to have dealt with them.

Even after it became obvious that Cliff wasn't holding his own in the first team, Matt Busby must have harboured hopes that he was a late developer because he kept him on the staff for another five and a half years.

Finally he was released to join Southport, for whom his older brother Wilf had played in goal.

BORN	PRESTON 4TH MAY 1929
POSITION	WINGER
JOINED UNITED	DEC. 1950 FROM LEYLAND MOTORS
UNITED DEBUT	WBA (A) DIV. 1 - 18/08/1951
UNITED HONOURS	DIV. 1 1951/2
UNITED FAREWELL	ARSENAL (H) DIV. 1 - 03/09/1952
LEFT UNITED FOR	CARLISLE UTD. SEPT. 1952 - £5,000

ERNIE BOND		
COMP.	APPS	GLS
LEAGUE	20	4
FAC	1	0
TOTAL	21	4

49. ERNIE BOND

OTHER CLUBS:
CARLISLE UNITED 52/3-58/9 (194, 23); COWDENBEATH 58/9.

It's not a word used often in connection with footballers, but left-winger Ernie Bond could realistically be described as petite. Tiny, slim and neat, he had pace and he could deliver the ball effectively from the touchline, but I never saw him as a world-beater and wasn't surprised when he left Old Trafford for the lower divisions.

Mind, it should be stressed that though Ernie didn't spend long in the United first team, he made the most of his stay, picking up a Championship medal in 1951/52, when he made nearly all his appearances for the club.

Ernie started the season in the side, then dropped out when Harry McShane switched from right to left flank following the arrival of Johnny Berry. But then Harry was injured and Ernie returned for a spell, before Matt handed the number-11 shirt first to Jack Rowley and then, unexpectedly, to Roger Byrne.

50. JOHNNY BERRY

OTHER HONOURS:
4 ENGLAND CAPS 1953-56.

OTHER CLUBS:
BIRMINGHAM CITY 47/8-51/2 (103, 5).

JOHNNY BERRY		
COMP.	APPS	GLS
LEAGUE	247	37
FAC	15	4
EUROPE	11	3
OTHERS	3	1
TOTAL	276	45

BORN	ALDERSHOT, HAMPSHIRE 1ST JUNE 1926
DIED	FARNHAM, SURREY 16TH SEPTEMBER 1994
POSITION	WINGER
JOINED UNITED	AUGUST 1951 FROM BIRMINGHAM C - £25,000
UNITED DEBUT	BOLTON W. (A) DIV. 1 - 01/09/1951
UNITED HONOURS	DIV. 1 1951/2, 1955/6, 1956/7.
UNITED FAREWELL	LUTON TOWN (A) DIV. 1 - 26/12/1957
RETIRED	DUE TO INJURIES RECEIVED IN MUNICH AIR CRASH

You could have 'em all, any winger you might care to name, but I'd always be happy with little Johnny Berry in my side. I'm not saying that he was literally the greatest – after all, there are fellers like Stan Matthews, Tom Finney and George Best to consider – but if you had Berry, then you had a player and a half who would never let you down in any situation.

'He had an insatiable appetite for the game, and if it hadn't been for Matthews and Finney he would have won far more than his four England caps.'

Johnny was as tough as old boots, ready to run through brick walls, without question the hardest flankman I've seen in my life. He was brave in an era when we weren't used to brave wingers, and it was like having an extra player in your team.

Often he was too courageous for his own good, such as one day at Stamford Bridge when Stan Willemse hacked chunks out of him. But Berry kept on running at him, taking him on and being hammered every time. I was playing alongside him at inside-right and shouted: 'Give it to me, you run into space for the return,' but he was having none of it. He grated under his breath to me: 'Doc, I'm having him. Does he think he's going to kick me out of the game? Over my dead body!'

So he kept going at Willemse, and eventually he did catch him, because Johnny would never give in. But it would be wrong to give the impression that he was merely physical, because Berry was some fabulous footballer as well.

He could play on either wing, though usually on the right; he had a trick to go past players and cross from the byline; he could cut inside for goal; he loved

A WINGER WITH ATTITUDE: Having left Blackpool's Tommy Garrett toiling in his wake, Johnny Berry delivers a trademark cross.

taking penalties, he didn't know what nerves were. On top of that he had an insatiable appetite for the game, and if it hadn't been for Matthews and Finney he would have won far more than his four England caps.

Sadly, the injuries he received at Munich prevented him from playing again and we shall never know whether he would have won back his place from young Kenny Morgans, who had recently ousted him.

But even though Johnny was in his 32nd year, I can't believe in my wildest imaginings that he was finished. He didn't know the meaning of the word.

What was he like off the pitch? He could be a bit awkward, a bit of a rum case, but in general he mixed well with the lads. He loved a drink, loved a smoke, thought we were all idiots for playing golf, enjoyed a game of snooker; Johnny was all right.

Poignantly, when great United players are mentioned, he tends to be forgotten. Certainly he's never received the accolades that should have been his by rights, probably because he wasn't actually a Babe, having been signed by Matt Busby from Birmingham City when he was 25. Yet he was as much to do with the success of the Babes as any man at Old Trafford. For Johnny Berry, no praise could be too high.

BORN	HORWICH, LANCASHIRE 21ST MARCH 1928
DIED	HORWICH, LANCASHIRE JULY 1979
POSITION	INSIDE-FORWARD
JOINED UNITED	JULY 1951 FROM BURY (AMATEUR)
UNITED DEBUT	PRESTON N.E. (H) DIV. 1 - 29/09/1951
UNITED FAREWELL	DERBY CO. (H) DIV. 1 - 06/10/1951
LEFT UNITED FOR	BURY JULY 1952 (AMATEUR)

JOHN WALTON		
COMP.	APPS	GLS
LEAGUE	2	0
TOTAL	2	0

51. JOHN WALTON

OTHER CLUBS:
BURY 49/50-50/1 (26, 4) AND 52/3-53/4 (29, 2);
BURNLEY 54/5-55/6 (18, 2);
COVENTRY CITY 56/7-57/8 (13, 0);
CHESTER 59/60 (1, 0).

John Walton was an England amateur international with a typical Corinthian attitude to playing football. I remember being alongside him in the reserves at Blackpool one day and throughout the game he was applauding the efforts of Bill Slater, another top amateur.

If I heard him say 'Well played, Bill!' once then I must have heard it 20 times. I told him: 'For pity's sake, he's on the other side. We're supposed to be tackling him and getting the ball off him, not telling him how well he's doing!'

If John had his way, when you got the ball you would be allowed to do party tricks; then it would go to the opposition and they could do their party tricks. It's fair to say that his attitude to winning and losing was not the same as the rest of us. To us it was our living, to him it was something else.

John was a skilful inside-forward and a nice lad, but he wasn't cut out for professional football and it was the right decision when he gave up the game to concentrate on his teaching career.

52. ROGER BYRNE

OTHER HONOURS:
33 ENGLAND CAPS 1955-57.

ROGER BYRNE		
COMP.	APPS	GLS
LEAGUE	245	17
FAC	18	2
EUROPE	14	0
OTHERS	3	1
TOTAL	280	20

BORN	GORTON, MANCHESTER 8TH FEBRUARY 1929
DIED	MUNICH 6TH FEBRUARY 1958
POSITION	FULL-BACK
JOINED UNITED	MARCH 1949 FROM JUNIOR FOOTBALL
UNITED DEBUT	LIVERPOOL (A) DIV. 1 - 24/11/1951
UNITED HONOURS	DIV. 1 1951/2, 1955/6, 1956/7.
UNITED FAREWELL	RED STAR BELGRADE EC - 05/02/1958

Roger Byrne was a magnificent performer who played a gigantic part in Manchester United's history, yet it's astonishing to reflect that in the summer before he made his debut he might easily have been allowed to leave the club.

At that point he turned out mainly at left-half for the reserves and his career appeared to be going nowhere, but then there was an injury crisis, with Matt Busby losing John Aston, Billy Redman and Billy McGlen in the run-up to a game at Liverpool, so Roger was pressed into duty at left-back.

The position fitted him like a glove, he barely missed a match for the next six seasons and he matured into a top international, playing in 33 consecutive England games before losing his life at Munich.

The strange thing was that if you took an inventory of Roger's attributes, then you would never have thought he could have become an outstanding left-back.

True, he had exceptional pace and a good right side, but he had no left side to speak of, he wasn't much of a tackler and he wasn't an accomplished header of the ball. Despite all that, I haven't seen a better full-back in the last 50 years. Somehow the role seemed to suit him down to the ground; he moved on to a different plane when he was converted and he continued to grow into the position as the decade wore on.

At one point, though, Matt amazed everyone by temporarily shifting Roger from his new job, not long after giving it to him. It was early in April 1952, United's title challenge was slipping and the manager decided that changes had to be made. So he shuffled John Aston to left-back, shifted Jack Rowley to centre-forward and stuck Roger on the left wing, where he responded by scoring seven goals in six games on the

ROGER BYRNE LEADS THE WAY: as United run out to face Birmingham, Roy Warhurst is carrying the ball for City, followed by England goalkeeper Gil Merrick and Peter Murphy.

way to clinching the Championship.

Was it inspiration or was it luck? Well, when a move like that succeeds, anybody can call it what they want; if it had failed, it would have been seen as stupidity. I'd guess that Matt thought Roger's pace out wide would give the

'I don't think there's any doubt that, if he had lived, he would have succeeded Billy Wright as England skipper for the foreseeable future.'

attack an extra dimension, and he was proved correct. Roger, who succeeded John Carey as captain, was a popular lad but he always had a certain arrogance about him. He could be very cutting, a bit of an awkward beggar, though no one was allowed to step out of line with the boss, not even the skipper.

I recall an incident in a practice game at The Cliff when Matt shouted something and Roger told him to 'f*** off.' By lunchtime Byrne was on the transfer list, and he wasn't taken off until he had apologised.

Much has been written about his leadership skills, and, yes, we all looked up to Roger but that was because he was such a fine player. Okay, it's a hobby-horse of mine, but I maintain that it's good footballers, not good captains, that make successful teams. It's a funny thing, but when you look back, there were never any good captains of bad teams!

For all that, Roger was identified as officer material and I don't think there's any doubt that, if he had lived, he would have succeeded Billy Wright as England skipper for the foreseeable future.

53. JACKIE BLANCHFLOWER

OTHER HONOURS:
12 NORTHERN IRELAND CAPS 1954-58.

BORN	BELFAST 7TH MARCH 1933
DIED	MANCHESTER 2ND SEPTEMBER 1998
POSITION	CENTRE-HALF, WING-HALF, INSIDE-FORWARD
JOINED UNITED	MAY 1949 FROM IRISH JUNIOR FOOTBALL
UNITED DEBUT	LIVERPOOL (A) DIV. 1 - 24/11/1951
UNITED HONOURS	DIV. 1 1955/6
UNITED FAREWELL	TOTTENHAM H. (H) DIV. 1 - 30/11/1957
RETIRED	DUE TO INJURIES RECEIVED IN MUNCIH AIR CRASH

JACKIE BLANCHFLOWER		
COMP.	APPS	GLS
LEAGUE	105	26
FAC	6	1
EUROPE	5	0
OTHERS	1	0
TOTAL	117	27

Jackie Blanchflower was a charmer of a man, and a very fine all-round footballer. He arrived at Old Trafford from Northern Ireland as a schoolboy wing-half and he made his first-team debut in that position, doing pretty well. Then he was switched to inside-forward when United had a few casualties, myself included. Later still, when I was back in contention and Billy Whelan and Bobby Charlton were on the scene, Jackie moved to centre-half, where he played some of his best football.

He wasn't a giant by any stretch of the imagination, and he had no pace at all, but he was a natural ball-player with both feet, he was excellent in the air and he was adept at controlling or re-directing the ball with his chest.

Perhaps most importantly, Jackie had a natural instinct for the game and a great knowledge of it, as he demonstrated by adapting successfully to so many different positions.

There was a purple patch, in 1953/54 and 1954/55, when he was scoring a lot of goals from inside-right and he was setting up plenty for his team-mates, too. However, it looked as though Matt Busby had decided that centre-half was to be his role, and from 1956 onwards he was vying with Mark Jones for the number-five shirt. As I've mentioned already, as players they were contrasting types – Mark a traditional rugged stopper and Jackie less physical but more skilful and subtle – and both of them made out a strong case for a regular slot.

Jackie had helped to clinch the title in the spring of 1957 and played in the FA Cup Final defeat by Aston Villa, extending his reputation for

'As players they were contrasting types: Mark (Jones) a traditional rugged stopper and Jackie less physical but more skilful and subtle – and both of them made out a strong case for a regular slot.'

TEN PAST FOUR AND ALL TO PLAY FOR: airborne Jackie Blanchflower escapes the attentions of Bolton defenders Bryan Edwards (centre) and former Red Devil Johnny Ball to smack a header goalwards at Burnden Park in September 1954.

versatility by going in goal when Ray Wood was injured, and he was still first choice at the start of the following season. But then Mark fought back and Jackie was out of the side at the time of Munich, though it was impossible to imagine that such a gifted individual, still only 24 years old, wouldn't come bouncing back at some stage. Who knows, he might have battled on against Mark or returned to one of his former roles; certainly he was good enough to threaten the places of several people.

As it turned out, tragically, he suffered terrible injuries at Munich and he never played again, so we shall never know the answer.

Jackie was the brother of Danny Blanchflower, who captained Spurs to the League and FA Cup double in 1960/61, but there were few similarities beyond their surname and the fact that they were both cultured footballers. Jackie was two-footed while Danny relied on his right; Danny was a showman while Jackie was the opposite; the pair of them didn't seem to be close in any way.

BORN	BELFAST 22ND DECEMBER 1933
DIED	MANCHESTER, JUNE 1978
POSITION	WINGER
JOINED UNITED	1950 FROM IRISH JUNIOR FOOTBALL
UNITED DEBUT	WOLBVERHAMPTON W. (A) DIV. 1 - 04/10/1952
UNITED FAREWELL	PRESTON N.E. (A) DIV. 1 - 21/01/1956
LEFT UNITED FOR	GRIMSBY TOWN JUNE 1956

JOHNNY SCOTT		
COMP.	APPS	GLS
LEAGUE	3	0
TOTAL	3	0

54. JOHNNY SCOTT

OTHER HONOURS:
2 NORTHERN IRELAND CAPS 1958.

OTHER CLUBS:
GRIMSBY TOWN 56/7-62/3 (241, 51);
YORK CITY 63/4 (21, 3).

One of Jackie Blanchflower's Irish contemporaries, Johnny was a skilful outside-right who could unsettle defenders. But he was a bit of a moaner, and I believe that if he had brought as much enthusiasm to the game as, say, Johnny Berry, then he would have been far more successful.

He played only three League games for United and there were more than three years between his first appearance and his last, reflecting the savage competition for places at Old Trafford in the mid 1950s, in Scott's case from Berry and Kenny Morgans.

After leaving United, Johnny went on to excel for Grimsby Town, under the management of Allenby Chilton, proving that he had staying power as well as talent, and also underlining what a terrific player Berry must have been to shut him out so comprehensively at United.

Johnny, who rose to international status during his Blundell Park days, left the game after his retirement, later dying in an horrific accident on a building site.

55. EDDIE LEWIS

OTHER CLUBS:
PRESTON NORTH END 55/6-56/7 (12, 2);
WEST HAM UNITED 56/7-57/8 (31, 12);
LEYTON ORIENT 58/9-63/4 (142, 4).

EDDIE LEWIS		
COMP.	APPS	GLS
LEAGUE	20	9
FAC	4	2
TOTAL	24	11

BORN	MANCHESTER 3RD JANUARY 1935
POSITION	CENTRE-FORWARD
JOINED UNITED	1949 FROM SCHOOL FOOTBALL
UNITED DEBUT	WBA (A) DIV. 1 - 29/11/1952
UNITED FAREWELL	EVERTON (H) DIV. 1 - 07/09/1955
LEFT UNITED FOR	PRESTON N.E. DEC. 1955 - £10,000

Eddie Lewis came through at the same time as me, his senior debut arriving a week ahead of mine. But although we played together in the 'A' team, the youth team and the reserves, we were rarely on the same pitch for the first team.

He was a big, strong leader of the line who scored nine goals in 14 games during his debut season, which was a pretty fair strike-rate, but then Tommy Taylor arrived and he was never going to be in Tommy's class. No one was.

I thought Eddie might do well at Preston, but he didn't, and it amazed me in later years when he was converted successfully to full-back at Leyton Orient. I never had him down as a defender.

I got on well with Eddie, but he had some funny ideas. I remember scoring a goal for the reserves just before half-time, and as we walked off he said: 'I wish that had been me.' I asked him why and he said you had to score in the first half to get your name in the *Football Pink*. Why that should have mattered to him, I don't know.

He's been living in South Africa for many years, but occasionally comes over to see us when the ex-players hold a dinner-dance.

56. JOHN DOHERTY

OTHER CLUBS:
LEICESTER CITY 57/8 (12, 5).

JOHN DOHERTY		
COMP.	APPS	GLS
LEAGUE	25	7
FAC	1	0
TOTAL	26	7

BORN	MANCHESTER 12TH MARCH 1935
POSITION	INSIDE-FORWARD
JOINED UNITED	MAY 1950 FROM JUNIOR FOOTBALL
UNITED DEBUT	MIDDLESBROUGH (H) DIV. 1 - 06/12/1952
UNITED HONOURS	DIV. 1 1955/6
UNITED FAREWELL	WOLVERHAMPTON W. (A) DIV. 1 - 28/09/1957
LEFT UNITED FOR	LEICESTER CITY OCTOBER 1957 - £6,500

Modesty forbids me going into too much detail about this fellow Doherty, but there are one or two people with long memories who tell me that he could play a bit. What was I like? In a nutshell: good ability, two decent feet, a fair footballing brain, absolutely terrible knees. I could pass, and I always scored my share of goals, but those knees... oh dear.

I picked up my first injury on the day before my eighteenth birthday against Brentford in the second leg of the FA Youth Cup semi-final in 1953. I was supposed to be entering Her Majesty's armed forces the next day, to begin my National Service, and that was one date I had to make. I missed the cup final against Wolves, too, and they signed Billy Whelan in time to replace me.

So those knees didn't do all that well for me, and it was mostly downhill from there. I don't think there was a particular weakness, it was just one of those things. The first injury took a long time to get over,

'I have to remember that if it hadn't been for my dodgy knees I might well have been on the plane that crashed at Munich.'

although Matt Busby retained faith in me. He knew I could play, that I could always score goals, so obviously he felt I was worth the chance, and in due course I came back to win a title medal in 1955/56.

At the time I had just been discharged by the RAF, classified as medically unfit, and not many people expected me to play again. But I resumed training at United, and scored in a win against Wolves when deputising for Jackie Blanchflower, who was away on international duty.

He returned but I had made a mark and soon I was recalled. There followed a great little run of about ten matches before we were drubbed in the FA Cup by Bristol Rovers, after which the only person to be dropped was me. Obviously, it must have been my fault.

I got back in towards the end of the season, then had a good summer tour, but Matt didn't pick me at the start of the new term, and so we started having a few words. As might be expected, the manager won the argument and, even though I was still having problems with my knees, I accepted a move to Leicester, where I had the pleasure of linking up with Johnny Morris.

I started well at Filbert Street, scoring a few times, but then my left knee gave up on me and that was the end of it. Apart from a brief fling at Rugby Town, where they treated me royally, I never played again.

Such an injury would not be career-threatening to-day, but I'm not complaining. It's better to be a has-been than a never-was, and I enjoyed every minute of my career.

I have to remember, too, that if it hadn't been for my dodgy knees I might well have been on the plane that crashed at Munich. On such little details do our lives depend, and from that viewpoint I can consider my-self extraordinarily lucky. After all, I went on to have a happy life, with a wonderful wife and family, while lots of my mates were dead.

57. DAVID PEGG

OTHER HONOURS:
1 ENGLAND CAP 1957.

DAVID PEGG		
COMP.	APPS	GLS
LEAGUE	127	24
FAC	9	0
EUROPE	12	4
OTHERS	2	0
TOTAL	150	28

BORN	DONCASTER 20TH SEPTEMBER 1935
DIED	MUNICH 6TH FEBRUARY 1958
POSITION	WINGER
JOINED UNITED	SEPTEMBER 1950 FROM JUNIOR FOOTBALL
UNITED DEBUT	MIDDLESBROUGH (H) DIV. 1 - 06/12/1952
UNITED HONOURS	DIV. 1 1955/6, 1956/7
UNITED FAREWELL	CHELSEA (H) DIV. 1 - 14/12/1957

David Pegg was an extremely talented outside-left who was only 22 when he was killed at Munich, but who had already been awarded his first England cap. Had he lived, I think there might have been plenty more to follow.

Yet for all the natural ability with which he was so well endowed, and for all the progress he had made since he and I made our League debut on the same day, Peggy always had a certain cloud on his horizon . . . and it was called Albert Scanlon.

Both David and Albert wanted United's number-11 shirt, and both of them were good enough to do justice to it, but while both of them were exceedingly quick, they were radically different in their styles of play.

David liked to do a bit on the ball, dip a shoulder and send his man the wrong way, very intricate and clever, whereas Albert was much more direct, knocking the ball past his marker and then slinging over a cross.

At the time of the tragedy, David was on the sidelines and Albert was playing out of his skin, but somewhere down the line he'd have had the opportunity to regain his place.

Just how good was he? A fine player, certainly, though I don't think he had the capacity to develop along the lines of, say, Bobby Charlton. He used to play inside-left for the youth team, but it's hard for me to envisage him as a midfielder in the First Division.

As I picture him, Peggy will always be a winger. In many ways he was a bit like Ryan Giggs, hard to pin down and contributing his share of goals, though without being unkind to Ryan, David might have been better at supplying a final ball. That said, I'd give Giggsy the edge as an all-round player.

Off the park David was a personable lad, easy to get on with and a particularly close chum of his fellow Yorkshireman Tommy Taylor.

BORN	ST. HELENS
	5TH JANUARY 1932
POSITION	FULL-BACK, CENTRE-HALF
JOINED UNITED	MARCH 1950 FROM
	JUNIOR FOOTBALL
UNITED DEBUT	LIVERPOOL (A)
	DIV. 1 - 13/12/1952
UNITED HONOURS	EUROPEAN CUP 1967/8
	DIV. 1 1955/6, 1956/7,
	1964/5, 1966/7
	FA CUP 1962/3
UNITED FAREWELL	SOUTHAMPTON (H)
	DIV. 1 - 16/08/1969
RETIRED	JUNE 1970
	UNITED COACHING STAFF

BILL FOULKES		
COMP.	APPS	GLS
LEAGUE	563 (3)	7
FAC	61	0
EUROPE	52	2
OTHERS	6	0
TOTAL	685 (3)	9

58. BILL FOULKES

OTHER HONOURS:
1 ENGLAND CAP 1954.

MANAGER:
CHICAGO STING 1975-77;
TULSA ROUGHNECKS 1978-79;
SAN JOSE EARTHQUAKES 1980, ALL USA;
FARSTAD, STENJKER (TWICE), LILLESTROM,
VIKING STAVANGER, ALL NORWAY, 1980-88;
MAZDA, JAPAN, 1988-91.

Bill Foulkes had an absolutely unbelievable career, finishing up with just about every major medal it was possible to win, spread over nearly 17 years. It was an achievement all the more remarkable for the fact that he wasn't blessed with the natural talent of many of his contemporaries, as I think he would be the first to admit.

Yet while it could be argued that Bill lacked this particular skill, or that particular refinement, the only question that matters is an easy one to answer – was Matt Busby wrong 685 times? He wasn't, of course, so the conclusion must be that Foulkesy couldn't have been a bad player.

Bill was a big fellow and a fitness fanatic whose greatest attribute was his strength. He took some beating in the air, he wasn't slow across the ground and, though he was very right-sided, he coped with it. No one was more focused on the job, he always paid minute attention to detail in his preparation and, perhaps the defining aspect of his make-up, he was a ruthless beggar.

After Munich, with Matt having to rebuild his team, Bill was ideal for the job of centre-half, the rock at the core of United's defence. Yet he had started in the team five years previously as a right-back, facing one of the sternest tests on debut that the First Division had to offer in the form of Liverpool's Scottish international Billy Liddell.

He didn't let the side down, and he went on to earn two title medals and his only England cap in that position, but I'm convinced that his move from full-back to centre-half, a little while after he had survived the Munich disaster, was the best thing that ever happened to him. He was far more at ease in the middle where he could face the ball, and it came on to him, than in wide situations in which he had to twist and turn and be much more mobile.

Away from the game, Bill was a bit of a loner, and he could be single-minded to the point of being blinkered. For example, when he took up golf he pursued it with so much determination that in no time at all he was a scratch golfer, and that personified his outlook. If he was going to do anything, then

he would go at it with all guns blazing; there was no way he was going to shirk.

Summing up Bill's career, I look at his figures and his list of honours, and I am staggered. I have to say I wouldn't mind having them on my CV.

BORN	BARNSLEY 29TH JANUARY 1932
DIED	MUNICH 6TH FEBRUARY 1958
POSITION	CENTRE-FORWARD
JOINED UNITED	MAY 1953 FROM BARNSLEY - £29,999
UNITED DEBUT	PRESTON N.E. (H) DIV. 1 - 07/03/1953
UNITED HONOURS	DIV. 1 1955/6, 1956/7
UNITED FAREWELL	RED STAR BELGRADE (A) EC - 05/02/1958

TOMMY TAYLOR		
COMP.	APPS	GLS
LEAGUE	166	112
FAC	9	5
EUROPE	14	11
OTHERS	2	3
TOTAL	191	131

59. TOMMY TAYLOR

OTHER HONOURS:
19 ENGLAND CAPS 1953-57.

OTHER CLUBS:
BARNSLEY 50/1-52/3 (44, 26).

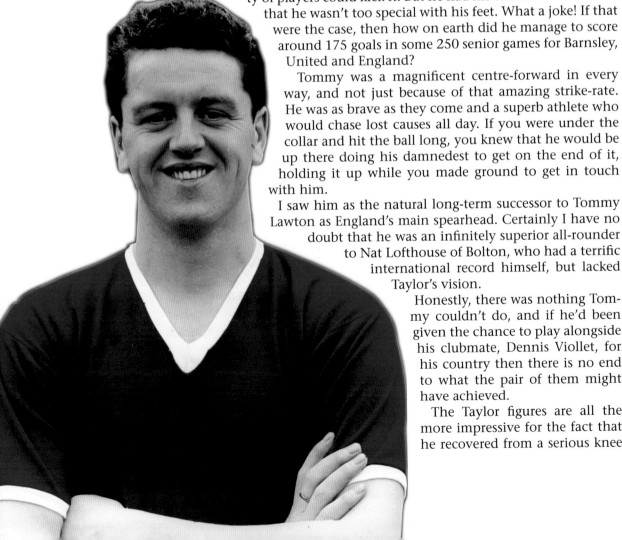

Tommy Taylor was one of the most underrated footballers to have played since the war. He did an absolutely stupendous job for Manchester United and I believe passionately that if he, Roger Byrne and Duncan Edwards had not died at Munich, then England would have gone very close to winning the World Cup in 1958.

No one could conceivably deny that he was brilliant in the air; he could hammer the ball harder with his head than plenty of players could kick it. But he had his critics who reckoned that he wasn't too special with his feet. What a joke! If that were the case, then how on earth did he manage to score around 175 goals in some 250 senior games for Barnsley, United and England?

Tommy was a magnificent centre-forward in every way, and not just because of that amazing strike-rate. He was as brave as they come and a superb athlete who would chase lost causes all day. If you were under the collar and hit the ball long, you knew that he would be up there doing his damnedest to get on the end of it, holding it up while you made ground to get in touch with him.

I saw him as the natural long-term successor to Tommy Lawton as England's main spearhead. Certainly I have no doubt that he was an infinitely superior all-rounder to Nat Lofthouse of Bolton, who had a terrific international record himself, but lacked Taylor's vision.

Honestly, there was nothing Tommy couldn't do, and if he'd been given the chance to play alongside his clubmate, Dennis Viollet, for his country then there is no end to what the pair of them might have achieved.

The Taylor figures are all the more impressive for the fact that he recovered from a serious knee injury while at his first club, just as Ruud van Nistelrooy did half a century later.

In fact, my first memory of Tommy was in a reserve match at Barnsley when he was on his comeback trail, not long before Matt Busby bought him. There was this big gormless beggar playing up front for them and he murdered us, totally destroyed us.

Talking of the Dutchman, Tommy's goals-to-games ratio is not far behind Ruud's. I know they say scoring goals is more difficult now, but how they work that out I don't know, because they play with a beach-ball now, and on perfect pitches, which ought to make the job a whole lot simpler.

Aside from his immeasurable worth as a player, Tommy was one of the most popular people at the club, a happy-go-lucky, bubbly character it was impossible to dislike.

He wasn't a golfer but he'd join the rest of the lads at the golf club we used to frequent after training. While most of us were on the course, probably he'd have a game of snooker with Mark and Duncan, then we'd all have a bit of lunch before going off to the pictures, pretty well the whole team together.

We had great times, and although I'd be lying if I said there was never any arguments, it was a super bunch of lads who made it a real pleasure to get up and go to work every day.

Obviously sometimes things happened at the club that we didn't like, but taken overall it was a fantastic way of life. Looking back, perhaps we should have been paying United.

A FINAL FLOURISH: Dennis Viollet (left) prepares to acclaim a brilliant goal by Tommy Taylor (number nine) in United¹s pulsating 5-4 victory over Arsenal at Highbury in February 1958. Five days later Tommy lost his life at Munich.

BORN	DUDLEY, WORCESTERSHIRE 1ST OCTOBER 1936
DIED	MUNICH 21ST FEBRUARY 1958
POSITION	WING-HALF
JOINED UNITED	JUNE 1952 FROM JUNIOR FOOTBALL
UNITED DEBUT	CARDIFF CITY (H) DIV. 1 - 04/04/1953
UNITED HONOURS	DIV. 1 1955/6, 1956/7
UNITED FAREWELL	RED STAR BELGRADE (A) EC - 05/02/1958

DUNCAN EDWARDS		
COMP.	APPS	GLS
LEAGUE	151	20
FAC	12	1
EUROPE	12	0
OTHERS	2	0
TOTAL	177	21

60. DUNCAN EDWARDS

OTHER HONOURS:
18 ENGLAND CAPS 1955-57.

Big Dunc – he wasn't bad, they tell me! Heaven only knows what his record might have been had it been allowed to run its natural course. He was a one-off, a phenomenon.

Yet a lot of people get confused when they talk about Duncan Edwards. They refer to him as a giant but, at least in terms of height, he wasn't, standing at something under six feet.

My God, though, he could play. He had a unique style about him, a certain presence, that could never be confused with anyone else's. He had supreme confidence in himself as a footballer, but that did not come over as brashness or arrogance, more like a kind of unshakeable certainty.

Duncan was a fearsomely strong lad, he covered acres of ground in every match, he was mad about fitness and he loved to train, loved to run. Looking at his physique, it was possible to imagine him playing for the next hundred years, and had he not lost his life at Munich, he would have had a profound effect on the future of both Manchester United and England.

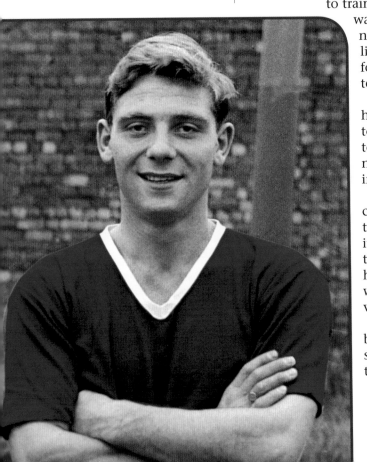

I'm sure that certain players would never have been bought, and with all due respects to another top-quality performer, there's got to be a fair chance that Bobby Moore would not have been a regular in the England side in 1966, let alone be captain.

I could rattle on indefinitely about Duncan Edwards' attributes without beginning to do him justice, but I must make a stab at it. He was gifted with both feet, majestic in the air, awesomely powerful and very, very hard; he was a genuinely great player and whether we shall ever see his like again, I very much doubt.

People wonder about his best position, but unquestionably it was left-half, a defensive midfield role if you like, breaking up the play and then driving forward. Some of his time was spent alongside the centre-half, but the United side of the 1950s didn't concern themselves unduly about conceding goals because they knew they'd always score loads – somehow the game was more for playing then than thinking about – so his time at the back was limited.

'He wasn't Superman, he didn't jump from the page of some comic book, but certainly he was a super player . . . the finest of his generation.'

For all that, a lot of rubbish is talked about what he did when he moved up front. People refer to him as a miracle man when he joined the attack, but in the main, in my experience, that's a story which has been exaggerated in the telling. He might have scored a few goals for the youth team, and for England under-23s, but he was hardly prolific for the United senior side.

But that's not to denigrate Duncan in any way. He wasn't Superman, he didn't jump from the page of some comic book, but certainly he was a super player, surely the finest of his generation.

Had he been spared, as the years passed he might have moved to the centre of defence, where I reckon he'd have been able to hold his own at the top level until he was 40. Then again, knowing his devotion to fitness, it's possible to picture him still charging all over the pitch at that stage. That was the thing about Duncan Edwards; the rules which governed mere mortals simply did not apply.

61. LES OLIVE

CLUB SECRETARY 1958-88

DIRECTOR SINCE 1988.

LES OLIVE		
COMP.	APPS	GLS
LEAGUE	2	0
TOTAL	2	0

BORN	SALFORD 27TH APRIL 1928
POSITION	GOALKEEPER
JOINED UNITED	1942 FROM SCHOOL FOOTBALL
UNITED DEBUT	NEWCASTLE UTD (A) DIV. 1 - 11/04/1953
UNITED FAREWELL	WBA (H) DIV. 1 - 18/04/1953
RETIRED	BECAME CLUB SECRETARY

Les Olive has had a tremendous influence on Manchester United down the years, though not principally through playing football.

When I joined the club straight from school to work in the office, Les was the chief office boy, or maybe I should call him the assistant secretary, and so he was my first boss.

As a player, his first-team career was limited to two games in goal, which was remarkable when you consider that his normal position in the junior teams was full-back or centre-half.

Even in a time of great emergency, with all the regular 'keepers injured, it is a tribute to Les's versatility that Matt Busby turned to him, not once but twice, and that United didn't lose either game. He played for United at every level, in any position in which they were short, and was the ultimate club-man.

Of course, it has been as an adminstrator that Les has made his principal impact, and it has been vast. He took over as club secretary following the death of Walter Crickmer at Munich in 1958, an enormous step for a fellow in his twenties, particularly with the club in such dire straits, and he did a wonderful job in a million and one different ways.

BORN	MANCHESTER 20TH SEPTEMBER 1933
DIED	JACKSONVILLE, FLORIDA 6TH MARCH 1999
POSITION	INSIDE-FORWARD
JOINED UNITED	AUGUST 1949 FROM JUNIOR FOOTBALL
UNITED DEBUT	NEWCASTLE UTD (A) DIV. 1 - 11/04/1953
UNITED HONOURS	DIV. 1 1955/6, 1956/7
UNITED FAREWELL	LEICESTER CITY (H) DIV. 1 - 11/11/1961
LEFT UNITED FOR	STOKE CITY JAN. 1962 - £25,000

DENNIS VIOLLET		
COMP.	APPS	GLS
LEAGUE	259	159
FAC	18	5
LC	2	1
EUROPE	12	13
OTHERS	2	1
TOTAL	293	179

62. DENNIS VIOLLET

OTHER HONOURS:
2 ENGLAND CAPS 1960-61.
OTHER CLUBS:
STOKE CITY 61/2-66/7 (182, 59);
BALTIMORE BAYS, USA;
LINFIELD, NORTHERN IRELAND, 69/70.
MANAGER:
CREWE ALEXANDRA 1971

I'll never tire of declaring that Dennis Viollet was a fantastic footballer, and that it was a criminal waste of talent that he was never called up to play for England alongside his Manchester United goal-scoring partner Tommy Taylor.

Even today I find it hard to credit that Dennis received only two caps, and both of them after Munich when poor Tommy was gone. It was yet another example of the outrageous shenanigans of the FA committee which used to pick the England team.

At a time when they were crying out for a proven marksman to play alongside the centre-forward, how could they ignore a man who averaged more than a goal every game in Europe, and far better than one in two over all competitions? It was a complete and utter disgrace.

'He didn't head the ball too often, but Tommy took care of that department, and together they were dynamite, made for each other. Dennis had total faith in the big feller, and that was important.'

After Munich Dennis provided even more evidence of his all-round ability by playing in a deeper role, but it didn't stop the flood of goals. In fact, in 1959/60 he scored 32 times in 36 outings, which is still the club's record for a League season.

You might say that Dennis was an unlikely looking striker because he was all skin and bone, but he was as fit as a flea and had tremendous pace, lovely control and a sharp brain. In all honesty, he was not a particularly brilliant striker of the ball, but he was an instinctive and deadly finisher who preferred to pass it into the net.

Dennis wore glasses, not on the pitch, of course, though some of us thought he should have done when floodlit football began because it caused him some problems at first, but he adapted and his tallies didn't seem to suffer.

BACK ON DUTY: though not fully recovered from the injuries he received at Munich, Dennis Viollet faced Bolton in the 1958 FA Cup Final. Here he is policed by an old pal of mine, John Higgins, whose son, Mark, played fleetingly for United in the mid 1980s.

He didn't head the ball too often, but Tommy took care of that department, and together they were dynamite, made for each other. Dennis had total faith in the big feller, and that was important.

Often you see a centre-forward jump for a high ball and his mate waits to see where it's going before making his move. Invariably, then, it's too late. But Dennis didn't hang around, he used to gamble on making an early run because he knew Tommy was going to win more than his fair share of headers, and it paid off over and over again.

Their record as a pair is staggering – more than 300 goals between them in the space of five seasons – and there would have been a lot more to come, but for Munich.

Sadly, Dennis left United when he still had a lot to give, having experienced a few non-footballing differences with the manager. He should have known, as many of us found out, that you could not beat Matt Busby. I could only conclude that the crash affected Dennis in more ways than he admitted, and unfortunately that was to have a bearing on his status at the club.

BORN	CARDIFF 17TH JULY 1932
DIED	SWANSEA 1ST MARCH 2001
POSITION	UTILITY FORWARD
JOINED UNITED	MAY 1952 FROM CARDIFF CITY (FREE)
UNITED DEBUT	PORTSMOUTH (A) DIV. 1 - 28/11/1953
UNITED HONOURS	DIV. 1 1955/6
UNITED FAREWELL	WOLVERHAMPTON W. (A) DIV. 1 - 04/10/1958
LEFT UNITED FOR	SWANSEA TOWN OCT. 1958 £7,500

BORN	BRAY, REPUBLIC OF IRELAND 20TH DECEMBER 1934
POSITION	WINGER
JOINED UNITED	APRIL 1952 FROM IRISH JUNIOR FOOTBALL
UNITED DEBUT & FAREWELL	TOTTENHAM H. (H) DIV. 1 - 13/02/1954
LEFT UNITED FOR	WATERFORD - JUNE 1956

COLIN WEBSTER		
COMP.	APPS	GLS
LEAGUE	65	26
FAC	9	4
EUROPE	5	1
TOTAL	79	31

63. COLIN WEBSTER

OTHER HONOURS:
4 WALES CAPS 1957-58.

OTHER CLUBS:
SWANSEA TOWN 58/9-62/3 (159, 65);
NEWPORT COUNTY 62/3-63/4 (31, 3).

Being kind to Colin Webster, he was a bit of a rascal, but there is no doubt that he could play. He came to United after being spotted by Dennis Viollet while doing his National Service at Catterick; Jimmy Murphy went to have a look and was sufficiently impressed to sign him.

Colin was quick, he could go past people, he had decent feet, he scored a few goals and, particularly after Munich, he played anywhere across the forward line, which made him a useful asset at a confused and traumatic time.

He took part in that incredibly emotional run to the 1958 FA Cup Final, scoring the winner against West Bromwich Albion in the quarter-final replay, and he was at Wembley for the defeat by Bolton.

Later in the year Jimmy, who was manager of Wales, called up Colin to replace the injured John Charles in the quarter-final of the World Cup against Brazil, but that proved to be the high-water mark of his career, as he left Old Trafford in the autumn.

To be honest, Colin was never my cup of tea. He had a tendency to leave his foot in a tackle when he shouldn't and he'd catch people when they weren't looking, which I didn't like.

NOEL MCFARLANE		
COMP.	APPS	GLS
LEAGUE	1	0
TOTAL	1	0

64. NOEL McFARLANE

OTHER CLUBS:
WATERFORD, REPUBLIC OF IRELAND.

Noel McFarlane took the eye when scoring twice as United beat Wolves 7-1 in the first leg of the 1953 FA Youth Cup Final, and he looked a fair prospect. But after a spell in the reserves he was offered only one opportunity at First Division level, for which he was judged a little lightweight. Noel was quick, rather reminiscent of Albert Scanlon in style, although he wasn't in Albert's class.

After a stint with Waterford he was forced to retire early with a health problem, but then recovered to play non-League football, mainly for Altrincham and Hyde United, well into his thirties. His son Ross is a professional golfer, who does a bit of work on Sky television.

65. IAN GREAVES

OTHER CLUBS:
LINCOLN CITY 60/1 (11, 0);
OLDHAM ATHLETIC 61/2-62/3 (22, 0).

MANAGER:
HUDDERSFIELD TOWN 1968-74;
BOLTON WANDERERS 1974-80;
OXFORD UNITED 1980-82;
WOLVERHAMPTON WANDERERS 1982;
MANSFIELD TOWN 1983-89.

IAN GREAVES		
COMP.	APPS	GLS
LEAGUE	67	0
FAC	6	0
EUROPE	2	0
TOTAL	75	0

BORN	SHAW, LANCASHIRE 26TH MAY 1932
POSITION	FULL-BACK
JOINED UNITED	MAY 1953 FROM BUXTON UNITED
UNITED DEBUT	WOLVERHAMPTON W. (A) DIV. 1 - 02/10/1954
UNITED HONOURS	DIV. 1 1955/6
UNITED FAREWELL	CHELSEA (H) DIV. 1 - 26/08/1959
LEFT UNITED FOR	LINCOLN CITY - DEC. 1960

When Ian Greaves got into United's title-winning side at right-back, at the expense of Bill Foulkes in the spring of 1956, there was no shortage of observers who thought he wouldn't drop out again.

But Matt Busby had other ideas, and it wasn't until the ranks had been depleted by the Munich disaster that Ian was given another run in the team, this time on the left.

He did very well, played in the FA Cup Final against Bolton, and he didn't miss too many games as United finished as runners-up to Wolves in 1958/59. Now it seemed that he might become a fixture, but he suffered from knee injuries and slipped out of the limelight.

Ian was more of a footballing full-back than Bill, and he was an awkward customer to go past, a bit nobbly. It was a shame that his fitness let him down in the end.

Later on he had a great run as manager of Huddersfield Town, where Henry Cockburn was his trainer, and then he impressed so much in charge of Bolton that he was linked strongly with the United vacancy when Tommy Docherty left in 1977.

I thought he would get it, and if he had I'd have expected him to make a success of it, because he's a strong character and a good man.

BORN	DUBLIN 9TH OCTOBER 1934
POSITION	FULL-BACK
JOINED UNITED	FEBRUARY 1952 FROM IRISH JUNIOR FOOTBALL
UNITED DEBUT & FAREWELL	WOLVERHAMPTON W. (A) DIV. 1 - 02/10/1954
LEFT UNITED FOR	BLACKBURN R. - AUG. 1956

PADDY KENNEDY		
COMP.	APPS	GLS
LEAGUE	1	0
TOTAL	1	0

66. PADDY KENNEDY

OTHER CLUBS:
BLACKBURN ROVERS 57/8 (3, 0);
SOUTHAMPTON 59/60 (2, 0).

L ife was not easy for young United full-backs in the mid 1950s, as the case of Paddy Kennedy illustrates. Apart from Roger Byrne and Bill Foulkes, there were Geoff Bent and Ian Greaves to climb over, and that was a tall order.

Paddy, whose only first-team chance came when Roger was away playing for England, was an Irish schoolboy international who was converted from centre-half to full-back at Old Trafford. He wasn't a bad player, but he wasn't in the right place at the right time.

BORN	HEYWOOD, LANCASHIRE 28TH JUNE 1933
POSITION	WING-HALF
JOINED UNITED	OCTOBER 1953 FROM JUNIOR FOOTBALL
UNITED DEBUT	ARSENAL (H) DIV. 1 - 20/11/1954
UNITED FAREWELL	DERBY COUNTY (A) FAC - 09/01/1960
LEFT UNITED FOR	LEEDS UNITED MARCH 1960 - £10,000

FREDDIE GOODWIN		
COMP.	APPS	GLS
LEAGUE	95	7
FAC	8	1
EUROPE	3	0
OTHERS	1	0
TOTAL	107	8

67. FREDDIE GOODWIN

OTHER CLUBS:
LEEDS UNITED 59/60-63/4 (107, 2);
SCUNTHORPE UNITED 65/6 (6, 1).

MANAGER:
SCUNTHORPE UNITED 1964-67;
NEW YORK GENERALS 1967-68;
BRIGHTON AND HOVE ALBION 1968-70;
BIRMINGHAM CITY 1970-75;
MINNESOTA KICKS 1976-79 AND 1980-81.

F reddie Goodwin was a lanky, leggy wing-half who played a few games before Munich, but his openings were severely limited by the presence of Duncan Edwards, Jeff Whitefoot and Eddie Colman.

He was never remotely in their class, but he had fair ability and was very constructive, a decent passer of the ball.

After the crash, Freddie became a regular in the team at right-half, playing in the FA Cup Final against Bolton, and he didn't miss a single game the following season when an under-strength United side astounded many people by finishing in second place in the First Division behind Wolves.

Despite that, he didn't survive Matt Busby's long-term rebuilding process, losing his place when Maurice Setters arrived during 1959/60, and he moved to Leeds, where he played a lot of games alongside Jack Charlton in central defence.

Freddie, who played nearly a dozen times as a fast bowler for Lancashire during the mid 1950s, went on to do pretty well in football management, both in England and in the States.

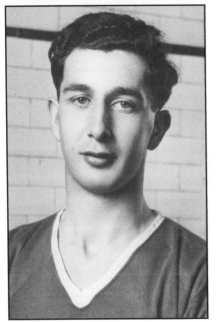

68. ALBERT SCANLON

OTHER CLUBS:
NEWCASTLE UNITED 60/1-61/2 (22, 0);
LINCOLN CITY 61/2-62/3 (47, 11);
MANSFIELD TOWN 62/3-65/6 (108, 21).

ALBERT SCANLON		
COMP.	APPS	GLS
LEAGUE	115	34
FAC	6	1
EUROPE	3	0
TOTAL	127	35

BORN	MANCHESTER 10TH OCTOBER 1935
POSITION	WINGER
JOINED UNITED	1950 FROM JUNIOR FOOTBALL
UNITED DEBUT	ARSENAL (H) DIV. 1 - 20/11/1954
UNITED FAREWELL	BRADFORD CITY (A) LC - 02/11/1960
LEFT UNITED FOR	NEWCASTLE UNITED NOV. 1960 - £18,000

Albert Scanlon, better known to his team-mates as Joe Friday; what a character! Though he was always a dreamer, he had the capacity to become a truly exceptional footballer, but there was something missing from his make-up which prevented him from taking that final step towards realising his full potential. As it was, he had a fair old career anyway, and he'll go down as a dashing, crowd-pleasing winger who, on his day, was so good he was frightening.

We called him Joe Friday after the detective hero of a 1950s TV series called *Dragnet*, a fellow who always knew the ins and outs of everything. That summed up Albert perfectly.

I first met him when he was picked in the Manchester Boys team for the final of the English Schools Shield against Swansea. He was like some little waif or stray from the city streets, telling tales of a tearaway life with a crowd of local kids, like how they'd stolen a car and the steering wheel had gone through his stomach when they crashed – and he had the scar to prove it.

To look at him and listen to him at that time, you'd have thought he'd do well to last until he was 18, never mind be playing for Manchester United, but Matt and Jimmy took him on because he was dripping with talent. I wondered whether he could apply himself enough to make it, but happily I was to find out that he could.

There were times when Albert must have driven Matt mad with the scrapes that he got into, but his saving grace was that he could play. He was a thrilling sight when he stuck the ball past his marker and galloped after it, and he had a great left peg.

People always ask me whether Dave Pegg would have got back in the side after Albert took his place for six weeks or so before Munich. The simple truth is that Peggy would only have regained his place if Albert had stopped doing it, and there was no sign of that at the time of the accident. Who can say?

His most famous game was United's last League outing before the disaster, when they beat Arsenal 5-4 with Albert flying through the mud at Highbury and tearing the defence to

shreds. He set up goals for Charlton, Viollet and Taylor, and although he didn't score himself that day, he did hit the target plenty of times, at a rather more prolific rate than Peggy.

Albert survived the crash, but was not well enough to play again that season. Then he bounced back and had two fantastic years, being ever-present and contributing 16 goals in a free-scoring forward line in 1958/59 – that was Bradley, Quixall, Viollet, Charlton and Scanlon – then excelling again in 1959/60.

He won an England under-23 cap and it seemed that he could join Dennis, Bobby, Bill Foulkes and Harry Gregg as the nucleus of the new team Matt was building, but then suddenly he was sold to Newcastle, where Charlie Mitten was the manager.

It seems there had been a few problems away from the game, and Albert had difficulty in dealing with them. That was a shame, and whatever the rights and wrongs, certainly he could count himself unlucky to be leaving without a major medal after six years in and out of the team.

Albert was a distinctive part of that Old Trafford scene and even now when I'm talking to Greggy he might ask after Joe Friday. Mind, I've known Harry lose his rag with Albert, such as the time on a tour of Holland when they were sharing a room and Greggy had forbidden him to smoke. When Harry walked in and found Albert puffing away, he grabbed him and held him out of the window, several floors up, threatening to drop him.

These days he's still the same old Albert: still comes to the ex-players do's, still drives us mad sometimes, still lives in another world, and still we love him to pieces.

69. GEOFF BENT

BORN	SALFORD 20TH SEPTEMBER 1932
DIED	MUNICH 6TH FEBRUARY 1958
POSITION	FULL-BACK
JOINED UNITED	MAY 1949 FROM JUNIOR FOOTBALL
UNITED DEBUT	BURNLEY (A) DIV. 1 - 11/12/1954
UNITED FAREWELL	TOTTENHAM H. (H) DIV. 1 - 06/04/1957

GEOFF BENT		
COMP.	APPS	GLS
LEAGUE	12	0
TOTAL	12	0

Geoff Bent was a very unfortunate lad, both during his career and in the circumstances leading up to his death at Munich.

He was a perpetual reserve left-back behind Roger Byrne, but there was a strong body of opinion which held that Roger should switch to the right in place of Bill Foulkes and that the number-three shirt should go to Geoff.

It never happened, and Geoff must have been fed up with hearing that he would have walked into any other side in the country, which was the truth because he was a fine player: quick, tidy on the ball, well-built and ready to put his foot in.

But then his luck got even worse. He wasn't due to make the fateful trip to Belgrade, but Roger sustained a minor injury in the League game against Arsenal and Geoff was drafted into the travelling party, just as cover, in place of Ronnie Cope.

So he got on the plane, didn't play against Red Star because Roger was fit after all, and then the poor lad was killed in the accident. You could say he died by default. But for the skipper's little strain, Geoff would have stayed at home and, in the circumstances, probably would have been looking at ten years as United's left-back.

So when we're all moaning and groaning about little everyday things, it would do us all good to remember Geoff Bent.

70. BILLY WHELAN

OTHER HONOURS:
4 REPUBLIC OF IRELAND CAPS 1956-57.

OTHER CLUBS:
HOME FARM, ROI

BILLY WHELAN		
COMP.	APPS	GLS
LEAGUE	79	43
FAC	6	4
EUROPE	11	5
OTHERS	2	0
TOTAL	98	52

BORN	DUBLIN, 1ST APRIL 1935
DIED	MUNICH, 6TH FEBRUARY 1958
POSITION	INSIDE-FORWARD
JOINED UNITED	MAY 1953 FROM HOME FARM, ROI
UNITED DEBUT	PRESTON N.E. (A) DIV. 1 - 26/03/1955
UNITED HONOURS	DIV. 1 1955/6, 1956/7
UNITED FAREWELL	CHELSEA (H) DIV. 1 - 14/12/1957

I always feel that I was slightly instrumental in Billy Whelan's death at Munich, on the basis that he came over to England from Dublin to play in the 1953 FA Youth Cup Final against Wolves because of my injuries.

His tremendous talent was apparent from the beginning and his goals-to-games ratio was phenomenal for an inside-forward, even given the fact that sometimes he would play in a slightly more advanced role than Dennis Viollet, the other inside man.

Yet for all his staggering success, Billy was out of the side in the weeks before the Munich tragedy, having been ousted by Bobby Charlton. In fact, United had suffered a poor run by their standards and the manager made wholesale changes for the home game with Leicester, bringing in Gregg, Morgans, Charlton and Scanlon for Wood, Berry, Whelan and Pegg. I remember it vividly because I was playing for Leicester that day and we went down 4-0.

It made you wonder what might have happened if there had been no air crash. Would Billy have moved Bobby, or Dennis, out of his way? Either one would have been a tall order and my guess is that he would have had to wait for an injury.

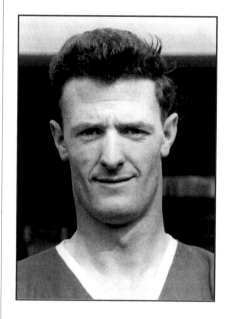

Sadly, and frustratingly, it's a question to which we can never supply the answer, but what we do know is that Billy had a huge amount to offer. He was never quick, but he had marvellous control and could beat defenders in very tight areas. He and I filled the same position but we were totally different in that respect, because where he loved to dribble, I preferred to pass.

One of Billy's best-remembered goals, on a Bilbao mudheap in the first leg of a European Cup quarter-final, involved an amazing shuffle past about five opponents before smacking in a shot from long distance. It was an important one, too, because it cut the Spaniards' lead to two goals and United fought back to win the tie in the second leg on a fantastic night at Maine Road.

As a person, Billy was quiet and relaxed, you couldn't help liking him. He was a regular churchgoer, having hailed from a staunchly Catholic background in Ireland, and so much is said about his gentle bearing that people who weren't lucky enough to see him play often wonder how he coped with the tough world of professional football. For instance, could he put his foot in?

My response is that he didn't need to. He was a lovely player in a wonderful side and his style was just right for what they were doing at the time.

Born	Manchester 7th June 1934
Position	Wing-half
Joined United	August 1950 from junior football
United Debut & Farewell	Everton (A) Div. 1 - 14/09/1955
Left united for	Chesterfield - July 1956

71. WALTER WHITEHURST

Walter Whitehurst		
Comp.	Apps	Gls
League	1	0
Total	1	0

Other clubs:
Chesterfield 56/7-59/60 (92, 2); Crewe Alexandra 60/1 (3, 1).

Walter Whitehurst was a creative and busy right-half, but what chance did he have at Old Trafford with such men as Jeff Whitefoot and Eddie Colman, not to mention Freddie Goodwin, ahead of him in the pecking order? I can recall his only appearance in the first team, which was against Everton at Goodison Park, because it was my comeback game after my long absence with knee trouble.

At the end of that season, during which the considerably younger Colman had established a regular place, Walter accepted the inevitable and brought his six-year stay with United to an end, beginning a worthy stint with Chesterfield of the Third Division North.

He went on to become a schoolteacher after leaving his final club, Crewe. At the time of writing we have not managed to entice Walter to a meeting of the Former Players Association, but we'll go on trying.

72. WILF McGUINNESS

OTHER HONOURS:
2 ENGLAND CAPS 1958-59.

MANAGER:
MANCHESTER UNITED 1969-70;
ARIS SALONIKA, GREECE, 1971-73;
PANARAIKI PATRAS, GREECE, 1973-74;
YORK CITY 1975-77; BURY (ACTING) 1989.

WILF McGUINNESS		
COMP.	APPS	GLS
LEAGUE	81	2
FAC	2	0
EUROPE	2	0
TOTAL	85	2

BORN	MANCHESTER 25TH OCTOBER 1937
POSITION	WING-HALF
JOINED UNITED	JANUARY 1953 FROM JUNIOR FOOTBALL
UNITED DEBUT	WOLVERHAMPTON W. (H) DIV. 1 - 08/10/1955
UNITED FAREWELL	EVERTON (A) DIV. 1 - 28/11/1959
RETIRED	1961 UNITED COACHING STAFF

To call Wilf McGuinness enthusiastic is the understatement of the century, but I wouldn't knock him for it. It's a quality that has taken him a long way. After all, Wilf captained Manchester Boys and England Boys, won two full caps, played 80-odd games for Manchester United and then managed the club, so he must have done something right.

'Brave and phenomenally wholehearted, he could stop more gifted footballers from playing, as he did on his debut when he dominated Peter Broadbent of Wolves and England.'

As a player he was an effective defensive wing-half, who was not brilliant with his feet but could win the ball, then pass it safely and sensibly. Brave and phenomenally wholehearted, he could stop more gifted footballers from playing, as he did on his debut when he dominated Peter Broadbent of Wolves and England, who was a bit useful. It's a game that lodges in my memory because I scored a goal with my head, which was like winning the pools – it didn't happen very often.

Wilf grew up at Old Trafford with a mountain to climb, because he was always in the shadow of another useful left-half, a young man called Duncan Edwards. He was only 12 months younger than Dunc, so you have to wonder what would have happened to Wilf if Dunc had lived. To be brutally honest, it was hard to envisage that he had a future at the club.

The picture changed dramatically after the accident and suddenly he looked as if he was a major part of Matt Busby's plans. That's when he won his caps, though it's fair to say I wasn't the only one surprised by his call-up. But then, in the situation where all those silly FA councillors picked manager Walter Winterbottom's team for him, I very rarely agreed with their selections, so what do I know?

But then Wilf's luck ran out when he suffered a badly broken leg and was forced to retire when he was still in his early twenties. He stayed at United as a coach, then went on to become manager when Matt stood down. I'll discuss that episode later in the book.

73. EDDIE COLMAN

BORN	SALFORD 1ST NOVEMBER 1936
DIED	MUNICH 6TH FEBRUARY 1958
POSITION	WING-HALF
JOINED UNITED	1952 FROM JUNIOR FOOTBALL
UNITED DEBUT	BOLTON W. (A) DIV. 1 - 12/11/1955
UNITED HONOURS	DIV. 1 1955/6, 1956/7
UNITED FAREWELL	RED STAR BELGRADE (A) ECC - 05/02/1958

EDDIE COLMAN		
COMP.	APPS	GLS
LEAGUE	85	1
FAC	9	0
EUROPE	13	1
OTHERS	1	0
TOTAL	108	2

Eddie Colman was an effervescent little lad from Salford who charmed the pants off the fans in the days of the Busby Babes. They called him Snakehips, and I think it was Harry Gregg who said that when Eddie performed a body-swerve, the crowd went one way and the main stand went the other.

He was just right for that side, but whether he would have been as valuable to a lesser team is debatable. You see, Eddie was the icing on the cake, doing the fancy bits, pulling off all sorts of tricks and entertaining the crowd. When he swivelled his hips, or dipped his shoulder, showing the opposition that he could do anything he liked, the supporters adored it.

But he wasn't going to win the ball too often, and he didn't score many goals – only two in more than 100 games was not many for an attacking wing-half in those days – though that didn't matter in a lovely side that was used to winning matches with something to spare. However, in a more ordinary team, he might just have been an unaffordable luxury.

Certainly Eddie was a beautiful passer, and if he was playing today I could imagine him bending the ball every which way. That just wasn't possible with the heavy leather lumps we used to use, especially in the middle of winter. I'd challenge any of the modern 'specialists' to surprise me on that score. Give Mr Beckham an old leather ball and I'll bet he couldn't swerve it round me. He might even bruise a metatarsal if he tried too hard!

Going back to Eddie, there was some talk at one point that Stan Cullis wanted to sign him, but I could no more imagine him playing for Wolves, with their hard-running long-ball game, than being the first man on the moon.

How could Cullis have thought of Colman when he had shown his preference for people like Ron Flowers and Eddie Clamp, such rigorous straight up-and-downers. I can't believe that Stan would have known what to do with Eddie. It would have been some contrast.

Both on the pitch and off it, Eddie Colman was Jack the Lad in the loveliest possible way. Invariably he was the height of fashion: if trilbies were in vogue, then Coley would have a trilby; if Sinatra was top of the charts then he'd be singing Sinatra's praises.

Would he have won England caps? Well, the prevailing policy would have had to have moved away from the likes of Flowers, Clamp and Ronnie Clayton of Blackburn Rovers. Coley was nothing like them, he was a different species, head to toe.

On the grounds of pure, unadulterated ability, he deserved to represent his country, though there a few other skilful unfortunates like him in the English game, including some who were quite a bit older. For instance, Ken Barnes of Manchester City and Bob Morton at Luton were smashing players, and they were never given a chance. I only wish that, in the case of Eddie Colman, we were not having to resort to guesswork.

74. RONNIE COPE

OTHER CLUBS:
LUTON TOWN 61/2-62/3 (28, 0).

RONNIE COPE		
COMP.	APPS	GLS
LEAGUE	93	2
FAC	10	0
LC	1	0
EUROPE	2	0
TOTAL	106	2

BORN	CREWE, CHESHIRE 5TH OCTOBER 1934
POSITION	CENTRE-HALF
JOINED UNITED	JUNE 1950 FROM JUNIOR FOOTBALL
UNITED DEBUT	ARSENAL (A) DIV. 1 - 29/09/1956
UNITED FAREWELL	EXETER CITY (H) LC - 26/10/1960
LEFT UNITED FOR	LUTON TOWN AUGUST 1961 - £10,000

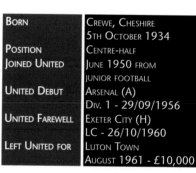

Ronnie Cope, one of nature's gentlemen, was an immensely accomplished footballing centre-half who played more than a century of games for United. But he was unlucky not to enjoy a far longer Old Trafford career.

His only problem was that he lacked ruthlessness. The truth is that Ronnie could have done with being nasty, but that just wasn't his way. He didn't want to hurt people, couldn't kick them, lacked the abrasive edge of competitiveness that most top-level stoppers count as an essential part of their armoury.

The game itself appeared to come easy to him. He was never flustered no matter how hectic the situation and usually he was able to play his way out of trouble.

I first ran across Ronnie when he and I were on opposite sides in county boys football; I was with Lancashire while he played for Cheshire. Then I picked him up from the railway

station on his first day at United, and we've been pals ever since.

But although we joined United at roughly the same time, he made his debut four years after me, a full six years after his arrival. Somehow Ronnie was always at the end of the line. At the time there was Allenby Chilton, Sammy Lynn and Mark Jones in front of him, a formidable barrier to progress, and he didn't get the breaks when he needed them.

The biggest slice of luck he ever had was not being on the plane that crashed at Munich. Ronnie had been selected for the trip, but then Geoff Bent replaced him at the last minute. He must have been upset at the time, and no one could have blamed him if he'd wondered what his future at United held, what with Mark Jones and Jackie Blanchflower vying for the number-five shirt. But all that was submerged by the accident, after which finally he got an extended opportunity.

He played in the 1958 FA Cup Final and held his own for two more years, before Matt decided to shift Bill Foulkes to the middle. Ronnie was only 26 and he joined Luton, where he didn't settle, before going non-League with Northwich Victoria.

It was a shame because Ronnie Cope was a far better player than that, but it never made him bitter. From that day to this, he has remained one of the nicest fellows I have known in the game.

75. BOBBY CHARLTON

BORN	Ashington, Northumberland 11th October 1937
POSITION	Inside-forward, Winger Midfielder
JOINED UNITED	January 1953 from Junior football
UNITED DEBUT	Charlton Athletic (H) Div. 1 - 06/10/1956
UNITED HONOURS	European Cup 1967/8 Div. 1 1956/7, 1964/5, 1966/7 FA Cup 1962/3
UNITED FAREWELL	Chelsea (A) Div. 1 - 28/04/1973
LEFT UNITED FOR	Preston N.E. May 1973 - Manager

BOBBY CHARLTON		
COMP.	APPS	GLS
LEAGUE	604 (2)	199
FAC	79	19
LC	24	7
EUROPE	45	22
OTHERS	5	2
TOTAL	757 (2)	249

OTHER HONOURS:
106 England caps 1958-70
World Cup winner 1966
European Footballer of the Year 1966
FWA Footballer of the Year 1966.

OTHER CLUBS:
Preston North End 74/5 (38, 8).

MANAGER:
Preston North End 1973-75;
Wigan Athletic (acting) 1983.

To conjure up in the mind's eye the remarkable gifts and staggering achievements of Bobby Charlton, and to come to any other conclusion than that he was one of the all-time greats, would be nonsensical. Beyond any shadow of a doubt, as an enduring talent over two decades he was among the best there has ever been.

Bobby caught the imagination of a generation of football-lovers because he played the game the way they wanted to watch it. When he drifted past his marker and hammered the

ball into the net from 25 yards, it was exciting and it was beautiful.

He was special from the moment he surfaced back in the early 1950s, even in the Manchester United context of being in the midst of so many glittering prospects. Whenever you looked at Bobby, you knew he was going to be a bit useful.

That said, he and I have never been particularly close, and there was one incident where we disagreed drastically. During a reserve game at Newcastle he told me he wanted the ball to his feet and I replied that he'd get it where I put it. That was on the basis that I was senior to him and, as far as I was concerned back then, I was the better player. There was no way he was going to tell me how to play the game.

But at half-time Jimmy Murphy gave me a rollocking; was I trying to get Bobby killed? My reply, which I suppose was a tad uncharitable, was: 'If necessary!' It was patched up soon enough, and I'm glad to say there has been no lasting animosity.

At that time Bobby was an attacking inside-forward, a goal-scorer with two exceptional feet, who was decent in the air, with loads of pace and the priceless knack of beating his man. Later on there were two further distinct phases to his career, first as a left-winger, then finally as a deep-lying play-maker.

'Alf (Ramsey) thought he was sending on stronger legs in the shape of Colin Bell; the only difference was that Franz Beckenbauer didn't give a monkey's about Bell, whereas he was terrified of Bobby.'

Where was he most effective? I always liked him as a front-man, and I thought he should have developed into the best outside-left in the world. But mostly when people talk about Bobby Charlton in the years to come, inevitably it will be as a midfielder because that's where he knew his greatest triumphs.

Did he have a weakness? Yes, and he'd be the first to admit it, he couldn't tackle a fish supper. He needed people who would get the ball for him, but once he had it there was nothing he couldn't do.

Also there were times early on when, maybe, he thought the glory was the be-all and end-all of the game; and it took him a while to learn that short could be as beautiful as long in terms of passing.

Was he a team player? A lot of rubbish is talked about that – and I mean generally, not particularly in his case. To me, good team players are people who do a decent job for the team. Bobby played more than 750 times for United and averaged a goal every three games. Now, bearing in mind that he was only up front for a few seasons, I'd say he wasn't a bad team player.

But magnificent though his club record is, I maintain that he was at his best in the international arena. There he was a *nonpareil*. At that level he tended to frighten opponents to death because they didn't come across many like him. Meanwhile in the First Division the likes of Norman Hunter wasn't going to be afraid of Bobby, because he faced him so frequently and knew his game so well.

Probably the greatest *faux pas* of Alf Ramsey's reign as England manager was substituting Bobby in the 1970 World Cup quarter-final against the Germans. Alf thought he was sending on stronger legs in the shape of Colin Bell; the only difference was that Franz Beckenbauer didn't give a monkey's about Colin Bell, whereas he was terrified of Bobby Charlton; and with good reason.

76. DAVID GASKELL

OTHER CLUBS:
WREXHAM 69/70-71/2 (95, 0).

DAVID GASKELL		
COMP.	APPS	GLS
LEAGUE	96	0
FAC	16	0
LC	1	0
EUROPE	5	0
OTHERS	1 (1)	0
TOTAL	119 (1)	0

BORN	WIGAN 5TH OCTOBER 1940
POSITION	GOALKEEPER
JOINED UNITED	1955 FROM JUNIOR FOOTBALL
UNITED DEBUT	MANCHESTER CITY (A) CS - 24/10/1956
UNITED HONOURS	FA CUP 1962/3
UNITED FAREWELL	TOTTENHAM H. (A) DIV. 1 - 10/09/1966
LEFT UNITED FOR	WREXHAM - JUNE 1969

When David Gaskell was a kid, there were high hopes that he would become Manchester United's goalkeeper for plenty of years to come. That optimism was fuelled when he tasted the limelight for the first time when he was only 16, being called from the crowd to replace the injured Ray Wood in the 1956 Charity Shield against Manchester City at Maine Road, but always there was a certain arrogance about him which didn't sit easily with me.

Undoubtedly he was talented, and no one questioned his agility or his courage, but I always had the feeling that he was a legend in his own head.

I never believed that David was as good as he thought he was, and although he picked up an FA Cup winner's medal in 1963 at the age of 22, he didn't go on to the glittering career which was once predicted for him.

Admittedly, a succession of injuries had something to do with that, but his approach was typified for me when he dropped his shorts and showed his backside to the crowd during one match when some fans had been annoying him. Who did he think he was? Where was his respect?

He spent a dozen or so years with the club, experiencing various fall-outs with the management which must have limited his appearances, and I'm not surprised.

Suffice it to say that David Gaskell would never be in my squad of players because I didn't like his attitude.

BORN	SHEFFIELD 15TH JANUARY 1938
POSITION	GOALKEEPER
JOINED UNITED	MAY 1953 FROM JUNIOR FOOTBALL
UNITED DEBUT & FAREWELL	BLACKPOOL (A) DIV. 1 - 27/10/1956
RETIRED	DECEMBER 1958

TONY HAWKSWORTH		
COMP.	APPS	GLS
LEAGUE	1	0
TOTAL	1	0

77. TONY HAWKSWORTH

Tony Hawksworth was an England schoolboy and youth international who wasn't massive for a goalkeeper, measuring around 5ft 9ins, but he was very agile. During the mid 1950s he played his part in three successive FA Youth Cup triumphs, but he never managed to mount a meaningful challenge to the likes of Ray Wood, Harry Gregg and David Gaskell, and he was granted only one first-team appearance before he left both the club and the professional game.

BORN	WEDNESBURY, STAFFS 3RD NOVEMBER 1936
DIED	MANCHESTER, 29TH SEPTEMBER 1991
POSITION	GOALKEEPER
JOINED UNITED	JUNE 1952 FROM JUNIOR FOOTBALL
UNITED DEBUT	WOLVERHAMPTON W. (A) DIV. 1 - 16/03/1957
UNITED FAREWELL	WBA (H) DIV. 1 - 29/04/1957
LEFT UNITED FOR	TRANMERE R. - NOV. 1959 £4,000 (FEE INCLUDED BOBBY HARROP)

GORDON CLAYTON		
COMP.	APPS	GLS
LEAGUE	2	0
TOTAL	2	0

78. GORDON CLAYTON

OTHER CLUBS:
TRANMERE ROVERS 59/60-60/1 (4, 0).

Gordon Clayton was one of Tony Hawksworth's young goalkeeping rivals, bigger and bulkier than the Yorkshireman but not as quick-footed and acrobatic. To be honest, neither of them were good enough to make the grade, a recurring theme among reserve net-minders during Matt Busby's reign.

Gordon, who won England recognition at junior levels and earned an FA Youth Cup winner's medal in 1953, was a close friend of Wilf McGuinness, and when Wilf became United's manager, he enlisted Gordon as a scout.

BORN	ABERDEEN 21ST FEBRUARY 1940
POSITION	CENTRE-FORWARD
JOINED UNITED	1956 FROM JUNIOR FOOTBALL
UNITED DEBUT	BURNLEY (H) DIV. 1 - 22/04/1957
UNITED FAREWELL	BIRMINGHAM CITY (H) DIV. 1 - 14/10/1961
LEFT UNITED FOR	PRESTON NORTH END OCT. 1961 - £18,000

ALEX DAWSON		
COMP.	APPS	GLS
LEAGUE	80	45
FAC	10	8
LC	3	1
TOTAL	93	54

79. ALEX DAWSON

OTHER CLUBS:
PRESTON NORTH END 61/2-66/7 (197, 114);
BURY 66/7-68/9 (50, 21);
BRIGHTON AND HOVE ALBION 68/9-70/1 (57, 26);
BRENTFORD 70/1 (10, 6).

If you look at Alex Dawson's scoring record – considerably better than a goal every two games taken over a 14-year League career – it is second to very few.

He was a big, strong lad who can be proud of his achievements for United at a particularly traumatic period in their history, the immediate aftermath of Munich, and his excep-

'Born to be a centre-forward...when the ball was there to be won he was like a bull on the rampage.'

tionally fine figures beg the question: just what did he have to do to prove himself worthy of a long-term place?

He stepped into the massive breach left by the death of the incomparable Tommy Taylor, and he didn't let the club down, always standing his corner, always delivering goals.

But Alex left United after Matt signed David Herd in 1961, going on to become something of a cult hero with Preston, where he was nicknamed the Black Prince of Deepdale. He was unlucky where FA Cup Finals were concerned, losing in 1958 with United, and then again in 1964 with Preston, though that day he scored against West Ham with a typical header.

When he started at Old Trafford Alex played a little bit at outside-right, but he was born to be a centre-forward, and that's the position in which he flourished. When the ball was there to be won he was like a bull on the rampage, and his fearlessness was a major part of his success in front of goal.

Of course, Munich afforded Alex early opportunities which he could not have expected in the normal course of events, but in the long run, probably, it did him no favours, heaping massive expectation on his young shoulders. Then again, no one could say that he didn't live up to them, especially as he scored all those goals without ever playing regularly for a strong United side. How would he have fared given the chance of teaming up with Best, Law and Charlton in the 1960s? It makes you wonder . . .

80. PETER JONES

OTHER CLUBS:
WREXHAM 59/60-66/7 (227, 7);
STOCKPORT COUNTY 66/7-67/8 (54, 1).

PETER JONES		
COMP.	APPS	GLS
LEAGUE	1	0
TOTAL	1	0

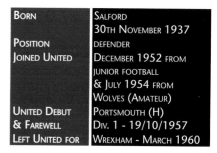

BORN	SALFORD 30TH NOVEMBER 1937
POSITION	DEFENDER
JOINED UNITED	DECEMBER 1952 FROM JUNIOR FOOTBALL & JULY 1954 FROM WOLVES (AMATEUR)
UNITED DEBUT & FAREWELL	PORTSMOUTH (H) DIV. 1 - 19/10/1957
LEFT UNITED FOR	WREXHAM - MARCH 1960

Peter Jones was asked to cope with one of the League's most dangerous wingers in his sole match for United, deputising at left-back for Roger Byrne. Portsmouth's Peter Harris was quick enough to catch pigeons and wasn't the opponent you would choose for a debut.

Not that Jonesy would have been overawed. He was a classy footballer who had excelled at centre-half when United won the FA Youth Cup in 1955, but eventually he succumbed to the red-hot competition for places at Old Trafford and went on to long and loyal service with Wrexham, most of it under the management of my chum Ken Barnes, once of Manchester City.

BORN	DERRY, N. IRELAND 25TH OCTOBER 1932
POSITION	GOALKEEPER
JOINED UNITED	DECEMBER 1957 FROM DONCASTER R. - £23,500
UNITED DEBUT	LEICESTER CITY (H) DIV. 1 - 21/12/1957
UNITED FAREWELL	STOKE CITY (A) DIV. 1 - 07/09/1966
LEFT UNITED FOR	STOKE CITY - DEC. 1966

HARRY GREGG		
COMP.	APPS	GLS
LEAGUE	210	0
FAC	24	0
LC	2	0
EUROPE	11	0
TOTAL	247	0

81. HARRY GREGG

OTHER HONOURS:
25 NORTHERN IRELAND CAPS 1954-63.

OTHER CLUBS:
LINFIELD, NORTHERN IRELAND;
COLERAINE, NORTHERN IRELAND;
DONCASTER ROVERS 52/3-57/8 (93, 0);
STOKE CITY 66/7 (2, 0).

MANAGER:
SHREWSBURY TOWN 1968-72;
SWANSEA CITY 1972-75;
CREWE ALEXANDRA 1975-78;
CARLISLE UNITED 1986-87.

Harry Gregg was one of the genuinely great goalkeepers, and that's not just my opinion. It is a view heartily endorsed by his award as the best 'keeper in the 1958 World Cup tournament, when he played such a gigantic part in Northern Ireland reaching the quarter-finals.

Expectations of Harry were high when he joined United for £23,500, which made him the world's most expensive player in his position, and although he didn't disappoint, he represented a serious culture shock for the club's defenders.

He was taking over from Ray Wood, essentially a line 'keeper, whereas Greggy was rather ahead of his time in being a box 'keeper, fiercely determined to dominate his area. Blanchflower, Jones, Edwards, Foulkes and Byrne were used to dealing with crosses outside the six-yard box, but all of a sudden there was this big fractious Irishman punching or catching anything that moved. He always went for the ball, and anyone who got in his way, be it friend or foe, was liable to be clattered.

When he made his debut, I was playing against him for Leicester City and I might have scored several early goals which would have spoiled his day. As it was Greggy kept me out, United won comfortably and he went from strength to strength.

But although he emerged as an undeniable top-notcher, probably we never saw the very best of him at United because of his terrible injury record. Bad luck comes into it, but also he paid the price for being so brave, often way above and beyond the call of duty, possibly to the point of recklessness sometimes.

Harry played so much, but he missed out when it mattered in terms of gathering honours and it's a downright travesty that he never won a medal. He didn't arrive until after the mid-1950s titles, then he was injured in the run-up to the 1963 FA Cup Final and although he was fit again in time for Wembley, Matt Busby stuck with David Gaskell.

Then Gaskell was out of the team which won the League in

64/5 but Pat Dunne had taken over. Now Pat's a nice lad, but no one could ever describe him as a better 'keeper than Greggy.

I know Matt Busby had a lot of time for him, but I think Harry's unyieldingly forthright approach to life led the pair into conflict, which did the Irishman no long-term favours. After all, in the end, no manager as strong as Matt Busby is going to lose an argument with a player.

'He paid the price for being so brave, often way above and beyond the call of duty, to the point of recklessness sometimes.'

Of course, in addition to his footballing contribution, Harry merits a unique niche in the United story through his courage at Munich, when he re-entered the crashed plane to rescue fellow survivors. He held himself together when people around him were panicking, and he saved lives in the process.

He was a larger-than-life personality who upset a few at the club, though generally he was popular. Stories abound about his antics, and I'm sure some of them are apocryphal, probably including the one about lighting up a cigarette during a game at Leicester.

I can vouch personally, though, for an even more outrageous one, when he dangled Albert Scanlon out of a hotel window, several floors up, for smoking in their room. I still talk to him regularly, and he still has his outspoken views on the game. Harry Gregg is not everybody's cup of tea, but he happens to be mine.

BORN	SWANSEA 16TH MARCH 1939
POSITION	WINGER
JOINED UNITED	JANUARY 1955 FROM JUNIOR FOOTBALL
UNITED DEBUT	LEICESTER CITY (H) DIV. 1 - 21/12/1957
UNITED FAREWELL	NOTTINGHAM F. (A) DIV. 1 - 25/02/1961
LEFT UNITED FOR	SWANSEA TOWN MARCH 1961 - £3,000

KENNY MORGANS		
COMP.	APPS	GLS
LEAGUE	17	0
FAC	2	0
EUROPE	4	0
TOTAL	23	0

82. KENNY MORGANS

OTHER CLUBS:
SWANSEA TOWN 60/1-63/4 (55, 8);
NEWPORT COUNTY 64/5-66/7 (125, 46).

Kenny Morgans (right) with Ray Wood on a European trip.

Kenny Morgans burst on to the scene as a slim, pacy, tricky 18-year-old right-winger deemed good enough, by Matt Busby, to remove the far more experienced and combative Johnny Berry from the team.

United had made an extremely disappointing start to the 1957/58 season, so the boss opted for drastic measures, and Kenny was one of them. In all honesty it surprised me, because while the lad was promising enough, I hadn't imagined him breaking through anything like that quickly.

He held his place during a run of much-improved performances leading up to Munich, but although he suffered no serious physical injuries in the crash, afterwards he never seemed to be the same person. He was only a kid and the trauma must have been overwhelming for him. I find it impossible to comprehend what he must have gone through.

He escaped from the disaster with his life, but in football terms he was horribly unlucky. The impetus of his career was halted brutally, and though later he had some productive years back home in Wales with Swansea and Newport, he never regained momentum at the top level.

BORN	BILSTON, STAFFS 3RD SEPTEMBER 1935
POSITION	WING-HALF
JOINED UNITED	FEBRUARY 1958 FROM ASTON VILLA - £18,000
UNITED DEBUT	SHEFFIELD WED. (H) FAC - 19/02/1958
UNITED FAREWELL	WOLVERHAMPTON W. (A) DIV. 1 - 04/10/1958
LEFT UNITED FOR	CHELSEA DEC. 1958 - £10,000

STAN CROWTHER		
COMP.	APPS	GLS
LEAGUE	13	0
FAC	5	0
EUROPE	2	0
TOTAL	20	0

83. STAN CROWTHER

OTHER CLUBS:
ASTON VILLA 56/7-57/8 (50, 4);
CHELSEA 58/9-59/60 (51, 0);
BRIGHTON AND HOVE ALBION 60/1 (4, 0).

Jimmy Murphy was desperate for players in the aftermath of Munich, and he must have thought Stan Crowther could do a job, but it was a signing I could never understand.

That said, Jimmy had precious little choice, with so many of the lads having lost their lives and Wilf McGuinness on the injured list, and he had to field a team for the FA Cup tie with Sheffield Wednesday only 13 days after the accident.

Stan was an enforcer, a ball-winning wing-half who had

faced United for Aston Villa in the 1957 FA Cup Final and that day, in fairness, he didn't do badly. He could put himself about, but he didn't have the class to be a Manchester United player, despite being an England under-23 international.

Perhaps Jimmy felt he needed to balance Ernie Taylor, his other signing at that time, who certainly wasn't going to kick anybody. Stan helped United to Wembley that season, but he didn't last long afterwards and I wasn't surprised.

Maybe being at United was all a bit too much for him, but at least he wrote himself into the record books as the only man to play for two teams in one season in the FA Cup, the FA having waived their normal rule because of the disaster.

84. ERNIE TAYLOR

OTHER HONOURS:
1 ENGLAND CAP 1953.

OTHER CLUBS:
NEWCASTLE UNITED 47/8-51/2 (107, 19);
BLACKPOOL 51/2-57/8 (217, 53);
SUNDERLAND 58/9-60/1 (68, 11).

ERNIE TAYLOR		
COMP.	APPS	GLS
LEAGUE	22	2
FAC	6	1
EUROPE	2	1
TOTAL	30	4

BORN	SUNDERLAND 2ND SEPTEMBER 1925
DIED	BIRKENHEAD, CHESHIRE 9TH APRIL 1985
POSITION	INSIDE-FORWARD
JOINED UNITED	FEBRUARY 1958 FROM BLACKPOOL - £8,000
UNITED DEBUT	SHEFFIELD WED. (H) FAC - 19/02/1958
UNITED FAREWELL	EVERTON (A) DIV. 1 - 18/10/1958
LEFT UNITED FOR	SUNDERLAND DECEMBER 1958

Ernie Taylor was an old-fashioned midfield general, a superb passer who knew the game inside out from all his years with Newcastle and Blackpool.

He was a bit of a wind-up merchant, too, and I remember playing against him at Bloomfield Road, when he upset Duncan Edwards. That was not a wise thing to do, though it wasn't Ernie who paid the price but poor Stan Matthews.

Now Ernie wasn't the sort that Duncan liked playing against. Ernie would get it and pass it, again and again, without giving Duncan time to get his foot in, and this time he made it worse by taking the mickey.

He asked: 'Where's this Edwards I've heard so much about, is he not playing today?' Duncan was getting really uptight, so Ernie carried on: 'Are you sure Edwards is here? I've not seen him all day.' Then Ernie gave the ball to Matthews and Duncan, by now in a real tizzy, ran at Stan and hit him like a train, head on. The most famous footballer in the world went up in the air like a rag doll and collapsed on the ground.

I thought Dunc had killed him. But when they picked Stan up he was still alive, and later when he mentioned Manchester United in his newpaper column, he wrote of 'youthful exuberance which sometimes exceeds the proper bounds.' My immediate thought was: 'Stan, it's Ernie you should be having a go at!'

All that aside, Ernie was a class act. He wasn't much bigger than a cotton reel, and his prime was behind him, but still he

Emergency recruit Ernie Taylor (left) is welcomed to Old Trafford by Munich survivor Johnny Berry.

was a wonderful director of midfield operations, whose constant vocal contributions were invaluable with so many youngsters around him.

BORN	SHEFFIELD 28TH OCTOBER 1939
POSITION	INSIDE-FORWARD
JOINED UNITED	1955 FROM JUNIOR FOOTBALL
UNITED DEBUT	SHEFFIELD WED. (H) FAC - 19/02/1958
UNITED FAREWELL	BURNLEY (H) DIV. 1 - 22/09/1962
LEFT UNITED FOR	SHEFFIELD WED. OCT. 1963 - £20,000

MARK PEARSON		
COMP.	APPS	GLS
LEAGUE	68	12
FAC	7	1
LC	3	1
EUROPE	2	0
TOTAL	80	14

85. MARK PEARSON

OTHER CLUBS:
SHEFFIELD WEDNESDAY 63/4-64/5 (39, 9);
FULHAM 65/6-67/8 (58, 7);
HALIFAX TOWN 68/9 (5, 0).

Mark Pearson, who was pitched into the deep end as a teenager on that incredibly emotional night when United met Sheffield Wednesday in the FA Cup less than two weeks after Munich, was much maligned.

Jimmy Murphy made the point that most youngsters had to be taught how to tackle, but Mark knew how to do it instinctively, making his challenges with the timing and expertise of a veteran from his very first day.

But, perversely, that was one of his problems. His tackles were so effective that people thought he was dirty. He wasn't: he was a damned fine footballer, who used the ball accurately and intelligently, and who looked as though he had what it took to make the grade at Old Trafford.

Mark's reputation took a terrible pounding after one match with Burnley when their chairman, Bob Lord, called him a teddy boy. It was ludicrous and grossly unfair. He could look after himself – he wasn't very big, so he had to – but he was always a quiet sort of lad with no malice about him. After the Burnley incident, though, this negative image got out of hand and he was persecuted because of it.

It was a crying shame because I'm convinced it was a major factor in Mark not developing into the outstanding player he might have become.

86. SHAY BRENNAN

OTHER HONOURS:
19 REPUBLIC OF IRELAND CAPS 1965-70.

OTHER CLUBS:
WATERFORD.

MANAGER:
WATERFORD 1970-74.

SHAY BRENNAN		
COMP.	APPS	GLS
LEAGUE	291 (1)	3
FAC	36	3
LC	4	0
EUROPE	24	0
OTHERS	3	0
TOTAL	358 (1)	6

BORN	MANCHESTER 6TH MAY 1937
DIED	TRAMORE, ROI 9TH JUNE 2000
POSITION	FULL-BACK
JOINED UNITED	1955 FROM JUNIOR FOOTBALL
UNITED DEBUT	SHEFFIELD WED. (H) FAC - 19/02/1958
UNITED HONOURS	EUROPEAN CUP 1967/8 DIV. 1 1964/5, 1966/7
UNITED FAREWELL	IPSWICH TOWN (A) FAC - 03/01/1970
LEFT UNITED FOR	WATERFORD, ROI PLAYER-MANAGER AUG. 1970

Lovely Seamus. He was an easy-going darling of a man and vastly underrated as a footballer in many quarters. In fact, he was an all-rounder of the highest quality, and possibly the best full-back in the country for four or five years in the mid 1960s.

'He didn't get involved with nasty stuff like kicking people, he didn't need to degrade himself with that. Shay almost seemed to charm the ball away from opponents.'

I knew Shay since his schooldays when he impressed me as a silkily skilled inside-forward without ever indicating that he would go on to the momentous career he ultimately enjoyed.

I'd even say, without being unkind to the memory of a man whom I loved dearly, that if there had been no Munich disaster then he might never have been heard of, there were that many exceptional players in front of him at the time.

When he made his entrance against Sheffield Wednesday in the first game after the crash, he was effectively a third-team inside-forward playing out of position at outside-left.

He finished that unforgettable night as the two-goal hero, but it wasn't plain sailing for Shay after that. For a while he was on the fringe of the team in bits-and-pieces roles, before finally settling as a full-back in 1960.

Now the talent which had characterised him as an inside-forward served him splendidly in his new position. He didn't get involved with nasty stuff like kicking people, he didn't need to degrade himself with that. Shay almost seemed to charm the ball away from opponents. His maxim might have been: 'Let them give me the ball and then I'll pass it.' He never seemed to be in a rush, either on the field or off it.

He was close to selection for several England squads, having made a favourable impression on Alf Ramsey, then later took the opportunity to play for the Republic of Ireland because of his ancestry. I used to joke with him that he was lucky, as he wasn't good enough for England so he could play for Ireland. He only laughed – that was Shay.

In 1967/68 he lost his place at United, with Tony Dunne moving to the right and Francis Burns taking over at left-back, but then he was recalled for the second leg of the European Cup semi-final against Real Madrid, with Franny losing out. Using all his experience, he shone against Francisco Gento and then, having barely played all season, he found himself in the European Cup Final, performing admirably yet again.

I must admit that Shay never struck me as management material – I'd have thought his players would have had to get their training in early, so he could get to the betting shop – but when he took over at Waterford he was highly successful, winning several major trophies, delighting in proving a few people wrong.

Shay was everybody's friend, being particularly close to Nobby Stiles and Bobby Charlton; they were like a three-ball. He loved the horses and the dogs, he loved a pint – he was always the first at the bar – and he loved golf, so that it was somehow appropriate when he died on the course.

You could never find a more popular Manchester United player than Seamus Brennan, and we may never see his like again. Bless him.

BORN	MANCHESTER 25TH AUGUST 1936
POSITION	WING-HALF
JOINED UNITED	1953 FROM JUNIOR FOOTBALL
UNITED DEBUT	WBA (H) FAC - 05/03/1958
UNITED FAREWELL	NEWCASTLE UNITED (H) DIV. 1 - 31/01/1959
LEFT UNITED FOR	TRANMERE R. - NOV. 1959 £4,000 (COMBINED FEE WITH GORDON CLAYTON)

BOBBY HARROP		
COMP.	APPS	GLS
LEAGUE	10	0
FAC	1	0
TOTAL	11	0

87. BOBBY HARROP

OTHER CLUBS:
TRANMERE ROVERS 59/60-60/1 (41, 2).

Bobby Harrop was a steady wing-half, reasonably skilful but with few frills to his game. Opportunity knocked for him after Munich, but he couldn't quite capitalise on it, proving unable to rise above competition from the likes of Freddie Goodwin, Stan Crowther and Shay Brennan, who was cropping up in several different positions.

In fairness, it was a difficult time to settle, a lot of players were feeling their way, and it wasn't the best of sides. When it became obvious that his future lay away from Old Trafford, Bobby, for whom there had been high hopes during his days as an England and Great Britain youth international, tried his luck with Tranmere, then played non-League football down south.

88. TOMMY HERON

OTHER CLUBS:
QUEEN'S PARK; PORTADOWN, NORTHERN IRELAND;
YORK CITY 61/2-65/6 (192, 6).

TOMMY HERON		
COMP.	APPS	GLS
LEAGUE	3	0
TOTAL	3	0

BORN	IRVINE, AYRSHIRE 31ST MARCH 1936
POSITION	FULL-BACK, WINGER
JOINED UNITED	MARCH 1958 PORTADOWN, N.IRELAND £8,000
UNITED DEBUT	PRESTON N.E. (H) DIV. 1 - 05/04/1958
UNITED FAREWELL	ARSENAL (A) DIV. 1 - 29/10/1960
LEFT UNITED FOR	YORK CITY - MAY 1961

Scot Tommy Heron was unearthed as a winger in Irish football, arriving at Old Trafford soon after the Munich tragedy. In that time of turmoil, Jimmy Murphy offered him an early debut on the left flank, but he made precious little impact and receded into obscurity for the next two years.

When he reappeared in the spring of 1960 he had been converted to left-back, and though he never looked like holding down the position for Manchester United, he went on to enjoy half a decade in the number-three shirt of York City.

89. ALBERT QUIXALL

OTHER HONOURS:
5 ENGLAND CAPS 1953-55.

OTHER CLUBS:
SHEFFIELD WEDNESDAY 50/1-58/9 (241, 63);
OLDHAM ATHLETIC 64/5-65/6 (37, 11);
STOCKPORT COUNTY 66/7 (13, 0).

ALBERT QUIXALL		
COMP.	APPS	GLS
LEAGUE	165	50
FAC	14	4
LC	1	2
EUROPE	3	0
OTHERS	1	0
TOTAL	184	56

BORN	SHEFFIELD 9TH AUGUST 1933
POSITION	INSIDE-FORWARD
JOINED UNITED	SEPTEMBER 1958 SHEFFIELD WED. £45,000
UNITED DEBUT	TOTTENHAM H. (H) DIV. 1 - 20/09/1958
UNITED HONOURS	FA CUP 1962/3
UNITED FAREWELL	BURNLEY (A) DIV. 1 - 26/12/1963
LEFT UNITED FOR	OLDHAM ATHLETIC SEPT. 1964 - £7,000

Albert Quixall moved to Manchester United as a so-called golden boy with a reputation second to none. He cost a European record fee and was expected to be one of the key men in the side Matt Busby was rebuilding after Munich.

It seemed like an appropriately ambitious and enterprising purchase because Albert had been an exuberant sort of player at Sheffield Wednesday, clearly wanting to be at the heart of every attacking move, and as a 25-year-old England international, the whole football world seemed to be at his feet.

He had tricky little skills, he had pace, he made goals and scored them, he had confidence and he had played inside-right to the great Stanley Matthews for his country. To all intents and purposes, he was the bee's knees; but things didn't work out quite as Matt and Albert had hoped.

Not that he was an unmitigated failure, at least not by normal standards; but judged against the expectations massaged by that enormous fee, he left a lot to be desired.

At first, understandably enough, he found it hard to settle into a team which was going through a period of painful transition – they went seven games without a win immediately after his arrival – but then they recovered and finished the 1958/59 season as title runners-up to Wolves.

He was playing in a pretty decent forward line, with Warren Bradley, Dennis Viollet, Bobby Charlton and Albert Scanlon, but somehow Quickie couldn't quite convince.

When he and Charlton were joined by Denis Law, David Herd and Johnny Giles, with Paddy Crerand pulling the strings in midfield, he could hardly have wished for better quality team-mates and they won the FA Cup in 1963, but still Albert never quite fulfilled all that early potential.

Sometimes I'd look at him and wonder if he had the necessary passion. He was never the sort to put his foot in, and that was fair enough because not everyone needs to be like that, but there was always something lacking.

Perhaps he was overawed by the size of the club and the scale of the task; maybe it took his breath away. Whatever the reason, what had looked like an exciting signing fizzled out rather sadly.

AN EXTRAVAGANTLY GIFTED INSIDE TRIO:
Matt Busby lines up with, left to right, Albert Quixall, Dennis Viollet and Bobby Charlton during 1958/59.

90. WARREN BRADLEY

OTHER HONOURS:
3 ENGLAND CAPS 1959.

OTHER CLUBS:
BURY 61/2-62/3 (13, 1).

WARREN BRADLEY		
COMP.	APPS	GLS
LEAGUE	63	20
FAC	3	1
TOTAL	66	21

BORN	HYDE, CHESHIRE 20TH JUNE 1933
POSITION	WINGER
JOINED UNITED	FEBRUARY 1958 FROM BISHOP AUCKLAND
UNITED DEBUT	BOLTON W. (A) DIV. 1 - 15/11/1958
UNITED FAREWELL	BURNLEY (H) DIV. 1 - 25/11/1961
LEFT UNITED FOR	BURY - MARCH 1962

Warren Bradley was an England amateur international winger who reached Old Trafford by a roundabout route. He had been on the books of Bolton, then distinguished himself in the colours of the famous amateurs Bishop Auckland, who supplied several players to help United out as they strove to regain their feet after Munich.

Warren was the only one to force his way into the team, and after taking a job as a teacher in Manchester, he became a part-time professional footballer. In some ways he was reminiscent of Johnny Berry, one of his predecessors in the number-seven shirt. They both had pace, crossed a decent ball, scored a few goals and weren't afraid of anything despite being not very big, but Warren didn't have Johnny's tricks or his exceptional all-round ability.

Still, he played a major part as United finished second to Wolves in the 1958/59 Championship race, holding his own with Quixall, Viollet, Charlton and Scanlon in a high-scoring and extremely fast-moving forward line.

He was rewarded with three full England caps and responded with two goals, so he never let his country down, just as he always did a sterling job for his club.

Outside of football, he went on to a wonderful career in education, including the headship of Dean's School in Bolton, one of the biggest in England, after which he became a schools inspector. I have had a lot to do with Warren, working together with him in the Manchester United Former Players Association – he has been the treasurer since we started in the 1980s – and he is as nice a fellow as you could wish to meet.

BORN	DUBLIN 8TH SEPTEMBER 1937
POSITION	FULL-BACK
JOINED UNITED	FEBRUARY 1956 FROM HOME FARM, ROI
UNITED DEBUT	LUTON TOWN (H) DIV. 1 - 22/11/1958
UNITED FAREWELL	EXETER CITY (H) LC - 26/10/1960
LEFT UNITED FOR	BRIGHTON HA - DEC. 1960

JOE CAROLAN		
COMP.	APPS	GLS
LEAGUE	66	0
FAC	4	0
LC	1	0
TOTAL	71	0

91. JOE CAROLAN

OTHER HONOURS:
2 REPUBLIC OF IRELAND CAPS 1959-60.

OTHER CLUBS:
HOME FARM, ROI;
BRIGHTON AND HOVE ALBION 60/1-61/2 (33, 0).

Joe Carolan was a more-than-useful full-back who was unlucky not to enjoy a far longer Old Trafford career than he did. Admittedly, had he stayed his chances might have been limited by the arrival of his countrymen Noel Cantwell and Tony Dunne, but he didn't do much wrong as United finished runners-up in 1958/59 and in seventh place the following season.

Like Shay Brennan, Joe seemed to find the game easy; he never flapped, never looked to be in a hurry, which was a reflection of his lovely laid-back character. So many Irishmen seem to have a wonderful attitude: that life is important, but not so important that you should worry about it.

It mystified me rather that Joe played 71 times over two seasons, barely missing a game and looking a good player in the process, only for the manager to decide that he wasn't the right man for the job. Why?

Perhaps it was because Matt felt he needed a leader and went for Noel Cantwell, which squeezed out Joe, who was only 23 and already a full international when he left. After that, surprisingly, he played most of his football in the non-League ranks but, knowing Joe, I'm sure he enjoyed it.

As a footnote I ought to mention that, together with my co-writer Ivan Ponting, who was working on his first book back in the late 1980s, I pronounced Joe dead and buried. Obviously our information was muddled somewhere down the line and since then I've been delighted to see him as hail and hearty as ever. Now that's what I call a comeback – God bless you, Joe!

BORN	COLWYN BAY 25TH OCTOBER 1938
POSITION	WINGER
JOINED UNITED	NOVEMBER 1956 FROM COLWYN BAY
UNITED DEBUT & FAREWELL	ASTON VILLA (A) DIV. 1 - 27/12/1958
LEFT UNITED FOR	WREXHAM - FEBRUARY 1960

REG HUNTER		
COMP.	APPS	GLS
LEAGUE	1	0
TOTAL	1	0

92. REG HUNTER

OTHER CLUBS:
WREXHAM 59/60-61/2 (34, 3).

Reg Hunter scored a goal in each leg as Manchester United overwhelmed West Ham 8-2 on aggregate in the 1957 FA Youth Cup Final, and must have felt he was on his way to a decent career in the game.

But Reg, a lively winger with plenty of skill, only had one

first-team opportunity, as a deputy for Warren Bradley, before being released to join Wrexham.

Perhaps he wasn't quite good enough for United, but it seemed surprising when he didn't last long at the Racecourse. Possibly the truth was that Reg's abilities weren't suited to the lower levels and that he might have thrived in, say, the Second Division.

93. JOHNNY GILES

OTHER HONOURS:
60 REPUBLIC OF IRELAND CAPS 1959-79.

OTHER CLUBS:
HOME FARM, ROI;
LEEDS UNITED 63/4-74/5 (383, 86);
WEST BROMWICH ALBION 75/6-76/7 (75, 3);
SHAMROCK ROVERS, REPUBLIC OF IRELAND, 77/8-82/3;
PHILADELPHIA FURY, USA, 78/9.

MANAGER:
WEST BROMWICH ALBION 1975-77 AND 1984-85;
PHILADELPHIA FURY 1978; SHAMROCK ROVERS 1977-83;
REPUBLIC OF IRELAND 1977-80; VANCOUVER WHITECAPS, CANADA, 1980-83.

JOHNNY GILES		
COMP.	APPS	GLS
LEAGUE	99	10
FAC	13	2
LC	2	1
OTHERS	1	0
TOTAL	115	13

BORN	DUBLIN 6TH NOVEMBER 1940
POSITION	INSIDE-FORWARD
JOINED UNITED	JULY 1956 FROM HOME FARM, ROI
UNITED DEBUT	TOTTENHAM H. (H) DIV. 1 - 12/09/1959
UNITED HONOURS	FA CUP 1962/3
UNITED FAREWELL	EVERTON (A) CS - 17/08/1963
LEFT UNITED FOR	LEEDS UTD. AUGUST 1963 - £37,500

John Giles was an inside-forward *par excellence*. He had two great feet, the shrewdest of football brains, and he made the game look easy. What a pity from Manchester United's point of view that he was not at Old Trafford in his magnificent pomp. He hailed from a footballing family – Con Martin, the famous Republic of Ireland star of the immediate post-war era, was his uncle – and from the moment he arrived in Manchester as a teenager it was evident that John had class to burn.

However, he was a strong-minded individual and had what proved to be unresolvable differences with Matt Busby, who persisted in playing him on the right wing. John didn't want that at any price, insisting that he was an inside-forward, and he went on to prove his point conclusively by playing hundreds of games for Leeds when they were one of the top teams in Europe.

Given the forceful personalities of the two men involved, it came as no surprise when John left United after being dropped by Matt – along with Albert Quixall and David Herd – following a comprehensive Charity Shield thrashing by Everton in 1963. Perhaps if the manager had omitted Quixall for the 1963 FA Cup Final and played Giles at inside-right, then he would not

TWO MEN WHO DIDN'T MINCE THEIR WORDS: Jimmy Murphy prepares to make his point to young John Giles.

have departed for Elland Road, where he became a far more influential player than ever he was at Old Trafford.

He might have stayed to form a midfield partnership with Paddy Crerand, with maybe Charlton and Law playing together up front and Best roaming everywhere. Doesn't sound a bad combination, does it? It's a funny thing about that Wembley team that United's two wingers, Giles and Charlton, both went on to become world-class midfielders, although there was a vast contrast in their methods of execution. I suppose you could say that John executed people, while Bobby didn't, which brings me to what I saw as Giles' only fault.

He could be a nasty beggar, which is an asset up to a point, but not if that point is exceeded. It was a trait which wasn't evident at Old Trafford, but it's my guess that when he went to Leeds, someone like Bobby Collins taught him a few tricks of the trade. It's strange because the Leeds manager, Don Revie, wouldn't have kicked anybody when he was a player, but his attitude changed completely when he took charge of Leeds.

For all that, John Giles will be remembered as a great performer, and as in the case of Johnny Morris some 14 years earlier, it was a crying shame that a compromise could not have been reached to prevent such an immense talent from slipping away.

> *'He might have stayed to form a midfield partnership with Paddy Crerand, with maybe Charlton and Law playing together up front and Best roaming everywhere. Doesn't sound a bad combination, does it?'*

A FINAL FLING: Playing in his unfavoured position on the right wing, John Giles fires a low cross beyond Leicester's Richie Norman during the 1963 FA Cup Final. The Irishman left Old Trafford soon afterwards.

94. MAURICE SETTERS

OTHER CLUBS:
EXETER CITY 53/4-54/5 (10, 0);
WEST BROMWICH ALBION 55/6-59/60 (120, 10);
STOKE CITY 64/5-67/8 (87, 5);
COVENTRY CITY 67/8-69/70 (51, 3); CHARLTON
ATHLETIC 69/70 (8, 1).

MANAGER:
DONCASTER ROVERS 1971-74.

MAURICE SETTERS		
COMP.	APPS	GLS
LEAGUE	159	12
FAC	25	1
LC	2	0
EUROPE	7	1
OTHERS	1	0
TOTAL	194	14

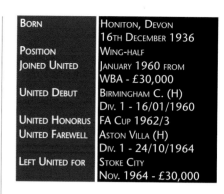

BORN	HONITON, DEVON 16TH DECEMBER 1936
POSITION	WING-HALF
JOINED UNITED	JANUARY 1960 FROM WBA - £30,000
UNITED DEBUT	BIRMINGHAM C. (H) DIV. 1 - 16/01/1960
UNITED HONORUS	FA CUP 1962/3
UNITED FAREWELL	ASTON VILLA (H) DIV. 1 - 24/10/1964
LEFT UNITED FOR	STOKE CITY NOV. 1964 - £30,000

But for the death of Duncan Edwards at Munich, never in a million years would Maurice Setters have joined Manchester United. Not that there was anything wrong with Maurice. He was excellent defensively, a formidable tackler and outstanding in the air for a relatively small man. But when the ball was at his feet, sometimes he would get a bit carried away and try to play a bit, which was not what he was paid to do.

His job was to stop the opposition scoring and then to pass the ball simply to Crerand or Charlton or Law, the artists of the team. That's something Bill Foulkes, for example, understood perfectly, but maybe Maurice thought his experience as an England under-23 international entitled him to embroider, which could result in possession being lost unnecessarily.

Whatever his reason, he didn't always fulfil the simple task of winning it and giving it, slipping a safe pass over five yards, or two yards or one yard; it didn't matter as long as it reached its destination.

He played in the 1963 FA Cup Final, taking a place which some people thought should have gone to Nobby Stiles, though in fairness to Maurice he had missed very few games during that season.

I think Maurice got to the point, when he became captain for a brief spell in the early 1960s, that he felt he was going to become a highly influential figure at the club. Now the truth was that, unless your name was Matt Busby, or perhaps Jimmy Murphy, you could forget about such ambitions. I believe Maurice misjudged that situation. Maybe there's a parallel to be drawn with Paul Ince in later years; he was allowed to leave by Alex Ferguson to the surprise of many outsiders, but not to those in the know.

For all that, Maurice was far from finished when Matt let him go after plumping for Nobby as Bill Foulkes' defensive partner. He did pretty well for Stoke and Coventry, then much later he returned to the limelight as assistant manager of the Republic of Ireland during Jack Charlton's successful reign.

BORN	MANCHESTER 25TH MARCH 1940
POSITION	WING-HALF, INSIDE-FORWARD
JOINED UNITED	1956 FROM JUNIOR FOOTBALL
UNITED DEBUT	LUTON TOWN (A) DIV. 1 - 09/04/1960
UNITED FAREWELL	NOTTINGHAM FOREST (H) DIV. 1 - 08/12/1962
LEFT UNITED FOR	PRESTON NORTH END MARCH 1963 - £11,500

NOBBY LAWTON		
COMP.	APPS	GLS
LEAGUE	36	6
FAC	7	0
LC	1	0
TOTAL	44	6

95. NOBBY LAWTON

OTHER CLUBS:
PRESTON NORTH END 62/3-67/8 (143, 22);
BRIGHTON AND HOVE ALBION 67/8-70/1 (112, 14);
LINCOLN CITY 70/1-71/2 (20, 0).

Norbert's a very unusual name yet Manchester United had two at the same time, both from the Collyhurst area, both of them firmly in the ranks of the good lads.

The similarities continue in that both could play at inside-forward or wing-half in their early years, but a difference arises in the length of their respective Old Trafford careers. Little Nobby Stiles spent a decade as a first-team regular, while his taller namesake was gone after some two and a half years in which he never quite managed to become a fixture.

Norbert Lawton's early progress was hampered by a life-threatening illness soon after he turned professional, but he recovered to emerge as a talented candidate for a place in Matt's new United.

He was a cultured passer and he didn't mind a tackle, without perhaps having quite the ruthless competitive edge of his fellow Norbert. He knew the way to goal, too, scoring a hat-trick at home to Nottingham Forest on Boxing Day 1961.

But fate wasn't kind to him with some niggling injuries, new players made it more difficult to get a game, and in the end he must have got tired of waiting, though that was nowhere near the end of the Nobby Lawton story.

He joined Alex Dawson at Preston and showed real stature over half a dozen seasons, captaining the side in the 1964 FA Cup Final, then going on to a creditable spell with Brighton.

BORN	ECCLES, LANCASHIRE 29TH NOVEMBER 1940
POSITION	CENTRE-HALF
JOINED UNITED	1957 FROM BLACKPOOL (AMATEUR)
UNITED DEBUT	BLACKBURN ROVERS (H) DIV. 1 - 20/08/1960
UNITED FAREWELL	NOTTINGHAM FOREST (A) DIV. 1 - 20/05/1963
LEFT UNITED FOR	CHARLTON ATHLETIC AUG. 1963 - £10,000

FRANK HAYDOCK		
COMP.	APPS	GLS
LEAGUE	6	0
TOTAL	6	0

96. FRANK HAYDOCK

OTHER CLUBS:
CHARLTON ATHLETIC 63/4-65/6 (84, 4);
PORTSMOUTH 65/6-68/9 (72, 1);
SOUTHEND UNITED 68/9-69/70 (33, 4).

Big Frank Haydock was a centre-half in the traditional stopper mould, a force to be reckoned with in the air or on the deck, and as a bonus he wasn't a bad passer, but he never managed to climb over Bill Foulkes to claim United's number-five shirt as his own.

Yet he was eight years younger than Bill, and it's difficult to see why Matt Busby let him go when he was still only 22. Maybe Frank became tired of being described as one of the most reliable deputy defenders in the First Division, so he decided to step down a level and try his luck with Charlton.

As it turned out, he didn't do badly away from Old Trafford, but never made the name for himself which some shrewd observers in Manchester had believed to be possible.

97. JIMMY NICHOLSON

OTHER HONOURS:
41 NORTHERN IRELAND CAPS 1960-71.

OTHER CLUBS:
HUDDERSFIELD TOWN 64/5-73/4 (281, 26); BURY 73/4-75/6 (83, 0).

JIMMY NICHOLSON		
COMP.	APPS	GLS
LEAGUE	58	5
FAC	7	1
LC	3	0
TOTAL	68	6

BORN	BELFAST 27TH FEBRUARY 1943
POSITION	WING-HALF
JOINED UNITED	1958 FROM IRISH JUNIOR FOOTBALL
UNITED DEBUT	EVERTON (A) DIV. 1 - 24/08/1960
UNITED FAREWELL	WBA (A) DIV. 1 - 15/12/1962
LEFT UNITED FOR	HUDDERSFIELD TOWN DEC. 1964 - £7,500

When Jimmy Nicholson crossed the Irish Sea to Manchester at the tender age of 15 he was hailed as the latest wonder-boy. There were even whispers that he might be 'the new Duncan Edwards', but obviously the people who said that knew nothing about Duncan Edwards.

It was a totally stupid comparison to make, and it was utterly irresponsible to saddle any young player with such a burden at the start of his footballing life.

Back in the real world, though his play bore no resemblance whatsoever to Duncan's, Jimmy was a decently talented wing-half who might have had a chance of fashioning a career at Old Trafford but for those daft artificial expectations.

He was an accurate and sometimes imaginative passer, he moved intelligently off the ball and he could time his tackles, and although there was immense competition for places there were plenty of people who thought him preferable to, say, Maurice Setters.

But after suffering a succession of injuries, and with Paddy Crerand and Nobby Stiles solidly established in the team, his United prospects diminished and he went to Huddersfield, where he spent ten highly productive years.

Much of his time at Leeds Road was served under the management of former Old Trafford full-back Ian Greaves, who rated him extremely highly, and I'm sure that Ian's assessment was a fair one.

BORN	MANCHESTER 18TH MAY 1942
POSITION	CENTRAL DEFENDER MIDFIELDER
JOINED UNITED	SEPTEMBER 1957 FROM JUNIOR FOOTBALL
UNITED DEBUT	BOLTON W. (A) DIV. 1 - 01/10/1960
UNITED HONORUS	EUROPEAN CUP 1967/8 DIV. 1 1964/5, 1966/7
UNITED FAREWELL	COVENTRY CITY (A) DIV. 1 - 13/04/1971
LEFT UNITED FOR	MIDDLESBROUGH MAY 1971 - £20,000

NOBBY STILES		
COMP.	APPS	GLS
LEAGUE	311	17
FAC	38	0
LC	7	0
EUROPE	36	2
OTHERS	3	0
TOTAL	395	19

98. NOBBY STILES

OTHER HONOURS:
20 ENGLAND CAPS 1965-70
WORLD CUP WINNER 1966
OTHER CLUBS:
MIDDLESBROUGH 71/2-72/3 (57, 2);
PRESTON NORTH END 73/4-74/5 (46, 1).
MANAGER:
PRESTON NORTH END 1977-81;
VANCOUVER WHITECAPS, CANADA, 1981-84;
WEST BROMWICH ALBION 1985-86.

All too often Nobby Stiles is portrayed as a one-dimensional destroyer, this snarling, kicking, bruising monster, but that fails dismally to do him justice. In fact, he was a splendid all-round footballer, who read the game with acute intelligence.

He was versatile, too, enjoying his greatest Manchester United days alongside Bill Foulkes in the middle of the back four, while playing in midfield for Alf Ramsey's England team that won the World Cup in 1966.

Nobby was ready to overcome any obstacle as he fought to establish his career. For instance, his eyesight was severely poor until he began wearing contact lenses, and he was far smaller than most of the opponents he was asked to mark. In fact, from a physical point of view he had very little going for him.

But the second son of Collyhurst undertaker Charlie Stiles did have two priceless assets: first, he could play; second, he had a heart like a lion. There appeared to be no set of circumstances which could faze him, and he was afraid of nothing or nobody.

Harry Gregg, a fair judge of character as well as football, could never praise him too highly, maintaining that for all the stars at United's disposal, Nobby was one of their most important players, and I have to agree.

Without Nobby, the course of football history might have been altered drastically. I truly believe that but for him, England might never have become world champions and, two years later in 1968, United might not have realised Matt Busby's dream of lifting the European Cup; and beyond that, surely Bill Foulkes' days at the core of the defence would not have lasted until his 38th year if it had not been for his mutually beneficial partnership with Nobby.

Matt eventually settled on centre-back as Nobby's best role, utilising all that strength and determination but also his almost uncanny knack of anticipating danger and snuffing it out. Meanwhile Alf could call on Bobby Moore or Norman Hunter to stand beside Jack Charlton, so he used Nobby's single-minded efficiency in midfield, where he would win the ball repeatedly and rarely or never squander possession by attempting something silly.

Nobby won two title medals in the mid 1960s and before that he counted himself unlucky to be left out of the 1963 FA Cup Final after playing for most of that season, either at wing-half or inside-forward.

To be honest, early in the decade when his place was not assured, though I could appreciate his quality and recognise that he would never be easy to play against, I wouldn't have envisaged the vast influence he would wield as the years went by.

Nobby is married to John Giles' sister, and while at one time it seemed that he had been outstripped by his brother-in-law, all of a sudden Nobby came up on the rails. That was typical of a man who would never give up, perhaps feeling a certain insecurity about what his life might be like without football.

He has been a credit to himself, his family, his club and his country, and that's not a bad way to be remembered.

99. IAN MOIR

OTHER CLUBS:
BLACKPOOL 64/5-66/7 (61, 12);
CHESTER 67/8 (25, 3);
WREXHAM 67/8-71/2 (150, 20);
SHREWSBURY TOWN 71/2-72/3 (25, 2);
WREXHAM 73/4-74/5 (15, 0).

IAN MOIR		
COMP.	APPS	GLS
LEAGUE	45	5
TOTAL	45	5

BORN	ABERDEEN 30TH JUNE 1943
POSITION	WINGER
JOINED UNITED	1958 FROM JUNIOR FOOTBALL
UNITED DEBUT	BOLTON WANDERERS (A) DIV. 1 - 01/10/1960
UNITED FAREWELL	BLACKPOOL (A) DIV. 1 - 14/11/1964
LEFT UNITED FOR	BLACKPOOL FEB. 1965 - £30,000

Ian Moir had so many tricks he could have made his living as a magician, and when Matt Busby gave him his first-team break at the age of 17, it was widely predicted that he would mature into something special.

After that Matt nursed him carefully until giving him a settled run at the expense of John Giles at the start of 1963/64 but then, after a few impressive performances, he didn't maintain his form and disappeared from the reckoning.

It was a shame because Ian was a lovely, happy-go-lucky lad, everybody wished him well, and he had bags of natural ability. Tall for a winger at 5ft 11ins, he was very quick and so skilful that sometimes he could mesmerise defenders, especially in training, where he looked like a world-beater.

I think Matt had a glorious vision of Ian on one wing and the young George Best on the other, but while the Irishman went

on getting better and better, the Scot just fell away, sadly unable to translate all that talent into solid achievement.

Why that should be I can only speculate. Perhaps he was a tad too easy-going, hoping to breeze through his career, but I may be doing him an injustice.

BORN	DUBLIN 24TH JULY 1941
POSITION	FULL-BACK
JOINED UNITED	APRIL 1960 FROM SHELBOURNE, ROI - £5,000
UNITED DEBUT	BURNLEY (A) DIV. 1 - 15/10/1960
UNITED HONORUS	EUROPEAN CUP 1967/8 DIV. 1 1964/5, 1966/7 FA CUP 1962/3
UNITED FAREWELL	IPSWICH TOWN (A) DIV. 1 - 17/02/1973
LEFT UNITED FOR	BOLTON W. - AUG. 1973

TONY DUNNE		
COMP.	APPS	GLS
LEAGUE	414	2
FAC	54 (1)	0
LC	21	0
EUROPE	40	0
OTHERS	5	0
TOTAL	534 (1)	2

100. TONY DUNNE

OTHER HONOURS:
33 REPUBLIC OF IRELAND CAPS 1962-76.

OTHER CLUBS:
SHELBOURNE, ROI;
BOLTON WANDERERS 73/4-78/9 (170, 0);
DETROIT EXPRESS, USA;
STENJKER, NORWAY.

Tony Dunne was a top-drawer full-back with speed to burn, comfortable on the ball, capable of operating equally effectively on either flank, and he did a superb job for Manchester United for a dozen years.

In fact, he could have carried on at Old Trafford for quite a bit longer, because when he was moved out by Tommy Docherty in 1973, he was still the best full-back at the club by some considerable distance.

Tony proved that he was far from finished in the most convincing way, by making nearly 200 League and cup appearances for Bolton over the next five years, taking his career total, including internationals, to something like 760, and helping Ian Greaves' side return to the top division in the process. Ian couldn't believe his luck in signing such a thoroughbred for nothing, and he maintained that when Tony finally retired at the age of 38, he was still as good as anyone who was knocking about.

During his prime with United, I'm sure that Bill Foulkes and Nobby Stiles loved having Tony at their side. He was an old-fashioned full-back whose instinct was to cover his central defenders and to block up any holes which might appear, a job which his pace enabled to him accomplish as effectively as anybody in the last 40 years.

Importantly, too, when Tony got the ball he didn't give himself problems by trying something fancy, instead looking for Crerand or Charlton so that they could do what they did best. Interestingly, when he went to Bolton, where they were not blessed with such gifted creators, Tony was encouraged by Ian Greaves to play a bit, and he found that he was good at it.

All the while, Docherty's decision to get rid of him, along with one or two other proven performers such as David Sadler and Brian Kidd, looked increasingly misguided. It's all very well trying to launch a new regime, but you have to have the material to do it, and at that stage he didn't.

Tony Dunne would have been pure gold for Docherty, as he had been all those years for Matt Busby.

101. HAROLD BRATT

OTHER CLUBS:
DONCASTER ROVERS 61/2-62/3 (54, 0).

HAROLD BRATT		
COMP.	APPS	GLS
LC	1	0
TOTAL	1	0

BORN	SALFORD 8TH OCTOBER 1939
POSITION	WING-HALF
JOINED UNITED	JULY 1955 FROM JUNIOR FOOTBALL
UNITED DEBUT & FAREWELL	BRADFORD CITY (A) LC - 02/11/1960
LEFT UNITED FOR	DONCASTER R. - MAY 1961

Y ou would go a long way to find a fitter footballer than Harold Bratt. He was an up-and-at-'em wing-half who was out to make the life of opposing inside-forwards as difficult as possible, but he was offered only the one chance by United before being transferred to Doncaster.

Later Harold joined the police, serving first as a constable and then a PE instructor. He comes to all the ex-players' do's, takes part in all the golf days, and in 2005 he remained in such fine physical condition that I'd swear he must have found the secret of eternal youth.

THE REBUILT UNITED SIDE IN 1963.
Left to right, back row: trainer Jack Crompton, Nobby Stiles, Shay Brennan, Noel Cantwell, Maurice Setters, Tony Dunne, Bill Foulkes, Paddy Crerand. Front row: Harry Gregg, John Giles, Albert Quixall, David Herd, Denis Law, Bobby Charlton, David Gaskell.

BORN	CORK, ROI
	28TH DECEMBER 1932
POSITION	FULL-BACK
JOINED UNITED	NOVEMBER 1960 FROM
	WEST HAM - £29,500
UNITED DEBUT	CARDIFF CITY (A)
	DIV. 1 - 26/11/1960
UNITED HONORUS	FA CUP 1962/3
UNITED FAREWELL	SOUTHAMPTON (A)
	DIV. 1 - 19/11/1966
LEFT UNITED FOR	COVENTRY CITY
	OCT. 1967 - MANAGER

NOEL CANTWELL		
COMP.	APPS	GLS
LEAGUE	123	6
FAC	14	2
EUROPE	7	0
OTHERS	2	0
TOTAL	146	8

102. NOEL CANTWELL

OTHER HONOURS:
36 REPUBLIC OF IRELAND CAPS 1953-67.
OTHER CLUBS:
CORK ATHLETIC, REPUBLIC OF IRELAND;
WEST HAM UNITED 52/3-60/1 (248, 11).
MANAGER:
COVENTRY CITY 1967-72;
REPUBLIC OF IRELAND NATIONAL TEAM 1967-68;
NEW ENGLND TEA MEN, USA, 1972 AND 1978-82;
PETERBOROUGH UNITED 1972-77 AND 1986-88.

Noel Cantwell was a truly major figure in the story of Manchester United during the 1960s. A vastly experienced, top-class international full-back, he was required by Matt Busby to act as a father figure to the other players on the field, filling much the same role as his fellow Irishman, John Carey, had done in the 1940s and 1950s.

He became skipper, but it's fair to say that his own best playing days were behind him; he retained his skills and he was in and out of the side quite a bit. Still it's significant that even when he wasn't first choice – and it wasn't easy holding down a full-back position with Tony Dunne and Shay Brennan on the scene – Noel continued as club captain, underlining his influence as a personality.

I think it might have been in Matt's mind that one day Noel might become his successor as manager. Maybe he wanted to monitor the Cantwell progress when he succeeded Jimmy Hill as boss of Coventry, where he did a decent job, as well as guiding the fortunes of the Republic of Ireland national side for a short spell. But the Irishman never came back and in the end his management career was a bit of a mish-mash.

Noel had emerged from the so-called West Ham coaching academy, with the likes of Malcolm Allison, John Bond, Ken Brown, John Smith, Frank O'Farrell, Malcolm Musgrove and Dave Sexton – the last three of whom would eventually work for United – and he thought deeply about the game.

When he arrived at Old Trafford, he expected some fascinating tactical insights from the manager, but in that he was disappointed. Noel could hardly believe what I

AERIAL BALLET: United skipper Noel Cantwell challenges Leicester and England goalkeeper Gordon Banks in the 1963 FA Cup Final.

'He will always be remembered as the captain who held up United's first trophy after the Munich disaster, when they beat Leicester in the 1963 FA Cup Final.'

had told him already, that Matt had signed him because he could play, and that was basically the extent of his strategy.

The way I put it to Noel was this: he had spent all those years at West Ham, where they had told him how to play, and he hadn't won a bowl of soup. In the meantime Matt had been telling his players nothing in the way of detailed tactics, yet his team had won the lot. Did that not speak volumes?

None of that should obscure the fact that Noel had been a fine footballer in his prime, a big fellow who was commanding enough in the air to play in the centre of defence, or even at centre-forward on occasion, but principally a composed and cultured full-back who was a delight to watch.

He will always be remembered as the captain who held up United's first trophy after the Munich disaster, when they beat Leicester in the 1963 FA Cup Final.

In recent years Noel, a typically eloquent Irish charmer, has been looking at players for the England set-up, thanks presumably to his continued links with Dave Sexton.

103. RONNIE BRIGGS

OTHER HONOURS:
2 NORTHERN IRELAND CAPS 1962-65.

OTHER CLUBS:
SWANSEA TOWN 64/5 (27, 0);
BRISTOL ROVERS 65/6-67/8 (35, 0).

RONNIE BRIGGS		
COMP.	APPS	GLS
LEAGUE	9	0
FAC	2	0
TOTAL	11	0

BORN	BELFAST 29TH MARCH 1943
POSITION	GOALKEEPER
JOINED UNITED	1958 FROM IRISH JUNIOR FOOTBALL
UNITED DEBUT	LEICESTER CITY (A) DIV. 1 - 21/01/1961
UNITED FAREWELL	ARSENAL (H) DIV. 1 - 16/04/1962
LEFT UNITED FOR	SWANSEA TOWN MAY 1964

Ronnie Briggs was a ginger-haired giant of an Ulsterman whose ability between the posts never matched either his stature or his overwhelming self-confidence.

He was given his chance because of injury to Harry Gregg and David Gaskell, and let in six at Leicester in his first game, then seven against Sheffield Wednesday in the FA Cup in his third.

Later he was capped by Northern Ireland, but he was never going to be good enough for United, and didn't last long at either Swansea or Bristol Rovers before descending to non-League football.

BORN	BOSTON, LINCOLNSHIRE 16TH FEBRUARY 1934
POSITION	GOALKEEPER
JOINED UNITED	FEBRUARY 1961 FROM QPR (AMATEUR)
UNITED DEBUT	ASTON VILLA (H) DIV. 1 - 04/02/1961
UNITED FAREWELL	NEWCASTLE UNITED (A) DIV. 1 - 11/03/1961
LEFT UNITED FOR	HENDON TOWN - 1961

MIKE PINNER		
COMP.	APPS	GLS
LEAGUE	4	0
TOTAL	4	0

104. MIKE PINNER

OTHER CLUBS:
ASTON VILLA 54/5-56/7 (4, 0);
SHEFFIELD WEDNESDAY 57/8-58/9 (7, 0);
QUEEN'S PARK RANGERS 59/60 (19, 0);
CHELSEA 61/2 (1, 0);
SWANSEA TOWN 61/2 (1, 0);
LEYTON ORIENT 62/3-64/5 (77, 0).

Matt Busby was so pleased with Ronnie Briggs during the injury absence of Harry Gregg and David Gaskell that he brought in Mike Pinner. Mike was an experienced England amateur international with more than half a century of caps to his credit, including appearances in the Sydney and Rome Olympics, but he was never going to be a fixture at Old Trafford.

Essentially he was happy to do Manchester United a favour in a crisis, and he performed steadily for four matches before going back to his work as a solicitor.

BORN	HAMILTON, LANARKSHIRE 15TH APRIL 1934
POSITION	CENTRE-FORWARD
JOINED UNITED	JULY 1961 FROM ARSENAL - £37,000
UNITED DEBUT	WEST HAM UTD (A) DIV. 1 - 19/08/1961
UNITED HONOURS	DIV. 1 1964/5, 1966/7 FA CUP 1962/3
UNITED FAREWELL	LIVERPOOL (H) DIV. 1 - 6/04/1968
LEFT UNITED FOR	STOKE CITY - JULY 1968

DAVID HERD		
COMP.	APPS	GLS
LEAGUE	201 (1)	114
FAC	35	15
LC	1	1
EUROPE	25	14
OTHERS	2	1
TOTAL	264 (1)	145

105. DAVID HERD

OTHER HONOURS:
5 SCOTLAND CAPS 1958-61.
OTHER CLUBS:
STOCKPORT COUNTY 50/1-53/4 (16, 6);
ARSENAL 54/5-60/1 (166, 97);
STOKE CITY 68/9-69/70 (44, 11);
WATERFORD, REPUBLIC OF IRELAND, 70/1.
MANAGER:
LINCOLN CITY 1971-72.

David Herd was a key player in Manchester United's multiple successes of the 1960s, just as his father Alex was integral to Manchester City's League title and FA Cup glory three decades earlier.

At the start of David's career and at the end of Alex's, they played together for Stockport County, and there can't be many footballing father-and-son pairings with a prouder record.

David scored goals by the bucketful wherever he went, and his figures stand scrutiny alongside anyone's, though strangely for a prolific centre-forward, he didn't get many with his head.

Against that he was a tremendous natural striker of the ball, packing an explosive shot which terrorised First Division goalkeepers for a decade and a half, and he was a quick and powerful mover who could control the ball and hold it when it was played up to him.

Also, aside from his own impressive tally, he proved the ideal foil for his fellow striker, Denis Law. The two of them created bags of chances for each other and must have been a dream for their team-mates to play behind.

Tellingly David, who scored twice in the 1963 FA Cup Final victory over Leicester, always found the net for ordinary teams as well as those that were riding high. For example, the Arsenal side of the late '50s were nothing to rave about, and neither were United when he arrived from Highbury in 1961.

Perversely, he took a lot of stick from the United crowd at times, never being the fans' favourite son despite all his goals. The likely explanation was that when things went wrong they were never going to get on the backs of their heroes, the likes of Charlton, Law and Best, but they needed a scapegoat so they turned on Herdy.

Unfortunately, after helping to win two League Championships, he suffered a badly broken leg in 1967 and was never quite the same force again, being supplanted in the United attack by the young Brian Kidd.

Away from the game David, who grew up in Manchester and was a childhood chum of Dennis Viollet, was a quiet, unassuming sort. For many years he was the co-proprietor of David Herd Motors in Davyhulme and he played cricket to a pretty high standard for several local clubs.

106. SAMMY McMILLAN

OTHER HONOURS:
2 NORTHERN IRELAND CAPS 1962.

OTHER CLUBS:
WREXHAM 63/4-67/8 (149, 52);
SOUTHEND UNITED 67/8-69/70 (77, 5);
CHESTER 69/70 (18, 0);
STOCKPORT COUNTY 70/1-71/2 (74, 29).

SAMMY McMILLAN		
COMP.	APPS	GLS
LEAGUE	15	6
TOTAL	15	6

BORN	BELFAST 20TH SEPTEMBER 1941
POSITION	FORWARD
JOINED UNITED	1957 FROM IRISH JUNIOR FOOTBALL
UNITED DEBUT	SHEFFIELD WED. (A) DIV. 1 - 04/11/1961
UNITED FAREWELL	BLACKBURN R. (H) DIV. 1 - 13/10/1962
LEFT UNITED FOR	WREXHAM DEC. 1963 - £8,000

Sammy McMillan was an honest trier who didn't do badly in the few games he played for United, some on the wing and some in the middle, but probably he lacked a bit of class for the top level.

He had all the enthusiasm in the world, he was brave and solidly-built, and he could hit the ball powerfully, but he was trying to prove his worth in an unsettled team and wasn't able to make enough of a mark.

Sammy's efforts earned him a couple of Northern Ireland caps while he was still at Old Trafford, and then he struck some of his best form on the 1963 close-season tour of Italy, only to fall prey to injury before slipping out of the first-team picture.

BORN	MANCHESTER 27TH OCTOBER 1942
POSITION	INSIDE-FORWARD
JOINED UNITED	1958 FROM JUNIOR FOOTBALL
UNITED DEBUT	EVERTON (A) DIV. 1 - 02/12/1961
UNITED FAREWELL	WOLVERHAMPTON W (H) DIV. 1 - 28/03/1964
LEFT UNITED FOR	LIVERPOOL APRIL 1964 - £25,000

PHIL CHISNALL		
COMP.	APPS	GLS
LEAGUE	35	8
FAC	8	1
EUROPE	4	1
TOTAL	47	10

107. PHIL CHISNALL

OTHER CLUBS:
LIVERPOOL 64/5 (6, 1);
SOUTHEND UNITED 67/8-70/1 (142, 28);
STOCKPORT COUNTY 71/2 (30, 2).

Phil Chisnall had the unusual, probably unique distinction of playing under Matt Busby, Bill Shankly and Alf Ramsey, three of the most illustrious names in the game's history; he started at United, moved on to Liverpool and featured for England at under-23 level.

Clearly Phil had natural ability. Certainly he could pass the ball and he could score goals, and when he was drafted in to replace Albert Quixall at inside-right for the first few months of 1963/64 he might have thought he was on the verge of a bright future.

But he never quite stamped his authority on the job, Matt bought Graham Moore from Chelsea, and though Phil had one or two isolated further opportunities, it proved to be a case of so near yet so far.

Busby sold him to Liverpool for £25,000, a sizeable fee for an unproven player in those days, and Shankly thought he had a winner. But it wasn't to be and Phil moved on to Southend, where he became an influential figure.

BORN	ABERDEEN 24TH FEBRUARY 1940
POSITION	INSIDE-FORWARD
JOINED UNITED	AUGUST 1962 FROM TORINO - £115,000
UNITED DEBUT	WBA (H) DIV. 1 - 18/08/1962
UNITED HONOURS	DIV. 1 1964/5, 1966/7 FA CUP 1962/3
UNITED FAREWELL	NORWICH CITY (H) DIV. 1 - 07/04/1973
LEFT UNITED FOR	MANCHESTER CITY JULY 1973

DENIS LAW		
COMP.	APPS	GLS
LEAGUE	305 (4)	171
FAC	44 (2)	34
LC	11	3
EUROPE	33	28
OTHERS	5	1
TOTAL	398 (6)	237

108. DENIS LAW

OTHER HONOURS:
55 SCOTLAND CAPS 1958-74.
EUROPEAN FOOTBALLER OF THE YEAR 1964.

OTHER CLUBS:
HUDDERSFIELD TOWN 56/7-59/60 (81, 16);
MANCHESTER CITY 59/60-60/1 (44, 21);
TORINO, ITALY, 61/2 (27, 10);
MANCHESTER CITY 73/4 (24, 9).

If any Manchester United fan told me that Denis Law was the finest footballer he had seen in his life, I would find it difficult to argue with him.

Yet I know plenty of people who maintain that we never saw the best of him at Old Trafford. They declare that he was even more brilliant during his first spell at City, playing as an old-fashioned inside-forward rather than as an out-and-out striker.

'For such a great goal-scorer, he was staggeringly unselfish, very rarely trying to score himself if he spotted a team-mate in a better position.'

But whatever your preference, his goals-to-games ratio was absolutely phenomenal, even in Italy, where it was virtually impossible to score heavily against blanket defences.

When I heap praise on Denis, which I am always liable to do because he deserves it, people ask me to compare him to Pele, and I find that impossible because I never saw enough of Pele to make a reasoned judgement. But I do point out that Pele played for a Brazil side that wasn't bad, and I believe that if Law had been in that team, with all those extravagant talents around him, there is nothing that he could not have achieved.

Matt Busby paid a British record £115,000 to sign Denis from Torino, but it was like getting him for nothing when you consider the vast impact he made at Old Trafford. He turned the place upside down, and was a dominant factor in transforming United from an ordinary side into the best in the land.

What made Denis Law special? Nothing physical, because there wasn't very much of him. But although he was extremely slender, he was as tough as old boots, frightened of nobody no matter what their size and strength. Beyond that, he had superb all-round ability: he was a demon in the air, incomparable for his size and weight; he had fabulous touch with both feet; his nous and knowledge of the game enabled him to take up dangerous positions instinctively; and he was a fantastic finisher.

For such a great goal-scorer, too, he was staggeringly unselfish, very rarely trying to score himself if he spotted a teammate in a better position, and that's a compliment you couldn't pay to many top marksmen down the years.

Then there were his courage and his competitiveness, both of which beggared belief. In truth, Denis could be a bit naughty at times, and he suffered a couple of long-term suspensions as a result. That said, I don't think he would have gone out of his way to hurt somebody who didn't deserve it. Mind, he had a good memory; most of the naughty ones do; they can always recall who tried to 'do' them and when, and they take the appropriate action.

Add it all together and you have the stuff of which heroes are made. Certainly I have never known another United player better loved by the Old Trafford fans, who christened him 'The King.' There's a pub in Denton called the King's Arm, and when you look at the sign, there's Law with his fist clenched. The first time I saw it I nearly smashed the car!

Normally I am not one for remembering individual goals, but I have two deathless images of Denis. One was a header against Everton at Old Trafford when he rose to meet a cross and the ball seemed to pass him, but somehow he appeared to extend himself backwards in mid-air to nod the ball downwards past 'keeper Gordon West. It was such a superhuman effort that even West applauded; how he reached it I'll never know.

My other memory is equally astonishing. He let a ball run past him in the inside-left-position and as a defender challenged him he dipped his shoulder, selling a perfect dummy; then another opponent attempted a tackle and Denis did exactly the same thing again before slipping the ball to Bobby Charlton, who scored. The Lawman had effectively gone past two people without touching the ball, then nicked it to Bobby. Incredible!

Denis won plenty with United but it's a crying sadness that he missed out on a European Cup winner's medal because of injury and I think they should have minted one specially for him.

Aside from his football, he's a smashing fellow, such a nice man, so very different from that spiky persona on the field. He's an exceptionally private person except in the company of those who know him well, and then he's the wickedest mickey-taker you could imagine. If you're a friend, you've got a chance with Denis. Otherwise forget it.

109. PADDY CRERAND

OTHER HONOURS:
16 SCOTLAND CAPS 1961-65.

OTHER CLUBS:
CELTIC 58/9-62/3 (81, 5).

MANAGER:
NORTHAMPTON TOWN 1976-77.

PAT CRERAND		
COMP.	APPS	GLS
LEAGUE	304	10
FAC	43	4
LC	4	0
EUROPE	41	1
OTHERS	5	0
TOTAL	397	15

BORN	GLASGOW 19TH FEBRUARY 1939
POSITION	WING-HALF
JOINED UNITED	FEBRUARY 1963 FROM CELTIC - £53,000
UNITED DEBUT	BLACKPOOL (H) DIV. 1 - 23/02/1963
UNITED HONOURS	EUROPEAN CUP 1967/8 DIV. 1 1964/5, 1966/7 FA CUP 1962/3
UNITED FAREWELL	MANCHESTER CITY (A) DIV. 1 - 05/05/1971
RETIRED	AUGUST 1971 UNITED COACHING STAFF

Not since the pre-Munich days of Jeff Whitefoot and Eddie Colman had United been blessed with a top-quality constructive wing-half, so the signing of Paddy Crerand was long overdue.

Paddy was a master of the art of passing, even though in Scottish football, where he made his name with Celtic, he was seen mainly as a ferocious tackler, while Jim Baxter was hailed as the principal creative player.

'Paddy took to the United scene like a duck to water, clearly enjoying being part of a massive club with correspondingly huge support, and his irrepressible enthusiasm was invaluable.'

Yet Matt Busby always loved the accuracy and intelligence of Paddy's distribution over both short and long distances, and he earmarked him as his playmaker from the start.

As a newcomer it took him a while to settle into English football because the game was played at a slower pace north of the border, but soon it became clear that United had acquired a thoroughbred.

Paddy was a shrewd tactician and, although heavily biased towards his right foot, he set up countless attacks by slipping unnoticed into the left-back position to take the ball from goalkeeper Alex Stepney. From there it seemed that he could find anyone he wanted, and in particular he developed a wonderful relationship with Denis Law (both on the field and off it), the pair of them bringing out the best in each other.

Also Paddy linked beautifully with Bobby Charlton, who wasn't a tackler but was brilliant on the ball and I believe that in the mid 1960s, when they were operating together in deep areas, the Scot played a crucial part in the Englishman's development. That's because Paddy was always a natural midfielder, while I think Bobby still had a bit to learn about the role at the outset of their partnership.

Much was made of Crerand's lack of pace, but he made up for that with what went on between his ears. He was always in position, and his pure knowhow would put him several strides ahead of most opponents. Importantly, Paddy was a leader because he always wanted the ball, and he was a forceful character, ever ready to say his piece and never prepared to run from an argument. Some said he had a big mouth, and certainly he wasn't afraid of confrontation, maybe even relishing it sometimes. He had a certain capacity to get himself in trouble, not so much with his tackling, but more with his demeanour. His immediate reaction to most situations was to speak now and think later, which landed him in trouble with officialdom from time to time.

After his arrival, Paddy took to the United scene like a duck to water, clearly enjoying being part of a massive club with correspondingly huge support, and his irrepressible enthusiasm was invaluable. I agree with the old saying that if Crerand played well, then United played well, though it does get used a bit glibly. After all, there were three European Footballers of the Year in that side and some other excellent performers, too. But Paddy was at the hub of everything, and United had no replacement for him if he couldn't turn out, which was not true of everybody.

BORN	Northwich, Cheshire 26th October 1944
DIED	2003
POSITION	Wing-half
JOINED UNITED	March 1960 from junior football
UNITED DEBUT & FAREWELL	Nottngham Forest (A) Div. 1 - 20/05/1963
LEFT UNITED FOR	York City - April 1964

DENNIS WALKER		
COMP.	APPS	GLS
LEAGUE	1	0
TOTAL	1	0

110. DENNIS WALKER

OTHER CLUBS:
York City 64/5-67/8 (153, 19);
Cambridge United 70/1-72/3 (56, 4).

Dennis Walker flickered only briefly in the First Division spotlight, wearing the number-11 shirt so that Bobby Charlton could be rested a few days before the 1963 FA Cup Final.

But though he featured on the wing that day, his customary position was the old-fashioned wing-half slot, or midfield if you like, which is where he served York City, faithfully and skilfully, before helping Cambridge United to gain entry to the League in 1970. Dennis was the first coloured lad to play for United.

111. DAVID SADLER

OTHER HONOURS:
4 ENGLAND CAPS 1967-70.

OTHER CLUBS:
PRESTON NORTH END 73/4-76/7 (105, 3).

DAVID SADLER		
COMP.	APPS	GLS
LEAGUE	266 (6)	22
FAC	22 (1)	1
LC	22	1
EUROPE	16	3
OTHERS	2	0
TOTAL	328 (7)	27

BORN	YALDING, KENT 5TH FEBRUARY 1946
POSITION	CENTRE-HALF, MIDFIELD OR CENTRE-FORWARD
JOINED UNITED	NOVEMBER 1962 FROM MAIDSTONE UNITED
UNITED DEBUT	SHEFFIELD WED. (A) DIV. 1 - 24/08/1963
UNITED HONOURS	EUROPEAN CUP 1967/8 DIV. 1 1966/7
UNITED FAREWELL	BURNLEY (A) DIV. 1 - 27/08/1973
LEFT UNITED FOR	PRESTON NORTH END NOV. 1973 - £25,000

When David Sadler came up from Maidstone as a 16-year-old England amateur international centre-forward in the early 1960s, you could have laid long odds against him playing for England as a centre-half and for United in the final of the European Cup as a defensive midfielder.

Perhaps he didn't have the pace to play at the top level up front, but he proved himself to be a versatile and immensely accomplished all-round footballer who developed both midfield and defensive games that would stand him in good stead. Indeed, he went on to win his full caps in the middle of the back four, which was his most effective position, and arguably he was unlucky not to finish with a more extensive collection than four.

David did a wonderful job for United over ten years, and he was anything but a spent force when he went to Preston, where he served under Bobby Charlton. Undoubtedly he could have continued to excel at Old Trafford, but like Tony Dunne and several others, David was never the happiest of bedfellows with the new manager, Tommy Docherty.

As a centre-forward, I have to say that David was very ordinary; not in terms of talent, it was just that he lacked the explosive acceleration needed to lead the attack.

But as a centre-half, he was terrific. He was never an old-fashioned, up-and-at-'em stopper, being more of a cultured operator, closer in style to, say, Jackie Blanchflower than to Mark Jones. He read the game shrewdly, he passed the ball accurately and perceptively, and he never, never lost his cool.

Now, that last-mentioned quality is the one that defines David Sadler. To me, he will al-

ways be Laid-back Louie, because he is such a relaxed character that the world could collapse around him and he would barely raise an eyebrow. That unflappable outlook, which I could never begin to emulate, has been a considerable asset in his work as the first (and only, at the time of writing) secretary of the Manchester United Former Players Association.

True, there are moments when I could scream at him to get his finger out, but no matter how agitated I might get, he merely responds with a gentle smile. David must be the world's hardest feller to fall out with, and thank God he is!

BORN	BELFAST 22ND MAY 1946
POSITION	FORWARD
JOINED UNITED	AUGUST 1961 FROM IRISH JUNIOR FOOTBALL
UNITED DEBUT	WBA (H) DIV. 1 - 14/09/1963
UNITED HONOURS	EUROPEAN CUP 1967/8 DIV. 1 1964/5, 1966/7
UNITED FAREWELL	QPR (A) DIV. 1 - 01/01/1974
LEFT UNITED FOR	DUNSTABLE TOWN JULY 1974

GEORGE BEST		
COMP.	APPS	GLS
LEAGUE	361	137
FAC	46	21
LC	25	9
EUROPE	34	11
OTHERS	4	1
TOTAL	470	179

112. GEORGE BEST

OTHER HONOURS:
37 NORTHERN IRELAND CAPS 1964-77.
EUROPEAN FOOTBALLER OF THE YEAR 1968;
FWA FOOTBALLER OF THE YEAR 1968.

OTHER CLUBS:
STOCKPORT COUNTY 75/6 (3, 2);
CORK CELTIC, REPUBLIC OF IRELAND, 75/6 (3, 0);
LOS ANGELES AZTECS, USA, 76-78 (54, 27);
FULHAM 76/7-77/8 (42, 8);
HIBERNIAN 79/80-80/1 (17, 3);
FORT LAUDERDALE STRIKERS, USA, 79 (19, 2);
SAN JOSE EARTHQUAKES, USA, 80 (26, 8);
GOLDEN BAY, USA;
BOURNEMOUTH 82/3 (5, 0).

You can't compare George Best to anyone else. He was a one-off talent, the type that you encounter once in a lifetime if you're lucky, and it's tragic from his own point of view – never mind about the wider loss to the game – that he destroyed himself so completely.

All we can do is to try to remember the good times, and George's greatness as a footballer, rather than dwell on the many negative aspects of his story. Unfortunately a lot of people, as they pull his memory to pieces, fail to appreciate the extent of his glory days. After all, George spent a dozen years at Old Trafford, and during that period he and the club scaled the heights together.

Also, I'd like to deal with another widespread misconception. It should be understood clearly that when he finished, he owed nothing to Manchester United; there can be no doubt that they had more than their money's worth out of the scrawny little waif who first crossed the Irish Sea back in 1961.

Even if judged purely by bald statistics, his contribution was exceptional, but mere figures don't even begin to describe the pure joy he inspired in those who watched him weaving his magic.

George was born with gifts beyond belief. He could do anything with either foot, he was wonderful in the air, he could tackle like a full-back and he was as brave as they come. I believe he could have filled any position in the team and I can't think of a single aspect of the game at which he didn't excel. In football terms, the lad was flawless.

You never talked about George in terms of a specific position. He might have worn a number seven, or a number 11 sometimes, but he could not be described merely as a winger. He just went out and played, roaming where the spirit took him and cutting defences to ribbons, pretty much at will.

Certainly there must have been plenty of times when he drove his team-mates mad by not passing the ball. You could accuse him of being greedy and, yes, he was. But how often would he beat three defenders and then, even as his colleagues were screaming at him for never giving them the ball, he would suddenly score a seemingly impossible goal. So not even his most scathing critics could ever say he hurt the team by his selfishness. Believe me, United benefited, royally and repeatedly.

In fact, there were a few seasons after they won the European Cup that George virtually carried the side single-handedly; without him they would have been mind-numbingly ordinary.

Manchester United would have been privileged to include such a player in their ranks at any stage of their history, but to be able to link him with two other European Footballers of the Year, Denis Law and Bobby Charlton, was downright incredible. Unquestionably no British club, and very few anywhere on the planet, have ever been able to field three such phenomenal talents at the same time.

One of the enduring sadnesses about George's career is that he was never able to perform on the highest international stage,

> 'How often would he beat three defenders and then, even as his colleagues were screaming at him for never giving them the ball, he would suddenly score a seemingly impossible goal.'

because Northern Ireland didn't reach World Cup finals. No one's to blame, it was just an accident of birth.

George's ability stands comparison with that of anyone who ever lived and I feel desperately sorry that he has been reduced to such criminally dire straits as he had reached in 2005. I must admit that it disturbs me, and to some degree disgusts me, that a genuine genius should fall so low.

Could the tragedy of George Best have been avoided if he had been managed differently in the early days? I don't know, but I would doubt it. Even to this day there is an arrogance about George which proclaims that he is always right, no matter what he does; that he can walk on water, that he is not subject to the normal rules. I'm not sure that Matt Busby, or anybody else, could have been expected to deal with that.

BORN	HENGOED, GLAMORGAN 7TH MARCH 1941
POSITION	INSIDE-FORWARD
JOINED UNITED	NOV. 1963 FROM CHELSEA - £35,000
UNITED DEBUT	TOTTENHAM HOTSPUR (H) DIV. 1 - 09/11/1963
UNITED FAREWELL	NOTTINGHAM FOREST (H) DIV. 1 - 25/04/1964
LEFT UNITED FOR	NORTHAMPTON TOWN DEC. 1965

GRAHAM MOORE		
COMP.	APPS	GLS
LEAGUE	18	4
FAC	1	1
TOTAL	19	5

113. GRAHAM MOORE

OTHER HONOURS:
21 WALES CAPS 1959-70.

OTHER CLUBS:
CARDIFF CITY 58/9-61/2 (85, 23);
CHELSEA 61/2-63/4 (68, 13);
NORTHAMPTON TOWN 65/6-66/7 (54, 10);
CHARLTON ATHLETIC 67/8-70/1 (110, 8);
DONCASTER ROVERS 71/2-73/4 (69, 3).

Jimmy Murphy, who had been manager of Wales, had been impressed by Graham Moore's work at his first club, Cardiff City, and when the lad arrived at Old Trafford from Chelsea, he brought with him a glowing reputation.

Of course, there were idiots who compared him to the great John Charles, just because he was a big, imposing Welshman with a lot of skill, though that was about as stupid as calling young Jimmy Nicholson the new Duncan Edwards. That aside, there was no doubt that Graham possessed bags of quality, but like so many players before him and plenty more since, he rarely made the best of his gifts at Old Trafford.

One exception was on his debut against Tottenham at Old Trafford, when he completed a potent inside-trio alongside David Herd and Denis Law, with the two Scots as the front pair and the newcomer shining as a deep-lying provider.

Sadly, in the months that followed Graham didn't come close to maintaining that early standard, perhaps being a trifle daunted by the vast expectations which go with the territory when you join United, and the fact that the team wasn't settled did nothing to help him. If Graham had been lucky enough to make his entrance in the following season, when they won the Championship, it might have made all the difference.

114. WILLIE ANDERSON

OTHER CLUBS:
ASTON VILLA 66/7-72/3 (231, 36);
CARDIFF CITY 72/3-76/7 (126, 12);
PORTLAND TIMBERS, USA, 76/7-81/2.

WILLIE ANDERSON		
COMP.	APPS	GLS
LEAGUE	7 (2)	0
FAC	2	0
EUROPE	1	0
OTHERS	0 (1)	0
TOTAL	10 (3)	0

BORN	LIVERPOOL 24TH JANUARY 1947
POSITION	WINGER
JOINED UNITED	MAY 1962 FROM JUNIOR FOOTBALL
UNITED DEBUT	BURNLEY (H) DIV. 1 - 28/12/1963
UNITED FAREWELL	LIVERPOOL (H) DIV. 1 - 10/12/1966
LEFT UNITED FOR	ASTON VILLA JAN 1967 - £20,000

Willie Anderson came through in the same wave of Old Trafford rookies as George Best, the Scouser occupying the right wing and the Irishman starting on the left as United won the FA Youth Cup in 1964.

At the time it was felt there was a fair chance that the two could go on developing together, but after they both made their senior debuts in 1963/64, their paths diverged.

Willie never had George's tricks but he had plenty of pace and, as he proved by the longevity of his subsequent service to Aston Villa and Cardiff, he had something about him.

However, his Old Trafford ambitions were hardly helped by the arrival of John Connelly, who would have been a difficult man to elbow aside. Then there was George, who could play on either flank, and young John Aston, who would soon begin to make his mark, so the competition was sharpish. The upshot was that Matt didn't need Willie as cover and he was allowed to leave, though that was no reflection on his ability, which was quite impressive.

115. WILF TRANTER

OTHER CLUBS:
BRIGHTON AND HOVE ALBION 65/6-67/8 (47, 1);
BALTIMORE BAYS, USA, 67/8;
FULHAM 68/9-71/2 (22, 0);
ST LOUIS STARS, USA, 71/2.

WILF TRANTER		
COMP.	APPS	GLS
LEAGUE	1	0
TOTAL	1	0

BORN	PENDLEBURY, LANCASHIRE 5TH MARCH 1945
POSITION	CENTRE-HALF
JOINED UNITED	MAY 1961 FROM JUNIOR FOOTBALL
UNITED DEBUT & FAREWELL	WEST HAM UNITED (A) DIV. 1 - 07/03/1964
LEFT UNITED FOR	BRIGHTON - MAY 1966

Wilf Tranter wasn't tall for a centre-half, but he deputised efficiently enough for Bill Foulkes when he was offered his sole senior outing by Matt Busby in the spring of 1964, helping to ensure a clean sheet at West Ham.

But at a time when United were on the verge of mounting a Championship challenge, it was always going to be difficult to break into the team on a regular basis, and Wilf went the way of Frank Haydock before him.

BORN	ST. HELENS
	18TH JULY 1938
POSITION	WINGER
JOINED UNITED	APRIL 1964 FROM
	BURNLEY £56,000
UNITED DEBUT	WBA (H)
	DIV. 1 - 22/08/1964
UNITED HONOURS	DIV. 1 1964/5
UNITED FAREWELL	BLACKPOOL (A)
	LC - 14/09/1966
LEFT UNITED FOR	BLACKBURN ROVERS
	SEPT. 1966 - £40,000

JOHN CONNELLY		
COMP.	APPS	GLS
LEAGUE	79 (1)	22
FAC	13	2
LC	1	0
EUROPE	19	11
TOTAL	112 (1)	35

116. JOHN CONNELLY

OTHER HONOURS:
20 ENGLAND CAPS 1959-66.

OTHER CLUBS:
BURNLEY 56/7-63/4 (216, 85);
BLACKBURN ROVERS 66/7-69/70 (149, 36);
BURY 70/1-72/3 (128, 37).

John Connelly was one of Matt Busby's best ever buys, a piece in the Championship jigsaw which ideally complemented the rest of a fabulous forward line, but I could never understand why he lasted only two years at Old Trafford.

Certainly the manager knew what he was getting with John, who had helped Burnley to win the title in 1959/60 and played regularly for England during his time at Turf Moor.

He offered pretty well the complete package. John was quick, he possessed fine touch with either foot, he crossed the ball accurately and intelligently, and he averaged better than a goal every three games, which is a fantastic rate for any winger. On top of that he was brave and he worked his socks off – echoes of Johnny Berry there – and he was comfortable on either flank. John was an instant success at Old Trafford, playing his first season on the right with the wandering George Best nominally on the left, Denis Law and David Herd up front and Bobby Charlton dropping deep. That was quite a combination.

That term John didn't miss a match in any competition, contributing 20 goals and picking up up the second Championship medal of his career. He performed brilliantly in his second season, too, particularly in the run to the European Cup semi-final, scoring eight times, including a hat-trick and a goal at the Stadium of Light as United beat Benfica 5-1 in what was arguably their greatest ever showing on foreign soil.

So there you have this excellent footballer in the prime of his playing days, a hell of a nice fellow who was popular with everybody at the club, and suddenly, just a couple of months after taking part in the World Cup finals, he's gone. He has spoken of differences of opinion with Matt, but whatever the reason for the premature exit it was a great shame for the club. John falls firmly into that category which also contains Johnny Morris and John Giles, top performers who should never have been allowed to get away.

It says a lot for John Connelly that after leaving United he went on to give marvellous value for money at Blackburn and Bury, proving himself the model professional to the last, eventually totting up well in excess of 600 senior games.

117. PAT DUNNE

OTHER HONOURS:
5 REPUBLIC OF IRELAND CAPS 1965-66.

OTHER CLUBS:
SHAMROCK ROVERS, REPUBLIC OF IRELAND, 62/3-63/4; PLYMOUTH ARGYLE 66/7-70/1 (152, 0); SHAMROCK ROVERS 70/1.

MANAGER:
SHELBOURNE, TURLES TOWN, BRAY WANDERERS ALL REPUBLIC OF IRELAND.

PAT DUNNE		
COMP.	APPS	GLS
LEAGUE	45	0
FAC	7	0
LC	1	0
EUROPE	13	0
OTHERS	1	0
TOTAL	67	0

BORN	DUBLIN 9TH FEBRUARY 1943
POSITION	GOALKEEPER
JOINED UNITED	MAY 1964 FROM SHAMROCK R. £10,500
UNITED DEBUT	EVERTON (A) DIV. 1 - 08/09/1964
UNITED HONOURS	DIV. 1 1964/5
UNITED FAREWELL	SUNDERLAND (A) DIV. 1 - 11/12/1965
LEFT UNITED FOR	PLYMOUTH ARGYLE FEB. 1967 - £5,000

Without being offensive towards a thoroughly likeable character who won a title medal during his brief stay in Manchester, I must say that Pat Dunne was a hit-and-miss 'keeper. When he was good he was very, very good, but when he was bad he was horrid.

He was a mystery man when he appeared on the United scene at the start of 1964/65, a close-season signing from Shamrock Rovers who few people could have envisaged so quickly becoming a first-team regular at the expense of Harry Gregg and David Gaskell, even though the two of them suffered abominable luck with injuries.

But Pat was given his opportunity in the autumn and surprised everybody by holding his place for the rest of the season, which ended with the club lifting a first League Championship since Munich.

Undoubtedly, there were games that United won because of him. He was magnificently athletic, capable of throwing himself to catch balls he had no right to reach, and he was faultlessly brave when facing a physical challenge.

But I wasn't ever convinced about his consistency when it came to handling crosses, which wasn't always calculated to inspire confidence in his fellow defenders, and Matt Busby must have come to a similar conclusion because he replaced him with Harry Gregg for most of the following season.

After that, though he was still in his early twenties, Pat never played another senior game for United, and with Alex Stepney firmly established as the new number-one, the Irishman left for Plymouth less than three years after joining the club.

I'm happy to say that Pat became a hero at Home Park, where there are folk who still talk about him with an affection bordering on reverence to this day. Later he went home to Ireland, where he played at a decent level until well into his forties, before concentrating on coaching.

It was a treat to see him again, after many years, at the Former Players Association golf day in September 2003.

118. ALBERT KINSEY

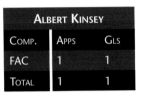

BORN	LIVERPOOL 19TH SEPTEMBER 1945
POSITION	FORWARD
JOINED UNITED	JUNE 1961 FROM JUNIOR FOOTBALL
UNITED DEBUT & FAREWELL	CHESTER (H) FAC - 09/01/1965
LEFT UNITED FOR	WREXHAM - MARCH 1966

ALBERT KINSEY		
COMP.	APPS	GLS
FAC	1	1
TOTAL	1	1

OTHER CLUBS:
WREXHAM 65/6-72/3 (253, 80);
CREWE ALEXANDRA 72/3-74/5 (32, 1).

Albert Kinsey was an England youth international, and he played in the same FA Youth Cup-winning side as George Best and David Sadler, but unlike them he didn't go on to sample first-team glory with Manchester United.

Still, he made an impression in his only senior game, scoring against Chester in the FA Cup, but he never did enough to suggest to Matt Busby that he was capable of challenging realistically for the places of the established front-men, David Herd and Denis Law.

Instead Albert achieved admirably with Wrexham, topping the Fourth Division scoring charts when they won promotion in 1970, netting the winner in the 1972 Welsh Cup Final and hitting the club's first goal in Europe in 1973.

119. JOHN FITZPATRICK

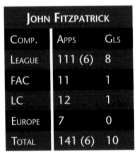

BORN	ABERDEEN 18TH AUGUST 1946
POSITION	WING-HALF, FULL-BACK
JOINED UNITED	SEPTEMBER 1961 FROM JUNIOR FOOTBALL
UNITED DEBUT	SUNDERLAND (A) DIV. 1 - 24/02/1965
UNITED FAREWELL	WOLVERHAMPTON W. (A) DIV. 1 - 16/09/1972
RETIRED	JULY 1973 - DUE TO INJURY

JOHN FITZPATRICK		
COMP.	APPS	GLS
LEAGUE	111 (6)	8
FAC	11	1
LC	12	1
EUROPE	7	0
TOTAL	141 (6)	10

John Fitzpatrick approached a century and a half of appearances for Manchester United, and he might have doubled that tally had he not suffered chronic knee problems which forced him to retire from the game at 26.

Maybe that fate had something to do with his way of playing – John was a fearsome tackler, very much of the muck-and-nettles school, some might even call him crude – which must have put tremendous pressure on his joints. Managers love to have players like John, people they know will give them 100 per-cent effort in every match, but he might not have done himself a lot of good in the long term.

Frequently he was compared to Nobby Stiles, for whom he deputised on his League debut, but he was never in that class. When Nobby won the ball, it was very rare for him to waste possession, but John never demonstrated the same ease of passing.

Often he was deployed as a man-marker in midfield, where he could be frighteningly ruthless, but arguably he was at his most effective as a full-back, which was his role for much of 1970/71 when he missed only seven League games.

Whatever else, he was in and out of the team between 1965 and 1972, a period when there was quite a bit going on at Old Trafford, some of it glorious and some of it diabolical, and he managed to hang on in there, carving a niche as someone who could be relied on.

So John was doubly unlucky in that he never picked up a medal, then he had to quit prematurely. Had he remained fit he might have been manna from heaven for the Tommy Docherty regime in the mid 1970s: after all he was Scottish, he could kick and he was relatively young.

What always surprised me about John was his line of business after he left football, when he became a wine-importer. Never could I have imagined him doing that. Now, I could have pictured him chipping one or two opponents over a vineyard wall if he'd got the opportunity, but obviously I did him an injustice.

THE CONVEYOR BELT CONTINUES: the Manchester United youth team lines up in the mid 1960s. Left to right, back row: Alan Duff, Jimmy Rimmer, Bobby Noble. Middle row: Peter McBride, David Farrar, John Fitzpatrick. Front row: Willie Anderson, Jim Ryan, David Sadler, Albert Kinsey, John Aston Jnr.

BORN	MANCHESTER 28TH JUNE 1947
POSITION	WINGER
JOINED UNITED	JULY 1962 FROM JUNIOR FOOTBALL
UNITED DEBUT	LEICESTER CITY (H) DIV. 1 - 12/04/1965
UNITED HONOURS	EUROPEAN CUP 1967/8 DIV. 1 1966/7
UNITED FAREWELL	CHELSEA (H) DIV. 1 - 22/01/1972
LEFT UNITED FOR	LUTON TOWN JULY 1972 - £30,000

JOHN ASTON JNR		
COMP.	APPS	GLS
LEAGUE	139 (16)	25
FAC	5 (2)	1
LC	12 (3)	0
EUROPE	8	1
OTHERS	2	0
TOTAL	166 (21)	27

120. JOHN ASTON JNR

OTHER CLUBS:
LUTON TOWN 72/3-77/8 (174, 31);
MANSFIELD TOWN 77/8 (31, 4);
BLACKBURN ROVERS 78/9-79/80 (15, 2).

No matter what else John Aston achieved in his career, he is always remembered for running the Benfica defence ragged as United won the European Cup in 1968, and that's got to be a satisfactory way to go down in history.

But it shouldn't be overlooked that he earned a title medal in 1966/67 after replacing John Connelly, which was no easy task, and although he was never such a complete player as his predecessor, he had plenty going for him.

Young Aston had outstanding pace, he crossed the ball reliably with his left peg and he never stopped grafting. On his day he could destroy pretty well any opposition – as Benfica discovered to their cost – but on another occasion, he might appear to be contributing precious little.

As he rose through the United ranks, John showed plenty of guts. His father, John Aston Snr, was his direct boss as a youth coach for part of that period and there was no way he was going to show favouritism towards his son, which must have made it hard for the boy. But he never flinched.

Then later there were days when he became the butt of senseless barrackers at Old Trafford, used as an aunt sally because so-called fans wanted to register their disapproval of a team display,

'The record books tell us that Charlton, Best and Kidd scored the goals, but John Aston was the undisputed man of the match, and that's a wonderful epitaph to any football life.'

but wouldn't criticise the stars.

A weaker character might have folded, but John coped manfully, and it was unfortunate that he broke his leg not long after the European triumph, which interrupted his momentum.

After that he never quite commanded a regular place in the long term and he switched to Luton, where he became a key player for half a decade.

But always, in John's case, we come back to that European final. The record books tell us that Charlton, Best and Kidd scored the goals, but John Aston was the undisputed man of the match, and that's a wonderful epitaph to any football life.

121. BOBBY NOBLE

BOBBY NOBLE		
COMP.	APPS	GLS
LEAGUE	31	0
FAC	2	0
TOTAL	33	0

BORN	MANCHESTER 18TH DECEMBER 1945
POSITION	FULL-BACK
JOINED UNITED	JUNE 1961 FROM JUNIOR FOOTBALL
UNITED DEBUT	LEICESTER CITY (H) DIV. 1 - 09/04/1966
UNITED HONOURS	DIV. 1 1966/7
UNITED FAREWELL	SUNDERLAND (A) DIV. 1 - 22/04/1967
RETIRED	MARCH 1969 DUE TO INJURY

Had it not been for an horrific car accident which almost claimed his life, Bobby Noble might have gone down in history as the finest full-back Manchester United ever had.

In making such a bold statement, I bear in mind the claims of Messrs Carey, Aston, Byrne, Brennan, Dunne, Irwin and maybe one or two others, but I am convinced that Bobby had the capacity to top the lot.

There was nothing that he lacked: he was a very tough guy with a ruthless streak, he moved like the wind, he was assured with both feet and he made intelligent decisions. There seemed no doubt that he would get into the England team, eventually replacing Ray Wilson, and then remain there for the foreseeable future.

I could never understand why Bobby didn't break into United's first team until he was 21, although I suppose Shay, Tony and Noel Cantwell represented quite a formidable barrier in the mid 1960s.

Certainly there was a point at which Bobby became frustrated, and he was confident enough to question Matt Busby about the delay, but the manager was adamant. There was no way his FA Youth Cup-winning skipper would be allowed to leave because his potential was limitless, but he would pick him

CRUNCH! Manchester City's Mike Summerbee feels the full abrasive force of a Bobby Noble tackle.

when he decided the time was right.

Duly Bobby won a regular place in the side during 1966/67, lining up at left-back while Dunne switched to the right in place of Brennan, and he couldn't have been more impressive in helping United to regain the Championship.

But then he crashed his car on the way home following a game with Sunderland in April and suffered terrible injuries to his head and chest. He survived, just, and when he got back on his feet he went down to the ground and tried to train.

What followed was a period of excruciating frustration as he discovered that he simply couldn't play the game any more. His timing and his edge had disappeared, he couldn't follow the flight of a ball, he could barely trap it, so he had to give up at the age of 23. It was enough to break anybody's heart.

In so many books about Manchester United, Bobby Noble gets no more than a minor footnote, which is no way to treat a major talent. I hope this goes some way towards setting the record straight.

BORN	STIRLING 15TH MAY 1945
POSITION	WINGER
JOINED UNITED	DECEMBER 1962 FROM JUNIOR FOOTBALL
UNITED DEBUT	WBA (A) DIV. 1 - 04/05/1966
UNITED FAREWELL	CHELSEA (H) DIV. 1 - 06/12/1969
LEFT UNITED FOR	LUTON TOWN - APRIL 1970 (1 OF 4 PLAYERS IN £35,000 DEAL)

JIM RYAN		
COMP.	APPS	GLS
LEAGUE	21 (3)	4
FAC	1	0
EUROPE	2	0
TOTAL	24 (3)	4

122. JIM RYAN

OTHER CLUBS:
LUTON TOWN 70/1-76/7 (184, 21);
DALLAS TORNADO, USA, 77-79;
WICHITA WINGS, USA, 79-84.
MANAGER:
LUTON TOWN 1990-91.

The perplexing case of Jim Ryan was strikingly similar to that of another Scottish winger, Ian Moir, a few seasons earlier. Both of them had all the skill in the world and often they lit up training sessions with their dazzling ability, only to be infuriatingly peripheral when it came to a match.

Jim was in and around the squad which won the European Cup in '68, but although he made some useful contributions, such as in the quarter-final first leg at home to Gornik, he never quite made the most of all that immense potential. Perhaps he didn't quite have the confidence to go with the talent which was evident to everyone. In the end, with Best, Aston and Willie Morgan on the scene, Jim slipped away to Luton, where he matured as a player and found the best form of his career.

Later he put in an enterprising stint as manager of Luton before Alex Ferguson asked him to return to Old Trafford to coach the reserves. At one point Jim rose to number-two in the pecking order, and even took charge of the first team when Alex was away, but he was content to return to a less prominent role, looking after young players. I don't think the limelight suits Jim Ryan, but that hasn't prevented him from going an admirable job for Manchester United.

123. ALEX STEPNEY

OTHER HONOURS:
1 ENGLAND CAP 1968.

OTHER CLUBS:
MILLWALL 63/4-65/6 (137, 0);
CHELSEA 66/7 (1, 0); DALLAS TORNADO, USA, 79-80.

ALEX STEPNEY		
COMP.	APPS	GLS
LEAGUE	433	2
FAC	44	0
LC	35	0
EUROPE	23	0
OTHERS	4	0
TOTAL	539	2

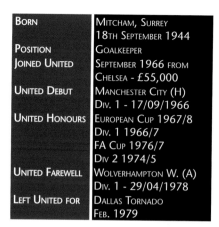

BORN	MITCHAM, SURREY 18TH SEPTEMBER 1944
POSITION	GOALKEEPER
JOINED UNITED	SEPTEMBER 1966 FROM CHELSEA - £55,000
UNITED DEBUT	MANCHESTER CITY (H) DIV. 1 - 17/09/1966
UNITED HONOURS	EUROPEAN CUP 1967/8 DIV. 1 1966/7 FA CUP 1976/7 DIV 2 1974/5
UNITED FAREWELL	WOLVERHAMPTON W. (A) DIV. 1 - 29/04/1978
LEFT UNITED FOR	DALLAS TORNADO FEB. 1979

Only Bobby Charlton, Bill Foulkes and now Ryan Giggs have made more appearances for Manchester United than Alex Stepney, whose career was sensational both in terms of achievement and longevity.

The only thing I've always found difficult to comprehend about Alex is why United didn't buy him from Millwall when he was available in May 1966; why wait for him to have one game for Chelsea before stepping in four months later?

He was needed at Old Trafford because although Matt Busby had put together yet another very fine side, he was not satisfied with Harry Gregg, who was struggling with terrible injury problems, David Gaskell or Pat Dunne.

Duly United won the title in Alex's first campaign at Old Trafford and Matt declared unhesitatingly that it had been the new 'keeper who made made the crucial difference. It was an exact repeat of the situation 15 years earlier, when he credited the arrival of Reg Allen as the Championship clincher.

Like Reg, Alex was a marvellous all-rounder. He wasn't bothered with trying to be flashy, that wasn't his style. He was a thorough craftsman who did his job in the simplest and best way imaginable.

Gordon Banks has said that a spectacular dive will invariably please the crowd, but it should be used only as a last resort. Whenever possible, sound positioning and the judgement of angles should come into play, and if they are employed successfully then nine times out of ten the goalkeeper can make difficult saves look simple. That was Alex all over.

I class goalkeepers in three categories: the good ones are those who save what they should; the great ones are those who save what they should and occasionally save what they shouldn't; and the bad ones are those who occasionally save what they shouldn't but, more importantly, they let in what they shouldn't, too.

Based on his performances for United over 12 years, Alex comes firmly into the second category. By any definition, he was a great goalkeeper.

Probably his best years came after his most famous save, when he prevented Eusebio from scoring a late winner for Benfica in the 1968 European Cup Final, and perhaps by the time he helped to win the FA Cup against Liverpool in 1977 he was beginning to pass his sell-by date.

It's telling that down the seasons some decent performers were thrown up against Alex, first Jimmy Rimmer and then Paddy Roche, but he resisted all their challenges, just kept rolling along, doing a consistently excellent job.

He was unlucky to get only one England cap, though that's explained by the fact that there were some rather decent 'keepers around, fellows like Gordon Banks, Peter Shilton and Ray Clemence. In another era, he would have needed an extra cabinet to house all his international headgear.

With the exception of Peter Schmeichel, no goalkeeper has done more to earn success for Manchester United. Harry Gregg might be judged the superior player, but the club won nothing with Greggy, and you can't argue with Alex's collection of medals.

If I was a manager and you offered me Alex Stepney to stand between my sticks, I would be highly delighted.

BORN	MANCHESTER 29TH MAY 1949
POSITION	STRIKER
JOINED UNITED	AUGUST 1964 FROM JUNIOR FOOTBALL
UNITED DEBUT	TOTTENHAM HOTSPUR (H) CS - 12/08/1967
UNITED HONOURS	EUROPEAN CUP 1967/8
UNITED FAREWELL	TOTTENHAM H. (H) DIV. 1 - 23/03/1974
LEFT UNITED FOR	ARSENAL AUG. 1974 - £110,000

BRIAN KIDD		
COMP.	APPS	GLS
LEAGUE	195 (8)	52
FAC	24 (1)	8
LC	20	7
EUROPE	16	3
OTHERS	2	0
TOTAL	257 (9)	70

124. BRIAN KIDD

OTHER HONOURS:
2 ENGLAND CAPS 1970.

OTHER CLUBS:
ARSENAL 74/5-75/6 (77, 30);
MANCHESTER CITY 76/7-78/9 (98, 44);
EVERTON 78/9-79/80 (40, 11);
BOLTON WANDERERS 80/1-81/2 (43, 14);
ATLANTA CHIEFS, USA, 81;
FORT LAUDERDALE STRIKERS, USA, 82-84;
MINNESOTA KICKS, USA, 84.

MANAGER:
PRESTON NORTH END 1986; BLACKBURN ROVERS 1998-99.

There was a time when I was convinced that Brian Kidd was destined to become one of Manchester United's longest-serving stars, but then he reached a crossroads in his career and he took a turning that dumbfounded me. It wasn't just that he left Old Trafford for Highbury, but that he went on to play for one club after another, never settling anywhere again.

To put this in perspective, let's examine Brian's situation in 1974. He was a local boy who, like Nobby Stiles, had learned the game on the playing fields of Collyhurst and Clayton and was United through and through.

He had burst on to the scene as a teenager, playing in a fabulous forward line alongside George Best, Denis Law and Bobby Charlton, and lived out the ultimate fantasy of scoring one of the goals which won the European Cup at Wembley on his 19th birthday.

By the time he was 25 the side had declined dramatically, but he was an England international with more than 250 United appearances to his credit. I thought he was a knock-in bet to become one of the club's foundation stones for the foreseeable future and, given that he was a quiet, home-loving lad, I'd have thought he'd have been one of the last in the world to move to London.

But out of the blue Tommy Docherty has sold him to Arsenal – which I think was a grave mistake from United's point of view at a time when they desperately needed players of his quality – and then he never stopped travelling.

It has always been a mystery to me. I know Brian quite well, and I have a hell of a lot of time for him, but he's a bit of an enigma. While he's a wicked practical joker who loves a laugh, he has always been unassuming, some might even say secretive, and I think I'd need a degree in psychology to fathom what happened in his career.

There is a theory that playing with so many world-class team-mates at an early age spoiled him for adjusting to mere mortals in later years, and there might be something in that. Then again, with Charlton, Law, Crerand and Stiles all reaching the veteran stage, Brian seemed ideally equipped to help Best shoulder the responsibility of taking the team further, but, sadly, it never happened.

How good was Kiddo? Very. Tall and strong, he had fair pace, was tremendous in the air and possessed an exceptionally fine left peg. Maybe he could have done a bit more with his right, because his main trick – that of dropping his right shoulder, then swerving left – eventually became predictable to opponents and he could have done with alternatives.

Also, for a player who spent almost all his time as a front-runner, he could have done with a few more goals in his locker, though in fairness he played a lot of his football for what was arguably the poorest United side in living memory in the early period of Docherty's reign.

You could say that there have not been too many who can point to such an impressive collection of clubs as Brian Kidd, and certainly he did wonderfully well after first breaking into the United team. But I am left with the nagging conviction that he could, and should, have taken his United career to an altogether more exalted plane.

BORN	GLENBOIG, LANARKSHIRE 17TH OCTOBER 1948
POSITION	FULL-BACK
JOINED UNITED	JUNE 1964 FROM JUNIOR FOOTBALL
UNITED DEBUT	WEST HAM UNITED (A) DIV. 1 - 02/09/1967
UNITED FAREWELL	EVERTON (H) DIV. 1 - 04/03/1972
LEFT UNITED FOR	SOUTHAMPTON JUNE 1972 - £50,000

FRANCIS BURNS		
COMP.	APPS	GLS
LEAGUE	111 (10)	6
FAC	11 (1)	0
LC	10 (1)	1
EUROPE	10 (1)	1
OTHERS	1	0
TOTAL	143 (13)	7

125. FRANCIS BURNS

OTHER HONOURS:
1 SCOTLAND CAP 1969.

OTHER CLUBS:
SOUTHAMPTON 72/3 (21, 0);
PRESTON NORTH END 73/4-80/1 (273, 9);
SHAMROCK ROVERS, REPUBLIC OF IRELAND, 81/2.

It's a measure of Francis Burns' considerable ability that he kept Shay Brennan out of the Manchester United side throughout most of 1967/68, and a measure of his ill-fortune that he lost his place again just as the triumphant European Cup campaign was reaching its climax.

When he came into the team at left-back, with Tony Dunne switching to the right to accommodate him, Frannie looked to be a genuine find. Young, eager and more of a tackler than Shay, he was a polished all-round footballer who was comfortable in possession of the ball and quite pacy.

As United progressed through the European rounds he continued to impress, only for Matt Busby to drop him for the second leg of the semi-final against Real Madrid, having decided that Shay's experience and knowhow was needed to counter the threat of Francisco Gento. Then Shay handled himself so brilliantly in Spain that he couldn't be left out against Benfica at Wembley, and poor Frannie can only have felt awful.

Confronted by such a crushing disappointment, a lot of people might have thrown a tantrum, but Frannie reacted with impeccable character, knuckling down to win his place back the following season.

Unfortunately then he began to suffer serious knee trouble at a time when such problems didn't receive the attention they do nowadays, and as a result, despite working phenomenally hard on his fitness, he began to lose impetus.

Even though he recovered sufficiently to win a Scotland cap, and was versatile enough to play at wing-half as well as full-back, he was unable to make himself indispensable to new manager Frank O'Farrell.

Had circumstances favoured him, he might have been classy enough to have forged a lengthy career at Old Trafford. As it was, although he did little at Southampton, Bobby Charlton took him to Preston, where he thrived into the 1980s before making a new life for himself in Australia.

126. FRANK KOPEL

OTHER CLUBS:
BLACKBURN ROVERS 68/9-71/2 (25, 0);
DUNDEE UNITED 71/2-81/2 (284, 7);
ARBROATH 81/2-83/4 (62, 1).

FRANK KOPEL		
COMP.	APPS	GLS
LEAGUE	8 (2)	0
FAC	1	0
EUROPE	1	0
TOTAL	10 (2)	0

BORN	FALKIRK 28TH MARCH 1949
POSITION	FULL-BACK
JOINED UNITED	SEPTEMBER 1964 FROM JUNIOR FOOTBALL
UNITED DEBUT	BURNLEY (H) DIV. 1 - 09/09/1967
UNITED FAREWELL	WATFORD (H) FAC - 25/01/1969
LEFT UNITED FOR	BLACKBURN ROVERS MARCH 1969 - £25,000

Frank Kopel was a stylish right-back who could join in comfortably when the ball was being passed around, while not neglecting his defensive duties. As such he looked to have the pedigree to become a long-term successor to Shay Brennan, but it was his misfortune to be breaking through during a severely unsettled period at Old Trafford, when there were countless comings and goings, and he didn't survive it.

Still United received a decent fee for a relative unknown, £25,000 from Blackburn, and although he didn't last long at Ewood Park he went on to distinguish himself for a decade with Dundee United. Happily we still see plenty of Frank, who travels down from Scotland for most of the events held by the Former Players Association.

127. ALAN GOWLING

OTHER CLUBS:
HUDDERSFIELD TOWN 72/3-74/5 (128, 58);
NEWCASTLE UNITED 75/6-77/8 (92, 30);
BOLTON WANDERERS 77/8-81/2 (149, 28);
PRESTON NORTH END 82/3 (40, 5).

ALAN GOWLING		
COMP.	APPS	GLS
LEAGUE	64 (7)	18
FAC	6 (2)	2
LC	7 (1)	1
TOTAL	77 (10)	21

BORN	STOCKPORT 16TH MARCH 1949
POSITION	CENTRE-FORWARD OR WING-HALF
JOINED UNITED	AUGUST 1965 FROM JUNIOR FOOTBALL
UNITED DEBUT	STOKE CITY (A) DIV. 1 - 30/03/1968
UNITED FAREWELL	STOKE CITY (H) DIV. 1 - 29/04/1972
LEFT UNITED FOR	HUDDERSFIELD TOWN JUNE 1972 - £25,000

I have a theory that Alan Gowling was never quite taken seriously enough in his early days with Manchester United. Had he been, then the club might have been rewarded with a reliable goal-scoring centre-forward at a time when they were toiling at the wrong end of the First Division, and needed one desperately.

How could this happen? Well, Alan was unusual in that he

divided his time between playing for United and working for an economics degree. Therefore he lived a double life, striving to do justice both to his studies and his football, which must have been incredibly hard graft.

In this situation, often he would have trained separately from the rest of the squad and he would have been out of the main swim of everyday events. Being a student, he would have been perceived as having plenty on his mind other than football; he might even have been viewed as a bit of an oddball, not maliciously, but it wouldn't have enhanced his prospects.

Despite all that, nobody could have made more of his ability than Alan. Tall, well-built and as strong as an ox, he had fair pace and no fear. True, you would never have described him as delicately skilful, but it didn't matter, he did well enough with a few bitty opportunities before being given more scope in 1970. He responded with eight goals in 17 League starts, including four at home to Southampton, and it seemed he had arrived.

But then a new boss, Frank O'Farrell, switched him to wing-half, which was a serious mistake because he didn't have the class for that position, even though he was given the England under-23 captaincy while filling it.

Of course, he could do a job there, or in any other slot, because he was honest and he was fit. Alan could never cheat on a manager; it wasn't part of his mentality.

The irony was that Frank wanted strikers and bought Ted MacDougall and the veteran Wyn Davies instead of persevering with young Gowling. Why convert Alan to something he

TURBULENT TIMES AHEAD: United line up with their new boss in the summer of 1971. Left to right, back row: John Fitzpatrick, Alan Gowling, Paul Edwards, Steve James, Jimmy Rimmer, Alex Stepney, Ian Ure, David Sadler, Tony Dunne, Bobby Charlton, manager Frank O'Farrell.
Front row: Francis Burns, Brian Kidd, George Best, Denis Law, Paddy Crerand, Willie Morgan, John Aston Jnr, Carlo Sartori.

wasn't cut out to be when the club needed exactly what he was already? It was plain daft. Had he been given the chance to settle in up front, he could have thrived at Old Trafford, as he did later for Huddersfield, Newcastle and Bolton.

Let's be fair to this lad. Whenever we hear about him he's either pigeon-holed as a peculiarity because he was a student, or dismissed as being awkward. Yet he played more than 500 senior games and scored a lot of goals; so maybe it's time Alan Gowling was given full credit for being a very useful professional footballer indeed.

128. JIMMY RIMMER

OTHER HONOURS:
1 ENGLAND CAP 1976.

OTHER CLUBS:
SWANSEA CITY ON LOAN 73/4 (17, 0);
ARSENAL 73/4-76/7 (124, 0);
ASTON VILLA 77/8-82/3 (229, 0);
SWANSEA CITY 83/4-85/6 (66, 0).

MANAGER: SWANSEA CITY 1995-96 (CARETAKER).

JIMMY RIMMER		
COMP.	APPS	GLS
LEAGUE	34	0
FAC	3	0
LC	6	0
EUROPE	2 (1)	0
TOTAL	45 (1)	0

BORN	SOUTHPORT 10TH FEBRUARY 1948
POSITION	GOALKEEPER
JOINED UNITED	MAY 1963 FROM JUNIOR FOOTBALL
UNITED DEBUT	FULHAM (H) DIV. 1 - 15/04/1968
UNITED FAREWELL	SOUTHAMPTON (A) DIV. 1 - 31/03/1973
LEFT UNITED FOR	ARSENAL APRIL 1974 - £40,000

For a long time Jimmy Rimmer was the only threat to the job security of Alex Stepney, having originally taken custody of the 'keeper's jersey when Alex was injured but then wearing it as first choice during the tail-end of Wilf McGuinness' managerial stint late in 1970.

It was a difficult time to make a breakthrough, and Jimmy didn't let the side down despite all the turbulence surrounding the club, showing himself to be a promising all-round operator. But as soon as Matt Busby resumed control of team affairs after Wilf's departure, Alex was back in at the younger fellow's expense. Maybe that was a case of 'Better the devil you know' on Matt's behalf. I'd say, though, that it was a reflection of Stepney's excellence, because he was an exceptional performer for United. That's not to say there was anything the matter with Rimmer, who went on to prove himself by high-quality service to Arsenal and Aston Villa, by winning an England cap, and by playing more than 500 senior games over an 18-year career.

Jimmy received a European Cup winner's medal as a substitute with United in 1968, played in both legs of the semi-final against AC Milan a year later, then earned another gong with Villa in 1982, though he was forced off with injury only ten minutes into the final against Bayern Munich. So although Jimmy didn't get much action on the big days, only Ray Clemence among English goalkeepers has finished up with more prizes from Europe's top club competition, and that's quite a distinction.

BORN	SAUCHIE, STIRLINGSHIRE 2ND OCTOBER 1944
POSITION	WINGER, MIDFIELDER
JOINED UNITED	AUGUST 1968 FROM BURNLEY - £117,000
UNITED DEBUT	TOTTENHAM HOTSPUR (H) DIV. 1 - 28/08/1968
UNITED HONOURS	DIV. 2 1974/5
UNITED FAREWELL	FULHAM (H) DIV. 2 - 12/04/1975
LEFT UNITED FOR	BURNLEY - JUNE 1975

WILLIE MORGAN		
COMP.	APPS	GLS
LEAGUE	236 (2)	25
FAC	27	4
LC	24 (1)	4
EUROPE	4	1
OTHERS	2	1
TOTAL	293 (3)	34

129. WILLIE MORGAN

OTHER HONOURS:
21 SCOTLAND CAPS 1967-74.

OTHER CLUBS:
BURNLEY 62/3-67/8 (183, 19) AND 75/6 (13, 0);
BOLTON WANDERERS 75/6-79/80 (155, 10);
CHICAGO STING, MINNESOTA KICKS, BOTH USA;
VANCOUVER WHITECAPS, CANADA;
BLACKPOOL 80/1-81/2 (42, 4).

The saddest thing about Willie Morgan was that he appeared to believe, in all honesty, that he was as good, if not better, than George Best. It was an immense shame because Willie was a fine player in his own right, and I'd have thought that to labour under such a colossal delusion must be very damaging to anyone's health. He arrived at United from Burnley in the immediate aftermath of the 1968 European Cup triumph, and might be excused for thinking that his timing was faultless.

He was joining a collection of world-class team-mates, some of whom were reaching the veteran stage, and it seemed reasonable to expect that Matt Busby was on the threshold of rebuilding with a new generation of top performers, including himself. It was an attractive scenario to someone of the confidence and ability of Willie Morgan.

Unfortunately United's brave new world never happened. It turned out that the team was already over the hill, perched on the top of a slippery slope which would lead to relegation, even if the decline was masked initially by a run to the semi-finals of the European Cup in 1969.

That was the wider issue, but Willie's personal chances were not enhanced by his George Best complex. Of course, he was entitled to his opinion, even if it was total rubbish. But why he wanted to perpetrate such a ludicrous myth was a mystery to me. Why compare himself to George, who was incomparable? Why not be the one and only Willie Morgan?

After all, he was a wonderful athlete, a gifted winger with plenty of tricks and an accomplished all-round sportsman. Indeed, in a sporting context, everything he's ever done he's done well, including running, golf and snooker.

I don't expect Willie would agree with me, but I felt the best football he ever played was at Bolton Wanderers, under the management of Ian Greaves in the late 1970s, as a right-sided midfielder rather than an old-fashioned winger. In that role he was superb.

At this stage I should point out, in all fairness to a United manager I didn't rate highly, that it was Frank O'Farrell who had originally converted Willie from the traditional role in which he had first flourished at Burnley. Actually I find it hard to give O'Farrell credit for anything he did at United, so perhaps the impetus came from Morgan himself, or maybe it was prevailing team circumstances which dictated the change.

After that Willie distinguished himself, first under O'Farrell and then under Tommy Docherty, and was rewarded by winning back his place in the Scotland team. At one point Docherty even described his fellow Scot as the best winger in the world; of course, that was before he fell out with him, dropped him and then appeared on the opposite side of an acrimonious court case.

In the early part of Docherty's reign, Willie was a high-quality footballer in a poor team, which must have been hugely frustrating for him. Then, as United began to taste renewed success, he was replaced by the young Steve Coppell, which will have been equally disappointing.

More happily, Willie always remained popular with the fans, who honoured him as his own man and a damned good player. They, at least, had sense enough not to draw daft parallels with a certain departed hero.

> *'Willie always remained popular with the fans, who honoured him as his own man and a damned good player.'*

130. CARLO SARTORI

OTHER CLUBS:
BOLOGNA, SPAL, LECCE, RIMINI, TRENTO, all Italy.

CARLO SARTORI		
COMP.	APPS	GLS
LEAGUE	26 (13)	4
FAC	9	1
LC	3 (2)	0
EUROPE	2	1
OTHERS	0 (1)	0
TOTAL	40 (16)	6

BORN	CALDERZONE, ITALY 10TH FEBRUARY 1948
POSITION	MIDFIELDER
JOINED UNITED	JULY 1963 FROM JUNIOR FOOTBALL
UNITED DEBUT	TOTTENHAM HOTSPUR (A) DIV. 1 - 09/10/1968
UNITED FAREWELL	WOLVERHAMPTON W. (H) DIV. 1 - 08/01/1972
LEFT UNITED FOR	BOLOGNA JANUARY 1973 - £50,000

Buona sera, Carlo! What a lovely man, and what an honest footballer. Carlo was a straight-up-and-down midfielder who wouldn't have known how to give less than 100 per-cent effort and endeavour every time he walked on to a football pitch, but he was never going to set the world on fire with his flair.

He was yet another player who suffered from trying to make his way at Old Trafford just as the Busby era was grinding to a halt, and efforts to replace the great man as manager ran into serial strife.

Still, he proved a useful fellow to have around the squad for nearly five years – for instance, it was his away goal against Anderlecht which earned United a European Cup quarter-final spot in 1969 – before he went home to Italy, where pretty soon he was called up for National Service in the army. That must have come as a kick in the pants, but knowing Carlo he would have made the best of it, and certainly it didn't stop him playing football.

He helped Bologna to win the Italian Cup and served a succession of other clubs over the next ten years before returning to the Manchester area, where he runs a very lucrative knife-sharpening business.

131. STEVE JAMES

OTHER CLUBS:
YORK CITY 75/6-79/80 (105, 1).

BORN	COSELEY, STAFFS
	29TH NOVEMBER 1949
POSITION	CENTRE-HALF
JOINED UNITED	JULY 1965 FROM
	JUNIOR FOOTBALL
UNITED DEBUT	LIVERPOOL (A)
	DIV. 1 - 12/10/1968
UNITED HONOURS	DIV. 2 1974/5
UNITED FAREWELL	BLACKPOOL (H)
	DIV. 2 - 26/04/1975
LEFT UNITED FOR	YORK CITY - JANUARY 1976

STEVE JAMES		
COMP.	APPS	GLS
LEAGUE	129	4
FAC	12	0
LC	17 (1)	0
EUROPE	2	0
TOTAL	160 (1)	4

Steve James was groomed by Manchester United as the successor to long-serving Bill Foulkes in the centre of defence, and for a couple of years there was no shortage of people at the club who thought that he might make the position his own. Certainly he was given plenty of chances to make an impression, even though most of them were in declining and, eventually, rank poor sides, but I never saw him as better than ordinary.

Steve was powerful in the air, as you would expect from such a tall lad, but he wasn't always commanding, certainly not in the way that Bill used to be. He played under Matt Busby, Wilf McGuinness, Frank O'Farrell and finally Tommy Docherty, who sometimes used him at left-back, preferring Jim Holton at centre-half.

Even when Jim suffered a broken leg during the Second Division campaign of 1974/75, Steve failed to assert himself decisively, losing out to the combination of Brian Greenhoff and Martin Buchan, and soon he was gone.

132. DON GIVENS

OTHER HONOURS:
56 REPUBLIC OF IRELAND CAPS 1969-82.

OTHER CLUBS:
LUTON TOWN 70/1-71/2 (83, 19);
QUEEN'S PARK RANGERS 72/3-77/8 (242, 76);
BIRMINGHAM CITY 78/9-80/1 (59, 10);
BOURNEMOUTH ON LOAN 79/80 (5, 4);
SHEFFIELD UNITED 80/1 (11, 3);
NEUCHATEL XAMAX, SWITZERLAND.

DON GIVENS		
COMP.	APPS	GLS
LEAGUE	4 (4)	1
LC	1	0
TOTAL	5 (4)	1

BORN	LIMERICK, ROI 9TH AUGUST 1949
POSITION	CENTRE-FORWARD
JOINED UNITED	SEPTEMBER 1965 FROM IRISH JUNIOR FOOTBALL
UNITED DEBUT	CRYSTAL PALACE (A) DIV. 1 - 09/08/1969
UNITED FAREWELL	WBA (A) DIV. 1 - 25/10/1969
LEFT UNITED FOR	LUTON TOWN APRIL 1970 - £35,000 (1 OF 4 PLAYERS IN THE DEAL)

Don Givens barely had a look-in with Manchester United but went on to enjoy a tremendous career after leaving Old Trafford, notably with Queen's Park Rangers, whom he helped to finish as First Division runners-up in 1975/76.

Hindsight is a wonderful thing, and it's easy from this distance to make the case that Don should have been offered more than his handful of opportunities in the autumn of 1969, when Wilf McGuinness was taking his first steps as chief coach.

Perhaps United made a mistake in letting him go, but with Denis Law, Brian Kidd and Alan Gowling on the scene it was always going to be difficult for Don to make an impact, and perhaps the move did him good.

133. PAUL EDWARDS

OTHER CLUBS:
OLDHAM ATHLETIC (ON LOAN, THEN PERMANENT) 72/3-77/8 (112, 7);
STOCKPORT COUNTY ON LOAN 76/7 (2, 0);
STOCKPORT COUNTY 78/9-79/80 (67, 2).

PAUL EDWARDS		
COMP.	APPS	GLS
LEAGUE	52 (2)	0
FAC	10	0
LC	4	1
TOTAL	66 (2)	1

BORN	CROMPTON, LANCASHIRE 7TH OCTOBER 1947
POSITION	DEFENDER
JOINED UNITED	DECEMBER 1963 FROM JUNIOR FOOTBALL
UNITED DEBUT	EVERTON (A) DIV. 1 - 19/08/1969
UNITED FAREWELL	SOUTHAMPTON (H) DIV. 1 - 25/11/1972
LEFT UNITED FOR	OLDHAM ATHLETIC MARCH 1973 - £15,000

Paul Edwards was built up as an outstanding prospect, playing for England at under-23 level and in more than half a century of games for United, but he didn't live up to those early expectations.

He was never the classiest of performers, being content to put his foot in and win the ball, then give it to someone who could play. Basically that's a sound policy for a defender, and one which has proved successful for many a stalwart down the years, but he was similar to Steve James in that he never really dominated.

In fairness to Paul, who was tall and strong but rather awkward looking, all knees and elbows, he never had the chance to feature regularly for a settled side.

He was deployed mostly at full-back by Wilf McGuinness,

then given a run at centre-half by Matt Busby, who paired him with Dave Sadler when it was decided to phase out Ian Ure.

In the end it was Tommy Docherty who sold Paul to Oldham, where he helped to win the Third Division title.

BORN	Ayr
	7TH DECEMBER 1939
POSITION	CENTRE-HALF
JOINED UNITED	AUGUST 1969 FROM
	ARSENAL £80,000
UNITED DEBUT	WOLVERHAMPTON W. (A)
	DIV. 1 - 23/08/1969
UNITED FAREWELL	MIDDLESBRROUGH (H)
	FAC - 02/01/1971
LEFT UNITED FOR	ST. MIRREN - AUG. 1972

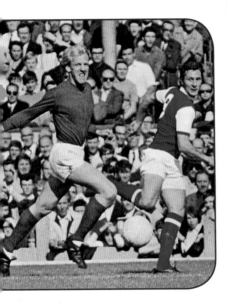

IAN URE		
COMP.	APPS	GLS
LEAGUE	47	1
FAC	8	0
LC	10	0
TOTAL	65	1

134. IAN URE

OTHER HONOURS:
11 SCOTLAND CAPS 1961–67.
OTHER CLUBS:
DUNDEE 58/9-62/3 (106, 0);
ARSENAL 63/4-69/70 (168, 2);
ST MIRREN 72/3 (3, 0).
MANAGER:
EAST STIRLINGSHIRE 1974–75.

I never fancied Ian Ure as the answer to Manchester United's central defensive problems following the retirement of Bill Foulkes.

You couldn't miss him on the field, with his bright blond air and arms and legs shooting out in all directions, but I don't think he was noticeable for the right reasons. Ian's methods were crude, to put it mildly, and I wouldn't have signed him if he were coming for nowt.

As to who actually did sign him, I can only speculate. Wilf McGuinness was in charge of the first team, but many believe to this day that Ure was a Busby recruit.

Whatever, he was effective in the very short term, helping to halt a run of defeats, but I could never see him lasting long, and he didn't.

Obviously not everyone shared my opinion of Ian, because he reached the semi-final of the European Cup with Dundee, won some Scotland caps and played plenty for Arsenal. Later he became a social worker in Barlinnie prison, Glasgow.

BORN	URMSTON, LANCASHIRE
	24TH DECEMBER 1952
POSITION	UTILITY
JOINED UNITED	MAY 1968 FROM
	JUNIOR FOOTBALL
UNITED DEBUT	IPSWICH TOWN (A)
	DIV. 1 - 19/09/1970
UNITED FAREWELL	QPR (A)
	DIV. 1 - 13/09/1975
LEFT UNITED FOR	CHARLTON A. - JAN. 1976

TONY YOUNG		
COMP.	APPS	GLS
LEAGUE	69 (14)	1
FAC	5	0
LC	5 (4)	0
TOTAL	79 (18)	1

135. TONY YOUNG

OTHER CLUBS:
CHARLTON ATHLETIC 75/6-76/7 (20, 1);
YORK CITY 76/7-78/9 (78, 2).

Once a player is labelled as a utility man, it always reduces his chances of making a lasting mark, and so it was with Tony Young.

Whether playing in midfield, which I think was his best position, or at full-back, he liked a tackle and he wasn't afraid of work, but he never quite managed to stamp his authority on any individual role.

Tony's big season at Old Trafford was 1972/73, during which he made 30 appearances in a side fighting for their First Division lives and playing some dreadful football. He started it as an in-and-out midfielder, then displaced Tommy O'Neil at right-back for the second half of the campaign, but his prospects dimmed midway through the relegation term that followed when Tommy Docherty brought in Alex Forsyth.

In 1974/75 Tony was on the periphery of the Second Division promotion team, but then he fell from favour altogether, surfacing briefly at Charlton before enlisting with Wilf McGuinness at York.

136. WILLIE WATSON

OTHER CLUBS:
MIAMI TOROS, USA, 73;
MOTHERWELL 73/4-77/8 (127, 2).

WILLIE WATSON		
COMP.	APPS	GLS
LEAGUE	11	0
LC	3	0
TOTAL	14	0

BORN	MOTHERWELL 4TH DECEMBER 1949
POSITION	FULL-BACK
JOINED UNITED	JUNE 1965 FROM JUNIOR FOOTBALL
UNITED DEBUT	BLACKPOOL (H) DIV. 1 - 26/09/1970
UNITED FAREWELL	TOTTENHAM H. (H) DIV. 1 - 28/10/1972
LEFT UNITED FOR	MIAMI TOROS - APRIL 1973

United's right-back slot was up for grabs in the early 1970s, especially after John Fitzpatrick was laid low by knee injuries, and Willie Watson was one of a posse of hopefuls who also included Tony Young, Tommy O'Neil and Ian Donald.

He was given brief opportunities by both Wilf McGuinness and Frank O'Farrell, but clearly he did not impress his third boss, Tommy Docherty, who dispensed with his services in quick time. In such circumstances it's difficult to judge Willie in United terms, but he went on to show decent mettle with Motherwell during the middle of the decade.

137. IAN DONALD

OTHER CLUBS:
PARTICK THISTLE 72/3 (1, 0);
ARBROATH 73/4-74/5 (4, 0).

IAN DONALD		
COMP.	APPS	GLS
LEAGUE	4	0
LC	2	0
TOTAL	6	0

BORN	ABERDEEN 28TH NOVEMBER 1951
POSITION	FULL-BACK
JOINED UNITED	MAY 1968 FROM JUNIOR FOOTBALL
UNITED DEBUT	PORTSMOUTH (H) LC - 07/10/1970
UNITED FAREWELL	LEICESTER CITY (A) DIV. 1 - 04/11/1972
LEFT UNITED FOR	PARTICK TH. - JAN. 1973

Like fellow right-back Willie Watson, Ian Donald was an early casualty of the Tommy Docherty regime, but unlike Willie he did not go on to make an impact as a player elsewhere. That surprised a few, who had noted his composure in several of his rare United outings.

However, a career in administration was mapped out for Ian, who emulated his father, Dick Donald, in becoming chairman of Aberdeen, his hometown club.

BORN	ST. HELENS 25TH OCTOBER 1952
POSITION	FULL-BACK
JOINED UNITED	AUGUST 1968 FROM JUNIOR FOOTBALL
UNITED DEBUT	MANCHESTER CITY (A) DIV. 1 - 05/05/1971
UNITED FAREWELL	DERBY COUNTY (A) DIV. 1 - 26/12/1972
LEFT UNITED FOR	SOUTHPORT - AUG. 1973

TOMMY O'NEIL		
COMP.	APPS	GLS
LEAGUE	54	0
FAC	7	0
LC	7	0
TOTAL	68	0

138. TOMMY O'NEIL

OTHER CLUBS:
BLACKPOOL ON LOAN 72/3 (7, 0);
SOUTHPORT 73/4-77/8 (197, 16);
TRANMERE ROVERS 78/9-79/80 (74, 10);
HALIFAX TOWN 80/1-81/2 (40, 2).

Frank O'Farrell obviously thought a great deal of little Tommy O'Neil, standing by him at right-back for virtually the whole of 1971/72. He was a natural all-round sportsman, having won schoolboy international honours at both soccer and rugby, but I'd call him hard-working and tenacious rather than classy and it didn't surprise me when he didn't linger long at the top level.

Tommy didn't survive the managerial change from O'Farrell to Docherty, but he went on to do a creditable job in the lower divisions, notably at Southport, and after leaving the League he played on for many more seasons, captaining St Helens Town when they won the FA Vase at Wembley in 1987.

BORN	BELFAST 2ND AUGUST 1954
POSITION	MIDFIELDER, FORWARD
JOINED UNITED	AUGUST 1969 FROM IRISH JUNIOR FOOTBALL
UNITED DEBUT	MANCHESTER CITY (A) DIV. 1 - 06/11/1971
UNITED HONOURS	FA CUP 1976/7 DIV. 2 1974/5
UNITED FAREWELL	EVERTON (H) DIV. 1 - 06/01/1982
LEFT UNITED FOR	STOKE CITY FEB. 1982 - £350,000

SAMMY McILROY		
COMP.	APPS	GLS
LEAGUE	320 (22)	57
FAC	35 (3)	6
LC	25 (3)	6
EUROPE	10	2
OTHERS	1	0
TOTAL	391 (28)	71

139. SAMMY McILROY

OTHER HONOURS:
88 NORTHERN IRELAND CAPS 1972-86
OTHER CLUBS:
STOKE CITY 81/2-84/5 (133, 14);
MANCHESTER CITY 85/6 (12, 1);
ORGRYTE, SWEDEN, 86;
MANCHESTER CITY 86/7 (1, 0);
BURY 86/7-87/8 (43, 6);
FC MOEDLING, AUSTRIA, 88;
BURY 88/9-89/90 (57, 2);
PRESTON NORTH END 89/90 (20, 0).
MANAGER:
MACCLESFIELD TOWN 1993-2000;
NORTHERN IRELAND NATIONAL TEAM 2000-03; STOCKPORT COUNTY 2003-04.

Sammy McIlroy didn't get the Manchester United he deserved. He gave terrific service at Old Trafford, but he possessed vast untapped potential and I am convinced that had his career coincided with the peak years of either Matt Busby or Alex Ferguson, then his talent would have blossomed even more luxuriantly.

As it was he played under no fewer than six United managers – Matt, Wilf McGuinness, Frank O'Farrell, Tommy Docherty, Dave Sexton and Ron Atkinson – and he suffered from the constant changes and consequent lack of stability. That roll-call of bosses is astonishing for a club which had known exactly what it was doing and where it was going for the previous quarter of a century, and it's a telling illustration of the turmoil which enveloped Old Trafford for so long.

Sammy was the last of the Busby Babes and he made a fantastic start by scoring as a 17-year-old debutant in a 3-3 with Manchester City at Maine Road. Obviously Matt thought a lot of him to give him his entrance in such a huge game, but the hullaballoo which greeted his success didn't make life any easier for him. Because he came from Belfast it was inevitable that, having made an immediate impact, he was going to be touted as another George Best. Of course, that was crazy, not only because there could never be another Best, but also because Sammy was a totally different type of player.

At first I don't think United knew where to deploy him, and they toyed with him as an out-and-out striker before he settled down to thrive as a clever, attacking wing-half, or midfielder to coin the modern description.

Despite that, he scored a few goals early on before his impetus was interrupted by injuries received in a serious car accident. He did well to fight back from that, particularly as it happened in the dismal days soon after Docherty took over, but we didn't begin to see the best of him until Jimmy Greenhoff arrived to partner Stuart Pearson up front and Sammy moved back to replace Gerry Daly.

The principal McIlroy attributes were lovely skills with the odd trick thrown in, a first-class engine and useful pace, but he wasn't quite robust enough to be a front-man, who spends much of the time riding ferocious challenges with his back to goal.

It suited Sammy to be facing the ball, and we saw him at his best in the 1979 FA Cup Final when he scored the incredible equaliser near the end against Arsenal, dancing past a couple of tackles before slipping his shot past Pat Jennings. If United had won the Cup we wouldn't have heard the last of that goal, but because of Alan Sunderland's late winner, Sammy's effort tended to be swept under the carpet. Now it's deep in the archives, a neglected gem.

Less than three years later, it was difficult to credit when Ron Atkinson let Sammy go. He was only 27 but, with the experience of more than 400 games for United behind him, he should have been approaching his best years. What he needed at that point was an extended opportunity to move up to the next level, and it was the least he had earned.

Super Sam: the gifted Irishman on his way past several Arsenal defenders to score one of the great Wembley goals towards the climax of the 1979 FA Cup Final. Sadly his feat was largely forgotten due to the Gunners' dramatic late winner.

BORN	Aberdeen 6TH MARCH 1949
POSITION	Central Defender Full-back
JOINED UNITED	March 1972 from Aberdeen - £125,000
UNITED DEBUT	Tottenham Hotspur (A) Div. 1 - 04/03/1972
UNITED HONOURS	FA Cup 1976/7 Div. 2 1974/5
UNITED FAREWELL	Watford (A) Div. 1 - 04/12/1982
LEFT UNITED FOR	Oldham Ath - Aug. 1983

MARTIN BUCHAN		
COMP.	APPS	GLS
LEAGUE	376	4
FAC	39	0
LC	30	0
EUROPE	10	0
OTHERS	1	0
TOTAL	456	4

140. MARTIN BUCHAN

OTHER HONOURS:
34 SCOTLAND CAPS 1971-78
SCOTTISH FOOTBALLER OF THE YEAR 1971
OTHER CLUBS:
ABERDEEN 66/7-71/2 (136, 9);
OLDHAM ATHLETIC 83/4-84/5 (28, 0).
MANAGER:
BURNLEY 1985

Martin Buchan was an exceptional defender, good enough to have graced any of the club's great teams down the decades, and it was a shame that he never got the chance.

Sometimes I ponder what heights his career might have scaled, and how many medals he might have collected, if he'd been fortunate enough to play alongside, say, Allenby Chilton, Steve Bruce or Gary Pallister.

As it was Martin found himself betwixt and between, caught in a deeply unsatisfying era in which he went to a few finals, captaining United to victory in the FA Cup against Liverpool in 1977, and picking up a Second Division gong. That was all right, but it was a haul which failed to reflect his stature.

Martin was brought to Old Trafford by Frank O'Farrell during difficult times, and at first I've no doubt that he could scarcely credit what he had got himself into. On joining Manchester United, he expected to be surrounded by high-quality players and, with a handful of exceptions, it just wasn't the case.

Also, perhaps even worse, he'd have been stunned by the general lack of enthusiasm for playing football, which seems a pretty strange thing to say, but that's the way it was under O'Farrell.

It must have been a chronic shock to his sytem, and no one could have blamed him if he was disillusioned, but he faced his responsibilities and straight away he began to show why he had been rated so highly in Scotland.

Martin's key asset was his tremendous pace, a priceless gift which got him out of plenty of scrapes, and that physical nimbleness was matched by an ability to read the game shrewdly. He wasn't bad in the air, although I wouldn't number that among his foremost qualities, and I wouldn't say he was the best passer from the back I've ever seen, but taken as a package, he was outstanding.

Unquestionably his forte was playing off the centre-half and when he was shunted to full-back by Tommy Docherty for a lengthy slice of the 1973/74 relegation season, I don't think he enjoyed it. It was never his natural role.

Martin was renowned for being strong-minded, having a will of his own, and sometimes he rubbed people up the wrong way, notably the winger Gordon Hill, whom he clipped around the ear for not chasing back on one famous occasion.

Now Martin was a reasonably bright fellow and sometimes he was neither kind nor tolerant to people who weren't quite as quick on the uptake. He never wasted a chance to take the mick and he could be merciless, arguably not the nicest of traits, especially if you're captain of the team.

Consequently, although people had to respect him as a player, they didn't necessarily like him as a person. Often he was his own worst enemy because he wanted to be clever; he didn't generate too much warmth and that was a shame, because basically he's not a bad lad, as I discovered when he was manager of Burnley (very briefly) and I was his chief scout.

During that period, he said to me one morning: 'JD, if you had money in the bank, a good pension and other ways to earn a living, if you were me would you be manager of Burnley?'

My immediate and honest answer was: 'No. You're not cut out for it. Pack it in. Go and do something you enjoy.' I'd had plenty of chances to witness his lack of patience with various human frailties – there was one occasion when he ended up fighting with a player who'd come to his office to talk about a transfer – and I harboured no doubts about my advice, which he took shortly afterwards.

Later he worked for Puma, now he represents the PFA, and I think it's fair to say he has mellowed a little. But no matter who Martin Buchan upset during his decade at Old Trafford, none of them could deny that he was a truly major player.

BORN	IPSWICH 17TH JANUARY 1945
POSITION	WINGER
JOINED UNITED	MARCH 1972 FROM NOTT'M F. - £200,000
UNITED DEBUT	HUDDERSFIELD TOWN (H) DIV. 1 - 11/03/1972
UNITED FAREWELL	WEST HAM UNITED (H) DIV. 1 - 15/03/1973
RETIRED	DECEMBER 1973 DUE TO INJURY

IAN STOREY-MOORE		
COMP.	APPS	GLS
LEAGUE	39	11
LC	4	1
TOTAL	43	12

141. IAN STOREY-MOORE

OTHER HONOURS:
1 ENGLAND CAP 1970.
OTHER CLUBS:
NOTTINGHAM FOREST 63/4-71/2 (236, 105);
CHICAGO STING, USA, 75.

Ian Storey-Moore was made to measure for Manchester United and it was a crying shame that his career was cut off by injury just as he was entering his prime.

He was one of the most devastating attackers in the country as demonstrated by his goal record for Nottingham Forest, which was all the more impressive when you remember that much of his time was spent in a wide position.

Ian was tall, fast and powerful with bags of ability, a player who frightened defenders to death when he ran at them. I have no doubt that, granted decent fortune, he'd have become one of the United's top performers of the 1970s.

I look back at the early part of that decade and shudder at what went on at the club, and Ian might just have been the one who made the difference, linking up with the likes of George Best, Brian Kidd and Willie Morgan.

In my opinion, Frank O'Farrell didn't get many things right when he was manager at Old Trafford, but recruiting Ian could have been a glorious exception. The dismal anti-climax of his premature retirement offered a vivid contrast to the dramatic manner of his arrival. Most United fans had already watched his televised signing by Derby County, with Brian Clough getting him to put pen to paper on the pitch before a game, then the next thing we knew he was doing the same at Old Trafford. We all had a laugh about it at the time, wondering how many clubs he was planning to join in front of the cameras.

Ian was a Suffolk lad who later became a bookmaker at Southwell racecourse before taking over as chief scout for his first club, Nottingham Forest.

RELEGATION FIGHTERS: the United squad that narrowly beat the drop in 1972/73. Left to right, back row: trainer Tommy Cavanagh, manager Tommy Docherty, David Sadler, Denis Law, Jim Holton, Alex Stepney, Mick Martin, George Graham, Wyn Davies, Alex Forsyth, Martin Buchan, assistant manager Paddy Crerand. Front row: Willie Morgan, Ted MacDougall, Tony Young, Bobby Charlton, Lou Macari, Brian Kidd, Ian Storey-Moore.

142. JOHN CONNAUGHTON

OTHER CLUBS:
HALIFAX TOWN ON LOAN 69/70 (3, 0);
TORQUAY UNITED ON LOAN 71/2 (22, 0);
SHEFFIELD UNITED 73/4 (12, 0);
PORT VALE 74/5-79/80 (191, 0).

JOHN CONNAUGHTON		
COMP.	APPS	GLS
LEAGUE	3	0
TOTAL	3	0

BORN	WIGAN 23RD SEPTEMBER 1949
POSITION	GOALKEEPER
JOINED UNITED	JANUARY 1965 FROM JUNIOR FOOTBALL
UNITED DEBUT	SHEFFIELD UTD. (A) DIV. 1 - 04/04/1972
UNITED FAREWELL	MANCHESTER CITY (H) DIV. 1 - 12/04/1972
LEFT UNITED FOR	SHEFFIELD UTD. OCTOBER 1972

John Connaughton, who played all his three games for United in the space of eight days, was a better goalkeeper than people gave him credit for, but it was always going to be difficult for him to displace Alex Stepney at Old Trafford.

He didn't find a niche with Sheffield United, either, but he gave excellent service to Port Vale, for whom he spent half a decade as a virtual ever-present, and then he did well for Altrincham when they were one of the top non-League sides in the country.

Later John built up a successful wastepaper recycling business, which left him plenty of time to concentrate on his golf.

143. WYN DAVIES

OTHER HONOURS:
34 WALES CAPS 1963-73.

OTHER CLUBS:
WREXHAM 60/1-61/2 (55, 22);
BOLTON WANDERERS 61/2-66/7 (155, 66);
NEWCASTLE UNITED 66/7-70/1 (180, 40);
MANCHESTER CITY 71/2-72/3 (45, 8); BLACKPOOL 73/4-74/5 (36, 5);
CRYSTAL PALACE ON LOAN 74/5 (3, 0); STOCKPORT COUNTY 75/6 (30, 7);
CREWE ALEXANDRA 76/7-77/8 (55, 13).

WYN DAVIES		
COMP.	APPS	GLS
LEAGUE	15 (1)	4
FAC	1	0
TOTAL	16 (1)	4

BORN	CAERNARVON 20TH MARCH 1942
POSITION	CENTRE-FORWARD
JOINED UNITED	SEPTEMBER 1972 FROM MANCHESTER C. £25,000
UNITED DEBUT	DERBY COUNTY (H) DIV. 1 - 23/09/1972
UNITED FAREWELL	WEST HAM UTD. (H) DIV. 1 - 20/01/1973
LEFT UNITED FOR	BLACXKPOOL - JUNE 1973

Big Wyn Davies was a battle-hardened Welsh international centre-forward who had forged a formidable reputation at the top level and, aged 30 when he arrived, he was hardly an old man; in fact, he should have been at the peak of his powers. So why did he fail to make an impact at Old Trafford?

The answer is that he never had a hope in hell, because he came at the end of Frank O'Farrell's reign, then almost immediately discovered that he wasn't part of the plans of the new manager, Tommy Docherty. After starting out at Wrexham, where he played under my mate Ken Barnes, Wyn had emerged as a star with Bolton and Newcastle, then fitted in exceedingly well at Manchester City in a fine side which included Francis Lee, Colin Bell and Mike Summerbee.

I know a lot of people at City who maintain to this day that

Malcolm Allison was wrong to get rid of him, essentially in favour of Rodney Marsh, after which the team went downhill. Wyn was fantastic in the air, he would run through brick walls for his side and he had vast experience. But whereas O'Farrell fancied him, Docherty didn't, and he was out of Old Trafford less than a year after he arrived.

If he'd been given the opportunity to settle in alongside the nippier Ted MacDougall, with George Best, Ian Storey-Moore and Willie Morgan providing the ammunition, who knows what he might have achieved.

BORN	INVERNESS 8TH JANUARY 1947
POSITION	CENTRE-FORWARD
JOINED UNITED	SEPTEMBER 1972 FROM BOURNEMOUTH £200,000
UNITED DEBUT	WBA (A) DIV. 1 - 07/10/1972
UNITED FAREWELL	IPSWICH TOWN (A) DIV. 1 - 17/02/1973
LEFT UNITED FOR	WEST HAM UNITED MARCH 1973 - £150,000

144. TED MacDOUGALL

TED MacDOUGALL		
COMP.	APPS	GLS
LEAGUE	18	5
TOTAL	18	5

OTHER HONOURS:
7 SCOTLAND CAPS 1975.

OTHER CLUBS:
YORK CITY 67/8-68/9 (84, 34);
BOURNEMOUTH 69/70-72/3 (146, 103);
WEST HAM UNITED 72/3-73/4 (24, 5); NORWICH CITY 73/4-76/7 (112, 51);
SOUTHAMPTON 76/7-78/9 (86, 42); BOURNEMOUTH 78/9-79/80 (52, 16);
BLACKPOOL 79/80-80/1 (13, 0).

Ted MacDougall's game was simplicity itself. He scored goals, sometimes in prodigious amounts. For example, at Bournemouth he averaged better than two strikes in every three games, and his manager, John Bond, described him as the deadliest finisher he had ever seen.

But at Manchester United he was blighted by the same misfortune that befell Wyn Davies, his partner. Frank O'Farrell, the manager who had bought him, was sacked; Tommy Docherty, the new boss, didn't want him and lost no time in pointing him towards the exit door.

Now it could be argued that Ted didn't bring anything to the party but goals, but does that matter? Some suggested that the Old Trafford stage was too big for him, but I don't see how they can reach that conclusion when he wasn't given the chance to prove his worth.

As it was his goals-to-games ratio wasn't far off one in three, and that was for a team at the bottom of the table whose confidence must have been somewhere near the zero mark.

It was a fair premise on O'Farrell's part that Ted, being very quick, could capitalise on Wyn's knockdowns, and with George Best and company to back them up then United could have had a pretty potent forward line.

After leaving the club Ted went on to earn Scotland caps. Had he been given a meaningful chance in Manchester, he night have won more, but we shall never know. How frustrating is that?

145. ALEX FORSYTH

OTHER HONOURS:
10 Scotland caps 1972-75.

OTHER TEAMS:
Partick Thistle 70/1-72/3 (52, 5);
Glasgow Rangers 78/9-80/1 (25, 5);
Motherwell 82/3 (19, 0);
Hamilton Academical 83/4-84/5 (63, 9).

ALEX FORSYTH		
COMP.	APPS	GLS
LEAGUE	99 (2)	4
FAC	10	1
LC	7	0
EUROPE	0 (1)	0
TOTAL	116 (3)	5

BORN	Swinton, Berwickshire 5th February 1952
POSITION	Full-back
JOINED UNITED	December 1972 from Partick Thistle £100,000
UNITED DEBUT	Arsenal (A) Div. 1 - 06/01/1973
UNITED HONOURS	Div. 2 1974/5
UNITED FAREWELL	WBA (A) Div. 1 - 22/10/1977
LEFT UNITED FOR	Glasgow Rangers Aug. 1978

Alex Forsyth was the first of many Scottish signings made by Tommy Docherty on taking over as manager of Manchester United late in 1972.

Earlier in the year, as Scotland boss, Docherty had given the young Partick Thistle right-back his full international debut, and now he thought he was tying up United's number-two shirt for the foreseeable future.

Very quickly Alex became a favourite of the Stretford End because he never stopped trying, he liked a tackle, and when he stormed forward, as he loved to do at every available opportunity, he was a beautiful striker of the ball.

He had very tidy feet, too, being far more comfortable with the ball than many a defender, and he could play either side. So right from the off he appeared to be a considerable improvement on a clutch of full-backs who would soon be cleared out, people like Tommy O'Neil, Willie Watson and Ian Donald.

Coming into a team under pressure near the bottom of the First Division, Alex did well for several seasons, and he formed a decent partnership with Stewart Houston, another Scot brought in by Docherty.

In the long run, though, Alex lost his place to young Jimmy Nicholl, who was an outstanding prospect, and he barely played in his last two seasons at Old Trafford before leaving to join Glasgow Rangers.

BORN	BARGEDDIE, LANARKSHIRE 30TH NOVEMBER 1944
POSITION	MIDFIELDER
JOINED UNITED	DECEMBER 1972 FROM ARSENAL £120,000
UNITED DEBUT	ARSENAL (A) DIV. 1 - 06/01/1973
UNITED FAREWELL	BRISTOL CITY (A) DIV. 2 - 09/11/1974
LEFT UNITED FOR	PORTSMOUTH - NOV. 1974 (EXCHANGE FOR RON DAVIES)

GEORGE GRAHAM		
COMP.	APPS	GLS
LEAGUE	41 (2)	2
FAC	2	0
LC	1	0
TOTAL	44 (2)	2

146. GEORGE GRAHAM

OTHER HONOURS:
12 SCOTLAND CAPS 1971-73.

OTHER CLUBS:
ASTON VILLA 62/3-63/4 (8, 2);
CHELSEA 64/5-66/7 (72, 35);
ARSENAL 66/7-72/3 (227, 60);
PORTSMOUTH 74/5-76/7 (61, 5);
CRYSTAL PALACE 76/7-77/8 (44, 2);
CALIFORNIA SURF, USA, 78.

MANAGER:
MILLWALL 1982-86; ARSENAL 1986-95; LEEDS UNITED 1996-98;
TOTTENHAM HOTSPUR 1998-2001.

George Graham . . . or Gorgeous George as some called him . . . I never quite understood how the manager, Tommy Docherty, expected him to improve the team.

True, he was an extremely accomplished footballer, a 28-year-old Scottish international who had played his part in Arsenal winning the League and FA Cup double only a season and a half earlier, but that in itself begged a question. If he had a lot to offer, why were Arsenal letting him go when he was in his pomp?

During his days with Aston Villa and Chelsea, George had been a centre-forward, but at Arsenal he was converted into a midfielder and that's where he was deployed by United.

When he arrived Docherty described him as 'another Gunter Netzer' and my reaction was that he and I must have been watching different Gunter Netzers.

Of course, George could play; he could push the ball around, he was effective in the air, and at his other clubs he showed he could score goals. But he didn't seem to be the right man for United at that time. To be blunt, the side wasn't good enough to absorb a George Graham; they faced a battle to get out of trouble at the wrong end of the First Division and they didn't need the occasional 'fancy dan' tricks which were a part of his game.

He played with an upright stance, with his head in the air, and people called it elegant, but it was a style which didn't appeal to me. I couldn't see why he came to United unless he was looking for an easy billet, which didn't prove to be the case, or the deal made very sound financial sense to him.

In the end he achieved very little in Manchester before joining Portsmouth in exchange for Ron Davies, another transaction which puzzled me. If Docherty had acquired 'another Gunter Netzer', at the considerable cost of £120,000, why was he swapping him for a centre-forward whose best days were so far behind him that he was never given a first-team start throughout his stay at Old Trafford?

147. JIM HOLTON

OTHER HONOURS:
15 SCOTLAND CAPS 1973-74.

OTHER CLUBS:
SHREWSBURY TOWN 71/2-72/3 (67, 4);
MIAMI TOROS, USA, ON LOAN 76;
SUNDERLAND 76/7 (15, 0);
COVENTRY CITY 76/7-79/80 (91, 0).

JIM HOLTON		
COMP.	APPS	GLS
LEAGUE	63	5
FAC	2	0
LC	4	0
TOTAL	69	5

BORN	LESMAHAGOW, LANARKSHIRE 11TH APRIL 1951
DIED	WARWICK 4TH OCTOBER 1993
POSITION	CENTRE-HALF
JOINED UNITED	JANUARY 1973 FROM SHREWSBURY T. £80,000
UNITED DEBUT	WEST HAM UTD. (H) DIV. 1 - 20/01/1973
UNITED HONOURS	DIV. 2 1974/5
UNITED FAREWELL	SHEFFIELD WED. (A) DIV. 2 - 07/12/1974
LEFT UNITED FOR	SUNDERLAND SEPT. 1976 - £40,000

The first time I saw Jim Holton he was playing for Harry Gregg at Shrewsbury Town and he looked like a walking mountain range. Oh, he was a big, rugged beggar, and pretty soon I was having strong words about him to Greggy.

I was managing the non-League club, Bangor, at the time and we were playing Shrewsbury in a pre-season friendly. They had Jim at centre-half, with another tough nut, the former Manchester City man Alf Wood, playing up front, and in the first half the pair of them were more than a little naughty, kicking lumps out of my lads.

I had to warn Harry at half-time that unless he reined them in, I'd have to let my own dogs loose in the second half. I did have a couple who could have caused some damage, and he would have been sorry. Fortunately reason prevailed, things calmed down and we had a reasonable game of football, but by then Big Jim had made a considerable impression.

Greggy told me he'd spoken to United about a deal and, in all honesty, at first sight I thought Holton left a lot to be desired. He was just so incredibly raw. But from that rough diamond – perhaps wild man would be a more accurate description – soon he improved out of all recognition, developing into an extremely useful First Division defender who picked up 15 Scotland caps in a short space of time.

When he appeared at Old Trafford for his debut against West Ham, he was a total unknown to most people, but before long the fans were treating him as some sort of saviour. The United defence had been terrible in recent months, but now, although Jim was exceedingly rough and ready, he created a genuine feeling that he was capable of shoring up the holes.

His forte was his aerial power, while on the deck he was formidably strong, but I'm not sure he knew how to tackle. At times he

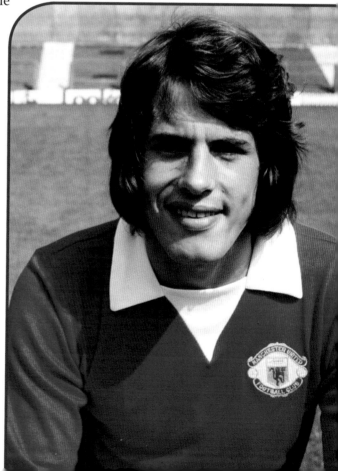

'(The fans) loved him, made him a folk hero and sang the song: "Six foot two, eyes of blue, Big Jim Holton's after you" and, believe it or not, his eyes were brown!'

looked like a dirty so-and-so because he was so clumsy, and he couldn't seem to do anything about it, but I'm positive that he never set out to hurt anyone. There wasn't a malicious bone in his body.

For all his technical short-comings, you knew that he would give you everything, and the fans understood it, too. They loved him, made him a folk hero and sang the song: 'Six foot two, eyes of blue, Big Jim Holton's after you' And, believe it or not, his eyes were brown!

It seemed that Jim had come from nowhere, and sadly he disappeared almost as quickly. After playing for just under two years, he broke his leg in a 4-4 at Sheffield Wednesday and he never kicked another ball for United's first team, eventually moving on to Sunderland.

After his fateful injury at Hillsborough, he had suffered a couple more breaks, including the time when he drove through the back wall of his garage, which sounds comical but must have been demoralising for poor Jim.

There was even worse to come. After starting a new life running a pub in the Coventry area, he suffered a heart attack after a training run and died at the age of 42. What a tragedy.

BORN	EDINBURGH 4TH JUNE 1949
POSITION	MIDFIELDER, STRIKER
JOINED UNITED	JANUARY 1973 FROM CELTIC £200,000
UNITED DEBUT	WEST HAM UTD (H) DIV. 1 - 20/01/1973
UNITED HONOURS	FA CUP 1976/7 DIV. 2 1974/5
UNITED FAREWELL	BOURNEMOUTH (A) FAC - 02/01/1984
LEFT UNITED FOR	SWINDON TOWN - JULY 1984 PLAYER/MANAGER

LOU MACARI		
COMP.	APPS	GLS
LEAGUE	311 (18)	78
FAC	31 (3)	8
LC	22 (5)	10
EUROPE	9 (1)	1
OTHERS	1	0
TOTAL	374 (27)	97

148. LOU MACARI

OTHER HONOURS:
24 SCOTLAND CAPS 1972-78.

OTHER CLUBS:
CELTIC 68/9-72/3 (58, 26);
SWINDON TOWN 84/5-85/6 (36, 3).

MANAGER:
SWINDON TOWN 1984-89;
WEST HAM UNITED 1989-90;
BIRMINGHAM CITY 1991;
STOKE CITY 1991-93;
CELTIC 1993-94; STOKE CITY 1994-97;
HUDDERSFIELD TOWN 2000-02.

Lou Macari made his debut against West Ham in the same match as Jim Holton and, like the big man, he endeared himself to his new fans instantly, in Lou's case by scoring a late equaliser.

He had joined United after upsetting Bill Shankly by turning down Liverpool and I've often wondered about that, because

Liverpool were by far the stronger club at that time. Perhaps he thought it would be easier in Manchester, that he wouldn't have as much to prove, because our team was nothing then.

Lou was a striker in those days – he had played in partnership with Kenny Dalglish at Celtic – but soon after his arrival at Old Trafford he was converted to midfield, where he spent the rest of his career. What a hell of a career it was, too, with an average of nearly a goal every four games over some 400 appearances and 11 years.

Lou is a tiny little fellow and it seemed to me right from the outset that it would be a virtual impossibility for him to survive as a front-man in our First Division, unless he turned out to be another Jimmy Greaves, which certainly he didn't.

But when he switched positions he was a revelation. Lou had neat and tidy feet, a terrific engine, he was ready to put himself about a bit, he wasn't short of pace and his experience of having played up front was invaluable to him in his new role as a provider. His positional play as an attacker was very sharp, because he had been there and done it himself.

Probably he peaked in 1975/76, when United went close to becoming champions in the first season after winning promotion, and he wasn't too far away from being voted Footballer of the Year, the award actually going to Kevin Keegan.

But despite plenty of exciting moments, and winning the FA Cup and the Second Division title, it's a fact that he played for the club in what was basically an ordinary period by Manchester United standards. I wonder if ever he compares their record with Liverpool's in the 1970s and regrets his decision.

As a character, Lou has always struck me as being a tad unusual. He was a teetotaller, who as a manager always discouraged his players from taking a drink, even banned alcohol from the team coach. But he was a gambler, so betting was all right in his book. Oh well, it takes all sorts.

BORN	DUBLIN 9TH JULY 1951
POSITION	MIDFIELDER
JOINED UNITED	JANUARY 1973 FROM BOHEMIANS - £25,000
UNITED DEBUT	EVERTON (H) DIV. 1 - 24/01/1973
UNITED FAREWELL	OLDHAM ATH. (H) DIV. 2 - 31/03/1975
LEFT UNITED FOR	WBA - OCT. 1975

MICK MARTIN		
COMP.	APPS	GLS
LEAGUE	33 (7)	2
FAC	2	0
LC	1	0
TOTAL	36 (7)	2

149. MICK MARTIN

OTHER HONOURS:
51 REPUBLIC OF IRELAND CAPS 1972-83.

OTHER CLUBS:
HOME FARM AND BOHEMIANS, BOTH ROI;
WEST BROMWICH ALBION 75/6-78/9 (89, 11);
NEWCASTLE UNITED 78/9-82/3 (147, 5);
VANCOUVER WHITECAPS, CANADA, 84;
CARDIFF CITY 84/5 (7, 0); PETERBOROUGH UNITED 84/5 (12, 0);
ROTHERHAM UNITED 85/6 (5, 0); PRESTON N.E. 85/6 (35, 0).

At £25,000, Mick Martin was one of Tommy Docherty's bargains, and he was the odd man out among the new manager's five major signings in the space of a month in that he wasn't a Scot. Mick was an unknown quantity to most supporters when he arrived from the Republic of Ireland, but he had a sound footballing pedigree, being the son of Con Martin, one of Eire's most famous sporting sons, and a cousin of John Giles.

After being given his debut in the same month that he crossed the Irish Sea, he played most of his games in midfield, although actually he was a natural defender, potentially a very fine one. Docherty tried to make him into a hard-nut in the centre of the park, but it never really worked. Back at Bohemians he had shone in defence, and later he excelled occasionally for his country at centre-half, notably against England when he contained Stuart Pearson pretty effectively.

It's a shame that Mick never got a chance at the back for United, because I'm sure he'd have done a top-class job. Unquestionably I'd have preferred him to Brian Greenhoff as a partner for Martin Buchan. I believe Mick and Martin could have been an ideal combination, one which could have thrived for quite a few seasons.

Sadly, Mick was allowed to slip away to link up with Giles at West Bromwich Albion, with Manchester United never having seen him at his best.

BORN	BELFAST 3RD MARCH 1951
POSITION	FORWARD
JOINED UNITED	OCTOBER 1972 FROM PORTADOWN, N.IRELAND £20,000
UNITED DEBUT	SOUTHAMPTON (A) DIV. 1 - 31/03/1973
UNITED FAREWELL	SOUTHAMPTON (H) DIV. 1 - 08/12/1973
LEFT UNITED FOR	SWINDON TOWN NOV. 1974

TREVOR ANDERSON		
COMP.	APPS	GLS
LEAGUE	13 (6)	2
TOTAL	13 (6)	2

150. TREVOR ANDERSON

OTHER HONOURS:
22 NORTHERN IRELAND CAPS 1973-78.

OTHER CLUBS:
PORTADOWN, NORTHERN IRELAND;
SWINDON TOWN 74/5-77/8 (131, 34); PETERBOROUGH UNITED 77/8-78/9 (49, 6);
LINFIELD, NORTHERN IRELAND.

Trevor Anderson was Frank O'Farrell's last signing as manager of Manchester United, but he wasn't blooded until Tommy Docherty took over, and then he was treated with a disdain which I could never fathom.

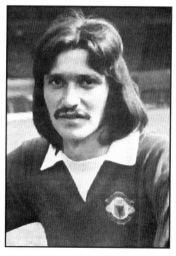

He started with some promising performances in the spring of 1973, the highlight of which was scoring an unexpected winner at Elland Road, which went a long way towards ensuring that relegation was avoided that season. Unfortunately, it proved to be only a temporary reprieve.

Trevor was an elegant player, very slight but with no shortage of smooth skills, and I am convinced that he was a far better bet for long-term success at Old Trafford than some of those brought in later by Docherty, the likes of Tommy Baldwin and Alan Foggon.

I think it was ridiculous that a lad who could clearly play the game should be discarded so quickly without being given the extended opportunity he deserved.

I don't know if there was an element of the manager rejecting him because he had been the protege of O'Farrell, an old pal from their days together as Preston's wing-halves, but whatever Docherty's reasoning, I'd contend that it was faulty.

When Trevor returned to Northern Ireland, having done well for both Swindon and Peterborough, he scored plenty of goals for Linfield, but was left to wonder what might have been if United had never sacked Frank O'Farrell.

151. PETER FLETCHER

OTHER CLUBS:
HULL CITY 74/5-75/6 (36, 5);
STOCKPORT COUNTY 76/7-77/8 (51, 13);
HUDDERSFIELD TOWN 78/9-81/2 (99, 37).

PETER FLETCHER		
COMP.	APPS	GLS
LEAGUE	2 (5)	0
TOTAL	2 (5)	0

BORN	MANCHESTER 2ND DECEMBER 1953
POSITION	STRIKER
JOINED UNITED	AUGUST 1969 FROM JUNIOR FOOTBALL
UNITED DEBUT	STOKE CITY (A) DIV. 1 - 14/04/1973
UNITED FAREWELL	WOLVERHAMPTON W. (H) DIV. 1 - 23/02/1974
LEFT UNITED FOR	HULL CITY - MAY 1974 (VALUED AT £30,000 IN EXCHANGE DEAL FOR STUART PEARSON)

Poor Peter Fletcher made his debut for United in the accursed year of 1973, when the Old Trafford scene was changing with bewildering rapidity. That made life extremely difficult, especially for the club's youngsters, and he suffered with the rest. It was a shame because he was a more-than-useful prospect, a leggy centre-forward with a bit of skill about him.

No matter what profession you follow, you need opportunity to succeed, and Tommy Docherty barely gave Peter the merest sniff. In the end he went to Hull when Stuart Pearson travelled in the opposite direction, and later he helped Huddersfield to win the Fourth Division title before being forced to retire with back problems. He's a nice lad and he deserved better.

BORN	BARNSLEY 1ST APRIL 1954
POSITION	CENTRAL DEFENDER
JOINED UNITED	JANUARY 1971 FROM JUNIOR FOOTBALL
UNITED DEBUT	SHEFFIELD UNITED (H) DIV. 1 - 23/04/1973
UNITED HONOURS	DIV. 2 1974/5
UNITED FAREWELL	ASTON VILLA (A) DIV. 2 - 22/02/1975
LEFT UNITED FOR	HUDDERSFIELD TOWN JAN. 1976

ARNOLD SIDEBOTTOM		
COMP.	APPS	GLS
LEAGUE	16	0
FAC	2	0
LC	2	0
TOTAL	20	0

152. ARNOLD SIDEBOTTOM

OTHER CLUBS:
HUDDERSFIELD TOWN 75/6-77/8 (61, 5);
HALIFAX TOWN 78/9 (21, 2).

I remember Tommy Docherty saying that Arnold Sidebottom would play for England, and he was right, but he didn't mean with a cricket ball in his hand!

The manager went even further, claiming that he had the three best young centre-halves in Britain in Steve James, Jim Holton and Arnold. Well, if he believed that sincerely, then why didn't he give young Sidebottom more of a chance?

Personally, I never thought he looked the part. He seemed very spindly for a central defender, looking rather like a schoolboy playing with grown-ups, and it was hard to envisage him dominating big, tough centre-forwards. Without wishing to be unkind, it might be said that as a footballer, Arnold was a good cricketer.

Certainly I was delighted when he made a name for himself as a fast bowler with Yorkshire, when he was selected for a Test against Australia in 1985, and when his son, Ryan, emulated him for both county and country.

BORN	DUBLIN 30TH APRIL 1954
POSITION	MIDFIELDER
JOINED UNITED	APRIL 1973 FROM BOHEMIANS - £20,000
UNITED DEBUT	ARSENAL (A) DIV. 1 - 25/08/1973
UNITED HONOURS	DIV. 2 1974/5
UNITED FAREWELL	DERBY COUNTY (H) DIV. 1 - 05/02/1977
LEFT UNITED FOR	DERBY COUNTY MARCH 1977 - £180,000

GERRY DALY		
COMP.	APPS	GLS
LEAGUE	107 (4)	23
FAC	9 (1)	5
LC	17	4
EUROPE	4	0
TOTAL	137 (5)	32

153. GERRY DALY

OTHER HONOURS:
48 REPUBLIC OF IRELAND CAPS 1973-86.

OTHER CLUBS:
BOHEMIANS, REPUBLIC OF IRELAND;
DERBY COUNTY 76/7-79/80 (112, 31);
NEW ENGLAND TEAMEN, USA, 78-79;
COVENTRY CITY 80/1-83/4 (84, 15);
LEICESTER CITY ON LOAN 82/3 (17, 1);
BIRMINGHAM CITY 84/5-85/6 (32, 1);
SHREWSBURY TOWN 85/6-86/7 (55, 8); STOKE CITY 86/7-87/8 (22, 1);
DONCASTER ROVERS 88/9 (39, 4).

Gerry Daly was Tommy Docherty's world-beater. One minute the manager was trumpeting the Irishman's praises to the heavens, but the next they had differences of opinion and suddenly Gerry was sold to Derby. Ironically, he was joined there by Docherty only a few months later.

Undoubtedly Gerry was a nice footballer, the type the crowd love to get behind. He could beat a man, he had pace to get away and he scored plenty of goals for a midfielder, even if a lot of them came from the penalty spot. He was a potent striker of the ball, knocking in a few from distance, and he could spot a pass and make it accurately.

When the team was going forward, I couldn't find fault with Gerry, but I don't think he knew what defending was, and maybe that's what cost him his place in the end.

For a while in the mid 1970s he looked as if he might be carving a long-term place for himself with United and, such was his ability, he might have become a truly major player.

But he turned out to be the one early casualty from the side which almost won the First Division in 1975/76. They got off to a disappointing start in 1976/77 and Docherty opted to bring in Jimmy Greenhoff to partner Stuart Pearson at the front and moved Sammy McIlroy back into midfield at the expense of Daly.

He might be called unlucky, but I have to say that, week-in and week-out, if I'd been offered any two out of Greenhoff, McIlroy and Daly, then I'd have taken Greenhoff and McIlroy every time. I am convinced that when the going got tough, Sammy would always give the team more than Gerry in terms of marking and tackling.

Still, Daly showed his quality with an extensive international career which lasted 13 years, but he never really settled after leaving Old Trafford, doing the rounds with eight clubs before going into non-League management with Telford.

CATCH ME IF YOU CAN: the elusive Gerry Daly ghosts between two Derby County defenders, David Nish (left) and Steve Powell.

BORN	Barnsley 28th April 1953
Position	Defender, Midfielder
Joined United	August 1968 from junior football
United Debut	Ipswich Town (A) Div. 1 - 08/09/1973
United Honours	FA Cup 1976/7 Div. 2 1974/5
United Farewell	Wolverhampton W. (H) Div. 1 - 07/05/1979
Left United for	Leeds United Aug. 1979 - £350,000

Brian Greenhoff		
COMP.	APPS	GLS
LEAGUE	218 (3)	13
FAC	24	2
LC	19	2
EUROPE	6	0
OTHERS	1	0
TOTAL	268 (3)	17

154. BRIAN GREENHOFF

OTHER HONOURS:
18 England caps 1976-80.
OTHER CLUBS:
Leeds United 79/80-81/2 (72, 1);
Hong Kong football;
Rochdale 82/3-83/4 (16, 0).

I think Brian Greenhoff was a lucky lad to collect 18 England caps. He wasn't the worst player in the world, but to me he was never in that kind of class.

It's very unfair to him, and no doubt he gets sick of hearing such comparisons, but I can never help noting that impressive total of appearances for his country, and then looking at his brother, Jimmy, who never won a single cap.

Yet Jimmy was a magnificent footballer, on a totally different plane to Brian, and I found their contrasting international fortunes exceedingly strange. I could never begin to make sense of it. They say that football is all about opinion and that was never more true than in the case of the Greenhoffs. My views and those of the England management could hardly have been farther apart.

Brian was first called into the United team as a young midfielder by Tommy Docherty, and that was where he played most of his games for England. But he enjoyed his greatest success for the club alongside Martin Buchan in central defence, where he replaced the injured Jim Holton for a few seasons, and also he had a spell at full-back not too long before Dave Sexton sold him to Leeds.

Wherever he was asked to line up, Brian invariably did a good and faithful job for his side. He was utterly honest, always gave his very best and made the most of every last scrap of ability at his disposal. I suppose I preferred him as an up-and-down wing-half, in a mainly defensive role, because I never felt he

'He was utterly honest, always gave his very best and made the most of every last scrap of ability.'

was strong enough aerially to be a centre-half. He wasn't the biggest and I would never, not in my wildest imaginings, have used him in the middle of a back four.

Not that he was a big, ugly type of player and, together with Buchan, he always tried to play the ball out from the back, but I never thought he dominated centre-forwards in the manner of, say, an Allenby Chilton or a Mark Jones. In the end Brian lost out when Sexton brought in Gordon McQueen. That must have been disappointing, and so must his stay at Elland Road, which was blighted by a succession of injuries.

155. GEORGE BUCHAN

OTHER CLUBS:
ABERDEEN 68/9-72/3 (29, 2);
BURY 74/5-75/6 (65, 6).

GEORGE BUCHAN		
COMP.	APPS	GLS
LEAGUE	0 (3)	0
LC	0 (1)	0
TOTAL	0 (4)	0

BORN	ABERDEEN 2ND MAY 1950
POSITION	FORWARD
JOINED UNITED	MAY 1973 FROM ABERDEEN
UNITED DEBUT	WEST HAM UTD. (H) DIV. 1 - 15/09/1973
UNITED FAREWELL	MIDDLESBROUGH (H) LC - 08/10/1973
LEFT UNITED FOR	BURY AUG. 1974 - £11,500

I have always liked George Buchan, the younger brother of Martin, as a character rather more than as a footballer. He was very quick, and he could play either wide or through the middle, but it didn't surprise me that he never started a game for United because I never thought he was good enough.

George, who followed Martin first to Pittodrie and then to Old Trafford, netted with the first kick of his United debut – as a substitute for George Graham – only for the 'goal' to be disallowed for offside. Eventually Tommy Docherty told him there was no place for him at the club unless he wanted to drive the reserve team coach, so he went to Bury for a couple of seasons before succeeding in a new career as a teacher.

156. CLIVE GRIFFITHS

OTHER CLUBS:
PLYMOUTH ARGYLE ON LOAN 74/5 (11, 1);
TRANMERE ROVERS 75/6-76/7 (59, 0);
CHICAGO STING, USA, 76-79;
TULSA ROUGHNECKS, USA, 80.

CLIVE GRIFFITHS		
COMP.	APPS	GLS
LEAGUE	7	0
TOTAL	7	0

BORN	PONTYPRIDD 22ND JANUARY 1955
POSITION	CENTRAL DEFENDER
JOINED UNITED	JUNE 1970 FROM JUNIOR FOOTBALL
UNITED DEBUT	BURNLEY (A) DIV. 1 - 27/10/1973
UNITED FAREWELL	IPSWICH TOWN (H) DIV. 1 - 29/12/1973
LEFT UNITED FOR	CHICAGO STING APRIL 1976

Clive Griffiths knew his best footballing days after leaving Old Trafford, playing for Bill Foulkes in Chicago and at Tulsa. He was a pretty ordinary central defender who, although he won Wales caps at schoolboy and under-23 level, never looked remotely likely to make the First Division grade. His immediate post-United days were spent at Plymouth, where he made little impact, but then Clive helped Tranmere to earn promotion from the Fourth Division in 1975/76 before bowing out of English football.

BORN	DUNOON, ARGYLLSHIRE 20TH AUGUST 1949
POSITION	FULL-BACK
JOINED UNITED	DECEMBER 1973 FROM BRENTFORD - £55,000
UNITED DEBUT	QPR (A) DIV. 1 - 01/01/1974
UNITED HONOURS	DIV. 2 1974/5
UNITED FAREWELL	IPSWICH TOWN (A) DIV. 1 - 01/03/1980
LEFT UNITED FOR	SHEFFIELD UTD - JULY 1980

STEWART HOUSTON		
COMP.	APPS	GLS
LEAGUE	204 (1)	13
FAC	22	1
LC	16	2
EUROPE	6 (1)	0
TOTAL	248 (2)	16

157. STEWART HOUSTON

OTHER HONOURS:
1 SCOTLAND CAP 1975.
OTHER CLUBS:
CHELSEA 67/8-69/70 (9, 0);
BRENTFORD 71/2-73/4 (77, 9);
SHEFFIELD UNITED 80/1-82/3 (94, 1);
COLCHESTER UNITED 83/4-85/6 (107, 5).
MANAGER:
ARSENAL, CARETAKER, 1995 AND 1996;
QUEEN'S PARK RANGERS 1997.

Stewart Houston was an accomplished left-back, tall enough to line up in central defence at need, and the fact that he was Scottish qualified him to play for Tommy Docherty – excuse my spot of sarcasm – during United's gruesome relegation campaign of 1973/74.

In fact, Stewart was one of Docherty's better buys – the pair of them knew each other from their time together at Chelsea – and I was surprised that he received only the one international cap.

He was tough and resilient, and his size and ability in the air proved important to a defence which was lacking in inches, especially at dead-ball situations when he could mark the big fellows.

Also, when given the chance, he could play a bit of football, passing the ball impressively from the back. He didn't panic, he thought about what he was doing and with his reliably accurate delivery he was capable of picking out Stuart Pearson and Jimmy Greenhoff, who so often made intelligent runs ahead of him.

Overall Stewart did a marvellous job in what was an extremely poor team, certainly during his early months at Old Trafford, and he was a key factor in the improvement that followed.

Sadly he broke his leg at Bristol City in the spring of 1977, which cost him a place in the FA Cup Final, thus allowing young Arthur Albiston to step in and excel against Liverpool.

Stewart recovered to play on and off for three more seasons, continuing to prove his worth, although in the end it was inevitable that the steady rise of Arthur would see him off.

By the time he left to join Sheffield United in 1980, though, no one could deny that he had given fabulous value for the relatively modest fee that Docherty had paid for him.

Later Stewart coached extensively, working with his old mate George Graham at both Arsenal and Tottenham.

158. PAUL BIELBY

OTHER CLUBS:
HARTLEPOOL UNITED 75/6-77/8 (93, 8);
HUDDERSFIELD TOWN 78/9 (31, 5).

PAUL BIELBY		
COMP.	APPS	GLS
LEAGUE	2 (2)	0
TOTAL	2 (2)	0

BORN	DARLINGTON 24TH NOVEMBER 1956
POSITION	WINGER
JOINED UNITED	JULY 1972 FROM JUNIOR FOOTBALL
UNITED DEBUT	MANCHESTER CITY (A) DIV. 1 - 13/03/1974
UNITED FAREWELL	CHELSEA (A) DIV. 1 - 30/03/1974
LEFT UNITED FOR	HARTLEPOOL UNITED DEC. 1975

ommy Docherty had enough faith in Paul Bielby to give him his senior entrance in a Manchester derby at Maine Road, a pretty daunting prospect for the 17-year-old winger, who had impressed quite a few good judges with his performances for the England youth team.

The United manager was absolutely desperate at the time, with relegation looming and his team playing abysmally, which was hardly the ideal scenario for the boy to bed in. As it turned out, he couldn't make an impact and he spent a handful of seasons in the lower divisions before leaving the League.

159. JIM McCALLIOG

OTHER HONOURS:
5 SCOTLAND CAPS 1967-71.

OTHER CLUBS:
CHELSEA 64/5-65/6 (7, 2);
SHEFFIELD WEDNESDAY 65/6-68/9 (150, 19);
WOLVERHAMPTON WANDERERS 69/70-73/4 (163, 34);
SOUTHAMPTON 74/5-76/7 (72, 8);
CHICAGO STING, USA, 77; LINCOLN CITY 78/9 (9, 0).

MANAGER:
HALIFAX TOWN 1990-91.

JIM McCALLIOG		
COMP.	APPS	GLS
LEAGUE	31	7
FAC	1	0
LC	5 (1)	0
TOTAL	37 (1)	7

BORN	GLASGOW 23RD SEPTEMBER 1946
POSITION	MIDFIELDER
JOINED UNITED	MARCH 1974 FROM WOLVES - £60,000
UNITED DEBUT	BIRMINGHAM CITY (A) DIV. 1 - 16/03/1974
UNITED HONOURS	DIV. 2 1974/5
UNITED FAREWELL	BRISTOL CITY (H) DIV. 2 - 01/02/1975
LEFT UNITED FOR	SOUTHAMPTON FEB. 1975 - £40,000

im McCalliog was a far better player than the evidence of his 11 months at Old Trafford might suggest. He was an old-fashioned inside-forward, adept at linking the play between midfield and attack and occasionally getting on the end of things, and when he joined the club he had proved his quality with Sheffield Wednesday, Wolves and Scotland.

In the event, he gave some smashing performances for United, but he was never consistent, and the good days were interspersed with some extremely ordinary ones.

When Tommy Docherty signed him in the spring of 1974, with the team on the verge of dropping into the Second Division, Jim's international career was over but he was still only 27, and there was no reason to believe he was a spent force.

My message to him would have been: 'McCalliog, you're at a big club now, and we need you to perform. You've got the ability, so get on with it.'

He did offer United fans some brief rays of hope with a few

goals that spring, his arrival coinciding with a belated change of policy from dourly defensive to having a go, but it wasn't enough.

So Jim went down with United, played pretty well for half the next season in the Second Division, but then he lost his place and was sold to Southampton in the February.

Just over a year later, of course, Jim had the last laugh on Docherty when he set up Southampton's winning goal for Bobby Stokes in the 1976 FA Cup Final against United.

Unquestionably McCalliog had the quality to have thrived at Old Trafford. Was the reason down to him, or was it the fault of the management? Let's just say his case was not an isolated one, which suggests that playing for Manchester United at that time was an occupation fraught with peril.

BORN	HULL 21ST JUNE 1949
POSITION	STRIKER
JOINED UNITED	MAY 1974 FROM HULL CITY (VALUED AT £170,000 IN EXCHANGE INVOLVING PETER FLETCHER)
UNITED DEBUT	ORIENT (A) DIV. 2 - 17/08/1974
UNITED HONOURS	FA CUP 1976/7 DIV. 2 1974/5
UNITED FAREWELL	SOUTHAMPTON (A) DIV. 1 - 30/04/1979
LEFT UNITED FOR	WEST HAM UNITED AUG. 1979 - £220,000

STUART PEARSON		
COMP.	APPS	GLS
LEAGUE	138 (1)	55
FAC	22	5
LC	12	5
EUROPE	6	1
OTHERS	1	0
TOTAL	179 (1)	66

160. STUART PEARSON

OTHER HONOURS:
15 ENGLAND CAPS 1976-78.
OTHER CLUBS:
HULL CITY 69/70-73/4 (129, 44);
WEST HAM UNITED 79/80-81/2 (34, 6).
MANAGER:
WEST BROMWICH ALBION, CARETAKER, 1991.

I always used to say that if they were knock-kneed they couldn't play, but Stuart Pearson, perhaps not the most elegant of movers, proved me wrong.

Tommy Docherty never made a better signing than Pancho. He was a delightful footballer who gave Manchester United five years of marvellous service, and then they made a £50,000 profit when they sold him after knee problems had forced him out of the team.

The supporters loved him; he was a hero to them, a dashing centre-forward who provided wonderful entertainment. It doesn't always follow that such a favourite of the fans rejoices in equally high regard from those who make their living in the game, but in Stuart's case it did.

Fellow professionals thought the world of him because he was a supremely unselfish performer whose lovely, deft style encouraged fluent play and enabled his team-mates to flow around him.

He was always looking for angles, roaming out wide to play people in. His movement was so effective that often he made a hopeful punt out of defence look like a brilliant pass. Invariably he was available to provide an outlet for a player under pressure, and he would chase lost causes all day.

'He was always looking for angles, roaming out wide to play people in. His movement was so effective that often he made a hopeful punt out of defence look like a brilliant pass.'

Stuart's strength, combined with his great touch, enabled him to hold the ball up while reinforcements arrived, and he was very quick, too.

Crucially, he and Jimmy Greenhoff were a superb pair, an absolute pleasure to watch. So much of their work was tremendously subtle, delivering smart little lay-offs to bring others into play and, as a duo, they were as good as anything knocking about in their era.

I know they weren't the most prolific of scorers, but they were never in a side of the very highest quality, and the fact that the goals were spread pretty well, with the wingers and midfielders all chipping in, was pretty much down to their contribution.

Not that Stuart's goal record is anything to be ashamed of. He top-scored as United climbed out of the Second Division, then did so again as they just missed the title in 1975/76, and he smacked a shot past Ray Clemence to put the team on the way to beating Liverpool in the 1977 FA Cup Final.

Arguably he should have won more England caps, because it's hard to imagine that there were many better players around, though he made his 15 appearances in a short space of time and then suffered injuries.

That was a shame because he should have been in his pomp in 1979 when Dave Sexton sold him to West Ham, but he wasn't finished, laying on the goal that beat Arsenal in the 1980 FA Cup Final. That said, whether his killer ball to Trevor Brooking was really intended as a cross might best be discussed over a quiet drink!

But whatever the disappointment of his early departure from Old Trafford, Stuart Pearson will always be a name that conjures up happy memories. He was a class act.

BORN	EDINBUIRGH 14TH JULY 1957
POSITION	FULL-BACK
JOINED UNITED	JULY 1972 FROM JUNIOR FOOTBALL
UNITED DEBUT	MANCHESTER CITY (H) LC - 09/10/1974
UNITED HONOURS	FA CUP 1976/7, 1982/3, 1984/5 DIV. 2 1974/5
UNITED FAREWELL	CHELSEA (A) DIV. 1 - 13/02/1988
LEFT UNITED FOR	WBA - AUGUST 1988

ARTHUR ALBISTON		
COMP.	APPS	GLS
LEAGUE	364 (15)	6
FAC	36	0
LC	38 (2)	1
EUROPE	26 (1)	0
OTHERS	3	0
TOTAL	467 (18)	7

161. ARTHUR ALBISTON

OTHER HONOURS:
14 SCOTLAND CAPS 1982-86.

OTHER CLUBS:
WEST BROMWICH ALBION 88/9 (43, 2);
DUNDEE 89/90 (10, 0);
CHESTERFIELD 90/1 (3, 1);
CHESTER CITY 91/2-92/3 (68, 0);
MOLDE, NORWAY, 93/4;
AYR UNITED 93/4 (1, 0).

You would never meet a lovelier lad than Arthur Albiston, he's one of nature's gentlemen – and he just happened to be one of the finest full-backs ever to play for Manchester United.

He turned out nearly 500 times for the club, which puts him among the top ten in terms of appearances, and that's a record which could, and should, have been stretched much further.

Without any question, Alex Ferguson unloaded Arthur when he still had plenty to give, because he was only 31 and as fit as a flea when he was released in 1988. It was like the Tony Dunne situation all over again. I know there were youngsters waiting for their chance, but you don't lightly dispense with top quality.

Towards the end of Albiston's days at Old Trafford it was beyond my comprehension that sometimes the manager would pick Colin Gibson ahead of him. To my mind, there was no contest between the two – the Scot was the better player by a vast distance.

Arthur Albiston was a superb performer, dating back to his early first-team outings as a teenager, including his cool display against Liverpool in the 1977 FA Cup Final after being brought in as a replacement for the injured Stewart Houston.

'Arthur Albiston was a gem, and he never received a fraction of the credit which he deserved.'

That day a lot of pundits predicted he would be run off his feet by Steve Heighway, but he coped brilliantly. His ability, there for all to see, was matched by his temperament, and as the years rolled by he proved worthy of following in a long line of exceptional Manchester United left-backs, the likes of John Aston, Roger Byrne and Tony Dunne.

In fact, if I was asked to pick my greatest ever United side and I was told that I must include Arthur, then I wouldn't be the slightest bit upset. He would be in the frame automatically, and I could be sure that he'd never let me down.

His attributes? He wasn't very big though he wasn't bad in the air for his size, he had a fair turn of speed and a more-than-decent left peg. Arthur would win the ball and give it sensibly, he was quite capable of joining in when the team was moving forward and there was never the remotest possibility that he would cheat on his manager or team-mates.

Also, for all his amiable nature, he never shirked a tackle and he could be relied upon to look after any of his mates who might have needed help from time to time, like Gordon Hill, for example.

Arthur Albiston was a gem, and he never received a fraction of the credit which he deserved.

162. RON DAVIES

OTHER HONOURS:
29 WALES CAPS 1964-74.

OTHER CLUBS:
CHESTER 59/60-62/3 (94, 44);
LUTON TOWN 62/3-63/4 (32, 21);
NORWICH CITY 63/4-65/6 (113, 58);
SOUTHAMPTON 66/7-72/3 (240, 134);
PORTSMOUTH 73/4-74/5 (59, 18);
ARCADIA SHEPHERDS, SOUTH AFRICA, 74/5;
MILLWALL 75/6 (3, 0).

RON DAVIES		
COMP.	APPS	GLS
LEAGUE	0 (10)	0
TOTAL	0 (10)	0

BORN	HOLYWELL, FLINTSHIRE 25TH MAY 1942
POSITION	STRIKER
JOINED UNITED	NOVEMBER 1974 FROM PORTSMOUTH (EXCHANGE FOR GEORGE GRAHAM)
UNITED DEBUT	SUNDERLAND (H) DIV. 2 - 30/11/1974
UNITED FAREWELL	ASTON VILLA (A) DIV. 2 - 22/02/1975
LEFT UNITED FOR	ARCADIA SHEPHERDS, SA MARCH 1975

How Manchester United could have done with Ron Davies in his top-drawer prime, when he used to murder centre-halves as a matter of routine. He had this terrible habit of not taking time to do anything; the ball would come in and, whoosh, it would be gone before the poor devil marking him could move.

But his best days were passed by the time he moved to Old Trafford and the deal remains an unfathomable mystery to me. Tommy Docherty took Ron in exchange for George Graham, for whom he'd paid £120,000 not that long ago, and then never gave him a start before packing him off to South Africa. What sort of business is that?

BORN	GATESHEAD 10TH JUNE 1945
POSITION	STRIKER
JOINED UNITED	JANUARY 1975 (LOAN) FROM CHELSEA
UNITED DEBUT	SUNDERLAND (A) DIV. 2 - 18/01/1975
UNITED FAREWELL	BRISTOL CITY (H) DIV. 2 - 01/02/1975
LEFT UNITED FOR	CHELSEA - FEBRUARY 1975

TOMMY BALDWIN		
COMP.	APPS	GLS
LEAGUE	2	0
TOTAL	2	0

163. TOMMY BALDWIN

OTHER CLUBS:
ARSENAL 64/5-66/7 (17, 7);
CHELSEA 66/7-74/5 (187, 74);
MILLWALL ON LOAN 74/5 (6, 1);
BRENTFORD 77/8 (4, 1).

The employment of Tommy Baldwin for a two-match loan early in 1975 puzzled me as much as the perplexing case of Ron Davies. Okay, so Stuart Pearson was injured and cover was needed, but what sort of message does the recruitment of an unremarkable Chelsea discard send to United's own reserves?

Apart from youngsters such as David McCreery, who was a striker at the time, Davies himself might have appreciated the opportunity. But Baldwin was selected twice before returning goalless to Stamford Bridge and the fans were left to shake their heads in bewilderment at Tommy Docherty's latest whim.

BORN	DUBLIN 4TH JANUARY 1951
POSITION	GOALKEEPER
JOINED UNITED	OCTOBER 1973 FROM SHELBOURNE - £15,000
UNITED DEBUT	OXFORD UNITED (A) DIV. 2 - 08/02/1975
UNITED FAREWELL	SOUTHAMPTON (A) DIV. 1 - 05/12/1981
LEFT UNITED FOR	BRENTFORD - AUG. 1982

PADDY ROCHE		
COMP.	APPS	GLS
LEAGUE	46	0
FAC	4	0
LC	3	0
TOTAL	53	0

164. PADDY ROCHE

OTHER HONOURS:
8 REPUBLIC OF IRELAND CAPS 1972-75.
OTHER CLUBS:
SHELBOURNE, REPUBLIC OF IRELAND;
BRENTFORD 82/3-83/4 (71, 0);
HALIFAX TOWN 84/5-88/9 (189, 0).

Paddy Roche is a delightfully affable, modest Irishman who was a far more accomplished goalkeeper than his press cuttings might suggest. In fact, the only reason I would leave him out of my team is that I thought he was unlucky – and if there's one thing any side needs, it's a lucky 'keeper.

Unfortunately for Paddy, there were a couple of high-profile occasions when he carried the can for some extremely sloppy defending in front of him. For example, he was slaughtered by the newspapers following a game at Anfield during 1975/76, and if I'd have been him I'd have strangled Brian Greenhoff afterwards. Brian kept going for balls which he should have left for Paddy, and when he missed them the 'keeper was left hopelessly exposed.

Not surprisingly his confidence suffered badly and he was dropped, while Brian, the real culprit, escaped without criticism.

Contrary to public perception, Paddy was not a line 'keeper

but one who liked to come out and claim the ball. In common with any other goalie who ever lived, he made one or two mistakes, but in general he had a safe pair of hands.

I admired Paddy as a 'keeper and I thought he possessed the basic attributes to merit a long career at Old Trafford. As it was, he went on to do well for Brentford, then even better for Halifax, and he was 38 when he retired.

Looking back he might feel he should have left United earlier, having understudied first Alex Stepney and then Gary Bailey over a lot of seasons. Had he done so, he might have achieved rather more at a higher level.

165. STEVE COPPELL

OTHER HONOURS:
42 ENGLAND CAPS 1977-83.

OTHER CLUBS:
TRANMERE ROVERS 73/4-74/5 (38, 10).

MANAGER:
CRYSTAL PALACE 1984-93
AND, AS TECHNICAL DIRECTOR, 1995-96;
MANCHESTER CITY 1996;
CRYSTAL PALACE 1997-98 AND 1999-2000;
BRENTFORD 2001-02;
BRIGHTON AND HOVE ALBION 2002-03; READING 2003-.

STEVE COPPELL		
COMP.	APPS	GLS
LEAGUE	320 (2)	54
FAC	36	4
LC	25	9
EUROPE	11 (1)	3
OTHERS	1	0
TOTAL	393 (3)	70

BORN	LIVERPOOL 9TH JULY 1955
POSITION	WINGER, MIDFIELDER
JOINED UNITED	FEBRUARY 1975 FROM TRANMERE R. - £60,000
UNITED DEBUT	CARDIFF CITY (H) DIV. 2 - 01/03/1975
UNITED HONOURS	FA CUP 1976/7
UNITED FAREWELL	SUNDERLAND (A) DIV. 1 - 04/04/1983
RETIRED	OCT. 1983 DUE TO INJURY

Stevie Coppell, the man who replaced Willie Morgan, was a very simple sort of player. He would receive the ball, go past his marker and cross it; alternatively he would carry it towards an opponent, then pass it and run into space for the return.

If he was dispossessed, or if the team had lost it, then he'd be the first to be on his bike, working hard to get it back. Nothing complicated, but very efficient, very effective.

If you're talking about sheer, unadulterated talent, perhaps he left a bit to be desired. But if you're looking for somebody to play outside-right, week-in, week-out, always giving 100 percent, never shirking any task, no matter how difficult or unglamorous it might be, then Stevie Coppell has got to be your man.

I think he was hugely underrated during his time at Manchester United, though he did collect 42 England caps by the time he was 28, when a knee in-

'If you asked me to choose between Stevie and David Beckham for the right-flank role, I wouldn't have to debate for a second. I'd go for Coppell like a shot.'

jury he picked up against Hungary forced him to retire when he might have had half a dozen years left in him.

Jimmy Murphy, that most perceptive judge of a footballer, was responsible for Stevie coming to Old Trafford. He spotted him playing for Tranmere and recommended him to Tommy Docherty, who had sense enough to take the advice.

Pretty soon he was in the team and he startled a few defenders and thrilled a lot of fans with his freshness and the directness of his attacking; then later, under Dave Sexton, he adapted his game to take on more defensive responsibility, and he was a success in that role, too, although I'd argue that he was asked to do too much. I don't believe wide players can be expected to operate as both wingers and full-backs at the same time, although Stevie was an exceptional athlete and managed it better than most.

In the end he played nearly 400 games for United, scoring plenty of goals along the way, and had he remained fit we might have been looking at 600 or even 700 appearances. Undoubtedly he would have lasted through Ron Atkinson's reign and might well have survived into Alex Ferguson's.

I'll go back again to the pleasurable pastime of picking an all-time United side, and if I was asked if I'd select Stevie on the right wing, then probably I'd say 'no.' After all, there have been a few outstanding candidates for the job down the years, including Jimmy Delaney, John Berry, John Connelly, you might even say George Best, although he could play anywhere.

But if you re-phrased your approach, and told me that I *had* to have Stevie, I would just say 'Thank you very much' and be quite satisfied. I'd be happy in the knowledge that I could rely on him to perform to a consistently high level, no matter what the circumstances, and that's a priceless asset.

Certainly if you asked me to choose between Stevie and David Beckham for the right-flank role, I wouldn't have to debate for a second. I'd go for Coppell like a shot.

166. JIMMY NICHOLL

OTHER HONOURS:
73 NORTHERN IRELAND CAPS 1976-86.

OTHER CLUBS:
SUNDERLAND ON LOAN 81/2 (3, 0);
TORONTO BLIZZARD, 82-83;
SUNDERLAND 82/3 (29, 0);
GLASGOW RANGERS 83/4 (17, 0);
WEST BROMWICH ALBION 84/5-85/6 (56, 0);
GLASGOW RANGERS 86/7-88/9 (65, 0);
DUNFERMLINE ATHLETIC 89/90-90/1 (24, 0);
RAITH ROVERS 90/1-95/6 (128, 7).

MANAGER: RAITH ROVERS 1990-96; MILLWALL 1996-97; RAITH ROVERS 1997-99.

JIMMY NICHOLL		
COMP.	APPS	GLS
LEAGUE	188 (9)	3
FAC	22 (4)	1
LC	14	1
EUROPE	10	1
OTHERS	1	0
TOTAL	235 (13)	6

BORN	HAMILTON, CANADA 28TH FEBRUARY 1956
POSITION	FULL-BACK
JOINED UNITED	NOVEMBER 1971 FROM IRISH JUNIOR FOOTBALL
UNITED DEBUT	SOUTHAMPTON (A) DIV. 2 - 05/04/1975
UNITED HONOURS	FA CUP 1976/7
UNITED FAREWELL	TOTTENHAM HOTSPUR (A) DIV. 1 - 21/11/1981
LEFT UNITED FOR	TORONTO BLIZZARD, CANADA APRIL 1982

Matt Busby once told me that Jimmy Nicholl's best position would be alongside the centre-half, a role he filled often for Northern Ireland, and who am I to argue with the opinion of such an eminent football man?

But I always thought Jimmy was a cracking full-back and I could never see why he was shipped out of Old Trafford, aged only 26 but with nearly 250 appearances to his credit. I believe that he should have doubled his tally for the club, and I'm convinced that if United had retained faith in him, he would be viewed now as one of the top right-backs in their history.

Jimmy was blessed with magnificent ability in both feet, an unusual bonus for a defender, and he passed with more precision than many a midfielder. In fact, he made the whole game look very easy, always appearing to be comfortable and in total control when he was on the ball. He was more than competent in the air, too, helped by his international experience in the centre.

His critics might say that he lacked a bit of pace, but he had a useful backside, which he was adept at employing to ease his opponents out of the way, and not too many wide-men gave him a chasing.

Jimmy won his place in Tommy Docherty's side at the expense of Alex Forsyth and with all due respect to Alex, who was no mug, it's not difficult to see why they let him go as the young Irishman matured so impressively.

Eventually he was an unexpected victim of a managerial change. Dave Sexton, who had used him regularly, was sacked and the new boss, Ron Atkinson, was keen to sign John

Gidman, which made Jimmy surplus to requirements.

There was nothing wrong with Gidman, but sometimes I think managers over-complicate matters by making wholesale changes when they are not necessary. Certainly, if I went into a club and inherited Jimmy Nicholl in his prime, then I wouldn't have been looking for another right-back.

After leaving the club, Jimmy travelled here, there and everywhere, and he didn't finish playing League football until he was 40, carrying on for no fewer than 14 additional years.

But he was United through and through, and it beggars my imagination what he might have achieved at Old Trafford had he been been allowed to continue with the job he had grown into, since his teens, with such assurance.

BORN	BELFAST 3RD NOVEMBER 1946
POSITION	MIDFIELDER
JOINED UNITED	JULY 1975 FROM NOTTINGHAM FOREST
UNITED DEBUT	WOLVERHAMPTON W. (A) DIV. 1 - 16/08/1975
UNITED FAREWELL	STOKE CITY (A) DIV. 1 - 10/05/1977
LEFT UNITED FOR	WATERFORD, ROI JUNE 1978

TOMMY JACKSON		
COMP.	APPS	GLS
LEAGUE	18 (1)	0
LC	4	0
TOTAL	22 (1)	0

167. TOMMY JACKSON

OTHER HONOURS:
35 NORTHERN IRELAND CAPS 1968-77.

OTHER CLUBS:
GLENTORAN, NORTHERN IRELAND;
EVERTON 67/8-70/1 (32, 0);
NOTTINGHAM FOREST 70/1-74/5 (81, 6);
WATERFORD, REPUBLIC OF IRELAND.

Tommy Docherty's explanation for signing Tommy Jackson was that his young United team had just risen out of the Second Division and he needed a man of experience to be a calming influence.

It was a wonderful theory, but it might have helped to have chosen someone who could play at the top level. Nothing against the lad personally, but I wouldn't have brought in Tommy Jackson in a million years.

I just can't work out what Docherty saw in him, but I can perceive the dead hand of the coach, Tommy Cavanagh, in this signing. Jackson was 28 and what had he done? Played a few games for Everton and a few more for Nottingham Forest without setting the world alight. In Manchester United terms, he was a nothing player.

I understand the attraction of bringing in someone who could stand in the middle of the park and push the ball about while offering guidance to the youngsters. But it needed to be someone of genuine stature, in the manner of Ernie Taylor, who was so influential for a brief time after the Munich disaster. Tommy was a typical Cavanagh recruit – too ordinary for words.

168. DAVID McCREERY

OTHER HONOURS:
67 NORTHERN IRELAND CAPS 1976-90.

OTHER CLUBS:
QUEEN'S PARK RANGERS 79/80-80/1 (57, 4);
TULSA ROUGHNECKS, USA, 81-82;
NEWCASTLE UNITED 82/3-88/9 (243, 2);
HEART OF MIDLOTHIAN 89/90-90/1 (29, 0);
HARTLEPOOL UNITED 91/2 (30, 0);
CARLISLE UNITED 92/3-93/4 (35, 0);
HARTLEPOOL UNITED 94/5 (9, 0).

MANAGER: CARLISLE UNITED 1992-93; HARTLEPOOL UNITED 1994-95.

DAVID McCREERY		
COMP.	APPS	GLS
LEAGUE	48 (38)	7
FAC	1 (6)	0
LC	4 (4)	1
EUROPE	4 (3)	0
OTHERS	0 (1)	0
TOTAL	57 (52)	8

BORN	BELFAST 16TH SEPTEMBER 1957
POSITION	MIDFIELDER, FORWARD
JOINED UNITED	SEPTEMBER 1972 FROM IRISH JUNIOR FOOTBALL
UNITED DEBUT	BIRMINGHAM CITY (A) DIV. 1 - 19/08/1975
UNITED HONOURS	FA CUP 1976/7
UNITED FAREWELL	CHELSEA (H) DIV. 1 - 16/05/1979
LEFT UNITED FOR	QPR AUG. 1979 - £200,000

David McCreery was as honest a footballer as the day is long. Curiously for such a little fellow, when he first came into the reckoning it was as a deputy centre-forward to Stuart Pearson, and I wasn't surprised when he switched to midfield.

He had amazing pace, which is why he was nicknamed 'The Road Runner', and although he never claimed a regular place for United, he never ever let the team down.

If Tommy Docherty needed a player to do a specific marking job, somebody who could gallop, then David was the man he turned to automatically.

His statistics make unusual reading in that he won more caps for Northern Ireland than he made starts for United, and that his substitute appearances for the club more or less equalled the times he was in the team from the kick-off. That must have been enormously frustrating, but he never complained, and he was an ideal character to have about any squad.

Eventually he was released by Dave Sexton and linked up again with Docherty at Queen's Park Rangers, but it was at Newcastle that his career really took off.

Wherever he was, David earned every penny that he was paid. He would graft all day and he wouldn't even comprehend the concept of cheating, which would be totally alien to his nature and his lovely outlook on life. If you were a manager, and you had a few like David McCreery at your club, then you would have a chance. He was the salt of the earth.

BORN	MANCHESTER 8TH DECEMBER 1957
POSITION	MIDFIELDER
JOINED UNITED	APRIL 1974 FROM JUNIOR FOOTBALL
UNITED DEBUT	BRENTFORD (H) LC - 10/09/1975
UNITED FAREWELL	LEEDS UTD (A) DIV. 1 - 11/10/1975
RETIRED	1979 - DUE TO INJURY

TONY GRIMSHAW		
COMP.	APPS	GLS
LEAGUE	0 (1)	0
LC	0 (1)	0
TOTAL	0 (2)	0

169. TONY GRIMSHAW

OTHER CLUBS:
BALLYMENA UNITED, NORTHERN IRELAND, ON LOAN 78/9.

Tony Grimshaw had a tremendous amount of talent, but shortly after Tommy Docherty promoted him to the senior reckoning he suffered a broken leg which put him out for two seasons.

Sadly his career never recovered from that shattering blow and he never played again in English senior football. That represented a chronic loss because he was a beautiful passer with a touch of flair, the type who can bring a game to life, a natural for Manchester United. Tony's story is a poignant one, the sort the game throws up all too often.

BORN	SUNBURY-ON-THAMES, MIDDX 1ST APRIL 1954
POSITION	WINGER
JOINED UNITED	NOVEMBER 1975 FROM MILLWALL £80,000
UNITED DEBUT	ASTON VILLA (H) DIV. 1 - 15/11/1975
UNITED HONOURS	FA CUP 1976/7
UNITED FAREWELL	ARSENAL (A) DIV. 1 - 01/04/1978
LEFT UNITED FOR	DERBY COUNTY APRIL 1978 - £275,000

GORDON HILL		
COMP.	APPS	GLS
LEAGUE	100 (1)	39
FAC	17	6
LC	7	4
EUROPE	8	2
OTHERS	1	0
TOTAL	133 (1)	51

170. GORDON HILL

OTHER HONOURS:
6 ENGLAND CAPS 1976-77.
OTHER CLUBS:
MILLWALL 72/3-75/6 (86, 20);
CHICAGO STING, USA, 75;
DERBY COUNTY 77/8-79/80 (24, 5);
QUEEN'S PARK RANGERS 79/80-80/1 (14, 1);
MONTREAL MANIC, CANADA;
CHICAGO STING, NEW YORK ARROWS, KANSAS COMETS,
TACOMA STARS, ALL USA;
HJK HELSINKI, FINLAND; TWENTE ENSCHEDE, HOLLAND.

Gordon Hill might be termed an enigma; or to put it another way, he was scatterbrained. But my, how he could play. He had a left peg to die for and, for a winger, his scoring record was nothing short of sensational.

For instance, in 1976/77 Gordon topped the goal charts for a team which included Stuart Pearson, Jimmy Greenhoff, Lou Macari and a few more who knew how to find the net. That season, he scored 22 times in 55 starts, a tally that most centre-forwards would be proud of, and a lot of his strikes were spectacular. When Gordon arrived at Old Trafford, and lined up on the left flank with Stevie Coppell on the right, they were as exciting a pair as could be found anywhere. I shall never forget his scintillating performance in the 1976 FA Cup semi-final, when he scored the two goals that beat Derby County. Whatever they say about him – and although essentially he's a nice lad, he can be a pain in the backside with his eccentric approach to life – he was a lovely player and a great entertainer.

Certainly Manchester United did well out of him, because he was hugely instrumental in turning the team around: he helped to win the FA Cup in 1977 and then they sold him for a profit of nearly £300,000, a lot of money in the 1970s. But just as Gordon flourished under Tommy Docherty, who bought him from Millwall, so he ran into severe problems when Dave Sexton took over as manager.

His difficulty was that he was a traditional outside-left. Now, back in Sexton's playing days, a winger would get the ball, beat his man, reach the byline and get his cross in, then he'd get out his pipe and put his feet up until he received the ball again. But by the time Gordon appeared on the scene, Dave had been to school with the FA. He had learned from the likes of the great coaching guru Charles Hughes – of whom nobody had ever heard as a player but who purported to know everything about football – that a winger had to work up and down ceaselessly.

That didn't suit Gordon Hill and I can understand why. I'll argue with anybody that you can't expect a player to perform to a high standard at both ends of the pitch. Everybody has to have a rest, but that's something Dave wouldn't allow Gordon to do. But even allowing for his differences with Dave Sexton, I could never understand what happened to Gordon after he left Old Trafford. Having performed brilliantly over three seasons for Manchester United, he was plagued by injuries at Derby and QPR, but then he disappeared to the States and never surfaced in England again.

I had to ask: what in the name of God is going on? He should have been a major player in his own country, and he should have won more caps, although competing for a place with Peter Barnes did not make that easy. I suppose the explanation for his career path can only lie in his nature. Shall we call it idiosyncratic?

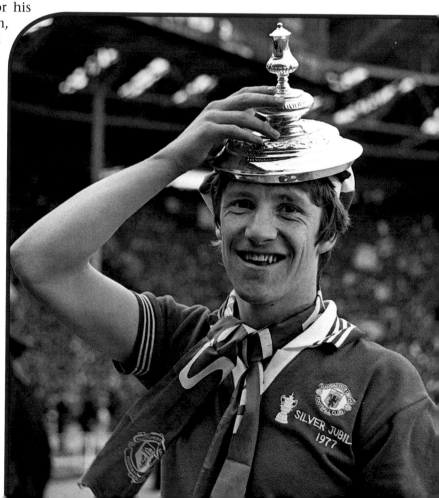

A MAGICAL MOMENT: Gordon 'Merlin' Hill celebrates after Liverpool had been defeated in the 1977 FA Cup Final.

BORN	CARLISLE 2ND MAY 1957
POSITION	MIDFIELDER
JOINED UNITED	APRIL 1972 FROM
	JUNIOR FOOTBALL
UNITED DEBUT & FAREWELL	WOLVERHAMPTON W. (H) DIV. 1 20/12/1975
LEFT UNITED FOR	CHICAGO STING, APR. 1977

JIMMY KELLY		
COMP.	APPS	GLS
LEAGUE	0 (1)	0
TOTAL	0 (1)	0

171. JIMMY KELLY

OTHER CLUBS:
CHICAGO STING, INITIALLY ON LOAN, 76-77,
LOS ANGELES AZTECS 78-80,
TULSA ROUGHNECKS 80, ALL USA;
TORONTO BLIZZARD, CANADA, 81.

Most people thought we would be hearing a lot more of Jimmy Kelly after he broke into the United side as a substitute for Brian Greenhoff against Wolves just before Christmas 1975.

Certainly he gave a tidy all-round performance that day, passing crisply and covering plenty of ground in midfield, but he was never given another opportunity at that level and the next time I became aware of him he was playing in Chicago for Bill Foulkes, who spoke highly of him.

BORN	HARTLEPOOL 13TH NOVEMBER 1958
POSITION	STRIKER
JOINED UNITED	MARCH 1975 FROM
	JUNIOR FOOTBALL
UNITED DEBUT	ASTON VILLA (A) DIV. 1 - 21/02/1976
UNITED FAREWELL	LEICESTER CITY (A) DIV. 1 - 24/04/1976
LEFT UNITED FOR	ASHTON UNITED MARCH 1977

PETER COYNE		
COMP.	APPS	GLS
LEAGUE	1 (1)	1
TOTAL	1 (1)	1

172. PETER COYNE

OTHER CLUBS:
CREWE ALEXANDRA 77/8-80/1 (134, 47);
SWINDON TOWN 84/5-88/9 (110, 30);
ALDERSHOT ON LOAN 89/90 (3, 0).

As a teenager in Manchester United's junior sides, Peter Coyne couldn't stop scoring goals. In fact, when Tommy Docherty bet him that he wouldn't hit the target 40 times in 1975/76, the manager was forced to reach for his back pocket before March was out.

So no one was surprised when Peter found the net on his first senior start, but quite a few were disappointed when he failed to carry on from there. Amazingly, when he left the club he moved into non-League football, though later he returned with Crewe, where he demonstrated that he hadn't lost the scoring knack.

It's possible that Peter enjoyed the game, but that he wasn't particularly bothered at which level he played.

173. ALAN FOGGON

OTHER CLUBS:
NEWCASTLE UNITED 67/8-70/1 (61, 14);
CARDIFF CITY 71/2-72/3 (17, 1);
MIDDLESBROUGH 72/3-75/6 (115, 45);
ROCHESTER LANCERS AND HARTFORD BI-CENTENNIALS,
BOTH USA, ON LOAN 76; SUNDERLAND 76/7 (8, 0); SOUTHEND UNITED 77/8 (22, 0);
HARTLEPOOL UNITED ON LOAN 77/8 (18, 2).

ALAN FOGGON		
COMP.	APPS	GLS
LEAGUE	0 (3)	0
TOTAL	0 (3)	0

BORN	CHESTER-LE-STREET, CO. DURHAM 23RD FEBRUARY 1950
POSITION	FORWARD
JOINED UNITED	JULY 1976 FROM MIDDLESBROUGH £27,000
UNITED DEBUT	BIRMINGHAM CITY (H) DIV. 1 - 21/08/1976
UNITED FAREWELL	MIDDLESBROUGH (H) DIV. 1 - 18/09/1976
LEFT UNITED FOR	SUNDERLAND SEPT. 1976 - £25,000

How on earth anybody allowed Tommy Docherty to spend £27,000 on Alan Foggon I shall never understand. What frightened me was that he should lay out that sort of money, and then never give the lad a start.

He arrived with a reputation for being quick, combative and a goal-scorer, and he could point to considerable experience, having scored for Newcastle in their European Fairs Cup Final triumph of 1969, then compiled a decent record at Middlesbrough.

But at Old Trafford, Foggon lasted a month and made only a handful of substitute appearances before joining Sunderland. What was the point of that?

174. COLIN WALDRON

OTHER CLUBS:
BURY 66/7 (20, 1); CHELSEA 67/8 (9, 0);
BURNLEY 67/8-75/6 (308, 16);
SUNDERLAND 76/7-77/8 (20, 1);
TULSA ROUGHNECKS 78, PHILADELPHIA FURY 78,
ATLANTA CHIEFS 79, ALL USA;
ROCHDALE 79/80 (19, 1).

COLIN WALDRON		
COMP.	APPS	GLS
LEAGUE	3	0
LC	1	0
TOTAL	4	0

BORN	BRISTOL 22ND JUNE 1958
POSITION	CENTRAL DEFENDER
JOINED UNITED	MAY 1976 FROM BURNLEY
UNITED DEBUT	SUNDERLAND (A) LC - 04/10/1976
UNITED FAREWELL	SUNDERLAND (H) DIV. 1 - 10/11/1976
LEFT UNITED FOR	SUNDERLAND - FEB. 1977 INITIALLY ON LOAN

When Colin Waldron left Bury for Chelsea in his late teens, he was feted as a top footballing centre-half of the future and he went on to give long and creditable service to Burnley.

As he was only 27 when he left Turf Moor for Old Trafford, it was fair to suppose that there was plenty of mileage left in him but, just as mysteriously as in the case of Alan Foggon, he was moved on by Tommy Docherty in a matter of months, having barely played.

How did this manner of doing business benefit Manchester United in any way? Even after all these years, I would like to know.

BORN	ELGIN, MORAYSHIRE 8TH APRIL 1958
POSITION	CENTRAL DEFENDER
JOINED UNITED	JULY 1974 FROM NAIRN COUNTY
UNITED DEBUT	AJAX (H) UEFA - 29/09/1976
UNITED FAREWELL	TOTTENHAM HOTSPUR (A) LC - 29/08/1979
RETIRED	JULY 1980

STEVE PATERSON		
COMP.	APPS	GLS
LEAGUE	3 (3)	0
LC	2	0
EUROPE	0 (2)	0
TOTAL	5 (5)	0

175. STEVE PATERSON

OTHER CLUBS:
HONG KONG AND JAPANESE FOOTBALL.
MANAGER:
INVERNESS CALEDONIAN THISTLE 1995-2003;
ABERDEEN 2003-04.

Steve Paterson has proved a canny manager, leading Inverness Caledonian Thistle from obscurity to the Scottish First Division, then taking over at Aberdeen.

Perhaps the fact that he didn't make much impact as a centre-half with United was down to a serious ankle injury which put him on the sidelines after Tommy Docherty had not been afraid to throw him in against the likes of Ajax and Juventus.

Later he never really looked like challenging Gordon McQueen, Martin Buchan and Kevin Moran, and after failing a medical with Sheffield Wednesday in 1980, he headed for the Far East. Eventually Steve ended his playing days back where they had started, in the Highland League, then began his managerial ascent with Elgin City.

BORN	BELFAST 29TH NOVMEBER 1954
POSITION	WINGER
JOINED UNITED	OCTOBER 1976 FROM TOTTENHAM H. £30,000
UNITED DEBUT	NORWICH CITY (H) DIV. 1 - 23/10/1976
UNITED FAREWELL	BIRMINGHAM CITY (A) DIV. 1 - 23/08/1980
LEFT UNITED FOR	TULSA ROUGHNECKS FEBRUARY 1981

CHRIS MCGRATH		
COMP.	APPS	GLS
LEAGUE	12 (16)	1
LC	0 (2)	0
EUROPE	3 (1)	0
TOTAL	15 (19)	1

176. CHRIS McGRATH

OTHER HONOURS:
21 NORTHERN IRELAND CAPS 1974-79.
OTHER CLUBS:
TOTTENHAM HOTSPUR 73/4-75/6 (38, 5);
MILLWALL ON LOAN 75/6 (15, 3);
TULSA ROUGHNECKS, USA, 81-82;
SOUTH CHINA, HONG KONG.

When Chris McGrath joined Manchester United he wasn't quite 22 years old, he had already started a collection of Northern Ireland international caps and there was no denying that he was a promising winger with plenty of pure skill. So on the face of it, he didn't seem a bad buy. But somehow Chris's Old Trafford career never took off and he never made the most of all that potential. He could go past a man, sometimes two or three, but usually he would ruin his good work by losing possession, which used to frustrate players and fans alike.

Chris was a quiet boy, and perhaps he just wasn't suited to the cut and thrust of top-level competition. Maybe it was telling that when he left United it was to play in Tulsa, then in Hong Kong, rather than remain in the game's mainstream for which his ability appeared to qualify him.

177. JONATHAN CLARK

OTHER CLUBS:
DERBY COUNTY 78/9-80/1 (53, 3);
PRESTON NORTH END 81/2-86/7 (110, 10);
BURY 86/7 (14, 1);
CARLISLE UNITED 87/8-88/9 (49, 2).

JONATHAN CLARK		
COMP.	APPS	GLS
LEAGUE	0 (1)	0
TOTAL	0 (1)	0

BORN	SWANSEA 12TH NOVEMBER 1958
POSITION	MIDFIELDER
JOINED UNITED	MARCH 1975 FROM JUNIOR FOOTBALL
UNITED DEBUT & FAREWELL	SUNDERLAND (H) DIV. 1 - 10/11/1976
LEFT UNITED FOR	DERBY COUNTY SEPT. 1978 - £50,000

When Jonathan Clark was 14, he was going to be the new superstar of English football. I can remember watching him at The Cliff, loving his classy passing, and thinking to myself that he must have a chance. Certainly Tommy Docherty fancied him for his life, so much so that when the lad couldn't break through with United, Doc took him to Derby.

But although Jonathan finished up playing more than 200 League games in total, the majority of them were in the lower divisions, and he never made anything like the splash that was expected of him. It was a pity because he was a naturally gifted footballer, but whereas he dazzled among the schoolboys, he didn't shine so brightly among the men.

ONWARD SEXTON'S SOLDIERS: left to right, back row: Kevin Moran, Jimmy Nicholl, Gordon McQueen, Paddy Roche, Gary Bailey, Steve Paterson, Ashley Grimes, Joe Jordan. Middle row: physiotherapist Laurie Brown, Sammy McIlroy, Andy Ritchie, Mike Duxbury, Tom Connell, Jimmy Greenhoff, Stewart Houston, trainer Tommy Cavanagh, manager Dave Sexton. Front row: Mickey Thomas, Tom Sloan, Lou Macari, Martin Buchan, Ray Wilkins, Steve Coppell, Arthur Albiston.

BORN	BARNSLEY 19TH JUNE 1946
POSITION	STRIKER
JOINED UNITED	NOVEMBER 1976 FROM STOKE CITY £120,000
UNITED DEBUT	LEICESTER CITY (A) DIV. 1 - 20/11/1976
UNITED HONOURS	FA CUP 1976/7
UNITED FAREWELL	NORWICH CITY (A) DIV. 1 - 06/12/1980
LEFT UNITED FOR	CREWE ALEXANDRA DECEMBER 1980

JIMMY GREENHOFF		
COMP.	APPS	GLS
LEAGUE	94 (3)	26
FAC	18 (1)	9
LC	4	1
EUROPE	2	0
OTHERS	1	0
TOTAL	119 (4)	36

178. JIMMY GREENHOFF

OTHER CLUBS:
LEEDS UNITED 62/3-68/9 (96, 19);
BIRMINGHAM CITY 68/9 (31, 14);
STOKE CITY 69/70-76/7 (274, 76);
CREWE ALEXANDRA 80/1 (11, 4);
TORONTO BLIZZARD, CANADA, 81;
PORT VALE 81/2-82/3 (48, 5);
ROCHDALE 82/3-83/4 (16, 0).

MANAGER:
ROCHDALE 1983-84.

Every night when Jimmy Greenhoff puts his head on the pillow, he could be excused for thinking: 'Now God, could you please explain to me why I never got an England cap?' I wish I could answer the question for him, but it's utterly beyond me.

Jimmy was one hell of a footballer but he wasn't in the slightest bit showy; rather he was a classical performer, one for the connoisseur.

The first thing you noticed about him was that he was so neat and tidy with his feet; it was almost beyond belief. No matter how the ball came to him, you could pretty well guarantee that it would stick.

True, he wasn't the heaviest of scorers for a front man, but he was such a beautifully subtle passer, so deadly in his positional play, so adept at setting up team-mates, that he must have been a dream to play alongside. When he came to United he was 30 and it might be argued that his peak had been reached at Stoke, where he had done wonders for Tony Waddington's team and where they loved him.

Even if that was the case, then certainly he found an overwhelmingly impressive second wind at Old Trafford, and when

he linked up with Stuart Pearson, it was like he had found a blood brother. They were on exactly the same wavelength, seeming to know instinctively where each other was going to run. Between them, they must have been a nightmare to mark.

Jimmy scored some colossally crucial goals for United, such as the delicate stooping header past Ray Clemence to beat Liverpool in a 1979 FA Cup semi-final replay at Goodison Park, though he knew nothing about the most important of all, the winner against the same opponents two years earlier in the final when a Lou Macari shot was deflected in off his chest.

Jimmy suffered pelvic problems and towards the end of his stay in Manchester he was written off by the surgeons a couple of times, but although he was a little bit slower after each comeback, still he had the sheer class to upset top-quality opponents right to the end.

Invariably Jimmy was used as a striker by United, but he was excellent also as a creative midfielder, a role he filled for part of his time at Stoke. I don't know whether Tommy Docherty or Dave Sexton ever considered playing him in a deeper position; I suppose it would have been a shame to remove him from the front line.

Even when he wasn't actually putting the ball into the net himself, he was largely responsible for the team not going short overall. If we employed the American system of 'assists' I think there would have been very few players in the First Division who would have outstripped the older Greenhoff.

It is impossible to replicate what Jimmy had, and there is no way that his brand of ability could be coached into a lesser performer. Either you're born with it or you're not. He was an absolute craftsman and it was a rare pleasure to watch him go about his business. Jim's a cracking fellow, too, so modest and unassuming, just the type of hero every dad would like his son to emulate.

BORN	DUBLIN 2ND AUGUST 1957
POSITION	MIDFIELDER, FULL-BACK
JOINED UNITED	MARCH 1977 FROM BOHEMIANS - £20,000
UNITED DEBUT	BIRMINGHAM CITY (A) DIV. 1 - 20/08/1977
UNITED FAREWELL	TOTTENHAM HOTSPUR (A) DIV. 1 - 11/05/1983
LEFT UNITED FOR	COVENTRY CITY AUG. 1983 - £200,000

ASHLEY GRIMES		
COMP.	APPS	GLS
LEAGUE	62 (28)	10
FAC	5	1
LC	6	0
EUROPE	4 (2)	0
TOTAL	77 (30)	11

179. ASHLEY GRIMES

OTHER HONOURS:
17 REPUBLIC OF IRELAND CAPS 1978-88.

OTHER CLUBS:
BOHEMIANS, REPUBLIC OF IRELAND;
COVENTRY CITY 83/4 (32, 1);
LUTON TOWN 84/5-88/9 (87, 3);
OSASUNA, SPAIN, 90/1; STOKE CITY 91/2 (10, 1).

I never quite worked out Ashley Grimes. What was he, first and foremost, a left-back or a left-sided midfielder? My personal view is that his best position was wide on the left, where I saw him put in some tremendous displays. He could pick out terrific passes with his left peg, the incisive sort of delivery that puts attackers in behind their markers.

Ashley's main problem was that he never quite managed to stake his claim for a regular long-term berth in the team. Always he seemed to be a six- or eight-game man, holding the fort until someone else came back from injury or suspension.

Certainly he was an invaluable fellow to have about the place, ready to fill in for anybody up the left-hand side of the team, but that sort of remit is never what a player wants for himself. Quite understandably, anyone worth his salt demands a position of his own, where he can feel secure.

Though he was competent enough at left-back, Ashley was never going to oust Arthur Albiston, and further forward he didn't quite fit the bill either for Dave Sexton or Ron Atkinson. After playing a key part in United's progress to the 1983 FA Cup Final, he must have been bitterly disappointed not to get a place at Wembley, and pretty soon afterwards he accepted a move to Coventry. Later he did have his day at Wembley, when he helped Luton to beat Arsenal in the League Cup Final of 1988.

BORN	NOTTINGHAM 26TH JANUARY 1960
DIED	RINGWOOD, HAMPSHIRE MARCH 1992
POSITION	FULL-BACK
JOINED UNITED	MAY 1976 FROM JUNIOR FOOTBALL
UNITED DEBUT & FAREWELL	WBA (A) DIV. 1 - 22/10/1977
LEFT UNITED FOR	QPR - JULY 1979

MARTYN ROGERS		
COMP.	APPS	GLS
LEAGUE	1	0
TOTAL	1	0

180. MARTYN ROGERS

OTHER CLUBS:
QUEEN'S PARK RANGERS 79/80 (2, 0).

Martyn Rogers' story is a particularly sad one. As a schoolboy he played for England and must have been brimming with hope when Dave Sexton called him up at the age of 17 to stand in at left-back for the injured Arthur Albiston.

That was to be his only chance at Old Trafford, but Tommy

Docherty remembered him from their United days together and took him to Queen's Park Rangers. Unfortunately he never became established at Loftus Road, either, soon being released by new boss Terry Venables. But worse was to come for poor Martyn, who was to die at the horribly premature age of 32.

181. ANDY RITCHIE

OTHER CLUBS:
BRIGHTON AND HOVE ALBION 80/1-82/3 (89, 23); LEEDS UNITED 82/3-86/7 (136, 40); OLDHAM ATHLETIC 87/8-94/5 (217, 82); SCARBOROUGH 95/6-96/7 (69, 17); OLDHAM ATHLETIC 96/7-97/8 (25, 2).

MANAGER:
OLDHAM ATHLETIC 1998-2001; BARNSLEY 2005-.

ANDY RITCHIE		
COMP.	APPS	GLS
LEAGUE	26 (7)	13
FAC	3 (1)	0
LC	3 (2)	0
TOTAL	32 (10)	13

BORN	MANCHESTER 28TH NOVEMBER 1960
POSITION	STRIKER
JOINED UNITED	SEPT. 1977 FROM JUNIOR FOOTBALL
UNITED DEBUT	EVERTON (A) DIV. 1 - 26/12/1977
UNITED FAREWELL	TOTTENHAM HOTSPUR (A) DIV. 1 - 06/09/1980
LEFT UNITED FOR	BRIGHTON OCT. 1980 - £500,000

The sale of Andy Ritchie was one of the worst moves Manchester United have made since the war. Here was a lad who had made 26 League starts and scored 13 goals, and they sold him to Brighton for £500,000.

I've heard it argued that the fee was pretty hefty for a teenager, but that fails to recognise that he was a genuine rarity, a natural top-quality finisher, and that he had at least another ten years to give the club.

How short-sighted can a manager be? If the boy was worth all that money to Brighton, who were going through a good patch but realistically could never match United's ambitions, then he must have been worth twice that to us.

Andy was only 17 when he was blooded by Dave Sexton on Boxing Day 1977, he was 18 when he banged in his first hat-trick (against Leeds) and 19 when he grabbed his second (against Spurs). Reasonable evidence, I'd submit, that United were on to a pretty good thing.

He wasn't the biggest of lads, but he was blessed with a strong build; he wasn't lightning quick, but he could accelerate when he had to; he was a skilful receiver and passer of the ball, and he appreciated other people on the pitch. But most important of all, Andy had this golden gift, this wonderful instinct for finding the net, something that is precious and can never be instilled into a footballer.

Coaching can help with some aspects of the game, dead-ball kicking for instance, but scoring goals is something that's either in your body, in your very being, or it isn't. It's an art form. Even Jimmy Greaves, arguably the finest finisher there has ever been, couldn't teach it – so if somebody who can do it can't teach it, how the hell can somebody teach it who can't

do it?

In the case of Andy, and in a wider sense, one of Sexton's most ridiculous mistakes was in retaining Tommy Cavanagh, the coach appointed earlier by Tommy Docherty. It was Cavanagh who talked Dave into selling Andy, and he was proud of it! My language when he told me that was not fit for family consumption.

Happily for Andy, after leaving United he succeeded everywhere he played, especially at Oldham when they were a club on the rise, and he kept going into his late thirties. What he might have achieved had he stayed at Old Trafford, linking up with better players, I tremble to contemplate.

Just to underline the stupidity of the decision to sell him, Andy is an absolutely smashing character, who wouldn't even know how to cause a manager trouble, and he loved Manchester United.

I had wondered about Sexton for a while, but it was this deal which convinced me that there was a serious flaw in his managerial make-up. How he could be influenced by Cavanagh, whose judgement of players was debatable, into parting with a gem like Andy Ritchie is beyond me. To call it a blunder is an understatement. In footballing terms, it was a major catastrophe.

BORN	CARLUKE, LANARKSHIRE 15TH DECEMBER 1951
POSITION	STRIKER
JOINED UNITED	JANUARY 1978 FROM LEEDS UNITED £350,000
UNITED DEBUT	WBA (H) FAC - 28/01/1978
UNITED FAREWELL	NORWICH CITY (H) DIV. 1 - 25/04/1981
LEFT UNITED FOR	AC MILAN, ITALY JULY 1981 - £175,000

JOE JORDAN		
COMP.	APPS	GLS
LEAGUE	109	37
FAC	11 (1)	2
LC	4	2
EUROPE	1	0
TOTAL	125 (1)	41

182. JOE JORDAN

OTHER HONOURS:
52 SCOTLAND CAPS 1972-82.

OTHER CLUBS:
MORTON 68/9-70/1 (12, 2);
LEEDS UNITED 71/2-77/8 (169, 35);
AC MILAN, ITALY, 81/2-82/3 (52, 12);
VERONA, ITALY, 83/4 (12, 1);
SOUTHAMPTON 84/5-86/7 (48, 12);
BRISTOL CITY 86/7-89/90 (57, 8).

MANAGER:
BRISTOL CITY 1988-90; HEART OF MIDLOTHIAN 1990-93;
STOKE CITY 1993-94; BRISTOL CITY 1994-97, PORTSMOUTH (CARETAKER) 2004.

I thought Joe Jordan was a bad, bad signing for Manchester United. He had been closely identified with Leeds and players develop something of the personality of any club where they spend a lot of time. Now, Leeds were one of United's closest rivals and I never felt wholly comfortable seeing Joe in a red shirt.

I gather that the majority of fans at Elland Road hated to see their hero crossing the Pennines to Old Trafford, but I can assure them there were plenty of folks in Manchester who were equally unhappy with the position.

Joe was a tall fellow, extremely strong and resilient and, in all fairness, he could be immensely effective in the air. Some of his more vitriolic critics – and he had a few – called him a carthorse, but he was never that, being capable of receiving the ball comfortably and of looking after it while other players ran into position.

I suppose he could be pretty fearsome when he was facing goal, but he didn't have any tricks, there was nothing special about him. Hand on heart, and without a shred of prejudice against Leeds, I felt he was no better than ordinary after coming to Manchester.

Certainly it bothered me that, for a main striker, he didn't score enough, though it might surprise a lot of people that his goals-to-games ratio at Old Trafford was a considerable improvement on what he managed at Elland Road.

Another problem I had with Joe was his heavy bias to his left side. I'm all for a balanced attack but his instinct was to move in that direction no matter what the situation, and then Dave Sexton made things worse by the barmy addition of another 'southpaw' in Garry Birtles.

Some reckon that Joe improved after his transfer, but I never bought into that theory because I maintain that it's a rare footballer who becomes better at the basics when he has reached his mid twenties.

I'm not disputing that he was integral to a successful set-up at Elland Road, and he wouldn't have won half a century of Scotland caps if he couldn't play, but no one will ever make me accept that Joe Jordan was a suitable acquisition for Manchester United.

183. GORDON McQUEEN

OTHER HONOURS:
30 SCOTLAND CAPS 1973-81.

OTHER CLUBS:
ST MIRREN 70/1-72/3 (57, 5);
LEEDS UNITED 72/3-77/8 (140, 15);
SEIKO, HONG KONG.

MANAGER:
AIRDRIEONIANS 1987-89.

GORDON McQUEEN		
COMP.	APPS	GLS
LEAGUE	184	20
FAC	21	2
LC	16	4
EUROPE	7	0
OTHERS	1	0
TOTAL	229	26

BORN	KILBIRNIE, AYRSHIRE 26TH JUNE 1952
POSITION	CENTRAL DEFENDER
JOINED UNITED	FEBRUARY 1978 FROM LEEDS UNITED - £500,000
UNITED DEBUT	LIVERPOOL (A) DIV. 1 - 25/02/1978
UNITED HONOURS	FA CUP 1982/3
UNITED FAREWELL	COVENTRY CITY (H) DIV. 1 - 12/01/1985
LEFT UNITED FOR	SEIKO, HK. - AUG. 1985 PLAYER/COACH

Gordon McQueen was a big, useful centre-half. That said, he always looked very leggy to me, cumbersome rather than comfortable, although I know that's a bit unjust because he did a pretty good job for Manchester United over a seven-year period.

Like his mate, Joe Jordan, he was indoctrinated in all things Leeds, which didn't recommend him to me, but he became very popular at Old Trafford and every now and again the crowd would erupt when he dashed forward like something out of the Charge of the Light Brigade.

But even while the fans were going wild with delight, I'd be cursing and thinking: 'For God's sake cross that ball and get back where you belong!' Perhaps it's fair to say that Gordon's positional play was not his strongest suit.

In fact, he was a ball-watcher and frequently prone to wander, which didn't make for a feeling of security at the back.

I could never quite understand why Dave Sexton was so keen to sign him, especially at the vast expense of £500,000. The size of the fee was mind-boggling for a defender at the time, and it wasn't even as though he was a footballing centre-half after the manner of, say, Paul McGrath, who came along a little later.

I thought there were plenty of better players knocking about, who would have been both available and considerably cheaper. If Jim Holton hadn't broken his leg a few years earlier, I don't suppose United would have been in the market for Gordon, and the two of them make a fascinating comparison.

Both were towering figures in the traditional stopper mould, but while Jim was raw and had something to learn, I preferred him to his fellow Scot.

At least you knew what you were getting with Holton, because he was a straight-up-and-downer, and you could safely bet on where he was going to be.

On the plus side for Gordon, he contributed quite a few goals with his commanding presence in opponents' penalty boxes and there was always a buzz of excitement from the supporters as he trundled forward at set pieces.

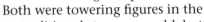

TRICKY: with uncharacteristic delicacy, Gordon McQueen tiptoes around the fallen Brian Talbot of Ipswich Town.

184. GARY BAILEY

OTHER HONOURS:
2 ENGLAND CAPS 1985

OTHER CLUBS:
KAISER CHIEFS, SOUTH AFRICA, 78.

GARY BAILEY		
COMP.	APPS	GLS
LEAGUE	294	0
FAC	31	0
LC	28	0
EUROPE	20	0
OTHERS	2	0
TOTAL	375	0

BORN	IPSWICH 9TH AUGUST 1958
POSITION	GOALKEEPER
JOINED UNITED	JANUARY 1978 FROM WITTS UNIVERSITY, SA
UNITED DEBUT	IPSWICH TOWN (H) DIV. 1 - 18/11/1978
UNITED HONOURS	FA CUP 1982/3, 1984/5
UNITED FAREWELL	SHEFFIELD WEDNESDAY (A) DIV. 1 - 21/03/1987
RETIRED	SEPT. 1987 - DUE TO INJURY

Gary Bailey was big, blond and overflowing with self-belief. In fact, I'd go as far as to say that if he was ever going to fall in love with anybody, then I'd be surprised if it wasn't himself.

But that mustn't obscure the fact that he was a fine goalkeeper who played 375 games for United in the space of nine years and would have made many more appearances if his career hadn't been halted by a knee injury at the age of 29.

Gary came from nowhere as far as most fans were concerned, being thrown in at the deep end when a deal to sign Jim Blyth from Coventry collapsed because of a failed medical.

That was a lucky escape for United because they had agreed to pay no less than £440,000 for Blyth, who didn't impress me in the slightest, and he wasn't able to play many games after the deal fell through.

Gary's first match was against Ipswich, with whom his father, another 'keeper name of Roy Bailey, had won the Championship back in 1961/62. After that the boy never looked back, making the place his own for the next eight years until his knee let him down.

Tall, muscular and athletic, he cut an imposing figure between the posts. Always ready to leave his line, he was a reliable catcher, he was brave, and if it hadn't been for Peter Shilton I'd guess he'd have picked up rather more than his couple of England caps.

Perhaps Gary Bailey fell slightly short of the very top class because of what was between his ears. I always got the impression that he thought he was the bee's knees, that somehow the game was all about him, and I think that sort of arrogance can be counter-productive.

BORN	BALLYMENA, N. IRELAND 10TH JULY 1959
POSITION	MIDFIELDER
JOINED UNITED	AUG. 1978 FROM BALLYMENA, N. IRELAND
UNITED DEBUT	IPSWICH TOWN (H) DIV. 1 - 18/11/1978
UNITED FAREWELL	COVENTRY CITY (H) DIV. 1 - 08/11/1980
LEFT UNITED FOR	CHESTER - AUG. 1982

TOM SLOAN		
COMP.	APPS	GLS
LEAGUE	4 (7)	0
LC	0 (1)	0
TOTAL	4 (8)	0

185. TOM SLOAN

OTHER HONOURS:
3 NORTHERN IRELAND CAPS 1979.
OTHER CLUBS:
BALLYMENA UNITED; CHESTER 82/3 (44, 3).

The United coach Tommy Cavanagh reckoned that Tom Sloan was going to be a world-beater. In fact, without wishing to be unkind to the lad, he was a midfield playmaker who couldn't play, certainly not at the top level.

Cavanagh had his own ideas about what made a decent footballer and when he told me, down at The Cliff training ground, that Sloan was special, then I expected the worst and I wasn't wrong.

The point is made in that here was an Irishman who spent four years at Manchester United and won only three caps. Normally that combination of club and country makes any player an automatic choice for Northern Ireland. My case rests.

BORN	MOCHDRE, NORTH WALES 7TH JULY 1954
POSITION	MIDFIELDER
JOINED UNITED	NOVEMBER 1978 FROM WREXHAM £300,000
UNITED DEBUT	CHELSEA (A) DIV. 1 - 25/11/1978
UNITED FAREWELL	CRYSTAL PALACE (H) DIV. 1 - 04/04/1981
LEFT UNITED FOR	EVERTON - AUGUST 1981 EXCHANGE FOR JOHN GIDMAN

MICKEY THOMAS		
COMP.	APPS	GLS
LEAGUE	90	11
FAC	13	2
LC	5	2
EUROPE	2	0
TOTAL	110	15

186. MICKEY THOMAS

OTHER HONOURS:
51 WALES CAPS 1977-86.
OTHER CLUBS:
WREXHAM 71/2-78/9 (230, 33);
EVERTON 81/2 (10, 0);
BRIGHTON AND HOVE ALBION 81/2 (20, 0);
STOKE CITY 82/3-83/4 (57, 14);
CHELSEA 83/4-84/5 (44, 9);
WEST BROMWICH ALBION 85/6 (20, 0);
DERBY COUNTY ON LOAN 85/6 (9, 0);
WICHITA WINGS, USA; SHREWSBURY TOWN 88/9 (40, 1); LEEDS UNITED 89/90 (3, 0);
STOKE CITY 89/90-90/1 (46, 7); WREXHAM 91/2-92/3 (34, 2).

Mickey Thomas was brought into the United side by Dave Sexton as a direct replacement for Gordon Hill on the left flank, and the two players could hardly have offered a more vivid contrast. Chalk is more similar to cheese than Mickey was to Gordon.

The little Welshman would do more running in one game than Hill would do in a month, but sometimes the result of all that effort was of debatable value.

Unquestionably Mickey was a wonderfully workmanlike footballer and he didn't lack ability, possessing a respectable left peg, so it's no surprise that he accumulated half a century of Welsh caps.

But he played at outside-left as though he was an old-fashioned left-half, a hive of industry who harassed anything that moved; whereas Gordon played at outside-left in the time-honoured manner, which meant that if he lost the ball then he was never going to fight to get it back.

Gordon appeared to think that retrieving possession was beneath his dignity, but we have to remember that he scored at least three times as many goals as Mickey. You pays your money and you takes your choice.

Mickey was a Dave Sexton-type of player whose attitude on the pitch couldn't be faulted, and he had his marvellous moments, such as delivering the perfect cross for Jimmy Greenhoff to nod an FA Cup semi-final replay winner against Liverpool at Goodison in 1979. But if you ask how regularly he damaged opponents at the attacking end of the field, then the answer has to be: 'Nowhere near as often as Gordon.'

In the end Mickey left United to become one of the game's wanderers, never regaining the stability that he'd known at his first club, Wrexham, and he got into a few scrapes away from the game. These days I see him often at Old Trafford and he's an endearingly cheerful soul, every bit as hyperactive now as he was in his playing days, and I wish him well.

187. TOM CONNELL

OTHER HONOURS:
1 NORTHERN IRELAND CAP 1978.

OTHER CLUBS:
COLERAINE AND GLENTORAN, NORTHERN IRELAND

TOM CONNELL		
COMP.	APPS	GLS
LEAGUE	2	0
TOTAL	2	0

BORN	NEWRY, N. IRELAND 25TH NOVEMBER 1957
POSITION	FULL-BACK
JOINED UNITED	AUG. 1978 FROM COLERAINE, N. IRELAND
UNITED DEBUT	BOLTON WANDERERS (A) DIV. 1 - 22/12/1978
UNITED FAREWELL	LIVERPOOL (H) DIV. 1 - 26/12/1978
LEFT UNITED FOR	GLENTORAN, N. IRELAND JUNE 1982

I'm afraid the case of Tom Connell is identical to that of his fellow Ulsterman, Tom Sloan, in that he was nowhere near as good as the coach made him out to be.

Certainly he was never up to playing for Manchester United, and after making his two appearances in the space of five days, deputising for Stewart Houston at left-back, he was never picked for the first team again. Instead he spent several years in the reserves before going home to Ireland.

BORN	DUBLIN 29TH JULY 1956
POSITION	CENTRAL DEFENDER
JOINED UNITED	FEBRUARY 1978 FROM PEGASUS, ROI
UNITED DEBUT	SOUTHAMPTON (A) DIV. 1 - 30/04/1979
UNITED HONOURS	FA CUP 1982/3, 1984/5
UNITED FAREWELL	NORWICH CITY (A) DIV. 1 - 05/03/1988
LEFT UNITED FOR	SPORTING GIJON, SPAIN AUGUST 1988

KEVIN MORAN		
COMP.	APPS	GLS
LEAGUE	228 (3)	21
FAC	18	1
LC	24 (1)	2
EUROPE	13 (1)	0
OTHERS	1	0
TOTAL	284 (5)	24

188. KEVIN MORAN

OTHER HONOURS:
71 REPUBLIC OF IRELAND CAPS 1980-94

OTHER CLUBS:
BOHEMIANS AND PEGASUS, BOTH REPUBLIC OF IRELAND;
SPORTING GIJON, SPAIN, 88/9;
BLACKBURN ROVERS 89/90-93/4 (147, 10).

It's clear that Alex Ferguson allowed Kevin Moran to leave Old Trafford too soon, even though the courageous one-time Gaelic footballer was 32 at the time.

After enjoying a productive ten-year stint with Manchester United, he disappeared for a spell in the Spanish sun with Gijon, but then re-surfaced at Blackburn, where he was good for another five terrific seasons. Under Kenny Dalglish, he played a massive part in the Rovers renaissance, earning promotion from the First Division and then proving that he still had the physical prowess required to flourish in the Premiership.

Kevin excelled at Ewood Park because he had learned so much down the years. Whereas in the early part of his career he had been a neck-or-nothing merchant, as he gained experience he found out that sometimes he could stand off his man instead of diving in and selling himself.

Undoubtedly in his youth he suffered a lot of injuries through his sheer bravery, throwing himself into reckless challenges while not appearing to worry overmuch whether he made contact with the ball or the fellow he was marking.

Unfortunately, he will always be remembered as the first man to be dismissed in an FA Cup Final, against Everton in 1985 when Peter Reid went flying through the air.

Nobody felt more sorry for Kevin than Reidy, who certainly didn't want him sent off. Both of the players involved were as honest as the

day is long but the referee was an officious sort, a policeman by profession and by nature, and an unwelcome slice of history was made.

189. RAY WILKINS

OTHER HONOURS:
84 ENGLAND CAPS 1976-86.

OTHER CLUBS:
CHELSEA 73/4–78/9 (179, 30);
AC MILAN 84/5–86/7 (73, 2);
PARIS ST GERMAIN 87/8 (10, 0);
GLASGOW RANGERS 87/8–89/90 (70, 2);
QUEEN'S PARK RANGERS 89/90–93/4 (154, 7);
CRYSTAL PALACE 94/5 (1, 0);
QUEEN'S PARK RANGERS 94/5–96/7 (21, 0);
WYCOMBE WANDERERS 96/7 (1, 0); HIBERNIAN 96/7 (16, 0);
MILLWALL 96/7 (3,0); LEYTON ORIENT 96/7 (3, 0).
MANAGER: QUEEN'S PARK RANGERS 1994–96; FULHAM AS CHIEF COACH 1997–98.

RAY WILKINS		
COMP.	APPS	GLS
LEAGUE	158 (2)	7
FAC	10	1
LC	14 (1)	1
EUROPE	8	1
OTHERS	1	0
TOTAL	191 (3)	10

BORN	HILLINGDON, MIDDLESEX 14TH SEPTEMBER 1956
POSITION	MIDFIELDER
JOINED UNITED	AUGUST 1979 FROM CHELSEA £825,000
UNITED DEBUT	SOUTHAMPTON (A) DIV. 1 - 18/08/1979
UNITED HONOURS	FA CUP 1982/3
UNITED FAREWELL	NOTTINGHAM FOREST (A) DIV. 1 - 16/05/1984
LEFT UNITED FOR	AC MILAN, ITALY JUNE 1984 - £1.5M

Ray Wilkins always looked a classy player, but I feel that by the time he joined Manchester United he was not moving forward with the same penetration that had distinguished him as a youthful prodigy with Chelsea.

He was still a beautiful passer, but too many of his deliveries seemed to go sideways or backwards, which was a waste, and eventually earned him the distinctly uncomplimentary nickname of 'The Crab' from Ron Atkinson.

Undoubtedly Ray had the ability to split defences with the so-called killer ball, but during his stay at United he rarely tried it, let alone achieved it. I felt he was lying too deep, presumably under orders, and as well as restricting the destructive possibilities of his distribution, it also cost him chances to go for goal. Surely, for a fellow who could strike the ball so cleanly, his return of a mere ten goals in nearly 200 games for the club was disappointing, and it compared pretty unfavourably with his return at Stamford Bridge.

At the time Dave Sexton bought him for a record fee, Ray was still only 22 and the general feeling was that he would graduate to become England captain for the foreseeable future. So although he cost an awful lot of money – Dave wasn't bad at spending vast sums – the perception was that it would be cash well spent.

But somewhere along the line, all that exciting talent became a trifle diluted, perhaps by a surfeit of coaching. Certainly for me, he never quite fulfilled his ultimate potential to become one of the outstanding midfield generals in the world, settling instead for the mantle of a

rather pedestrian wing-half. Not that Ray didn't represent extremely high quality, as he demonstrated not only at United, but also at AC Milan, whom he joined in 1984 after five years at Old Trafford, and after that at Queen's Park Rangers.

During his stint at Loftus Road there was some conjecture, or perhaps it was only newspaper talk, that he might return to Old Trafford, where the team was in need of creativity. But I could never see it happening. Alex Ferguson liked his midfielders to be box-to-box merchants, and Ray was never that.

Later on he surprised me by playing on for such a long time at a lower level, something which few footballers of Ray's repute tend to do. Perhaps he just couldn't bear the thought of stopping, even when he was 40 at Leyton Orient, but at that stage I think there's an element of outstaying your welcome.

Off the pitch, Ray's a likeable individual, though I wish he would lighten up a bit in his occasional role as a television pundit. I tend to find him boring rather than scintillating; surely he can't be that serious 24 hours a day!

BORN	CETINJE, YUGOSLAVIA 18TH SEPTEMBER 1952
POSITION	CENTRAL DEFENDER MIDFIELDER
JOINED UNITED	JAN 1980 FROM RED STAR BELGRADE £350,000
UNITED DEBUT	DERBY COUNTY (A) DIV. 1 - 02/02/1980
UNITED FAREWELL	LEICESTER CITY (A) DIV. 1 - 07/02/1981
LEFT UNITED FOR	BUDUCNOST, YUGOSLAVIA NOV. 1982 - AFTER LOAN

NIKKI JOVANOVIC		
COMP.	APPS	GLS
LEAGUE	20 (1)	4
FAC	1	0
LC	2	0
EUROPE	2	0
TOTAL	25 (1)	4

190. NIKKI JOVANOVIC

OTHER HONOURS:
YUGOSLAVIA CAPS.
OTHER CLUBS:
RED STAR BELGRADE AND BUDUCNOST, YUGOSLAVIA

Nikki Jovanovic was United's first foreign import and, although he was an established Yugoslavian international, he was by no means a household name. Sadly, his stay at Old Trafford offered him precious little chance of becoming one.

He had a bit of a problem with the language, which couldn't have helped, and he never really had a settled position, which was not his fault but the manager's. When he made such a major purchase, Dave Sexton should have known where he was going to play the lad.

Nikki was a big, strapping fellow and most people knew him as a central defender, but often Dave played him in midfield. Perhaps putting defenders in advanced positions was part of his precious coaching theory, but I could never agree with it. I know there has got to be a blend of abilities, but for me the midfield is primarily for expression.

All this is not to imply that Nikki was a bad footballer. In fact, he was comfortable on the ball and was talented enough to use it, but I think United did him a disservice on occasions by playing him in the wrong role. At times he was on a hiding to nothing and it was hardly a surprise that he made no lasting impression.

Here's quite a common problem, which may or may not be relevant to Nikki's case, I can't be sure. A player is recommended to a club, and because he doesn't look a world-beater in his first few games, people start casting aspersions, talking the manager into experimenting before the newcomer has had a fair chance to acclimatise.

At that point the manager has to have the strength of his own convictions and have faith in his player over a reasonable period of time. If he doesn't then the footballer becomes a victim of impatience and indecision and, inevitably, pretty soon he moves on.

191. MICK DUXBURY

OTHER HONOURS:
10 ENGLAND CAPS 1983-84.

OTHER CLUBS:
BLACKBURN ROVERS 90/1-91/2 (27, 0);
BRADFORD CITY 91/2-93/4 (66, 0).

MIKE DUXBURY		
COMP.	APPS	GLS
LEAGUE	274 (25)	6
FAC	20 (5)	1
LC	32 (2)	0
EUROPE	17 (1)	0
OTHERS	2	0
TOTAL	345 (33)	7

BORN	ACCRINGTON, LANCASHIRE 1ST SEPTEMBER 1959
POSITION	FULL-BACK, MIDFIELDER
JOINED UNITED	JULY 1976 FROM JUNIOR FOOTBALL
UNITED DEBUT	BIRMINGHAM CITY (A) DIV. 1 - 23/08/1980
UNITED HONOURS	FA CUP 1982/3, 1984/5
UNITED FAREWELL	NOTTINGHAM FOREST (A) DIV. 1 - 02/05/1990
LEFT UNITED FOR	BLACKBURN R. - AUG. 1990

Whether you call him a versatile utility man, or a failed midfielder who became a full-back, Mick Duxbury did an excellent job for Manchester United over ten years and under three managers.

As in the cases of Arthur Albiston and Kevin Moran, I believe he was released prematurely by Alex Ferguson after he had taken over as manager from Ron Atkinson. After all, Mick was only 31, with vast experience and a sound character, and I think he would have been eminently suited to become the old head of the reserve team, passing on invaluable knowhow to the promising youngsters that Alex was bringing through.

My only reservation on that score is that I'm not sure whether he was enough of a shouter on the field to exert the necessary influence; Alex would know that better than me. In Mick's own prime, although he could play anywhere in midfield or defence – he wore eight different numbers on his back during 1980/81,

his debut season – undoubtedly his premier position was right-back, which is where he won all ten of his England caps in the space of 11 months.

Mick made an impressive start in international football, but then he dropped a few rickets and his confidence seemed to evaporate. Perhaps he was marginally short of class for the very highest level, but that doesn't alter the fact that he was a damned good First Division operator whom any club would have been delighted to accommodate.

He picked up his two FA Cup medals with Ron Atkinson and then he went through the leanest period of the Ferguson regime in the shadow of Viv Anderson, who was Alex's first signing. I suppose the fact that the new manager brought in Viv so quickly indicates that he didn't see Mick as top class, which reminds us that football is a sport dominated by opinion. But certainly Alex, like everyone else who had dealings with Mick Duxbury, will acknowledge that he was a magnificent servant to the club.

BORN	GLASGOW 22ND APRIL 1963
POSITION	STRIKER
JOINED UNITED	JUNE 1979 FROM JUNIOR FOOTBALL
UNITED DEBUT	LEICESTER CITY (H) DIV. 1 - 13/09/1980
UNITED FAREWELL	TOTTENHAM HOTSPUR (A) DIV. 1 - 11/05/1983
LEFT UNITED FOR	PORTSMOUTH - JULY 1984

192. SCOTT McGARVEY

SCOTT McGARVEY		
COMP.	APPS	GLS
LEAGUE	13 (12)	3
TOTAL	13 (12)	3

OTHER CLUBS:
WOLVERHAMPTON WANDERERS ON LOAN 83/4 (13, 2); PORTSMOUTH 84/5-85/6 (23, 6); CARLISLE UNITED, FIRST ON LOAN 85/6-86/7 (35, 11); GRIMSBY TOWN 86/7-87/8 (50, 7); BRISTOL CITY 88/9 (26, 9); OLDHAM ATHLETIC 89/90 (4, 1); WIGAN ATHLETIC ON LOAN 89/90 (3, 0); MAZDA, JAPAN, 90.

Scott McGarvey might be described as a bit of a legend in his own memory. He had plenty of talent, but what he did with it at times, God only knows. He was the next bright young striker to emerge after Andy Ritchie, but he was unlike Andy in that he couldn't apply his gifts consistently to the business of scoring goals and winning matches.

It's a hard thing to say, but I think Scott became rather carried away with being a footballer without putting enough into it. His career path after leaving Old Trafford shows that he never settled anywhere for very long, which suggests that maybe he didn't have the necessary commitment. Undoubtedly Scott was not short of the attributes demanded of a successful marksman. He had a fine first touch, he was a clean striker of the ball, he was quick enough and he had decent stature.

There were a lot of people at Old Trafford who believed he had a hell of a chance of making it to the top, particularly Dave Sexton, Tommy Cavanagh and another coach, Syd Owen, who was convinced that he would mature into a world-beater. So it added up to a sad waste. In Scott McGarvey's mind he was good enough, he had the talent to be good enough, but he lacked application.

193. GARRY BIRTLES

OTHER HONOURS:
3 ENGLAND CAPS 1980.

OTHER CLUBS:
NOTTINGHAM FOREST 76/7-80/1 (87, 32)
& 82/3-86/7 (125, 38);
NOTTS COUNTY 87/8-88/9 (63, 9);
GRIMSBY TOWN 89/90-91/2 (69, 9).

GARRY BIRTLES		
COMP.	APPS	GLS
LEAGUE	57 (1)	11
FAC	4	1
LC	2	0
TOTAL	63 (1)	12

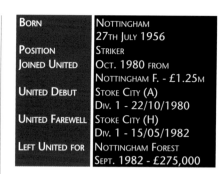

BORN	NOTTINGHAM 27TH JULY 1956
POSITION	STRIKER
JOINED UNITED	OCT. 1980 FROM NOTTINGHAM F. - £1.25M
UNITED DEBUT	STOKE CITY (A) DIV. 1 - 22/10/1980
UNITED FAREWELL	STOKE CITY (H) DIV. 1 - 15/05/1982
LEFT UNITED FOR	NOTTINGHAM FOREST SEPT. 1982 - £275,000

I felt sorry for Garry Birtles. He was signed for a huge fee by Dave Sexton, with all the consequent expectations that entails, and then was asked to play alongside Joe Jordan, who was never going to be his ideal partner.

They were both strongly left-sided players, and both of them would move in that direction at every opportunity, which meant they were bound to get in each other's way.

Garry had done well at Nottingham Forest, though it should be understood that a lot of people excelled there but not elsewhere. Brian Clough had a set pattern of play which suited his team, and if you were at Cloughie's club you either did what he said or you were on your bike.

It was perfect for Garry because that pattern was predominantly left-sided, and it called for him to make constant runs along the left flank with, say, Trevor Francis making the runs in the central areas.

When he tried a similar strategy at United it failed because he and Joe were often covering the same ground. It might be thought that I'm insulting the intelligence of everyone involved if I suggested that an experienced coach such as Dave Sexton did not foresee that problem, which is why I was, and I remain, bewildered by the whole situation.

I can't conceive that he had to throw Joe and Garry into the same team to realise that this confusing duplication was bound to come about, because it's impossible to teach new fundamentals to mature players.

Poor Garry made the worst imaginable start for a striker, not scoring until his 30th game, and although I was never his biggest fan, he was better than that. He demonstrated that much by his improved strike-rate when Jordan left and he linked up with Frank Stapleton, who gravitated naturally to the right. Here was solid evidence that, in tandem with Joe, Garry simply hadn't had a fair crack of the whip.

But that didn't alter what was an unbelievable scenario regarding United's strike-force. At one point they had two men in their mid twenties, Jordan and Birtles, who were never especially prolific; and one in his teens, Andy Ritchie, who scored goals for fun.

What did they do? They sold the one who was young and prolific. Could that ever make sense? Not to me. Finally, to compound the madness, Garry was sent back to Forest with United taking a loss of £1 million. It beggared belief.

194. ANTO WHELAN

OTHER CLUBS:
BOHEMIANS, SHAMROCK ROVERS (TWICE), CORK, BRAY WANDERERS, SHELBOURNE, ALL REPUBLIC OF IRELAND.

ANTO WHELAN		
COMP.	APPS	GLS
LEAGUE	0 (1)	0
TOTAL	0 (1)	0

BORN	DUBLIN 23RD NOVEMBER 1959
POSITION	DEFENDER
JOINED UNITED	AUG. 1980 FROM BOHEMIANS, ROI, £30,000
UNITED DEBUT & FAREWELL	SOUTHAMPTON (H) DIV. 1 - 29/11/1980
LEFT UNITED FOR	SHAMROCK ROVERS JUNE 1983

It's impossible to pass realistic judgement on the first-team career of the young Irishman Anto Whelan because it lasted only a few minutes, after he was called on as a substitute for the injured Kevin Moran against Southampton.

Clearly Dave Sexton rated the lad, or he wouldn't have paid £30,000 for him, but it was always going to be a difficult job to get past the likes of such experienced and high-quality central defenders as Kevin, Gordon McQueen, Paul McGrath and Martin Buchan, and Anto gave up the ghost after three years in United's reserves.

195. JOHN GIDMAN

OTHER HONOURS:
1 ENGLAND CAP 1977.
OTHER CLUBS:
ASTON VILLA 72/3-79/80 (197, 9);
EVERTON 79/80-80/1 (64, 2);
MANCHESTER CITY 86/7-87/8 (53, 1);
STOKE CITY 88/9 (10, 0);
DARLINGTON 88/9 (13, 1).

JOHN GIDMAN		
COMP.	APPS	GLS
LEAGUE	94 (1)	4
FAC	9	0
LC	5	0
EUROPE	7 (2)	0
OTHERS	1 (1)	0
TOTAL	116 (4)	4

BORN	LIVERPOOL 10TH APRIL 1954
POSITION	FULL-BACK
JOINED UNITED	AUGUST 1981 FROM EVERTON IN EXCHANGE FOR MICKEY THOMAS
UNITED DEBUT	COVENTRY CITY (A) DIV. 1 - 29/08/1981
UNITED HONOURS	FA CUP 1984/5
UNITED FAREWELL	LEICESTER CITY (H) DIV. 1 - 26/04/1986
LEFT UNITED FOR	MAN.CITY - OCTOBER 1986

Most clubs would have been happy to have John Gidman as their right-back, and most crowds would have loved him as much as they did at Old Trafford. Now, coming from a Mancunian, that's not an ungenerous tribute to a Scouser!

John was a swashbuckling right-back who liked nothing better than to bomb down the touchline. He had impressive pace and skills to match, but he didn't allow his adventurous forward sorties to compromise his defensive duties, and there was a touch of flamboyance about him which made him a natural entertainer. That's not something you can say about a lot of defenders.

Clearly Ron Atkinson, another Liverpudlian, fancied John to bits because he lost no time in making him his first signing after taking over as manager of Manchester United, and I suppose John reflected Ron's footballing philosophy to a fair extent.

The down-side to that was that it cost Jimmy Nicholl his future at the club, which has to go down as part of the game's rich tapestry of amazing happenings. I wouldn't say that John's arrival weakened the side in any way, but Jimmy was a couple of years younger and well bedded in at United. I don't know why Ron saw so little in him, but that's his prerogative.

I'm surprised that John, who was an apprentice at Anfield before being released by Bill Shankly and starting afresh with Aston Villa, never won more than a single England cap. Apart from a firework accident which nearly cost him an eye when he was 20, he never suffered many injuries, at least not until he came to United, where his fitness record became patchy.

John was overjoyed to play a part in beating his former club, Everton, in the 1985 FA Cup Final, and was looking forward to a tilt at the League title during the following season, only to break his leg in the second game, at Ipswich.

He bounced back from that but then Johnny Sivebaek arrived and Gidman went to Maine Road on a free transfer. These days he lives in Spain, reportedly in deep contentment.

196. FRANK STAPLETON

OTHER HONOURS:
70 REPUBLIC OF IRELAND CAPS 1976-90.

OTHER CLUBS:
ARSENAL 74/5-80/1 (225, 75);
AJAX, HOLLAND, 87/8 (4, 0);
DERBY COUNTY ON LOAN 87/8 (10, 1);
LE HAVRE, FRANCE, 88/9;
BLACKBURN ROVERS 89/90-90/1 (81, 13);
ALDERSHOT ON LOAN 91/2 (1, 0);
HUDDERSFIELD TOWN 91/2 (5, 0);
BRADFORD CITY 91/2-93/4 (68, 2).

MANAGER:
BRADFORD CITY 1991-94.

FRANK STAPLETON		
COMP.	APPS	GLS
LEAGUE	204 (19)	60
FAC	21	7
LC	26 (1)	6
EUROPE	14 (1)	5
OTHERS	2	0
TOTAL	267 (21)	78

BORN	DUBLIN 10TH JULY 1956
POSITION	STRIKER
JOINED UNITED	AUGUST 1981 FROM ARSENAL FOR £900,000
UNITED DEBUT	COVENTRY CITY (A) DIV. 1 - 29/08/1981
UNITED HONOURS	FA CUP 1982/3, 1984/5
UNITED FAREWELL	WIMBLEDON (H) DIV. 1 - 02/05/1987
LEFT UNITED FOR	AJAX - AUGUST 1987

Frank Stapleton was a very fine centre-forward for Arsenal, and he was by no means a disaster for Manchester United. But given the shining reputation he had forged at Highbury, the Old Trafford fans never saw quite the influential player they expected.

Here was a man with the same name, the same qualities and the same number on his back, but the fact was that often he played in a different position for United.

For Arsenal, invariably, Frank lined up in the middle, but at United he spent loads of his time in wide areas which, I believe, limited his effectiveness. Not that he was selected on the wing, just that he seemed to drift there during games, and it surprised me.

His great strength was upstairs, but the way he played for Ron Atkinson meant that he was not always best placed to make the most of his prodigious aerial expertise.

Of course, Frank was an immensely gifted all-round footballer with an assured touch, very good at holding the ball and at neat lay-offs which kept attacks moving. His work wasn't always spectacular but it meant a lot to the team.

He was never an especially prolific marksman, neither for club nor country – though for a while he was the Republic of Ireland's leading scorer – and while he wasn't the quickest, you don't get to play 500 games in the front line for Arsenal and Manchester United without being a reasonably sharp mover.

In view of the vast expectations he brought with him when he moved north, some critics have described Frank as a disappointment for United, but I think that's unduly harsh. It should always be remembered that when things don't appear to run smoothly for a player, it's not always his fault.

In Stapleton's case, for instance, was all the running wide his own idea or was it one of the team's tactical ploys? I would imagine there was some managerial influence in there somewhere.

Frank played alongside an assortment of striking partners at Old Trafford – including Garry Birtles, Norman Whiteside, Mark Hughes, Alan Brazil, Peter Davenport and Terry Gibson – but the one I'd have liked to link him with was Gary Lineker.

I'm told by a reliable source that Atkinson was once offered Lineker but said he didn't need him because he'd got Alan Brazil. Now I know Ron liked people who could play and I could never understand why he preferred Brazil to Lineker, who could have made a massive difference to United in the mid 1980s.

Frank was Ron's first really big signing, one he had been forced to make by the loss of Joe Jordan to AC Milan. Personally I thought it was an acceptable change. If I was offered either Joe or Frank for my team, I'd go for Frank every time.

Later Frank managed Bradford City, with Stuart Pearson as his assistant, and then went on to coach for Sam Allardyce at Bolton.

197. REMI MOSES

OTHER CLUBS:
WEST BROMWICH ALBION 79/80-81/2 (63, 5).

REMI MOSES		
COMP.	APPS	GLS
LEAGUE	143 (7)	7
FAC	11	1
LC	22 (2)	4
EUROPE	12 (1)	0
OTHERS	0 (1)	0
TOTAL	188 (11)	12

BORN	MANCHESTER 14TH NOVEMBER 1960
POSITION	MIDFIELDER
JOINED UNITED	SEPTEMBER 1981 FROM WBA FOR £650,000
UNITED DEBUT	SWANSEA CITY (H) DIV. 1 - 19/09/1981
UNITED FAREWELL	WIMBLEDON (H) DIV. 1 - 09/05/1988
RETIRED	JUNE 1988 - DUE TO INJURY

I never saw in Remi Moses what Ron Atkinson appeared to see. To me he was an exceptionally ordinary performer and not a United player by any stretch of the imagination.

Remi was touted as a terrific ball-winner, and perhaps he was, but I've always believed there's not a lot of point in winning the ball if you don't know what to do with it when you've got it.

If you pay £650,000, which was a lot of money in 1981, I think you were entitled to more than a lad who wasn't afraid to put his foot in. Perhaps Remi was never any more than the sprat thrown to West Bromwich Albion so that United could catch the mackerel, the man they really wanted, Bryan Robson.

I know that Ron thought the world of Remi, and all managers have their pet players. He's entitled to his opinion and he won't shake me from mine. That said, there's no doubt that Remi had rotten luck with injuries after he arrived at Old Trafford, and in the end he was forced to retire with ankle trouble when he was only 27. Having faced similar heartache myself, I wouldn't wish that on anyone.

His fitness problems cost him the chance of an FA Cup Final appearance in 1985 – he had missed the 1983 final because of suspension – and also he was forced to withdraw from an England squad after being called up by Bobby Robson. He never did win a cap.

Remi was unusual in that he was born in Manchester, then started his career at West Bromwich before returning to his home city to join United. He was always a quiet, shy fellow, and that hasn't changed, because strenuous efforts to contact him by the Former Players Association have failed.

BORN	CHESTER-LE-STREET, CO. DURHAM 11TH JANUARY 1957
POSITION	MIDFIELDER
JOINED UNITED	OCTOBER 1981 FROM WBA FOR £1.5M
UNITED DEBUT	TOTTENHAM H. (A) LC - 07/10/1981
UNITED HONOURS	ECWC 1990/1 PREMIERSHIP 1992/3, 1993/4 FA CUP 1982/3, 1984/5, 1989/90
UNITED FAREWELL	COVENTRY CITY (H) DIV. 1 - 08/05/1994
LEFT UNITED FOR	MIDDLESBROUGH MAY 1994 PLAYER/MANAGER

BRYAN ROBSON		
COMP.	APPS	GLS
LEAGUE	326 (20)	74
FAC	33 (2)	10
LC	50 (1)	5
EUROPE	26 (1)	8
OTHERS	2 (1)	2
TOTAL	437 (25)	99

198. BRYAN ROBSON

OTHER HONOURS:
90 ENGLAND CAPS 1980-91.
OTHER CLUBS:
WEST BROMWICH ALBION 74/5-81/2 (198, 39);
MIDDLESBROUGH 94/5-96/7 (25, 1).
MANAGER:
MIDDLESBROUGH 1994-2001;
BRADFORD CITY 2003-04
WEST BROMWICH ALBION 2004-.

Signing Bryan Robson for £1.5 million, even though it was a British record fee in 1981 and seemed like riches beyond imagining at the time, was the equivalent of recruiting one of the world's top players on a free. I didn't agree with everything Bill Shankly said, but when he advised Ron Atkinson to pay West Bromwich Albion whatever it took to sign Robbo, he was spot on.

Bryan was one of the best players in Manchester United's history, and if you were naming the ten finest at Old Trafford since the war, he's got to be among them.

He was predominantly left-sided, and wasn't outstanding with his right foot, but apart from that he had everything. He was a monumental tackler, he was exceptionally strong in the air, he got on the end of things and scored goals more effectively than pretty well any other midfielder you could name. In fact, it was nothing short of phenomenal that he should hit the target nearly a century of times from midfield.

Ask any of his team-mates. They'll tell you, to a man, that if they were in trouble on the pitch (or off it, come to that) the odds were that he would be there to help them out. Bryan was everywhere, seeking out trouble and dealing with it. He didn't make a fuss about it, just got on and did his job to a standard that no one else in his generation could equal.

I was disappointed when Robbo left United because, although he was 37,

'They put Bryan back together so often he was like the Six Million Dollar Man, except he was worth more than that.'

he had plenty still to offer in terms of inspiration. I know he had an attractive player-management offer at Middlesbrough, and United had Paul Ince and Roy Keane, so I suppose it was not surprising. But I happen to believe that Robson at 37 was still a better player than Ince would be in the whole of his life.

What a pity that Bryan wasn't just a few years younger so he could have enjoyed all the modern success that United have had. Considering the service he gave the club, and the all pain he suffered on its behalf, it would have been lovely if could have enjoyed all the fruits. At least it was a nice touch when Steve Bruce, as skipper of United, insisted that the old feller joined him to receive the first Premier League trophy in 1993.

Comparing 'Captain Marvel' to Keane, I would say they were very close. Robbo got on the end of things better than Roy, but wouldn't you love a team with both of them in it?

When you look at Bryan's record, and take into account all the injuries he suffered, he was a giant of the modern game. But for all those unscheduled absences, the product of his own astonishing bravery, I'm sure he would have exceeded Bobby Moore's total of 108 England caps, which is still a record for an outfielder.

What amazed me was the way he would repeatedly return from serious injury, time and time again, raring to go, his energy, enthusiasm and will to win utterly undiluted. They put Bryan back together so often he was like the Six Million Dollar Man, except he was worth more than that.

It's all too easy to describe footballers as great, and I get sick of hearing it these days, but in Robbo's case it was more than justified. Yet for all the accolades that went his way so deservedly, he has remained a star off the field as well as on it.

BORN	BELFAST 7TH MAY 1965
POSITION	MIDFIELDER, STRIKER
JOINED UNITED	JUNE 1981 FROM IRISH JUNIOR FOOTBALL
UNITED DEBUT	BRIGHTON & HA (A) DIV. 1 - 24/04/1982
UNITED HONOURS	FA CUP 1982/3, 1984/5
UNITED FAREWELL	SOUTHAMPTON (A) DIV. 1 - 06/05/1989
LEFT UNITED FOR	EVERTON AUG. 1989 - £600,000

NORMAN WHITESIDE		
COMP.	APPS	GLS
LEAGUE	193 (13)	47
FAC	24	10
LC	26 (3)	9
EUROPE	11 (2)	1
OTHERS	2	0
TOTAL	256 (18)	67

199. NORMAN WHITESIDE

OTHER HONOURS:
38 NORTHERN IRELAND CAPS 1982-89.
OTHER CLUBS:
EVERTON 89/90-90/1 (29, 9).

Norman Whiteside had enormous God-given talent. Originally he was a front player, then he moved back to midfield with striking success, and that's where he gave his most influential performances.

He did it all very early, including taking Pele's record as the youngest man to appear in a World Cup tournament when he was only 16. Then, sadly, his injuries caught up with him, and at the tender age of 24 he was on his way out of United to join Everton, with very few miles left on his clock.

The one attribute Norman lacked was pace, which was why he was withdrawn from the role of spearhead, but he was endowed with tremendous ball skills, he was excellent in the air, he was as strong as a dozen oxes and, sure as hell, he was frightened of nobody.

Norman scored goals which were spectacular, many of them on the grandest of stages. He had all the class and composure of a top striker, even if it became evident pretty soon that he was short of acceleration. But even after he dropped back to become a midfielder, whenever he found himself in an advanced position, the expert striker took over and he could finish superbly.

Probably, towards the end of his United days, Norman strayed towards an over-physical approach, which gained him a lurid reputation. Indeed, when comparing two team-mates who never shirked a challenge in their lives, critics claimed that there was a certain malice in Whiteside that was never present in Bryan Robson.

My view is that maybe Norman was excessive at times, but that I could imagine his behaviour being fuelled by the frustration of his own ever-worsening injury situation. Certainly, by that stage of his career, he was wracked with aches and pains most of the time he was on a football pitch.

Whatever the rights and wrongs of that, and of his well-documented habit of taking a beer or two, Norman Whiteside was one hell of a player and a talisman for the fans who adored him.

Twice he played a massive part in

Norman Whiteside threatens the Arsenal goal with a left-foot thunderbolt despite the close attention of Kenny Sansom.

United winning the FA Cup, scoring in the finals of 1983 and 1985, and it would have been fitting for that group of players to have won the title. I think they deserved it, and undoubtedly they should have done it in 1985/86, when they won their first ten games and didn't lose until their 16th.

200. ALAN DAVIES

OTHER HONOURS:
11 WALES CAPS 1983-90.

OTHER CLUBS:
NEWCASTLE UNITED 85/6-86/7 (21, 1);
CHARLTON ATHLETIC ON LOAN 85/6 (1, 0);
CARLISLE UNITED ON LOAN 86/7 (4, 1);
SWANSEA CITY 87/8-88/9 (84, 8);
BRADFORD CITY 89/90 (26, 1);
SWANSEA CITY 90/1-91/2 (43, 4).

ALAN DAVIES		
COMP.	APPS	GLS
LEAGUE	6 (1)	0
FAC	2	0
EUROPE	0 (1)	1
TOTAL	8 (2)	1

BORN	MANCHESTER 5TH DECEMBER 1961
DIED	GOWER, S. WALES 4TH FEBRUARY 1992
POSITION	MIDFIELDER
JOINED UNITED	JULY 1978 FROM JUNIOR FOOTBALL
UNITED DEBUT	SOUTHAMPTON (H) DIV. 1 - 01/05/1982
UNITED HONOURS	FA CUP 1982/3
UNITED FAREWELL	EVERTON (A) DIV. 1 - 05/05/1984
LEFT UNITED FOR	NEWCASTLE UNITED JULY 1985 - £50,000

Alan Davies is the saddest case of all, God bless him, because he took his own life. He had an unusual United career in that twice he contested the FA Cup at Wembley, and he earned a winner's medal, yet he totalled only eight starts for the club. His big moment came against Brighton in 1983, when the game went to a replay in which he set up the opening goal for Bryan Robson.

Alan got his chance at Wembley because of Steve Coppell's knee trouble, though fundamentally he wasn't a natural winger, rather a central midfielder. He never became a regular first-teamer with United, being a tidy, workmanlike performer rather than an exceptional one, yet no one knows what might

BORN	VOLENDAM, HOLLAND 2ND JUNE 1951
POSITION	MIDFIELDER.
JOINED UNITED	AUGUST 1982 FROM IPSWICH TOWN
UNITED DEBUT	BIRMINGHAM CITY (H) DIV. 1 - 28/08/1982
UNITED HONOURS	FA CUP 1982/3
UNITED FAREWELL	WATFORD (A) DIV. 1 - 13/05/1985
LEFT UNITED FOR	AJAX - JUNE 1985

have happened had he not suffered horrendous luck with injuries.

Almost immediately after his joyful cup final experience, Alan played for Wales against Brazil, but then everything started to go downhill. He broke his ankle, and took a long time to get over it, then he moved to Newcastle where he suffered a fractured leg.

After that he played in the lower divisions and it was during his second stint at Swansea that he committed suicide. What possessed him to do such a thing, at the age of 31 and with a wife and family, only he and his maker will ever know.

The horror of Alan Davies' death serves to put football firmly into its rightful perspective. People talk so glibly about the game's so-called tragedies, but this was the real thing.

201. ARNOLD MUHREN

ARNOLD MUHREN		
COMP.	APPS	GLS
LEAGUE	65 (5)	13
FAC	8	1
LC	11	1
EUROPE	8	3
OTHERS	1	0
TOTAL	93 (5)	18

OTHER HONOURS:
23 HOLLAND CAPS 1978-88.

OTHER CLUBS:
AJAX AND TWENTE ENSCHEDE, BOTH HOLLAND; IPSWICH TOWN 78/9-81/2 (161, 21); AJAX 85/6-87/8.

Arnold Muhren was as fine a signing as Ron Atkinson ever made. In fact, despite all the stars who have graced Old Trafford during my lifetime, I don't think I've ever seen a footballer with a more devastatingly accurate left peg.

The Dutchman was blessed with extravagant skills, and he brought the best out of his high-quality team-mates. For example, Bryan Robson never carried more of a goal threat than when Arnie was at his side, pulling the strings.

Muhren had the priceless ability of picking people out and anticipating their runs into dangerous positions. It was almost as if he was thinking several frames ahead of the action.

He chipped in with quite a few goals, too, although admittedly a lot of them were from the penalty spot, for example in the 1983 FA Cup Final replay against Brighton.

Yet for all the magnificence of Muhren, and all the respect he enjoyed at Old Trafford, somehow he remained an unobtrusive figure. Since he's left United I've barely heard his name mentioned around the club. I'm quite amazed by that because he was an exceptionally superb performer, the sort that doesn't come along every season, and he deserves to be remembered with pride.

Okay, I go along with the view that he was probably more

effective at home than he was away, though a lot of talented players down the eras have fallen into that category. It's a fact that the team is set up to play differently when they are on their travels, tending to rely more on the counter-attack.

Arnold was already 31 when he arrived in Manchester, having forged an enviable reputation alongside his countryman Frans Thijssen at Ipswich. He enjoyed fabulous times with Ajax and Holland, and continued to excel on the international stage even after Ron let him go.

So, with the benefit of hindsight, did the manager dispense with his services a bit early? Well, he was in his mid-thirties and had barely played in his last term in Manchester, so the decision was understandable.

Whatever, he fulfils my most important requirement – he had quality. Arnie Muhren was a real Manchester United player. Had he joined the Red Devils instead of Ipswich, when he was 27 years old and on the verge of his prime, then he'd have been acclaimed as one of the club's greatest ever players.

As it was, he gave us a couple of wonderful years before slipping out of the picture

202. PETER BEARDSLEY

OTHER HONOURS:
59 ENGLAND CAPS 1986-96.

OTHER CLUBS:
CARLISLE UNITED 79/80-81/2 (104, 22);
VANCOUVER WHITECAPS, CANADA, 81 AND 83;
NEWCASTLE UNITED 83/4-86/7 (147, 61);
LIVERPOOL 87/8-90/1 (131, 46);
EVERTON 91/2-92/3 (81, 25);
NEWCASTLE UNITED 93/4-96/7 (129, 47);
BOLTON WANDERERS 97/8 (17, 2);
MANCHESTER CITY ON LOAN 97/8 (6, 0); FULHAM ON LOAN 97/8 (8, 1);
HARTLEPOOL UNITED 98/9 (22, 2).

PETER BEARDSLEY		
COMP.	APPS	GLS
LC	1	0
TOTAL	1	0

BORN	NEWCASTLE 18TH JANUARY 1961
POSITION	STRIKER
JOINED UNITED	SEPTEMBER 1982 FROM VANCOUVER WHITECAPS
UNITED DEBUT & FAREWELL	BOURNEMOUTH (H) LC - 06/10/1982
LEFT UNITED FOR	VANCOUVER WHITECAPS MAY 1983

I t will always remain a total mystery to me how Manchester United signed a thoroughbred footballer like Peter Beardsley and let him leave the club after only one game for the first team.

I saw him play for Carlisle at Wrexham round about 1980 and immediately I realised I was looking at a fantastic talent. I sought out Jimmy Murphy to tell him the good news, only to find he already knew, which was typical because very little escaped Jimmy.

But nothing was done at the time, Peter went to Vancouver, and Ron Atkinson signed him from there.

True, there were a lot of strikers at Old Trafford at the time, but Beardsley was much

'He's got to be one of the best English footballers of the last 20 years – yet United couldn't find a place for him... does that make any sort of sense?'

more than an out-and-out marksman. He scored plenty of goals but he set up even more, and he really was a class act.

The lad had been blessed with two great feet, he was aware of all the ever-changing options around him, and he used his body intelligently to protect the ball.

He's got to be one of the best English footballers of the last 20 years – yet United couldn't find a place for him. Here was a talented young man with the world at his feet, and Ron thought enough of him to bring him over from Canada, but then didn't think enough of him to play him. Does that make any sort of sense?

It was a strange deal in that the manager actually bought him from Vancouver, then sold him back to John Giles, who was to make a healthy profit for his club a little later when he sold Peter to Newcastle.

Unquestionably, from Manchester United's point of view, Peter Beardsley was a gem that got away.

DOES THE SHIRT FIT? Perhaps not, because Peter Beardsley did not hang around to wear it more than once! Peter with his wife, Sandra, at Old Trafford in September 1982.

203. PAUL McGRATH

OTHER HONOURS:
83 REPUBLIC OF IRELAND CAPS 1985-97.
PFA FOOTBALLER OF THE YEAR 1993.

OTHER CLUBS:
ASTON VILLA 89/90-95/6 (253, 9);
DERBY COUNTY 96/7 (24, 0);
SHEFFIELD UNITED 97/8 (12, 0).

PAUL McGRATH		
COMP.	APPS	GLS
LEAGUE	159 (4)	12
FAC	15 (3)	2
LC	13	2
EUROPE	4	0
OTHERS	1	0
TOTAL	192 (7)	16

BORN	EALING, LONDON 4TH DECEMBER 1959.
POSITION	CENTRAL DEFENDER
JOINED UNITED	APRIL 1982 FROM ST. PATRICK'S ATHLETIC £30,000
UNITED DEBUT	BRADFORD CITY (A) LC - 10/11/1982
UNITED HONOURS	FA CUP 1984/5
UNITED FAREWELL	SOUTHAMPTON (A) DIV. 1 - 06/05/1989
LEFT UNITED FOR	ASTON VILLA AUGUST 1989 - £450,000

Paul McGrath was one of the most talented central defenders the British game has seen for many a long day. He was a bit special.

When I first saw him, I was impressed by his pace and his natural ability, but it used to worry me that he took chances, a bit like Rio Ferdinand today. Paul thought it was against the rules to kick the ball into the stand, he always wanted to be doing something on it.

It might sound daft, but when he went to Aston Villa – at a time when he was more or less a cripple, barely able to train due to his long-standing knee problems – he probably became a better pure defender because he had to take fewer risks.

When he was coming through, Ron Atkinson deployed him occasionally in midfield, where his exceptional skill was always evident, and I've no doubt that he could have made a career in that position. He wouldn't have been a Robson or a Keane, but certainly he would have been better than average in Premiership terms.

Paul's wonky knees were always going to get the better of him in the end, but he was nearly 30 when he left Old Trafford, then he ended up playing more games for Villa than he did for United.

During his spell in the Midlands, he was voted PFA Footballer of the Year, an amazing achievement for a fellow supposedly in his dotage and needing crutches. In fact, there was a point during that season when it seemed he might pick up a championship medal at United's expense, so the lad didn't do badly.

Away from the game it's no secret that he

had problems regarding his drinking, and that led him into conflict with Alex Ferguson, which in turn precipitated his departure. But despite his social habits, and despite his creaking knees, Paul McGrath played for club and country until he wasn't too far off 40. Had he not drunk more than was good for him, and had he not been plagued with so many aches and pains, what might he have achieved? Anything. Anything at all.

'Had he not drunk more than was good for him, and had he not been plagued with so many aches and pains, what might he have achieved? Anything. Anything at all.'

There was even a point, after he received rave reviews for a faultless performance for the Football League in its centenary showpiece against the Rest of the World in 1987, that he was linked with a move to several of the top continental clubs.

So if he could hold his own, apparently effortlessly, against the likes of Diego Maradona and Michel Platini, why did Manchester United not build their defence around him for the foreseeable future?

I suppose it comes down to the fact that either he had to do things Alex Ferguson's way or depart, and he chose the latter course.

BORN	DARLINGTON 26TH AUGUST 1951
POSITION	GOALKEEPER
JOINED UNITED	FEBRUARY 1983 FROM BIRMINGHAM CITY INITIALLY ON LOAN
UNITED DEBUT	COVENTRY CITY (H) DIV. 1 - 02/04/1983
UNITED FAREWELL	NOTTS COUNTY (H) DIV. 1 - 27/12/1983
LEFT UNITED FOR	ALTRINCHAM - MAY 1985

JEFF WEALANDS		
COMP.	APPS	GLS
LEAGUE	7	0
LC	1	0
TOTAL	8	0

204. JEFF WEALANDS

OTHER CLUBS:
DARLINGTON 71/2 (28, 0);
HULL CITY 71/2-78/9 (240, 0);
BIRMINGHAM CITY 79/80-81/2 (102, 0);
OLDHAM ATHLETIC ON LOAN 84/5 (10, 0);
PRESTON NORTH END ON LOAN 84/5 (4, 0).

Jeff Wealands was an experienced, much-travelled 'keeper brought to Old Trafford by Ron Atkinson as cover for Gary Bailey, and he never let the club down in his handful of appearances. Jeff had already proved himself at Hull and Birmingham over more than a decade, and he was both a top-rate professional and a lovely lad.

After leaving the League he went on to do well for Altrincham and he still lives in the area, usually turning up for golf days organised by United's Former Players Association.

205. LAURIE CUNNINGHAM

OTHER HONOURS:
6 ENGLAND CAPS 1979-80.

OTHER CLUBS:
ORIENT 74/5–76/7 (75, 15); WEST BROMWICH ALBION 76/7–78/9 (86, 21);
REAL MADRID, SPAIN, 79/80-82/83; SPORTING GIJON, SPAIN, 83/4;
MARSEILLE, FRANCE, 84/5-85/6; LEICESTER CITY ON LOAN 85/6 (15, 0);
RAYO VALLECANO, SPAIN, 86/7; REAL BETIS, SPAIN, 87/8;
CHARLEROI, BELGIUM, 87/8; WIMBLEDON 87/8 (6, 2); RAYO VALLECANO, SPAIN, 88/9.

LAURIE CUNNINGHAM		
COMP.	APPS	GLS
LEAGUE	3 (2)	1
TOTAL	3 (2)	1

BORN	HOLLOWAY, LONDON 8TH MARCH 1956
DIED	MADRID, 15TH JULY 1989
POSITION	WINGER
JOINED UNITED	MARCH 1983 ON LOAN FROM REAL MADRID
UNITED DEBUT	EVERTON (A) DIV. 1 - 19/04/1983
UNITED FAREWELL	SWANSEA CITY (H) DIV. 1 - 07/05/1983
LEFT UNITED FOR	REAL MADRID RETURNED FOLLOWING LOAN

Laurie Cunningham is always a footnote in Old Trafford history, yet he was a hugely talented player who joined United when he was only 27, and therefore had ample opportunity to make a more lasting impact.

That said, I couldn't really understand why Ron brought him to United in the first place. Times were different then, and Real Madrid weren't signing players and sending them out on loan if they were doing a good job. It made me wonder how much Laurie's star had waned and how much Ron had seen of him in recent years.

I remember him in his West Bromwich Albion heyday as a quick and tricky customer, extremely elusive, difficult for defenders to track, one of the shining lights in a smashing side which contained top performers like Bryan Robson, Cyrille Regis, Tony Brown and Derek Statham.

I guess Ron was half hoping that he could bring Laurie back to his West Brom form, but it never happened. Having roamed Europe without settling, he appeared to be finished as a top-ranker. Perhaps he was one of that type who's a star at 18 but is all washed up by 28; certainly he made no significant contribution for Manchester United.

Tragically, only six years after leaving Old Trafford and still in the prime of life, Laurie was killed in a road accident in Spain.

BORN	GLASGOW 26TH OCTOBER 1952
POSITION	WINGER
JOINED UNITED	AUGUST 1983 LEEDS UTD - £30,000
UNITED DEBUT	LIVERPOOL (WEMBLEY) CS - 20/08/1983
UNITED FAREWELL	BURNLEY (H) LC - 26/09/1984
LEFT UNITED FOR	BRADFORD CITY JUNE 1985 (PLAYER/COACH)

ARTHUR GRAHAM

COMP.	APPS	GLS
LEAGUE	33 (4)	5
FAC	1	0
LC	6	1
EUROPE	6 (1)	1
OTHERS	1	0
TOTAL	47 (5)	7

206. ARTHUR GRAHAM

OTHER HONOURS:
10 SCOTLAND CAPS 1977-80.

OTHER CLUBS:
ABERDEEN 69/70-76/7 (228, 34);
LEEDS UNITED 77/8-82/3 (223, 37);
BRADFORD CITY 85/6-86/7 (31, 2).

Ron Atkinson recruited Arthur Graham as a stopgap when it became apparent that Steve Coppell's injury was more serious than had been hoped, and after Laurie Cunningham had failed to make his mark.

Arthur could play on either flank and he didn't do a bad job for United, toiling honestly, working up and back and doing his best to supply crosses for Frank Stapleton.

Of course, United never saw him at his peak, as he was past 30 when he arrived and nearing the end of a long and commendable career, in which the highlights had been experienced at Aberdeen and Leeds.

So he was never going to be a long-term prospect but Ron knew exactly what he was getting when he bought Arthur, a supremely honest professional who knew the ropes, and the former Scottish international didn't disappoint him.

He took the eye in the autumn of 1983, laying on a few goals for Frank, giving admirable value for his modest fee before fading into the background in 1984/85 following the purchase of Gordon Strachan and Jesper Olsen.

BORN	WREXHAM, DENBIGHSHIRE 1ST NOVEMBER 1963
POSITION	STRIKER
JOINED UNITED	JUINE 1980 FROM JUNIOR FOOTBALL; REJOINED FROM BARCELONA JULY 1988 - £1.6 MILLION
UNITED DEBUT	PORT VALE (H) LC - 26/10/1983
UNITED HONOURS	ECWC 1990/1 PREMIERSHIP 1992/3, 1993/4 FA CUP 1984/5, 1993/4 LEAGUE CUP 1991/2
UNITED FAREWELL	EVERTON (WEMBLEY) FAC - 20/05/1995
LEFT UNITED FOR	BARCELONA - AUGUST 1986 £2 MILLION CHELSEA - JULY 1995 £1.5 MILLION

MARK HUGHES

COMP.	APPS	GLS
LEAGUE	336 (9)	120
FAC	45 (1)	17
LC	37 (1)	16
EUROPE	30 (3)	9
OTHERS	5	1
TOTAL	453 (14)	163

207. MARK HUGHES

OTHER HONOURS:
72 WALES CAPS 1984-99.
PFA FOOTBALLER OF THE YEAR 1989, 1991.

OTHER CLUBS:
BARCELONA 86/7 (28, 4);
BAYERN MUNICH ON LOAN 87/8 (18, 6);
CHELSEA 95/6-97/8 (95, 25);
SOUTHAMPTON 98/9-99/00 (51, 2);
EVERTON 99/00-00/01 (18, 1);
BLACKBURN ROVERS 00/01-01/02 (50, 6).

MANAGER: WALES NATIONAL TEAM 1999-2004, BLACKBURN ROVERS 2004-.

What a player! Mark Hughes was something a bit special and, believe it or not in view of all the accolades he's received down the years, I think he was more than a tad underrated by a lot of people.

At least the fans didn't sell him short. They loved him. But I think the football world in general, and certainly the press, who do so much to create heroes, didn't realise just how exceptional he was.

I always said Mark was a scorer of great goals, rather than a great goal-scorer, meaning that for all his breathtaking strikes, the spectacular bicycle-kicks and the screamers from 30 yards, he didn't contribute too many scrappy tap-ins. But in fairness, he wasn't exactly short of goals during his two spells at Old Trafford.

The muscular Welshman was a tremendous talent, yet his breakthrough was something of a fluke in that he was a midfield player who appeared to be going nowehere. Then he was moved up front in an emergency and he proved a revelation.

I liked everything about Mark Hughes. He was devilishly strong, he had good feet, and he was effective in the air despite not being a giant of a man. He was an absolute master at the art of holding the ball up and bringing others into the game, as adept as anyone I've ever seen at playing with his back to goal. He suited Cantona; he suited the wingers, Giggs, Sharpe and Kanchelskis; he suited everybody.

In 1985/86, when United made a long unbeaten start to the First Division campaign, Mark couldn't stop scoring, but then details of a move to Barcelona seeped out, and in the New Year he could barely find the net at any price. Obviously he was deeply troubled, and so were the fans, who felt betrayed that Manchester United should be selling one of their top men to Barcelona. I couldn't understand it, either.

Here was a young lad who didn't seem to want to leave United, I'll always be convinced of that. Certainly he gave the impression that he

> *'He was an absolute master at the art of holding the ball up and bringing others into the game, as adept as anyone I've ever seen at playing with his back to goal. He suited Cantona; he suited the wingers, Giggs, Sharpe and Kanchelskis; he suited everybody.'*

just needed someone to put an arm round his shoulder and say that he was needed at Old Trafford. I might be wrong, but it seemed as if the opposite was happening, that he was actually being encouraged to leave. All the while the supporters were screaming blue murder and it seemed as if it was affecting the team. Understandably so.

When Alex Ferguson re-signed him for the club, Martin Edwards asked me what I thought, and I told him that it worried me because it didn't often work out when players returned to the scenes of their former exploits.

As it turned out, Mark had improved mightily, learning during his time in Spain and probably even more from his season with Bayern Munich. He came back to United as a much better all-round player.

I was a little disappointed when Alex sold him to Chelsea in 1995. I think he still had something to offer, as he proved by playing another 100 games for Chelsea, picking up three major cup medals in the process, then continuing at the top level, and helping Blackburn to win the League Cup when he was nearly 40.

Amazingly, Mark played more than 200 senior games after leaving Old Trafford for the second time. Perhaps he wouldn't have reached that total had he stayed, but he would have been a hell of a presence on the bench. Mind, that might not have been what he wanted at that stage of his career. He was a doer, not a watcher.

I was dumbfounded when Mark became a manager, his demeanour throughout his career having always signalled to me that he wouldn't want to be bothered with all the cares and intricacies involved. Off the pitch he's a very unassuming fellow, nothing like the fire-breathing Welsh dragon beloved of the fans, and I thought he'd opt for the quiet life.

Managing Wales is such a difficult job, but he did wonderfully well and the more I watched him, the more I believed he might have a chance of becoming one of the top men. Now he's been given the opportunity by Blackburn Rovers. He's got light years ahead of him to prove himself comprehensively, and it's not beyond the bounds of belief that he might end up back at Old Trafford. Who knows? I can't imagine a more popular choice.

208. MARK DEMPSEY

OTHER CLUBS:
SWINDON TOWN ON LOAN 84/5 (5, 0);
SHEFFIELD UNITED 86/7-87/8 (63, 8);
CHESTERFIELD ON LOAN 88/9 (3, 0);
ROTHERHAM UNITED 88/9-90/1 (75, 7).

MARK DEMPSEY		
COMP.	APPS	GLS
LEAGUE	1	0
EUROPE	0 (1)	0
TOTAL	1 (1)	0

BORN	MANCHESTER 14TH JANUARY 1964
POSITION	MIDFIELDER
JOINED UNITED	MAY 1980 FROM JUNIOR FOOTBALL
UNITED DEBUT	SPARTAK VARNA (H) ECWC - 02/11/1983
UNITED FAREWELL	IPSWICH TOWN (H) DIV. 1 - 07/12/1985
LEFT UNITED FOR	SHEFFIELD UNITED AUGUST 1986 - £20,000 INITIALLY ON LOAN

At one time there were high expectations of Mark Dempsey, who was a busy and enterprising young midfielder, but it never happened for him at Old Trafford and he went off to try his luck at Sheffield United.

Maybe had he joined a smaller club than Manchester United when he was a boy, he might have enjoyed a more rewarding career, as he indicated by collecting a Fourth Division championship medal with Rotherham in 1988/89.

Latterly he returned to Old Trafford as a youth coach.

209. GARTH CROOKS

OTHER CLUBS:
STOKE CITY 75/6-79/80 (147, 48);
TOTTENHAM HOTSPUR 80/1-84/5 (125, 48);
WEST BROMWICH ALBION 85/6-86/7 (40, 16);
CHARLTON ATHLETIC 86/7-90/1 (56, 15).

GARTH CROOKS		
COMP.	APPS	GLS
LEAGUE	6 (1)	2
TOTAL	6 (1)	2

BORN	STOKE 10TH MARCH 1958
POSITION	STRIKER
JOINED UNITED	NOVEMBER 1983 FROM TOTTENHAM H (LOAN)
UNITED DEBUT	WATFORD (H) DIV. 1 - 19/11/1983
UNITED FAREWELL	LIVERPOOL (A) DIV. 1 - 02/01/1984
LEFT UNITED FOR	TOTTENHAM HOTSPUR RETURNED AFTER LOAN JANUARY 1984

I have never understood the loan system for clubs like Manchester United. If you're manager at Old Trafford, you should make judgements without the insurance of being able to send someone back if you don't like him. It's something I disagree with completely.

Garth Crooks scored goals for everyone, including a couple in his brief and puzzling spell at United, but he never particularly appealed to me. I thought he was an ordinary player, while already at the club were far greater talents in the shape of Frank Stapleton, Norman Whiteside and the emerging Mark Hughes, with Alan Brazil on the horizon. The Crooks transfer left me scratching my head at the time, and I'm none the wiser now.

BORN	ABERDEEN
	17TH JUNE 1964
POSITION	CENTRAL DEFENDER
JOINED UNITED	JULY 1980
	FROM JUNIOR FOOTBALL
UNITED DEBUT	BOURNEMOUTH (A)
	FAC - 07/01/1984
UNITED FAREWELL	PORTSMOUTH (H)
	DIV. 1 - 07/05/1988
LEFT UNITED FOR	PORTSMOUTH
	AUGUST 1988

GRAEME HOGG		
COMP.	APPS	GLS
LEAGUE	82 (1)	1
FAC	8	0
LC	7 (1)	0
EUROPE	10	0
OTHERS	1	0
TOTAL	108 (2)	1

210. GRAEME HOGG

OTHER CLUBS:
WEST BROMWICH ALBION ON LOAN 87/8 (7, 0);
PORTSMOUTH 88/9-90/1 (100, 2);
HEART OF MIDLOTHIAN 91/2-94/5 (58, 3);
NOTTS COUNTY 94/5-97/8 (66, 0);
BRENTFORD 97/8 (17, 2).

Graeme Hogg was a big, gangly, quick, very left-sided centre-half, and at first he was pretty impressive. Indeed, there was a period in 1984/85 when he filled Kevin Moran's place on merit and he looked like the answer to everybody's prayers for a dominant figure at the heart of the defence.

Sadly it never worked out. Eventually Graeme proved very much second-best to the likes of Moran and Paul McGrath, and slipped down the pecking order. I suppose that, in such company, it wasn't surprising that he struggled. In the final analysis, he just wasn't good enough.

For all that, I expected him to enjoy rather more success than he did after leaving United. Somehow he never really became established in the long term at any of his subsequent clubs and my thought was: 'You're better than that, son, surely.'

Certainly it all went wrong for Graeme at United, where he had his differences with Alex Ferguson. In fact, he was one of the first at Old Trafford to complain publicly about the so-called 'hairdryer' treatment from Alex. Enough said.

BORN	NEATH, GLAMORGAN
	23RD SEPTEMBER 1964
POSITION	FULL-BACK OR MIDFIELDER
JOINED UNITED	JUNE 1981
	FROM JUNIOR FOOTBALL
UNITED DEBUT	NOTTINGHAM FOREST (A)
	DIV. 1 - 16/05/1984
UNITED HONOURS	ECWC 1990/1
	PREMIERSHIP 1992/3
	FA CUP 1989/90
UNITED FAREWELL	BURY (H)
	FAC - 05/01/1993
LEFT UNITED FOR	MIDDLESBROUGH
	MAY 1994

CLAYTON BLACKMORE		
COMP.	APPS	GLS
LEAGUE	150 (36)	19
FAC	15 (6)	1
LC	23 (2)	3
EUROPE	11	2
OTHERS	2	1
TOTAL	201 (44)	26

211. CLAYTON BLACKMORE

OTHER HONOURS:
39 WALES CAPS 1985-97.

OTHER CLUBS:
MIDDLESBROUGH 94/5-97/8 (53, 4);
BRISTOL CITY ON LOAN 96/7 (5, 1);
BARNSLEY 98/9 (7, 0);
NOTTS COUNTY 99/00 (21, 2).

By any standard, Clayton Blackmore enjoyed an accomplished and rewarding career at United, yet there was a time when it was believed genuinely that he might achieve even more.

In the mid 1980s, with the team needing a creative influence in midfield, there were plenty of people who thought he could provide the long-term answer. He was blessed with wonderful feet and, fleetingly, he suggested that he might make a go of that demanding central role. Yet it proved to be a short-lived phase, and in the end he made the majority of his appearances at full-back.

Clayton had one fantastic season in 1990/91, when he was practically ever-present at left-back, and he picked up a Cup Winners' Cup medal for his pains. During that run he was extremely consistent, and he scored an important goal against Montpellier with a long-range free-kick. But what he will always be remembered for even more vividly is clearing a Michael Laudrup shot off the line in the final against Barcelona when United were 2-1 in front near the end.

Given the fact that Clayton played nearly 250 times for the first team, it might sound daft to call him unlucky, but he was unfortunate in that he had such an encouraging run as a midfielder only to be edged out before he could realise his full potential.

Then, just when it looked as though he was destined for a long-term stay at full-back, that didn't materialise either, due to the arrival of Paul Parker and Denis Irwin's switch from right-back to left.

So, except in his one truly memorable campaign, Clayton was always on the fringe; even when he enjoyed a run of matches in the side, there was always the feeling that he was a reserve and that soon he would be replaced.

In the end he was a hugely versatile, immensely useful substitute, but he could be excused for feeling that, in another era, probably a lad with his gifts would have cemented his place and finished up as one of United's longest serving players.

Clayton, who was born with enviable all-round talent, being a hell of a golfer who plays off scratch, is an old mate of Mark Hughes, the pair of them having risen through the Old Trafford ranks together. It was natural enough, then, that he went on to help Sparky to coach Wales, with whom he won 39 caps himself.

> 'Clayton was always on the fringe; even when he enjoyed a run of matches in the side, there was always the feeling that he was a reserve and that he would be replaced.'

BORN	EDINBURGH 9TH FEBRUARY 1957
POSITION	MIDFIELDER
JOINED UNITED	AUGUST 1984 FROM ABERDEEN - £600,000
UNITED DEBUT	WATFORD (H) DIV. 1 - 25/08/1984
UNITED HONOURS	FA CUP 1984/5
UNITED FAREWELL	NOTTINGHAM FOREST (H) FAC - 18/03/1989
LEFT UNITED FOR	LEEDS UNITED MAR. 1989 - £300,000

GORDON STRACHAN		
COMP.	APPS	GLS
LEAGUE	155 (5)	33
FAC	22	2
LC	12 (1)	1
EUROPE	6	2
TOTAL	195 (6)	38

212. GORDON STRACHAN

OTHER HONOURS:
50 SCOTLAND CAPS 1980-92.

OTHER CLUBS:
DUNDEE 74/5-76/7 (60, 13);
ABERDEEN 77/8-83/4 (191, 54);
LEEDS UNITED 88/9-94/5 (196, 37);
COVENTRY CITY 94/5-96/7 (26, 0).

MANAGER:
COVENTRY CITY 1996-2001; SOUTHAMPTON 2001-04; CELTIC 2005-.

There was never any questioning Gordon Strachan's immense talent, but he was never one of my favourites. Ron Atkinson signed him from Aberdeen, where he had played under Alex Ferguson, and when they were reunited at Old Trafford, I think it was pretty clear there would be a parting of the ways between the two Scots. They just didn't get on.

When Strachan left Old Trafford at the age of 32 he had an immense impact at Elland Road, helping them to pip United to the League title in 1991/92, the last year before the Premiership was launched.

The surprising thing was that he did it with Howard Wilkinson as his manager. I wouldn't have thought Strachan's personality would have gelled with Wilkinson's, any more than it did with Ferguson's, which shows that you never can tell.

Strachan was basically a right winger most of his career, but like many people when they reach a certain age, he started playing a little bit deeper and it suited him.

Plainly he was not short of talent, as he showed during his United days by the chances that he created and the goals that he scored from the wing. He brought width to the team, his skills added to the variety of the attack and he helped to win the FA Cup in 1985.

But there was always something about him which I couldn't quite warm to. I could never make him out. Takes all sorts, I suppose.

213. ALAN BRAZIL

OTHER HONOURS:
13 Scotland caps 1980-83.

OTHER CLUBS:
Ipswich Town 77/8-82/3 (154, 70);
Tottenham Hotspur 82/3-83/4 (31, 9);
Coventry City 85/6 (15, 2);
Queen's Park Rangers 86/7 (4, 0);
FC Baden, Switzerland, 88/9.

ALAN BRAZIL		
Comp.	Apps	Gls
League	18 (13)	8
FAC	0 (1)	0
LC	4 (3)	3
Europe	2	1
Total	24 (17)	12

Born	Glasgow 15th June 1959
Position	Striker
Joined United	June 1984 from Tottenham H. £700,000
United Debut	Watford (H) Div. 1 - 25/08/1984
United Farewell	Birmingham City (H) Div. 1 - 01/01/1986
Left United for	Coventry City January 1986 exchange for Terry Gibson

Alan Brazil cost a lot of money, having been extremely impressive under Bobby Robson at Ipswich, scoring a goal virtually every other game.

But then he didn't fit in at Tottenham, and despite the fact that his United record is not at all bad on paper – most people would be satisfied with 12 goals in 24 starts – I can't get past the fact that, allegedly, Ron Atkinson was offered Gary Lineker by Leicester City, but took Alan instead. It still hurts my head to think about it. Brazil or Lineker? There's just no comparison.

To be fair to Alan, he was granted only 18 League games in two years, which was odd given such a heavy investment, and then Ron compounded a bizarre situation by doing an exchange deal with Coventry for Terry Gibson, more of whom later.

At Ipswich, alongside Paul Mariner, Brazil had done himself proud. But at United, forget him! He made no lasting impact whatsoever. I suppose Ron must have envisaged him playing alongside Frank Stapleton, but then Norman Whiteside and Mark Hughes came through from the youth ranks and that changed the picture.

Alan always looked on the burly side to me. I'm sure it was a misleading impression, but he never looked like a trained athlete. He never looked part of the team, either.

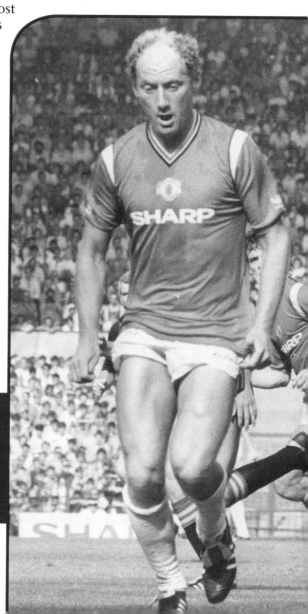

> 'To be fair to Alan, he was granted only 18 League games in two years, which was odd given such a heavy investment.'

BORN	FAKSE, DENMARK 20TH MARCH 1961
POSITION	WINGER
JOINED UNITED	JULY 1984 FROM AJAX - £350,000
UNITED DEBUT	WATFORD (H) DIV. 1 - 25/08/1984
UNITED HONOURS	FA CUP 1984/5
UNITED FAREWELL	DERBY COUNTY (A) DIV. 1 - 12/11/1988
LEFT UNITED FOR	BORDEAUX, FRANCE NOV. 1988 - £400,000

JESPER OLSEN

COMP.	APPS	GLS
LEAGUE	119 (20)	21
FAC	13 (3)	2
LC	10 (3)	1
EUROPE	6 (1)	0
OTHERS	1	0
TOTAL	149 (27)	24

214. JESPER OLSEN

OTHER HONOURS:
45 DENMARK CAPS 1980-90.

OTHER CLUBS:
NAESTVED, DENMARK; AJAX, HOLLAND, 82/3-83/4; BORDEAUX, FRANCE, 88/9-89/90; CAEN, FRANCE, 90/1-91/2.

When Ron Atkinson agreed to sign Jesper Olsen, midway through 1983/84, there was much talk that the Dane had been whisked from under the noses of Europe's leading clubs and the deal was presented to United's fans as a massive coup.

Ron even went as far as to describe him as the club's most exciting talent since George Best. I always shudder when I hear those words. Clearly, his new manager did him no favours there.

Of course, that wasn't the fault of Jesper Olsen, who wasn't a bad footballer. But I would say that he lacked sufficient strength for the English top division, offering too lightweight a presence, often drifting out of the action for frustratingly lengthy periods.

Probably I'm being unkind, but to me he was always a 'nearly man.' Sure, he had his impressive games. He could beat a defender and he carried a powerful shot for a little feller, but sometimes he seemed to disappear up blind alleys, not making the most of his extravagant ability. Often he had you on the edge of your seat, hinting that something extraordinary was about to happen, but it very rarely did.

> *'Jesper was typical of so many of the players Ron brought in . . . they flattered to deceive, sometimes doing well in the cup competitions but not doing the business over the long haul of 42 games which had to be negotiated to claim the title.'*

Ron's vision was Strachan on the right, balanced by Olsen on the left, and it was splendid on paper, but it never came into focus on the pitch.

Jesper was typical of so many of the players Ron brought in. Obviously Bryan Robson was the shining exception, but so many of the rest left unfulfilled, with gigantic question-marks against their names. They flattered to deceive, sometimes doing well in the cup competitions but not doing the business over the long haul of 42 games which had to be negotiated to claim the title.

The English game was a bit too harsh physically for Jesper Olsen. Technically there was no problem, but that was not enough.

215. BILLY GARTON

OTHER CLUBS:
BIRMINGHAM CITY ON LOAN 85/6 (5, 0).

BILLY GARTON		
COMP.	APPS	GLS
LEAGUE	39 (2)	0
FAC	3	0
LC	5 (1)	0
EUROPE	0 (1)	0
TOTAL	47 (4)	0

BORN	SALFORD 15TH MARCH 1965
POSITION	DEFENDER
JOINED UNITED	MAY 1981 FROM JUNIOR FOOTBALL
UNITED DEBUT	BURNLEY (H) LC - 26/09/1984
UNITED FAREWELL	COVENTRY CITY (A) DIV. 1 - 10/12/1988
RETIRED	MAY 1990 - DUE TO INJURY

Billy Garton's is a hard-luck story. He looked as if he had a genuine chance of making the grade, but then he suffered a debilitating illness which ruined his career.

After he had recovered enough to live a normal life, he had a spell as player-manager of non-League Hyde United, but by then any aspirations of glory had long since disappeared.

Billy was a talented central defender, who could also play at full-back. He was a contemporary of Graeme Hogg but, for me, he was always the better player of the two, more of a footballer, far more comfortable in possession.

He was useful upstairs, he had pace and he had tidy feet. He wasn't as big as Hogg, and perhaps might have made a name for himself playing alongside a physically commanding centre-half, maybe in the manner of Martin Buchan next to Jim Holton or Gordon McQueen.

It was such a shame that poor Billy was finished at 25.

BORN	BRANDON, CO. DURHAM 22ND JANUARY 1962
POSITION	GOALKEEPER
JOINED UNITED	JULY 1978 FROM JUNIOR FOOTBALL
UNITED DEBUT	COVENTRY CITY (H) DIV. 1 - 12/01/1985
UNITED FAREWELL	SHEFFIELD WEDNESDAY (A) DIV. 1 - 09/04/1985
LEFT UNITED FOR	MIDDLESBROUGH JULY 1985

STEVE PEARS		
COMP.	APPS	GLS
LEAGUE	4	0
FAC	1	0
TOTAL	5	0

216. STEVE PEARS

OTHER CLUBS:
MIDDLESBROUGH ON LOAN 83/4 (12, 0);
MIDDLESBROUGH 85/6-94/5 (327, 0);
HARTLEPOOL UNITED 96/7 (16, 0).

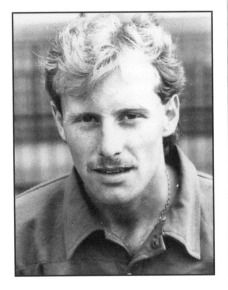

Steve Pears appeared only fleetingly on the first-team scene at Old Trafford, making his entrance in January and bidding Farewell in April, but in view of his subsequent success and longevity at Middlesbrough, how unlucky was he not to make the grade with United?

He had spent seven years at the club, and it seems that Ron Atkinson couldn't have rated him too highly, because he stuck to Gary Bailey and then recruited Chris Turner and Jeff Wealands.

Perhaps United made a slight mistake with Steve, and maybe he should have had more opportunities. Certainly he made considerable strides after leaving, being mentioned in dispatches as an England possible during his time at Ayrsome Park.

He was more of a shot-stopper than a dominator of his area, his style being to leave crosses to his defenders unless they landed in his six-yard box. That was the method generally in vogue at the time, as we seemed to have lost the tradition of goalkeepers leaving their line boldly, in the manner of Harry Gregg.

BORN	MANCHESTER 10TH JUNE 1957
POSITION	WINGER
JOINED UNITED	JULY 1985 FROM COVENTRY CITY - £50,000
UNITED DEBUT	NOTTINGHAM FOREST (A) DIV. 1 - 31/08/1985
UNITED FAREWELL	WIMBLEDON (A) DIV. 1 - 29/11/1986
LEFT UNITED FOR	MANCHESTER CITY JAN 1987 - £30,000

PETER BARNES		
COMP.	APPS	GLS
LEAGUE	19 (1)	2
LC	5	2
TOTAL	24 (1)	4

217. PETER BARNES

OTHER HONOURS:
22 ENGLAND CAPS 1977-82.

OTHER CLUBS:
MANCHESTER CITY 74/5–78/9 (115, 15);
WEST BROMWICH ALBION 79/80–80/1 (77, 23);
LEEDS UNITED 81/2 (31, 1); REAL BETIS, SPAIN, 82/3; LEEDS UNITED 83/4 (27, 4);
COVENTRY CITY 84/5 (18, 2); MANCHESTER CITY 86/7 (8, 0);
BOLTON WANDERERS ON LOAN 87/8 (2, 0); PORT VALE ON LOAN 87/8 (3, 0);
HULL CITY 87/8 (11, 0), FARENSE, PORTUGAL 88/9; BOLTON WANDERERS 88/9 (3, 0);
SUNDERLAND 88/9 (1, 0); TAMPA BAY ROWDIES, USA, 90;
CLIFTONVILLE, NORTHERN IRELAND, 92/3; MELBOURNE CITY, AUSTRALIA.

I knew Peter Barnes from childhood, being a good pal of his dad Ken, the Manchester City wing-half, and the boy was always bursting with talent. He could do amazing things with a football. Later I handled his transfer from Manchester City to West Brom, which was the first time I ever met Ron

Atkinson, who was in charge at The Hawthorns.

Ron loved Peter, but then a depressing thing happened – Allan Clarke took him from West Brom to Leeds, where he had no chance. He was everything Leeds didn't want at a time when they were a poor side. People tend to dismiss Peter's contribution to Manchester United as a brief burst after his best days had gone, yet he was only 28 when Ron took him to Old Trafford so there was plenty of time for him to make the enormous impact his gifts warranted.

Peter had pace, a great left peg and he could beat defenders from morning to night. He loved doing it and sometimes he made it look as though he could do it at will. Okay, he was never a chaser-back. Like me, he couldn't tackle a fish supper, but what of it? Peter excelled for England, too, and at first he looked like a world-beater on the international stage. As a pair of wingers, he and Stevie Coppell were seen as the future for their country.

It was bold and imaginative of Ron to take Peter, whose stock had fallen by the mid 1980s, but he knew what a superb player the lad could be from their previous days together. It takes a lot for me to become excited, but that's how I felt when I heard United had signed him.

So I wasn't surprised when he played magnificently as the side won their first ten games of 1985/86, shooting to the top of the First Division and not losing until their 16th. But then all of a sudden, when injuries bit into the squad and results started going wrong, it seemed there was only one person to blame and that, illogically, was the winger. So Peter Barnes was dropped. I could never understand it. If he was the catalyst for the team making such a breathtaking start, and I am sure that he was, then why was he the only fall guy? He had given United something they hadn't had for a long time – an outside-left who ran past people on a regular basis and crossed the ball accurately. They hadn't had anyone like that since Gordon Hill.

As pressure began to build Ron brought back Jesper Olsen, who had played the first four

'He had given United something they hadn't had for a long time – an outside-left who ran past people on a regular basis and crossed the ball accurately. They hadn't had anyone like that since Gordon Hill.'

matches. I would have persevered with Barnes, because sheer talent like he had does not go away. Why did Ron lose belief in him? Well, looking at his record, Ron lost belief in a lot of people he signed, which I felt was a disturbing trait. There's a pattern whereby the likes of Cunningham, Crooks, Beardsley, Brazil all came in and then were discarded almost instantly. I don't care how good you are, if they don't play you then you can't prove anything.

The saddest thing to me when I look at Peter's record is how, with all his natural gifts, he finished up roaming the world, looking for a game, and getting nowhere special. Perhaps he wasn't the strongest character in the world, but he could play. He always reminded me a little of Albert Scanlon. He needed a love and a cuddle; bollockings didn't help him.

In the end it was Alex Ferguson who got rid of him, although not before Ron had dispensed with him. Even though he played 22 times for England, I will always think of Peter as a remarkable performer who was allowed to slip away without making the most of his ability. Ron missed a trick and so did everybody else. The rotten shame is that Ron knew him so well, knew what made him tick, and should have known how to get the best out of him.

218. COLIN GIBSON

OTHER CLUBS:
ASTON VILLA 78/9-85/6 (185, 10);
PORT VALE ON LOAN 90/1 (6, 2);
LEICESTER CITY 90/1-93/4 (59, 4);
BLACKPOOL 94/5 (2, 0); WALSALL 94/5 (33, 0).

COLIN GIBSON		
COMP.	APPS	GLS
LEAGUE	74 (5)	9
FAC	8 (1)	0
LC	7	0
TOTAL	89 (6)	9

BORN	BRIDPORT, DORSET 6TH APRIL 1960
POSITION	FULL-BACK, MIDFIELDER
JOINED UNITED	NOV. 1985 FROM ASTON VILLA - £350,000
UNITED DEBUT	WATFORD (H) DIV. 1 - 30/11/1985
UNITED FAREWELL	WIMBLEDON (H) DIV. 1 - 30/04/1990
LEFT UNITED FOR	LEICESTER CITY DEC. 1990 - £100,000

Obviously Ron Atkinson didn't share my opinion, but I never thought Colin Gibson was a Manchester United player. I know he won a Championship medal with Aston Villa, for whom he did a decent job, but still I believe that he was ordinary in the extreme.

Although sometimes he was deployed in midfield, Colin was basically a left-back, and his presence was to the sore detriment of the wholly superior Arthur Albiston, who was in a different class.

I could never begin to understand why we needed Colin Gibson. Do managers think they are duty-bound to get rid of established players and sign their own? I suppose bosses want to put their own stamp on their teams, but surely to God, nobody could have thought Gibson a better player than Arthur. How was he going to improve the side? No idea. Pass.

219. CHRIS TURNER

OTHER CLUBS:
SHEFFIELD WEDNESDAY 76/7-78/9 (91, 0);
LINCOLN CITY ON LOAN 78/9 (5, 0);
SUNDERLAND 79/80-84/5 (195, 0);
SHEFFIELD WEDNESDAY 88/9-90/1 (75, 0);
LEEDS UNITED ON LOAN 89/90 (2, 0);
LEYTON ORIENT 91/2-94/5 (58, 0).

MANAGER:
LEYTON ORIENT 1994-95; HARTLEPOOL UNITED 1999-2002;
SHEFFIELD WEDNESDAY 2002-04, STOCKPORT COUNTY 2004-.

CHRIS TURNER		
COMP.	APPS	GLS
LEAGUE	64	0
FAC	8	0
LC	7	0
TOTAL	79	0

BORN	SHEFFIELD 15TH SEPTEMBER 1958
POSITION	GOALKEEPER
JOINED UNITED	AUGUST 1985 FROM SUNDERLAND - £250,000
UNITED DEBUT	ASTON VILLA (A) DIV. 1 - 14/12/1985
UNITED FAREWELL	WIMBLEDON (H) DIV. 1 - 09/05/1988
LEFT UNITED FOR	SHEFFIELD WEDNESDAY SEPT. 1988 - £175,000

Chris Turner was a pretty competent 'keeper but I always thought he lacked a bit of stature for the top level. He had a decent pair of hands, and was a terrific shot-stopper, but he never seemed to be in charge of his box.

He was a front-line 'keeper but I don't think he would have been signed in a million years if Gary Bailey had not been experiencing fitness problems. Ron Atkinson obviously thought a lot of him, to give Sunderland all that money, but he wouldn't have been my first choice to replace a player of Bailey's calibre.

It seems that Alex Ferguson must have agreed with me because later he favoured young Gary Walsh, then Jim Leighton, and Turner was allowed to return to his first club, Sheffield Wednesday, which later he was to manage.

220. NICKY WOOD

NICKY WOOD		
COMP.	APPS	GLS
LEAGUE	2 (1)	0
LC	0 (1)	0
TOTAL	2 (2)	0

BORN	OLDHAM 6TH JANUARY 1966
POSITION	FORWARD
JOINED UNITED	JUNE 1981 FROM JUNIOR FOOTBALL
UNITED DEBUT	EVERTON (A) DIV. 1 - 26/12/1985
UNITED FAREWELL	OXFORD UNITED (H) DIV. 1 - 04/04/1987
RETIRED	JAN 1989 - DUE TO INJURY

Poor Nicky Wood had to retire before his exceedingly promising career had the chance to get started properly. The lad had a lot going for him: he was quick, had a fine left foot, and was tall for a wide player, but he had a dodgy back and he had to pack in at the age of 22.

Earlier Nicky had cut a considerable dash for the England youth team and there was no shortage of sensible judges who reckoned he could do the same for United. He has my heartfelt sympathy.

BORN	BUXTON, DERBYSHIRE 29TH SEPTEMBER 1958
POSITION	CENTRAL DEFENDER
JOINED UNITED	DEC. 1985 FROM EVERTON - £60,000 FOLLOWING EARLIER RETIREMENT THROUGH INJURY
UNITED DEBUT	ROCHDALE (H) FAC - 09/01/1986
UNITED FAREWELL	SHEFFIELD WED. (H) DIV. 1 - 13/04/1986
LEFT UNITED FOR	BURY - INITIALLY ON LOAN £10,000

MARK HIGGINS		
COMP.	APPS	GLS
LEAGUE	6	0
FAC	2	0
TOTAL	8	0

221. MARK HIGGINS

OTHER CLUBS:
EVERTON 76/7-83/4 (152, 6);
BURY 86/7-87/8 (68, 0);
STOKE CITY 88/9-89/90 (39, 1).

In a footballing sense, Mark Higgins came back from the dead. He was an immensely promising centre-half with Everton who missed out on all that club's mid-1980s success under Howard Kendall because he was invalided out of the game through injury.

Astonishingly Ron Atkinson took a gamble by bringing Mark out of retirement, but it was a signing that always baffled me. United were paying £60,000 for a 27-year-old, previously written off by the medical men, and over whose future hung a tremendous doubt. Like quite a few of Ron's dealings, it seemed almost whimsical. Perhaps he had a hunch that if he could get Mark back to anything like he used to be, then he would have a bargain, but I couldn't see the logic.

What made it even more bizarre was that we weren't exactly short of centre-halves at the time; we had Paul McGrath, Kevin Moran, Graeme Hogg, Billy Garton . . . what was Ron thinking? It would be unfair to Mark to judge him on what he showed during his brief stint at Old Trafford. That was not the real Mark Higgins. He'd had his time at Everton, which unfortunately did not last. That was particularly poignant for me because I had known him since he was a boy, being an old friend of his late father, John, who played centre-half for Bolton Wanderers when they beat United in the 1958 FA Cup Final.

BORN	WALTHAMSTOW, LONDON 23RD DECEMBER 1962
POSITION	STRIKER
JOINED UNITED	JANUARY 1986 FROM COVENTRY C. - £400,000
UNITED DEBUT	WEST HAM UNITED (A) DIV. 1 - 02/02/1986
UNITED FAREWELL	TOTTENHAM HOTSPUR (A) DIV. 1 - 04/05/1987
LEFT UNITED FOR	WIMBLEDON AUG. 1987 - £200,000

TERRY GIBSON		
COMP.	APPS	GLS
LEAGUE	14 (9)	1
FAC	1 (1)	0
LC	0 (2)	0
TOTAL	15 (12)	1

222. TERRY GIBSON

OTHER CLUBS:
TOTTENHAM HOTSPUR 79/80-82/3 (18, 4);
COVENTRY CITY 83/4-85/6 (98, 43);
WIMBLEDON 87/8-92/3 (86, 22);
SWINDON TOWN on loan 91/2 (9, 1);
PETERBOROUGH UNITED 93/4 (1, 0);
BARNET 93/4-94/5 (32, 5).

Nothing against the lad personally, but Terry Gibson was never going to be a Manchester United player, in the true sense of that description, if he lived to be a thousand.

The club paid £400,000 for him and yet gave him only 14 League starts, which was incomprehensible enough. But what made the situation even more unreal was that after the tiny

little striker was signed, at a time when the team was struggling for goals, he *still* didn't get picked. I felt sorry for Terry,
who did very well at Coventry, averaging close to a goal every
two games. After all, he hadn't asked United to pay a small
fortune for him, and I imagine the transfer was as big a surprise
to him as it was to the rest of us.

The mystery deepens when you consider this: if Ron Atkinson thought Alan Brazil was a better striker than Gary Lineker,
then how on earth did he come to swap him for Terry Gibson?
It made no sense at all. Looking back, the move offers a telling
illustration of the changing climate of football. There is no
way Matt Busby would have been allowed to pay good money
for a player and then not use him. The directors would have
hung him for less.

223. JOHNNY SIVEBAEK

OTHER HONOURS:
87 DENMARK CAPS 1982-92.

OTHER CLUBS:
VEJLE, DENMARK;
ST ETIENNE AND MONACO, BOTH FRANCE;
ATALANTA AND PESCARA, BOTH ITALY.

JOHNNY SIVABAEK		
COMP.	APPS	GLS
LEAGUE	29 (2)	1
FAC	2	0
LC	1	0
TOTAL	32 (2)	1

BORN	VEJLE, DENMARK 25TH OCTOBER 1961
POSITION	FULL-BACK OR MIDFIELDER
JOINED UNITED	FEBRUARY 1986 FROM VEJLE, DEN. - £200,000
UNITED DEBUT	LIVERPOOL (A) DIV. 1 - 09/02/1986
UNITED FAREWELL	TOTTENHAM HOTSPUR (A) DIV. 1 - 04/05/1987
LEFT UNITED FOR	ST. ETIENNE AUG 1987 - £250,000

When Ron Atkinson signed Johnny Sivebaek, I
applauded. He appeared to me a thoroughbred
footballer and I thought he would prove an
admirable long-term acquisition at a time when the squad
needed considerable improvement. Just as the deal went
through, the fans were still marvelling at a recent much-tele-
vised wonder-goal Johnny had scored for Denmark, so everybody was happy. There seemed little doubt that the lad was the
bee's knees as a right-sided midfielder.

But only a few months after his recruitment, Big Ron was
sacked, Alex Ferguson arrived, and pretty soon Sivebaek was
history, which goes to show what an inexact science football
management is. Here were two well-respected managers with a
massive gulf in their judgements of the same player.

It's amazing how one man's meat can become another man's
poison so quickly. As for Johnny, most of his time at United
was spent as a full-back, a position from which he showed how
effective he might have been had he remained on the flank –
he was quick, he got wide and he delivered plenty of crosses.

Johnny was an accomplished footballer and I wish he'd been
granted a decent run of games, preferably in midfield because
I think he lacked a little bit defensively. But I don't think Ron
ever had any intention of playing him wide; he saw him as a
full-back.

BORN	BIRKENHEAD 24TH MARCH 1961
POSITION	STRIKER
JOINED UNITED	MARCH 1986 FROM NOTT'M F. - £570,000
UNITED DEBUT	QPR (A) DIV. 1 - 15/03/1986
UNITED FAREWELL	NORWICH CITY (A) DIV. 1 - 26/10/1988
LEFT UNITED FOR	MIDDLESBROUGH NOV 1988

PETER DAVENPORT		
COMP.	APPS	GLS
LEAGUE	73 (19)	22
FAC	2 (2)	0
LC	8 (2)	4
TOTAL	83 (23)	26

224. PETER DAVENPORT

OTHER HONOURS:
1 ENGLAND CAP 1985.

OTHER CLUBS:
NOTTINGHAM FOREST 81/2-85/6 (118, 54);
MIDDLESBROUGH 88/9-89/90 (59, 7);
SUNDERLAND 90/1-92/3 (99, 15);
AIRDRIEONIANS 93/4 (38, 8);
ST JOHNSTONE 94/5 (22, 4); STOCKPORT COUNTY 94/5 (6, 1);
MACCLESFIELD TOWN 97/8-98/9 (5, 1).

MANAGER:
MACCLESFIELD TOWN 2000.

Like Garry Birtles before him, Peter Davenport suffered in that he was used to Brian Clough's distinctive way of playing at Nottingham Forest. Moving from the City Ground to Old Trafford was like moving from one footballing culture to another, and the language was clearly totally different. They had nothing in common.

Peter was an England international with a highly impressive scoring record for his first club, yet after joining United, he seemed constantly to be straining to fit in. His place always seemed to be under question, and the situation worsened for him when the manager was changed. Not long after the arrival of Alex Ferguson, in came Brian McClair and Mark Hughes, and soon Peter was on his way out.

He was a central striker, but Alex usually deployed him in a wide position, which can't have been easy for a young man striving to make an impact and earn acceptance at such a big club. I felt sorry for Peter, because he was a useful footballer with more natural ability than, say, Birtles, who had made the same journey before him. I thought United got rid of him far too quickly.

He had good skill and enterprising movement, he was intelligent, knew what the game was about and could score goals, though he was slender, no sort of a giant, and wasn't brilliant upstairs. Peter Davenport was yet another who came and left before we knew much of him. It's a great shame, because we'll never know whether or not he had it in him to become a true United man.

225. GARY WALSH

OTHER CLUBS:
AIRDRIEONIANS ON LOAN 88/9 (3, 0);
OLDHAM ATHLETIC ON LOAN 93/4 (6, 0);
MIDDLESBROUGH 95/6-96/7 (44, 0);
BRADFORD CITY 97/8-02/03 (132, 0);
MIDDLESBROUGH ON LOAN 00/01 (3, 0);
WIGAN ATHLETIC 03/04- (3, 0).

GARY WALSH		
COMP.	APPS	GLS
LEAGUE	49 (1)	0
LC	7	0
EUROPE	6	0
TOTAL	62 (1)	0

BORN	WIGAN 21ST MARCH 1968
POSITION	GOALKEEPER
JOINED UNITED	JUNE 1983 FROM JUNIOR FOOTBALL
UNITED DEBUT	ASTON VILLA (A) DIV. 1 - 13/12/1986
UNITED FAREWELL	COVENTRY CITY (H) DIV. 1 - 03/01/1995
LEFT UNITED FOR	MIDDLESBROUGH AUG 1995 - £250,000

When I first laid eyes on Gary Walsh, I thought he was as fine a young goalkeeper as I had seen for many a long day.

I liked everything about him. He was big, strong and fearless, commanding his box in a manner which brought to mind Harry Gregg, which is praise indeed. I thought Gary had every chance of becoming a top performer, and I was mortified when he suffered two awful injuries which put his progress on hold.

He remains the only 'keeper I've seen in my life who looked a class act as a kid. Usually they all lack something, and the best ones learn as they go along, coming into their prime at around the age of 27. But Gary appeared to be in his pomp at 18, straight into it from boyhood.

Those mishaps knocked him back at a crucial stage of his development, and both his movement and his confidence were affected. Happily he didn't lose all his impetus because nine years after making his United debut, he moved to Middlesbrough for £250,000, so clearly Bryan Robson thought a lot of him.

Had Gary enjoyed better fortune, perhaps neither Jim Leighton nor Peter Schmeichel would have been bought by Alex Ferguson. They simply wouldn't have been needed if he had developed in the way that seemed possible when he was a teenager.

I'd say Gary Walsh was one of the unluckiest young men to play for United in the last 40 years, because he had talent to burn and I don't believe it came to full fruition. Still, he's kept going well, being number-two at Wigan during their successful push for promotion from Division One in 2004/05 at the age of 37.

BORN	DUBLIN 5TH SEPTEMBER 1964
POSITION	MIDFIELDER
JOINED UNITED	OCTOBER 1986 FROM SHAMROCK R. - £50,000
UNITED DEBUT	LEICESTER CITY (H) DIV. 1 - 20/12/1986
UNITED FAREWELL	ASTON VILLA (H) DIV. 1 - 05/11/1988
LEFT UNITED FOR	NEWCASTLE UNITED NOV. 1988 - £275,000

BORN	BRADFORD 6TH MARCH 1968
POSITION	MIDFIELDER, FULL-BACK
JOINED UNITED	JUNE 1984 FROM JUNIOR FOOTBALL
UNITED DEBUT	SOUTHAMPTON (A) DIV. 1 - 03/01/1987
UNITED FAREWELL	NOTTINGHAM FOREST (A) DIV. 1 - 27/03/1989
RETIRED	DEC. 1990 - DUE TO INJURY

Liam O'Brien		
COMP.	APPS	GLS
LEAGUE	16 (15)	2
FAC	0 (2)	0
LC	1 (2)	0
TOTAL	17 (19)	2

226. LIAM O'BRIEN

OTHER HONOURS:
16 REPUBLIC OF IRELAND CAPS 1987-96.
OTHER CLUBS:
SHAMROCK ROVERS, REPUBLIC OF IRELAND;
NEWCASTLE UNITED 88/9-93/4 (151, 19);
TRANMERE ROVERS 93/4-98/9 (181, 11).

The word 'nice' may seem a terrible description to give a footballer, but it sums up Liam O'Brien, who was never less than a pleasure to watch.

He was a tall, gangling, rather slender Irish lad with a bit of culture about him. Always ready to put his foot on the ball and dip his shoulder, he could pass both accurately and imaginatively, and he brought welcome intelligence to his game.

Ron Atkinson signed him shortly after he had helped Shamrock Rovers to the League of Ireland championship of 1985/86, but within a month O'Brien had a new boss in Alex Ferguson, who lost little time in giving him his debut.

Over the next two years there were a couple of spells of five or six games when Liam really began to look the part as a midfield provider, but in the end he was crowded out of contention by the sheer weight of competition and he joined Newcastle, with whom he performed impressively, as he did later at Tranmere.

Maybe if Liam had crossed the Irish Sea to join a club like, say, Coventry or Southampton, he would have stood out. But chances at United are limited and you have to make the most of them, often in the briefest window of opportunity. There's always going to be money spent to bring in top quality rivals for your place.

Tony Gill		
COMP.	APPS	GLS
LEAGUE	5 (5)	1
FAC	2 (2)	1
TOTAL	7 (7)	2

227. TONY GILL

Tony Gill was as unlucky as they come. Without question, he had displayed enough ability and application to prove he had a definite chance to become a top player.

Unfortunately, with the type of injury he picked up against Nottingham Forest, when his leg was shattered in a challenge with Brian Laws, there is no tomorrow in the footballing sense.

Tony could pass, he could tackle, he was willing to work, and

he was versatile, being capable of excelling either in midfield or at full-back.

Sometimes it's a curse to be adaptable because it prevents a player settling into his best position, but this lad seemed comfortable with it. He could do a bit of everything in the same way that Bryan Robson could, although I'm not suggesting he was another Robbo. They don't come along too often.

True, even without that horrendous collision at the City Ground in the spring of 1989, his road to success would have been hard because of the money that Alex Ferguson was spending to rebuild his team.

But Tony was one of the so-called Fergie's Fledglings – what a dreadfully contrived label that was – and as Alex was to demonstrate when he gave the next generation of boys their heads in the 1990s, he was not afraid to stand by his youngsters provided they were talented enough.

Later Tony became the youngest coach in the country at Bristol Rovers before losing his job through a management change and leaving the game to make a new life for himself with a Bristol-based office supplies company.

228. VIV ANDERSON

OTHER HONOURS:
30 ENGLAND CAPS 1978-88.

OTHER CLUBS:
NOTTINGHAM FOREST 74/5-83/4 (328, 15);
ARSENAL 84/5-86/7 (120, 9);
SHEFFIELD WEDNESDAY 90/1-92/3 (70, 8);
BARNSLEY 93/4 (20, 3); MIDDLESBROUGH 94/5 (2, 0).

MANAGER:
BARNSLEY 1993-94.

VIV ANDERSON		
COMP.	APPS	GLS
LEAGUE	50 (4)	2
FAC	7	1
LC	6 (1)	1
EUROPE	1	0
TOTAL	64 (5)	4

BORN	NOTTINGHAM 29TH AUGUST 1956
POSITION	FULL-BACK
JOINED UNITED	JULY 1987 FROM ARSENAL - £250,000
UNITED DEBUT	SOUTHAMPTON (A) DIV. 1 - 15/08/1987
UNITED FAREWELL	HALIFAX TOWN (H) LC - 10/10/1990
LEFT UNITED FOR	SHEFFIELD WEDNESDAY JAN 1991

Some people were quite surprised that Alex Ferguson should make a 30-year-old his first signing, and I must admit to being one of them. Perhaps that's the reason why Alex has won every prize in the book and I haven't!

It's just that when he already had two such accomplished full-backs as Mick Duxbury and Arthur Albiston, both internationals and both younger men, I could never understand why he needed to spend so much money on a player of Viv Anderson's age.

But the manager had been massively impressed by Anderson's attitude when United had beaten Arsenal during the previous season. That January afternoon at Old Trafford, Viv simply refused to take defeat lying down, proving himself a bad loser after Fergie's own heart and earning himself a move

to Manchester United in the process.

My initial reaction to the transfer does not signify the slightest criticism of Viv himself, a well-established international and England's first black player, who had nothing to prove after winning the League title and two European Cups with Nottingham Forest. You could say he had done it all yet his hunger still burned brightly, which is exactly what attracted Alex to him.

Certainly Viv didn't let his new boss down, proving an immensely valuable signing to Alex. In those first few years when he wasn't winning trophies, it was worth a lot to have someone as reliable and stable as Viv in the side.

He remained an extremely bubbly and competitive character, always wanting to play and to win, exuding that desire from every pore. Come hell or high water, he'd do everything in his power to make sure he didn't finish on the losing side.

Viv had a very individual gait, loping along almost as if he had a limp, but that was just his style of running. He was tall for a full-back and often, when a winger had apparently nipped past him, he would stick out a long leg to collect the ball.

Unfortunately he suffered quite a few injuries when he was at Old Trafford, which was ironic in that he was invariably fit for both Forest and Arsenal, as he was in his Sheffield Wednesday days after leaving United.

BORN	AIRDRIE, LANARKSHIRE 8TH DECEMBER 1963
POSITION	STRIKER OR MIDFIELDER
JOINED UNITED	JULY 1987 FROM CELTIC - £850,000
UNITED DEBUT	SOUTHAMPTON (A) DIV. 1 - 15/08/1987
UNITED HONOURS	ECWC 1990/1 PREMIERSHIP 1992/3, 1993.4, 1995/6, 1996/7 FA CUP 1989/90, 1993/4 LEAGUE CUP 1991/2
UNITED FAREWELL	LEEDS UNITED (H) PREM. - 04/05/1998
LEFT UNITED FOR	MOTHERWELL - JUNE 1998

BRIAN McCLAIR		
COMP.	APPS	GLS
LEAGUE	296 (59)	88
FAC	39 (6)	14
LC	44 (1)	19
EUROPE	17 (6)	5
OTHERS	3	1
TOTAL	399 (72)	127

229. BRIAN McCLAIR

OTHER HONOURS:
30 SCOTLAND CAPS 1986-93.
SCOTTISH FOOTBALLER OF THE YEAR 1987
SCOTTISH PFA FOOTBALLER OF THE YEAR 1987

OTHER CLUBS:
MOTHERWELL 81/2-82/3 (39, 15);
CELTIC 83/4-86/7 (145, 99);
MOTHERWELL 98/9 (11, 0).

I bet Alex Ferguson wishes he could buy two Brian McClairs every season. In fact, the fellow they call Choccy must be up there among the manager's top ten purchases during all the long years of his Old Trafford reign.

Not that McClair was an eye-catching performer, either as a striker or midfielder. You could go to a game and not notice that he'd played – other than the fact that he'd scored two goals. That's not being derogatory, some players are like that, unobtrusive but overwhelmingly professional.

In midfield he was a fetcher and carrier. He wasn't a hard man but he wasn't a coward; he didn't go around kicking people but he didn't run away from them, either.

Beyond that, Brian brought an exemplary attitude to everything he did. He was a wonderful man to have around the club and a perfect example for the youngsters as they rose through the ranks.

Brian joined United as an out-and-out marksman, having found the net freely for Celtic and been voted Scotland's player of the year in 1986/87. In his first English campaign he became the first United man since George Best to score 20 League goals in a season.

That term he was the only one expected to score goals, but then Mark Hughes returned to Old Trafford, so the emphasis shifted. Brian found it difficult, and he finished up shifting to midfield, where he toiled productively through many more hugely successful campaigns.

He lost his regular berth for a time when Roy Keane arrived in 1993/94, but he just soldiered on, earning a place in the team more often than not over the next five immensely rewarding years.

Whether Brian was a better front player than midfielder, I don't think matters particularly. To say he couldn't do this or that, as certain of his most vociferous critics were prone to do, was being needlessly pedantic. Suffice to say that he satisfied a demanding manager like Alex Ferguson for 11 years.

Perhaps it is possible to break down his game and be critical of one aspect or another, but that's all immaterial. Look at his record, count his honours and register the size of the smile on his boss's face. Brian McClair can look back on an absolutely magnificent career at the club.

The transaction which brought him to Old Trafford was referred to a transfer tribunal, with Celtic asking for £2 million, an astronomical sum at that time. In the end United parted with only £850,000, which represents one of the best deals anybody has completed in modern times.

These days Choccy, a quiet character with a highly individual sense of humour, is back with United after working under Brian Kidd at Blackburn. His responsibility is the reserves, and I hope the boys in his charge understand how fortunate they are. They could never wish for a more impeccable role model.

'Perhaps it is possible to break down his game and be critical of one aspect or another, but that's all immaterial. Look at his record, count his honours and register the size of the smile on his boss's face.'

BORN	CANNOCK, STAFFORDSHIRE 4TH OCTOBER 1969
POSITION	STRIKER
JOINED UNITED	JULY 1986 FROM JUNIOR FOOTBALL
UNITED DEBUT	WIMBLEDON (A) DIV. 1 - 21/11/1987
UNITED FAREWELL	QPR (A) FAC - 11/01/1989
LEFT UNITED FOR	BARNSLEY AUG. 1991 - £50,000

DEINIOL GRAHAM		
COMP.	APPS	GLS
LEAGUE	1	0
FAC	0 (1)	1
LC	0 (1)	0
TOTAL	1 (2)	1

230. DEINIOL GRAHAM

OTHER CLUBS:
BARNSLEY 91/2-93/4 (38, 2);
PRESTON NORTH END ON LOAN 92/3 (8, 0);
CARLISLE UNITED ON LOAN 93/4 (2, 1);
STOCKPORT COUNTY 94/5 (11, 2);
SCUNTHORPE UNITED 95/6 (3, 1).

Deiniol Graham was one of those unfortunate lads saddled with a label comparing him to a former great. In his case, because he was a Welsh schoolboy and youth international, he was dubbed the new Ian Rush, which was as wild and ridiculous as all such arbitrary tags tend to be.

After scoring freely at junior levels, he was given his first senior opportunity as an 18-year-old, but didn't make his mark and returned to the reserves. Just over a year on he was given another chance and netted an FA Cup equaliser against Queen's Park Rangers at Loftus Road, only to suffer a badly broken arm a few days later.

Sadly Deiniol was never offered another shot at first-team action, and when he moved on his subsequent career was dogged by injury.

BORN	HEXHAM, NORTHUMBERLAND 31ST DECEMBER 1960
POSITION	CENTRAL DEFENDER
JOINED UNITED	DEC. 1987 FROM NORWICH CITY - £800,000
UNITED DEBUT	PORTSMOUTH (A) DIV. 1 - 19/12/1987
UNITED HONOURS	ECWC 1990/1 PREMIERSHIP 1992/3, 1993/4, 1995/6 FA CUP 1989/90, 1993/4 LEAGUE CUP 1991/2
UNITED FAREWELL	LEEDS UNITED (H) PREM. - 17/04/1996
LEFT UNITED FOR	BIRMINGHAM CITY JUNE 1996

STEVE BRUCE		
COMP.	APPS	GLS
LEAGUE	309	36
FAC	41	3
LC	32 (2)	6
EUROPE	25 (1)	6
OTHERS	4	0
TOTAL	411 (3)	51

231. STEVE BRUCE

OTHER CLUBS:
GILLINGHAM 79/80-83/4 (205, 29);
NORWICH CITY 84/5-87/8 (141, 14);
BIRMINGHAM CITY 96/7-97/8 (72, 2);
SHEFFIELD UNITED 98/9 (10, 0).

MANAGER:
SHEFFIELD UNITED 1998-99;
HUDDERSFIELD TOWN 1999-2000;
WIGAN ATHLETIC 2001; CRYSTAL PALACE 2001;
BIRMINGHAM CITY 2001-.

Steve Bruce is a delightful Geordie character, a totally genuine family man, and what a good egg he proved to be for Manchester United down the years.

Alex Ferguson has made all sorts of star signings in his time at Old Trafford, but he hasn't struck many better bargains than the one he reached with Norwich City to recruit Steve.

I saw him play for his first club, Gillingham, when I was chief scout at Burnley. He was a wing-half in those days, but then he suffered an injury and finished up playing centre-half, where he went on to make his name. That was the best move he ever made because I'd say it's unlikely that he would have played for United in his former role.

Come December 1987, at a time when Paul McGrath was apparently on his way out, Alex was contemplating a new central defensive pairing, and Brucie proved to be the perfect first half of the combination. Eventually Gary Pallister arrived to join him, and although they offered a striking contrast in styles, with Pally being quicker and more of a ball player, they complemented each other ideally.

Steve was brave and honest, a lad who would never let the side down because he wouldn't know how and who often played with injuries that would have had other men on their knees. He was the sort you'd love to have beside you if you were fighting in the trenches, and his resolute backbone and unquenchable spirit made him a key defensive cornerstone of the modern Manchester United.

Admittedly he was never elegant, but no one should run away with the idea that Brucie was a mere clogger. He always tried to play, and he learned to read the game brilliantly, so that his accumulated experience and nous were worth an extra yard of pace by anyone's reckoning.

I think most people who know their football would agree that Steve was one of the unluckiest men on God's earth never to have played for England, and Bobby Robson has had the good grace to admit that he made a mistake in not selecting him. Mind, I'm not sure how much consolation that is when the lad's finished up without a cap.

Probably Graham Taylor was even more culpable than Robson, because arguably Brucie reached his peak in the early 1990s, when Taylor was in charge of the national team.

Happily, Steve made spectacular amends for that international travesty on the club front, doing an inspirational job for United over the best part of a decade.

In 1990/91 he even found time to score 19 goals, including 11 penalties, and he was a colossal influence as Barcelona were beaten in the final of the European Cup Winners' Cup.

He continued to thunder forward in 1992/93, never more effectively than at home to Sheffield Wednesday in the spring, when United were striving desperately to win their first Championship for more than a quarter of a century.

They were a goal down near the end, and you could feel the despair of the fans welling

up all over again. But then Brucie popped up with two late headers, the second of them seven minutes into stoppage time, and after that the team never looked back.

A year later he became the first Englishman in the 20th century to captain his side to the League and FA Cup double, and nobody could have deserved the honour more. It was always going to be difficult for Alex to find a worthy successor to Bryan Robson as skipper, but he found him in Brucie.

I'm proud to say that I got him his first job in management at Sheffield United, where he found it difficult dealing with the board. Since then he's moved around a bit but now I believe he's found his niche at Birmingham, with people who will back his judgement.

As to his next step, presuming that he makes one, if Steve carries on in his current vein at St Andrew's, then he's got to be in with a hell of a chance of taking over at Old Trafford when that post finally becomes vacant.

BORN	HYDE, CHESHIRE 5TH FEBRUARY 1968
POSITION	FULL-BACK
JOINED UNITED	JUNE 1985 FROM JUNIOR FOOTBALL
UNITED DEBUT	WIMBLEDON (H) DIV. 1 - 09/05/1988
UNITED HONOURS	FA CUP 1989/90
UNITED FAREWELL	LEICESTER CITY (H) LC - 27/10/1993
LEFT UNITED FOR	CELTIC JAN. 1994 - £250,000

LEE MARTIN		
COMP.	APPS	GLS
LEAGUE	56 (17)	1
FAC	13 (1)	1
LC	8 (2)	0
EUROPE	6 (6)	0
OTHERS	1	0
TOTAL	84 (26)	2

232. LEE MARTIN

OTHER CLUBS:
CELTIC 93/4-94/5 (19, 0);
BRISTOL ROVERS 96/7-97/8 (25, 0);
HUDDERSFIELD TOWN ON LOAN 97/8 (3, 0).

I thought Lee Martin was going to be one of the big United players of the 1990s. When he scored the winning goal in the 1990 FA Cup Final replay against Crystal Palace, he was only 22 and he looked as though he had everything going for him.

But then he suffered a back injury which shattered his impetus, Denis Irwin and Paul Parker prospered in the full-back positions, and all the while the Neville brothers were coming up on the rails.

THE SWEETEST MOMENT OF LEE MARTIN'S CAREER: the 22-year-old rattles home the winner against Crystal Palace in the FA Cup Final replay of 1990.

As a result Lee secured a move to Celtic, which didn't seem a bad destination if he had to leave Old Trafford, but he fell prey to more fitness problems, and the gremlins even followed him to Bristol Rovers, eventually causing early retirement.

Suddenly, a player who seemed set to be a long-term fixture with United, a level-headed type who might have matured into another Arthur Albiston, was out of the game.

Lee's approach was very similar to Arthur's, winning the ball and giving it simply, covering sensibly but unspectacularly, always efficient.

Probably his goal that beat Palace at Wembley seemed out of character, because you wouldn't have expected to see him in such an advanced position, crashing an unstoppable shot into the roof of the net at the end of a flowing move. When I saw that I had to blink to clear my head. Surely that wasn't Lee Martin, it must have been somebody else!

More typically, Lee was unobtrusively competent, exactly the type I would have expected to compile a mountain of appearances, but he ran out of luck. No one plays 500 games, like Arthur, without being born with a shamrock over their head.

Clearly, in a football sense, Lee wasn't blessed. Playing for United at the time he broke through, he could easily have been part of all the success they enjoyed during the 1990s, a truly magical period for the club. By now he could be polishing eight Championship medals and counting a big pile of money. Instead of that he finds himself out of the game and running a sports shop.

Lee encountered a few problems outside of football, but happily he's got them sorted out, and I wish him well. He's a nice, honest lad who has never tried to do anything but look after his family.

He's by far the youngest committee member of the Manchester United Former Players Association and I hope he continues to play an active part in the future.

THE FRUITS OF VICTORY: sadly, there were to be no more glory days for unlucky Lee Martin.

233. JIM LEIGHTON

OTHER HONOURS:
91 SCOTLAND CAPS 1982-98.

OTHER CLUBS:
ABERDEEN 78/9-87/8 (300, 0);
READING ON LOAN 91/2 (8, 0);
DUNDEE 91/2-92/3 (21, 0);
HIBERNIAN 93/4-96/7 (151, 0);
ABERDEEN 97/8-99/00 (82, 0).

JIM LEIGHTON		
COMP.	APPS	GLS
LEAGUE	73	0
FAC	14	0
LC	7	0
TOTAL	94	0

BORN	PAISLEY, RENFREWSHIRE 24TH JULY 1958
POSITION	GOALKEEPER
JOINED UNITED	JUNE 1988 FROM ABERDEEN - £750,000
UNITED DEBUT	QPR (H) DIV. 1 - 27/08/1988
UNITED FAREWELL	HALIFAX TOWN (A) LC - 26/09/1990
LEFT UNITED FOR	DUNDEE FEB 1992 - £150,000

Jim Leighton arrived at Old Trafford to tumultuous fanfares heralding the best goalkeeper in the country, a man who had thrived under Alex Ferguson at Aberdeen, accumulating an enviable collection of honours. He really was some-

thing as far as Alex was concerned.

Sure enough, Jim made a brilliant early impression. After a period when United had not had a settled 'keeper for a while, pretty well everybody liked what they saw.

But his form appeared to deteriorate after some injuries, then his Old Trafford career turned on the 1990 FA Cup Final. Jim was picked for the first match, was subjected to a barrage of hysterical criticism after conceding three goals and then was left out in favour of Les Sealey for the replay.

My opinion is that if he was considered good enough for the original match, then he should have been retained for the second.

I didn't think the goals conceded in the first game were his fault. I disagree with the manager over that. It's always very easy to blame the goalkeeper, but there are ten other people playing on the same side and somewhere along the line they have to accept a little bit of responsibility. On this occasion, I don't think they did.

It was an extremely harsh decision to drop Jim half-way through the FA Cup Final, and it is hardly surprising that he was bitter about it. But Alex was the manager, Alex made the decision, and Alex was right, because United won the Cup. It's always been the same in football: as long as you win, you'll never be wrong.

That said, I never thought Jim was as great a goalkeeper as he was made out to be in the first place. I thought he was all right, but nothing more. Certainly I didn't share Alex's view that he was the best in Britain. But to be fair, I never saw him as the ultimate culprit, either.

BORN	HALESOWEN, BIRMINGHAM 27TH MAY 1971
POSITION	WINGER, MIDFIELDER
JOINED UNITED	MAY 1988 FROM TORQUAY UTD - £200,000
UNITED DEBUT	WEST HAM UTD (H) DIV. 1 - 24/09/1988
UNITED HONOURS	ECWC 1990/1 PREMIERSHIP 1992/3, 1993/4, 1995/6 FAC 1993/4 LEAGUE CUP 1991/2
UNITED FAREWELL	NOTTINGHAM FOREST (H) PREM. - 28/04/1996
LEFT UNITED FOR	LEEDS UNITED AUGUST 1996 - £4.5M

LEE SHARPE		
COMP.	APPS	GLS
LEAGUE	160 (33)	21
FAC	22 (7)	3
LC	15 (8)	9
EUROPE	15 (2)	3
OTHERS	1	0
TOTAL	213 (50)	36

234. LEE SHARPE

OTHER HONOURS:
8 ENGLAND CAPS 1991-93.

OTHER CLUBS:
TORQUAY UNITED 87/8 (14, 3);
LEEDS UNITED 96/7-98/9 (30, 5);
SAMPDORIA, ITALY, ON LOAN 98/9 (3, 0);
BRADFORD CITY 98/9-01/02 (56, 4);
PORTSMOUTH ON LOAN 00/01 (17, 0);
EXETER CITY 02/03 (4, 1).

Potentially Lee Sharpe was Manchester United's finest left-winger since Charlie Mitten, but he blew the chance of a lifetime through lack of professionalism, failing to look after himself in the way that any top athlete should do.

Lee was endowed with a superb left peg and, unlike so many modern players, he was a wonderful crosser of a ball. So many times in a match he would go past his marker on the outside and then create a goal-scoring opportunity with a beautiful delivery from near the byline. Only rarely did he cut inside and take a pot himself, despite the fact that he carried a tremendous shot.

I'm convinced that, given a more disciplined approach, he could still have been a United player in 2005, still only 34 years old and with a record to rival that of Ryan Giggs. And who knows, with a fully committed Lee Sharpe to call on, United might have achieved even more than they have, if that's possible to envisage.

In an ideal world, I would have been more than happy to accommodate three wingers, Giggs, Sharpe and Andrei Kanchelskis, being thankful to have three such fabulous performers in my squad. It's not as though only 11 can play these days, when substitutes are used tactically. Any one of those three would be equally effective starting the game or getting up from the bench to change the course of a contest.

When he was breaking through, Lee, who was recommended to the club by former *Weekly News* reporter Len Noad, always had Ryan to contend with as a fellow left-winger, which might explain why Alex Ferguson played him at left-back in some of his early games. I didn't agree with that because I didn't rate Lee as a defender, it simply wasn't his forte.

Often comparisons are made between Giggs and Sharpe, and they offered a nice contrast. There was very little to choose between them in terms of pace, while Lee was the more reliable crosser and Ryan the more devastating dribbler. But how lovely for any manager to have two players who could do the same job so brilliantly yet so differently.

It's a travesty that Lee Sharpe's no longer in the game. We're talking here of a lad who had won six major honours with United by the age of 25 and had played for England, yet by his early thirties he was out of top-line football. How did that happen to this kid?

He should have had so much more to offer, but I think the manager discovered that he was doing one or two naughty things, not knuckling down to business as a professional foot-

SHARPE FINISH: Lee nets with a brilliant glancing header on the way to a hat-trick in United's 6-2 League Cup annihilation of Arsenal at Highbury in November 1990.

baller should.

Alex's judgement has been borne out in that Lee did virtually nothing in what remained of his career after joining Leeds for £4.5 million, which represented a massive profit on what United had paid to sign him from Torquay.

I know he suffered illness and injuries, but they were nothing to do with the start of his sad decline. That had rather more to do with inattention to the details of his professional life. What a shameful waste of talent.

BORN	WIGAN 28TH SEPTEMBER 1968
POSITION	MIDFIELDER
JOINED UNITED	JUNE 1985 FROM JUNIOR FOOTBALL
UNITED DEBUT	WEST HAM UNITED (H) DIV. 1 - 24/09/1988
UNITED FAREWELL	ATLETICO MADRID (A) ECWC - 23/10/1991
LEFT UNITED FOR	BOURNEMOUTH - JUNE 1993

RUSSELL BEARDSMORE		
COMP.	APPS	GLS
LEAGUE	30 (26)	4
FAC	4 (4)	0
LC	3 (1)	0
EUROPE	2 (3)	0
TOTAL	39 (34)	4

235. RUSSELL BEARDSMORE

OTHER CLUBS:
BLACKBURN ROVERS ON LOAN 91/2 (2, 0); BOURNEMOUTH 93/4-97/8 (178, 4).

Russell Beardsmore wasn't the size of two penn'orth of copper, but he was a perky little local lad and the crowd warmed to him immediately. As I said to Fergie, if you play your kids the supporters will always forgive you a few mistakes.

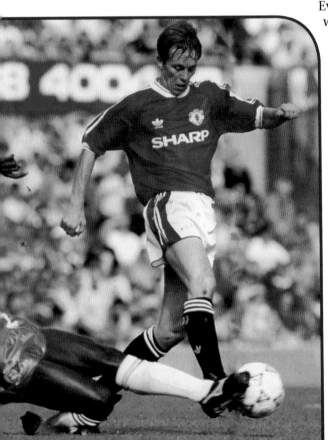

Even today, in this much more cosmopolitan world that we've had to get used to, the fans would prefer a few more locals to expensive nonentities from abroad.

Russell made a fantastic start to his United career, unforgettably lighting up Old Trafford with one incandescent performance in a 3-1 victory over Liverpool on New Year's Day 1989, first setting up goals for Brian McClair and Mark Hughes, then cracking home a super volley.

He wanted to be a central midfielder in the Paul Scholes mould, and undoubtedly he had the necessary skill. But unlike Scholesy, I don't think he had the strength. That said, he could do a pretty decent job playing wide.

I liked Russell. He had no real physique so he had to rely on being able to play the game, which he could do. Of course, he was facing a monumental task, given his lack of stature and the scale of the competition for places.

After his playing days were ended by injury, he coached youngsters for Sam Allardyce at Bolton.

236. MARK ROBINS

OTHER CLUBS:
NORWICH CITY 92/3-94/5 (67, 20);
LEICESTER CITY 94/5-96/7 (56, 12);
FC COPENHAGEN, DENMARK, ON LOAN 96/7;
READING ON LOAN 97/8 (4, 0);
ORENSE, SPAIN, 97/8; PANIONIOS, GREECE, 98/9;
MANCHESTER CITY ON LOAN 98/9 (2, 0);
WALSALL 99/00 (40, 6);
ROTHERHAM UNITED 00/01-03/04 (108, 44);
BRISTOL CITY ON LOAN 02/03 (6, 4);
SHEFFIELD WEDNESDAY 03/04 (15, 3).

MARK ROBINS		
COMP.	APPS	GLS
LEAGUE	19 (29)	11
FAC	4 (4)	3
LC	0 (7)	2
EUROPE	4 (2)	1
OTHERS	0 (1)	0
TOTAL	27 (43)	17

BORN	ASHTON-UNDER-LYNE, LANCS 22ND DECEMBER 1969
POSITION	STRIKER
JOINED UNITED	JULY 1986 FROM JUNIOR FOOTBALL
UNITED DEBUT	ROTHERHAM UNITED (H) LC - 12/10/1988
UNITED HONOURS	FA CUP 1989/90
UNITED FAREWELL	MIDDLESBROUGH (H) LC - 11/03/1992
LEFT UNITED FOR	NORWICH CITY AUGUST 1992 - £800,000

Mark Robins scored goals for fun from his childhood, which is why I tried to sign him for Burnley from junior football when I was chief scout at Turf Moor.

He was a marksman, pure and simple, possessing an unbelievable gift, an asset that can't be taught. If you lined him up with ten strikers and gave them all ten identical chances, he would convert more than most. Yet as an all-round footballer I don't think he was in the front rank.

Particularly in the Premiership, often a striker has to fashion his own opportunities, and I don't think Mark was able to do that often enough. But give him a sniff and he was deadly.

At United, Alex Ferguson always described him as the best finisher in the club, and I wouldn't argue with that. But even after paying his compliment, the manager obviously felt that the lad couldn't create enough off his own bat.

A couple of times he left Mark Hughes out of his side to accommodate Mark Robins, which proves that not even the greatest managers can be right all of the time.

237. MAL DONAGHY

OTHER HONOURS:
89 NORTHERN IRELAND CAPS 1980-94.

OTHER CLUBS:
LUTON TOWN 78/9-88/9 (410, 16);
LUTON TOWN ON LOAN 89/90 (5, 0);
CHELSEA 92/3-93/4 (68, 3).

MAL DONAGHY		
COMP.	APPS	GLS
LEAGUE	76 (13)	0
FAC	10	0
LC	9 (5)	0
EUROPE	2 (3)	0
OTHERS	1	0
TOTAL	98 (21)	0

BORN	BELFAST 13TH SEPTEMBER 1957
POSITION	DEFENDER
JOINED UNITED	OCTOBER 1988 FROM LUTON TOWN - £650,000
UNITED DEBUT	EVERTON (A) DIV. 1 - 30/10/1988
UNITED FAREWELL	TOTTENHAM HOTSPUR (H) DIV. 1 - 02/05/1992
LEFT UNITED FOR	CHELSEA AUGUST 1992 - £150,000

It came as a huge shock to me when Alex Ferguson signed Mal Donaghy. That's not to say I didn't rate his ability, just that I thought he was far too old to spend so much money on.

After all, he was in his 32nd year and, with every respect to Luton, he had never played for a top club. For all that, he was

a terrific professional who had looked after himself impeccably, United needed another defender, and he played very well, never letting the side down over some three and a half years.

Perhaps Jimmy Ryan, who was at Luton around that time but still maintained United connections, had input in that deal, knowing exactly how dedicated an individual Donaghy was. If that's the case, then all credit to Jimmy.

Mal was a very neat, straightforward and sensible operator who was never less than efficient alongside Steve Bruce, and when Gary Pallister arrived to replace him, he continued to provide reliable cover. Also he was capable of performing more than competently at full-back and his presence helped to give the manager time to form his long-term plans.

Even when he left Old Trafford at the grand old age of nearly 35, Mal secured another decent move by joining Chelsea, a fitting reward for one of the game's Mr Dependables.

BORN	DUNDEE, 13TH MAY 1961
POSITION	WINGER
JOINED UNITED	NOVEMBER 1988 FROM BRISTOL CITY - £170,000
UNITED DEBUT	SOUTHAMPTON (H) DIV. 1 - 19/11/1988
UNITED FAREWELL	DERBY COUNTY (H) DIV. 1 - 13/01/1990
LEFT UNITED FOR	SING TAO - MAY 1991

RALPH MILNE		
COMP.	APPS	GLS
LEAGUE	19 (4)	3
FAC	7	0
TOTAL	26 (4)	3

238. RALPH MILNE

OTHER CLUBS:
DUNDEE UNITED 79/80-86/7 (179, 44);
CHARLTON ATHLETIC 86/7-87/8 (22, 0);
BRISTOL CITY 87/8-88/9 (30, 6);
SING TAO, HONG KONG, 91/2.

I have to say that when Ralph came to United from Bristol City, where Joe Jordan was the manager, he must have thought he was the luckiest man in the world.

It seems that Alex Ferguson hadn't seen much of him recently but remembered some terrific displays he had given for Dundee United against Aberdeen in their Scottish days. So, with United having a bad time, he signed him from memory.

Soon some of the fans called him Michelin Man, because he appeared a trifle weighty and wasn't the quickest of movers on the left wing. In truth, nothing I saw ever convinced me that he was anything more than a very ordinary Third Division player.

The sad thing was that Alex played young Lee Sharpe, a natural winger, at left-back behind him and accommodated Ralph on the basis that he would help educate Lee. I never believed that could happen. If Ralph had been playing behind Lee, I could have understood it to some degree because the more experienced man might have protected the boy by doing some of his tackling.

In fairness to Ralph, the call from United must have given him the shock of his life. Obviously it was a temporary measure but I never understood it, although maybe there were financial constraints at that time and he was all Alex could afford. Still, that didn't alter the fact that Ralph Milne was never going to make a United footballer.

239. DAVID WILSON

OTHER CLUBS:
LINCOLN CITY ON LOAN 90/1 (3, 0);
CHARLTON ATHLETIC ON LOAN 90/1 (7, 2);
BRISTOL ROVERS 91/2-92/3 (11, 0).

DAVID WILSON		
COMP.	APPS	GLS
LEAGUE	0 (4)	0
FAC	0 (2)	0
TOTAL	0 (6)	0

BORN	BURNLEY 20TH MARCH 1969
POSITION	MIDFIELDER
JOINED UNITED	JUNE 1985 FROM JUNIOR FOOTBALL
UNITED DEBUT	SHEFFIELD WED. (H) DIV. 1 - 23/11/1988
UNITED FAREWELL	DERBY COUNTY (H) DIV. 1 - 15/04/1989
LEFT UNITED FOR	BRISTOL ROVERS - JULY 1991

David Wilson was one of the wave of youngsters daftly dubbed as Fergie's Fledglings, but sadly he never took flight in the first team, not even starting a match.

Some people reckoned he had what it took to make the grade as a constructive midfielder, but whether he was good enough was debatable, and certainly his subsequent record suggests that he wasn't of the highest class.

240. JOOLS MAIORANA

JOOLS MAIORANA		
COMP.	APPS	GLS
LEAGUE	2 (5)	0
FAC	0 (1)	0
TOTAL	2 (6)	0

BORN	CAMBRIDGE 18TH APRIL 1969
POSITION	WINGER
JOINED UNITED	DECEMBER 1988 FROM HISTON UNITED £30,000
UNITED DEBUT	MILLWALL (H) DIV. 1 - 14/01/1989
UNITED FAREWELL	TOTTENHAM H. (H) LC - 25/10/1989
RETIRED	1994 - DUE TO INJURY

Jools Maiorana was an amateur left-winger, playing his football for Histon United and working in the family clothes shop, when suddenly he was catapulted to prominence on Manchester United's left wing.

It was a fantasy sequence which started when the Red Devils went to Histon for a charity game. The 19-year-old was in the opposition and impressed enough to earn a contract, but there was to be no happy ending.

Sadly Maiorana suffered terrible injuries, and played his final senior game only ten months after his arrival, but United honoured his agreement, meaning that he didn't leave until five years later.

241. DEREK BRAZIL

OTHER CLUBS:
OLDHAM ATHLETIC ON LOAN 90/1 (1, 0);
SWANSEA CITY ON LOAN 91/2 (12, 1);
CARDIFF CITY 92/3-95/6 (115, 1).

DEREK BRAZIL		
COMP.	APPS	GLS
LEAGUE	0 (2)	0
TOTAL	0 (2)	0

BORN	DUBLIN 14TH DECEMBER 1968
POSITION	CENTRAL DEFENDER
JOINED UNITED	MARCH 1986 FROM IRISH JUNIOR FOOTBALL
UNITED DEBUT	EVERTON (H) DIV. 1 - 10/05/1989
UNITED FAREWELL	MILLWALL (A) DIV. 1 - 10/02/1990
LEFT UNITED FOR	CARDIFF CITY AUG. 1992 - £85,000

People around the club talked in glowing terms for a long time about Derek Brazil, believing him to be a terrific prospect at centre-half, but that was as far as it went.

He was never offered more than two first-team opportunities, both as substitute, and never remotely threatened to challenge Steve Bruce or Gary Pallister for their first-team slots. Still, considering he'd done nothing, United picked up decent money for him from Cardiff, where he played for four years.

BORN	NELSON, LANCASHIRE 24TH SEPTEMBER 1962
POSITION	MIDFIELDER
JOINED UNITED	JULY 1989 FROM NORWICH CITY - £750,000
UNITED DEBUT	ARSENAL (H) DIV. 1 - 19/08/1989
UNITED HONOURS	ECWC 1990/1 PREMIERSHIP 1992/3 FA CUP 1989/90 LEAGUE CUP 1991/2
UNITED FAREWELL	WIMBLEDON (H) PREM. -.20/11/1993
LEFT UNITED FOR	WEST BROMWICH ALBION JULY 1994

MICKY PHELAN		
COMP.	APPS	GLS
LEAGUE	88 (14)	2
FAC	10	1
LC	14 (2)	0
EUROPE	14 (3)	0
OTHERS	1	0
TOTAL	127 (19)	3

242. MICKY PHELAN

OTHER HONOURS:
1 ENGLAND CAP 1989.

OTHER CLUBS:
BURNLEY 80/1-84/5 (168, 9);
NORWICH CITY 85/6-88/9 (156, 9);
WEST BROMWICH ALBION 94/5-95/6 (21, 0).

Manchester United paid £750,000 for Micky Phelan from Norwich, yet a few years earlier, I had offered him to them for £60,000 during my time as Burnley's chief scout.

But Ron Atkinson thought Micky wasn't good enough for United so the boy went to Norwich City, for whom he excelled for three years before making them a handsome profit when finally he moved to Old Trafford.

Micky is a lad who deserved to get on. He loved the game to distraction, he was ready to work at it until he dropped, often coming back for extra training sessions in the afternoon. His whole life revolved around playing football and wherever he went he gave magnificent value for money.

There was nothing flamboyant about him, he wasn't spectacular in any way, and even when he moved to Old Trafford, nearly all the headlines went to Neil Webb, who arrived at roughly the same time.

But folk inside the game understood his value. He had a tremendous engine and a pair of exceedingly tidy feet; he could play in midfield, alongside the centre-half or at full-back, and he would always do an impeccable job.

In addition to his skill, versatility and stamina, the lad was a monument to dedication and honesty, a manager's dream. If you had 11 Micky Phelans in your team, you would be a very lucky man. Certainly you would never get relegated.

So there you have him – a good player, a lovely character, an asset to any squad, Micky has always been a credit to himself and his family. Since retiring he has done well as a coach, eventually becoming an assistant to Sir Alex Ferguson at Old Trafford.

243. NEIL WEBB

OTHER HONOURS:
26 ENGLAND CAPS 1987-90.

OTHER CLUBS:
READING 79/80-81/2 (72, 22);
PORTSMOUTH 82/3-84/5 (123, 34);
NOTTINGHAM FOREST 85/6-88/9 (146, 47)
& 92/3-93/4 (30, 3);
SWINDON TOWN ON LOAN 94/5 (6, 0);
GRIMSBY TOWN 96/7 (4, 0).

NEIL WEBB		
COMP.	APPS	GLS
LEAGUE	70 (5)	8
FAC	9	1
LC	14	1
EUROPE	11	1
OTHERS	1	0
TOTAL	105 (5)	11

BORN	READING 30TH JULY 1963
POSITION	MIDFIELDER
JOINED UNITED	JULY 1989 FROM NOTTINGHAM F. - £1.5M
UNITED DEBUT	ARSENAL (H) DIV. 1 - 19/08/1989
UNITED HONOURS	FA CUP 1989/90
UNITED FAREWELL	TORPEDO MOSCOW (A) UEFA - 29/09/1992
LEFT UNITED FOR	NOTTINGHAM FOREST NOV. 1992 - £800,000

United had been looking for a midfield creator for a long time, and in his early days at Old Trafford it seemed possible that they had found him in Neil Webb. But then he suffered a serious Achilles injury while playing for England and he was never the same again.

'Had he not damaged that Achilles, Neil might easily have been part of the side that swept all before it in the first half of the 1990s.'

Neil had lost what he needed most, which was that little bit of extra movement to leave his markers. When he couldn't do it any longer he remained a skilful performer but he looked comparatively pedestrian.

Unfortunately for him, after returning from his lengthy lay-off he experienced a disagreement with Alex Ferguson. In fact, he had a rough ride with managers because before Fergie he'd had to deal with Brian Clough. But whereas Cloughie couldn't afford not to play him at Forest, Alex could leave him out when he wanted to, and did so.

It was sad, because Neil Webb had plenty of ability, he could pass the ball perceptively and he knocked in a few goals.

We saw the best of the boy in his debut on the first day of 1989/90, when United beat Arsenal 4-1 and he contributed a memorable strike from long range. That was the day that Michael Knighton, who was apparently on the verge of buying the club, did his famous ball-juggling act in front of an incredulous Stretford End.

Neil, who grew up in a footballing family – his father Doug played for Reading, which was also his own first club – managed only four more League games before being struck down.

Eventually a United career which had started so magnificently ended messily in tears and recrimination. Had he not damaged that Achilles, Neil might easily have been part of the side that swept all before it in the first half of the 1990s. Football can be the cruellest of games.

BORN	RAMSGATE, KENT 30TH JUNE 1965
POSITION	CENTRAL DEFENDER
JOINED UNITED	AUGUST 1989 FROM MIDDLESBROUGH, £2.3M
UNITED DEBUT	NORWICH CITY (H) DIV. 1 - 30/08/1989
UNITED HONOURS	ECWC 1990/1 PREMIERSHIP 1992/3, 1993/4, 1995/6, 1996/7 FA CUP 1989/90, 1993/4, 1995/6 LEAGUE CUP 1991/2
UNITED FAREWELL	LEEDS UNITED (H) PREM. - 4/05/1998
LEFT UNITED FOR	MIDDLESBROUGH JULY 1998 - £2M

GARY PALLISTER		
COMP.	APPS	GLS
LEAGUE	314 (3)	12
FAC	38	2
LC	36	0
EUROPE	39 (1)	1
OTHERS	6	0
TOTAL	433 (4)	15

244. GARY PALLISTER

OTHER HONOURS:
22 ENGLAND CAPS 1988-96.
PFA FOOTBALLER OF THE YEAR 1992.

OTHER CLUBS:
MIDDLESBROUGH 85/6-89/90 (156, 5);
DARLINGTON ON LOAN 85/6 (7, 0);
MIDDLESBROUGH 98/9-00/01 (55, 1).

If all the world was full of Gary Pallisters, then what a lovely place it would be. Despite all his success, there are no airs and no graces about him. Invariably he's wearing a huge, disarming grin; he's always obliging and accessible; in short, he's magic, exactly how any boy would want his footballing hero to be.

The amazing thing about Gary as a player is that he cost Manchester United £2.3 million, put in nine years of fantastic service and won everything in sight, then he returned to Middlesbrough and United regained £2 million of their original investment. Now that's what I'd call a canny bit of business.

Gary had a truly fabulous career, but the only thing I'll never understand about it is why he played so few England games – and poor old Brucie played none – yet as a central defensive pair they were by far the best in the country for quite a few seasons. I suppose Tony Adams was the main obstacle, but I wouldn't have picked him because I'd have gone for a tried and tested club partnership.

After coming to Old Trafford from Ayrsome Park, Pally took a fair time to settle, but that was understandable. It must have been like coming from another world, and I imagine he felt weighed down by what was, at the time, a gigantic fee around his neck.

When he arrived he was slim to say the least, but United built him up and gradually he gained confidence to make the most of his ability. At first, too, it's fair to say that he was a big dozy beggar at times, but that was, shall we say, coached out of him, and he became one of the finest central defenders in Europe. He was marvellous in the air, he could play a bit with the ball at his feet, and when Pally got revved up he was very, very quick.

Gary and Steve Bruce were chalk and cheese in the same way that Blanchflower and Jones had been around 40 years earlier. Of course, we didn't play double centre-halves in the 1950s so Jackie and Mark rarely turned out together, while Pally and Brucie were able to complement each other perfectly in Alex Ferguson's team.

Funnily enough, in terms of size Gary was the Mark Jones of the equation, but in terms of how they played, he was the Jackie Blanchflower. Although he was the bigger of the two, Pally was very much the footballer; and while Brucie had the aura of a big man, with power and determination to match, actually he was no giant.

Crucially Steve was a born winner, I don't believe a thought of finishing second ever entered his head. Obviously Gary was a winner, too, but he wasn't as intense as Steve, maybe taking the attitude that losing the odd game was to be expected.

The two of them needed each other and together they were brilliant. They were good pals, which was a great starting point, and they stood the test of a supremely demanding boss. The fact that they did such a vital job for so long speaks volumes for their capability and their temperament.

In the end Pally was moved out following the purchase of Jaap Stam in 1998, but he carried on for another three years and eventually played in excess of 700 games in all senior football. Not bad for a lad who suffered from a dicky back throughout his career.

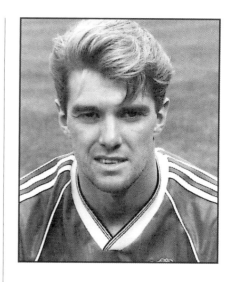

245. PAUL INCE

OTHER HONOURS:
53 ENGLAND CAPS 1992-2000.

OTHER CLUBS:
WEST HAM UNITED 86/7-89/90 (72, 7);
INTERNAZIONALE OF MILAN 95/6-96/7 (54, 9);
LIVERPOOL 97/8-98/9 (65, 14);
MIDDLESBROUGH 99/00-01/02 (93, 7);
WOLVERHAMPTON WANDERERS 02/03- (97, 7).

PAUL INCE		
COMP.	APPS	GLS
LEAGUE	203 (3)	25
FAC	26 (1)	1
LC	23 (1)	2
EUROPE	20	0
OTHERS	4	1
TOTAL	276 (5)	29

BORN	ILFORD, ESSEX 21ST OCTOBER 1967
POSITION	MIDFIELDER
JOINED UNITED	SEPTEMBER 1989 FROM WEST HAM UTD £1.7M
UNITED DEBUT	MILLWALL (H) DIV. 1 - 16/09/1989
UNITED HONOURS	ECWC 1990/1 PREMIERSHIP 1992/3, 1993/4 FA CUP 1989/90, 1993/4 LEAGUE CUP 1991/2
UNITED FAREWELL	EVERTON (WEMBLEY) FAC - 20/05/1995
LEFT UNITED FOR	INTERNAZIONALE (ITALY) JULY 1995 - £7M

If Paul Ince had been half as good as he thought he was, he'd have been some player. He was in the Manchester United team which won Premiership titles in 1992/93 and 1993/94 but, to my mind, he was never a really major influence.

Quite simply, he didn't have enough ability for that, falling miles short of, say, Bryan Robson or Roy Keane, both of whom

'Quite simply, he didn't have enough ability . . . falling miles short of, say, Bryan Robson or Roy Keane, both of whom were in a different class.'

were on a different planet in terms of class.

Ince was no more than a straight-up-and-downer with a streak of arrogance that was always far too wide for my liking. We had to put up with his lip from the moment he arrived – before that, in fact, when he posed for the cameras in a United shirt even before the transfer went through.

Yet pretty soon we discovered he was that good that Alex Ferguson couldn't find a midfield spot for him, so he shifted him to full-back for a time.

A little later, the inane way in which he portrayed himself as 'The Guv'nor' tended to rub me up the wrong way. That he should aspire to such a title when he was playing at the same club as Robbo defied belief. You might say that it betrayed an unbecoming sense of his own worth.

Undoubtedly the peak of his career was at Old Trafford, and he was never the same force after he left. In fact, he played nearly as many games for United as for all the rest of his clubs put together and, perhaps contrary to general perception, he never even made a century of League appearances for anyone else, moving on every couple of seasons.

Readers will have gauged that Ince was not one of my favourites, yet he compiled six major honours as a Red Devil, so clearly he wasn't all bad. For instance, he made telling contributions to important games when surging through from midfield, scoring or creating a goal just when it was needed, and it would be wrong to deny him the credit for that.

It's just that certain players you fancy, certain ones you don't – and Paul Ince was never one of my fancies.

246. DANNY WALLACE

OTHER HONOURS:
1 ENGLAND CAP 1986.

OTHER CLUBS:
SOUTHAMPTON 80/1-89/90 (255, 64);
MILLWALL ON LOAN 92/3 (3, 0);
BIRMINGHAM CITY 93/4-94/5 (16, 2);
WYCOMBE WANDERERS 94/5 (1, 0).

DANNY WALLACE		
COMP.	APPS	GLS
LEAGUE	36 (11)	6
FAC	7 (2)	2
LC	4 (3)	3
EUROPE	5 (2)	0
OTHERS	1	0
TOTAL	53 (18)	11

BORN	LONDON 21ST JANUARY 1964
POSITION	FORWARD
JOINED UNITED	SEPTEMBER 1989 FROM SOUTHAMPTON - £1.1M
UNITED DEBUT	PORTSMOUTH (A) LC - 20/09/1989
UNITED HONOURS	FA CUP 1989/90
UNITED FAREWELL	BRIGHTON (H) FAC - 23/01/1993
LEFT UNITED FOR	BIRMINGHAM CITY OCT. 1993 - £250,000

For the best part of a decade, since he was only 16, Danny Wallace had been serving up thrilling football for Southampton, and it came as a major disappointment when he didn't reproduce that form consistently following his £1 million-plus move to Manchester United.

Perhaps a clue to his contrasting level of performance is that the Saints often deployed him up front alongside the main striker, rather than on the left wing, where he spent all his time for the Red Devils.

Not that Danny's time at Old Trafford was wholly unproductive. He picked up an FA Cup winner's medal in 1990, putting in some splendid displays on the way to Wembley, notably at Newcastle where he slammed in a stunning goal from an acute angle.

Sadly that proved to be one of a few isolated flourishes instead of the sustained brilliance the supporters had been led to expect from the tiny little man. There was always a nagging feeling that he had looked a better player at The Dell than he did in Manchester.

But Danny always seemed to struggle with his fitness at United and, with the benefit of hindsight, I wonder whether he was already suffering the beginnings of the multiple sclerosis which became so sadly evident in later years.

That awful disease is a slow burner and perhaps it was starting to take effect before anyone realised it. I suppose we'll never know, but whatever the position, Danny went through some distressing times, suffering a lot of harsh judgements and coming under heavy pressure because he did not appear up to scratch.

Fast forwarding to the present day, I find it overwhelmingly sad when there's so much cash in the game, with people receiving such monumental wages, that it should be necessary to stage a special match to raise some money for the poor lad.

BORN	BETHNAL GREEN, LONDON 29TH SEPTEMBER 1957
DIED	19TH AUGUST 2001
POSITION	GOALKEEPER
JOINED UNITED	DECEMBER 1989 FROM LUTON TOWN INITIALLY ON LOAN REJOINED JAN 1993 FROM ASTON VILLA
UNITED DEBUT	QPR (A) DIV. 1 - 14/04/1990
UNITED HONOURS	ECWC 1990/1 FA CUP 1989/90
UNITED FAREWELL	ASTON VILLA (WEMBLEY) LC - 27/03/1994
LEFT UNITED FOR	ASTON VILLA - JULY 1991 BLACKPOOL - JULY 1994

LES SEALEY		
COMP.	APPS	GLS
LEAGUE	33	0
FAC	4 (1)	0
LC	9	0
EUROPE	8	0
OTHERS	1	0
TOTAL	55 (1)	0

247. LES SEALEY

OTHER CLUBS:
COVENTRY CITY 76/7-82/3 (158, 0);
LUTON TOWN 83/4-88/9 (207, 0);
PLYMOUTH ARGYLE ON LOAN 84/5 (6, 0);
ASTON VILLA 91/2 (18, 0);
COVENTRY CITY ON LOAN 91/2 (2, 0);
BIRMINGHAM CITY ON LOAN 92/3 (12, 0);
BLACKPOOL 94/5 (7, 0);
WEST HAM UNITED 95/6 (2, 0);
LEYTON ORIENT 96/7 (12, 0);
WEST HAM UNITED 96/7-97/8 (2, 0).

Les Sealey was loud and brash, a typical Cockney some might say, and he probably drove a few managers mad with his antics and his unorthodox style.

Certainly he wasn't a textbook performer, often repelling the ball with unexpected parts of his anatomy, and you wouldn't employ a video of Les in action in an attempt to tutor impressionable youngsters in the classic approach to goalkeeping.

But he was effective, and twice he held the fort successfully for Manchester United, first when Jim Leighton was axed after supposed errors in the FA Cup Final draw with Crystal Palace in 1990, then when Peter Schmeichel was unavailable in 1994.

Incredibly, Les played in four cup finals during his stop-go service at Old Trafford. Considering he started only slightly more than half a century of games overall, that's a pretty impressive ratio.

Personally I found the way he moved between clubs in a complicated series of loan deals quite confusing, and it was hard to fathom exactly whose player he was at times. I suppose United must have known but the fans were in a lot of doubt.

Les had an unusual career record, spending lengthy spells with Coventry and Luton, then winning honours with United and flitting from club to club towards the end of his playing days.

He will always be remembered most vividly for replacing Leighton ahead of the 1990 FA Cup Final replay, in which he made some useful saves against Crystal Palace on the way to picking up a winner's medal.

Les didn't have the substantial stature expected of a goalkeeper, but he was immensely brave, sometimes to the point of downright foolhardiness.

For instance, in the 1991 League Cup Final defeat by Sheffield Wednesday he cut his knee almost to the bone, but he played on. The injury put him in perilous doubt of his place in the Cup Winners' Cup Final against Barcelona, but he made light of medical advice to sit it out, and helped United to lift the trophy.

In view of his earlier career, which was worthy but not exceptional, Les Sealey must have been overjoyed at the late glory he sampled with United. He was the right man in the right place at the right time and, all credit to him, he made the most of it.

248. MARK BOSNICH

OTHER HONOURS: AUSTRALIA CAPS.

OTHER CLUBS:
CROATIA SYDNEY, AUSTRALIA;
ASTON VILLA 91/2-98/9 (179, 0);
CHELSEA 01/02 (5, 0).

MARK BOSNICH		
COMP.	APPS	GLS
LEAGUE	26	0
LC	1	0
EUROPE	7	0
OTHERS	4	0
TOTAL	38	0

BORN	SYDNEY, AUSTRALIA 13TH JANUARY 1972
POSITION	GOALKEEPER
JOINED UNITED	JUNE 1989 FROM CROATIA SYDNEY, REJOINED JULY 1999 FROM ASTON VILLA
UNITED DEBUT	WIMBLEDON (H) DIV. 1 - 30/04/1990
UNITED HONOURS	PREMIERSHIP 1999/2000
UNITED FAREWELL	SUNDERLAND (H) PREM. - 15/04/2000
LEFT UNITED FOR	CROATIA SYDNEY JUNE 1991 CHELSEA - JAN 2001

Mark Bosnich appears to have destroyed his career through his involvement with drugs, which is a tragic waste of a talented athlete and a sad comment on the times in which we live.

The lad had a brief flirtation with Manchester United while he was a university student in his teens, but it was later, under Ron Atkinson at Aston Villa, that he made his name. So it was considerably ironic when we paid a relative fortune to sign him for a second time, ten years after he had made his first appearance in a United shirt.

On the basis of his Villa days I thought he was an accomplished operator, and when Peter Schmeichel left I felt that Alex Ferguson had made a sensible move in recruiting the Australian. They already knew him at Old Trafford, and had played against him for long enough to know what he could do.

It should be remembered, too, that for all his subsequent difficulties, he had a decent run in 1999/2000, performing superbly on occasions, but even though he earned a Championship medal he wasn't an automatic choice for long.

He made some mistakes, which were well documented, but I always feel sorry for goalkeepers. Even the great centre-forwards can miss 100 chances in a season and get away with it, but when a 'keeper drops a clanger, sometimes there's no second chance.

True, Mark was never the greatest kicker during his second spell at Old Trafford, but that only appeared to have happened after his move. Maybe he was suffering from a leg injury; certainly he always seemed to be struggling.

Perhaps he was always going to suffer as the first man after the outstanding Schmeichel, but at least the Dane was gone rather than breathing down the newcomer's neck.

Eventually the Bosnich situation deteriorated until he wasn't even keeping out his much older deputy, Raimond van der Gouw. Of course, 'keepers are vulnerable, because there is only one such position in the team. If a replacement does well he can become a lucky charm, and perhaps that happened with Rai.

People say that Mark was more of a shot-stopper than a claimer of crosses, but with the advent of the accursed modern beach ball, life has become more and more difficult for 'keepers.

I believe fervently that the wayward movement of the new footballs is the reason we have no great 'keepers any more. It's made it a well-nigh impossible job. People talk about free-kickers moving the ball from 30 yards; my response is that they couldn't kick it in a straight line. It mightn't move the way the kicker wants it, but if he doesn't know where it's going, what chance does the goalkeeper have?

Getting back to specifics on Bosnich, eventually there was a big-time fall-out with Sir Alex Ferguson, for which the player has to take the rap. If you're going to be a professional footballer and work for a manager who is as successful as Fergie, then you have to be prepare to do as you're told.

The ultimate judgement on Mark Bosnich? As a top-class 'keeper who had already proved himself in the Premiership, but who failed to last with United, for whatever reasons, he can only be viewed as a sorry disappointment.

BORN	CORK
	31ST OCTOBER 1965
POSITION	FULL-BACK
JOINED UNITED	JUNE 1990 FROM
	OLDHAM ATH. - £650,000
UNITED DEBUT	LIVERPOOL (WEMBLEY)
	CS - 18/08/1990
UNITED HONOURS	EUROPEAN CUP 1998/9
	ECWC 1990/1
	PREMIERSHIP 1992/3,
	1993/4, 1995/6,
	1996/7, 1998/9,
	1999/2000, 2000/01
	FA CUP 1993/4, 1995/6
	LEAGUE CUP 1991/2
UNITED FAREWELL	CHARLTON ATHLETIC (H)
	PREM. - 11/05/02
LEFT UNITED FOR	WOLVERHAMPTON W.
	JULY 2002

249. DENIS IRWIN

DENIS IRWIN

COMP.	APPS	GLS
LEAGUE	356 (12)	22
FAC	42 (1)	7
LC	28 (3)	0
EUROPE	73 (2)	4
OTHERS	12	0
TOTAL	511 (18)	33

OTHER HONOURS:
56 REPUBLIC OF IRELAND CAPS 1990-99.

OTHER CLUBS:
LEEDS UNITED 83/4-85/6 (72, 1);
OLDHAM ATHLETIC 86/7-89/90 (167, 4);
WOLVERHAMPTON WANDERERS 02/03-03/04 (75, 2).

The name of Denis Irwin should gain an honourable mention in any list of the great players in Manchester United history. He's right up there with them all.

So what a tribute it is to the judgement of Leeds United that they had Denis as a youngster, played him more than 70 times in their first team, and then let him join Oldham on a free transfer when he was 20 years old.

Joe Royle took him to Boundary Park and he just went about his business as he's always done, gradually building a reputation.

He might have appeared ordinary to laymen, but those who knew the game could see what he was becoming, and one of those was Alex Ferguson. Perhaps a deciding factor was the way Denis handled himself in the two 1990 FA Cup semi-final meetings with United.

Ironically, in 1993 Leeds wanted Denis back, and when they phoned United to make what would inevitably prove an abortive inquiry, they demonstrated their acumen still further by striking the deal that took Eric Cantona to United. So we ended up with the best of both worlds – keeping Denis and signing Eric.

Apart from his attributes as a player, which should be obvious to anyone with a football brain, he's a lovely man with a calm temperament, someone who's always looked after himself and been a shining example to the youngsters rising through the ranks. All Alex had to say to the boys was: 'Take a leaf out of that man's book and you won't go far wrong.'

There was nothing whatsoever to complain about in Denis Irwin's game. Though he was naturally right-sided, he could play on either defensive flank with equal facility. He had pace, two decent feet and he never took chances, which made him an ideal all-round defender.

He never tried to kick people up in the air, he didn't come into conflict with referees, he played the game properly. When the ball needed kicking into touch, he'd kick it into touch. If there was somebody available, he'd pass it to them. He never made the game difficult.

There's an old saying that it's a very simple game, so why complicate it? If you wanted to illustrate that to youngsters, just sit them down and show them videos of Denis in action.

From the moment he arrived it was apparent how crisply he struck the ball, how sweetly he could cross it on the run, and that's something you can't teach. I'm sure that must be true or they'd have taught Ryan Giggs by now! The technique of delivery when standing still may be teachable, but curling your foot around the ball in full flight, that's a natural art.

People forget, but before David Beckham came along, Denis rattled in some tremendous free-kicks. In fact, he could do as much with a dead ball as Beckham ever could, but he lost that particular job.

How Manchester United could do with another Denis Irwin now. But you could say that about any team, in any era. The time you find out just how fine Denis Irwin was is when you haven't got him. As Joni Mitchell put it: 'You don't know what you've got 'til it's gone.'

BORN	GLASGOW 9TH FEBRUARY 1972
POSITION	MIDFIELDER
JOINED UNITED	JULY 1988 FROM JUNIOR FOOTBALL
UNITED DEBUT	SHEFFIELD UNITED (A) DIV. 1 - 26/02/1991
UNITED HONOURS	PREMIERSHIP 1992/3
UNITED FAREWELL	BLACKBURN ROVERS (H) PREM. - 26/12/1993
LEFT UNITED FOR	WOLVERHAMPTON W. JAN. 1994 - £500,000

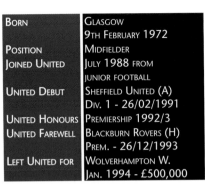

BORN	CARDIFF 29TH NOVEMBER 1973
POSITION	UTILITY FORWARD
JOINED UNITED	JULY 1990 FROM JUNIOR FOOTBALL
UNITED DEBUT	EVERTON (H) DIV. 1 - 02/03/1991
UNITED HONOURS	EUROPEAN CUP 1998/9 PREMIERSHIP 1992/3, 1993/4, 1995/6, 1996/7, 1998/9, 1999/2000, 2000/1, 2002/3 FA CUP 1993/4, 1995/6, 1998/9, 2003/4 LEAGUE CUP 1991/2

250. DARREN FERGUSON

DARREN FERGUSON		
COMP.	APPS	GLS
LEAGUE	20 (7)	0
LC	2 (1)	0
TOTAL	22 (8)	0

OTHER CLUBS:
WOLVERHAMPTON WANDERERS 93/4-98/9 (117, 4);
COSENZA, ITALY, ON LOAN;
SPARTA ROTTERDAM, HOLLAND, ON LOAN 98/9;
WREXHAM 99/00- (238, 22).

Darren Ferguson's only meaningful run in United's first team was at the start of one of the club's most momentous seasons in modern times, when they became Champions for the first time in more than quarter of a century.

Of course, given the situation that he was the manager's son, he would have had to have been another George Best to have lasted at Old Trafford. It was impossible. Normally you can allow a lad a couple of bad games, but that's not possible for the boss's boy. John Aston found it difficult enough having his father on the staff; for Darren there was no way.

In fact, he wasn't a bad midfielder. He had a decent left peg, he could pick out a pass, but he was never going to get 14 or 15 goals a season. In fact, in his 30 outings he didn't get any.

Whether he could have stood the test of time at United under normal circumstances, I wouldn't like to say. In all honesty, I doubt it. Certainly I would think it's in his make-up to want to try his hand at management at some time in the future. Should be interesting . . .

251. RYAN GIGGS

RYAN GIGGS		
COMP.	APPS	GLS
LEAGUE	396 (51)	92
FAC	46 (6)	9
LC	22 (5)	7
EUROPE	91 (5)	22
OTHERS	12 (1)	0
TOTAL	567 (68)	130

OTHER HONOURS:
51 WALES CAPS 1991-.

What an unbelievably magnificent career this young man has had, with no sign that it is about to end at the time of writing. Ryan Giggs seems as if he's been there forever, but when you look at him dancing past defenders, then he's still a spring chicken.

Ryan is the only man who has played in all of Alex Ferguson's eight Championship seasons to date, which puts him level with the all-time record of Liverpool's Alan Hansen, and we're still counting . . .

'When they're counting the club's legends, Ryan will always be in the mix, and he's still got power to add.'

The first time I saw him was as a schoolboy playing for England Boys in an old-fashioned left-half position. He was Ryan Wilson at that time – his dad was a very good rugby player, Danny Wilson – but when his parents split up he took his mother's maiden name.

Right from the beginning he has looked a top-quality act, and yet there are occasions when you watch him and say: 'That can't be Ryan Giggs.' When he has a bad 'un, he has a bad 'un. Thank God for Manchester United and his career, they don't come very often.

If you wanted to use someone as a yardstick as to how a young man should behave in the harsh glare of constant media attention, if he wants to be a professional footballer, then you need look no farther than Ryan Giggs.

He has been feted since his early teens, but he has never appeared to lose his natural humility. He has kept both feet planted firmly on the ground.

I compare him with Beckham and wonder why the Londoner couldn't have been more like Ryan. Why did he want this glamour-boy, pop-star image? It might do David Beckham a good turn if he took a long, cool look at his pal Mr Giggs. Surely he'd say: 'That's not a bad life he leads.' What more could anyone want?

Ryan is a supreme example of a young man with a lot of talent, who has looked after himself, and with a bit of luck and a following breeze, it'll be another five or six years before he retires. When that day comes, I hope he'll still be a Manchester United player, and I think he will be. I'm sure that he's perfectly happy at Old Trafford, where he is well rewarded but no better than he deserves.

From the early days Ryan could always go past people like the wind. He always had pace, that's what made him special. Beckham can't go past people, but is a great crosser, while Ryan runs past people for fun, but isn't the most reliable crosser in the world. If you could marry the two talents, you might have something approaching a George Best, which just goes to show what level

THE SHIRT'S GOT TO GO: Ryan Giggs celebrates his scintillating FA Cup semi-final replay winner against Arsenal in 1999.

George was on.

Ryan has been a superb footballer, a loyal servant and a wonderful example. There aren't many players you can say all that about. When they're counting the club's legends, Ryan will always be in the mix, and he's still got power to add.

Where would I play him? Always on the left wing. I'm not saying that's the only position he can fill, but certainly it's where he is most effective. As an inside-forward, or central midfielder, I'm not sure whether he could perform at the highest level.

I don't like him on the right, because he comes inside too much. Okay, people will mention his unforgettable FA Cup semi-final goal against Arsenal, when he cut in (albeit from the left) but that was a one-off. I like him when he beats people on the outside; there's not many who can live with him when he does that.

Sometimes he gets played as an extra striker, but I wouldn't use him there. Of course, he'll always do a decent job – with his attitude, I'd wager that he'd turn out at left-back if the manager asked him to do so for the good of the team – but it's not his forte.

His finishing? Not as deadly as it might be, but when someone is as gifted as Ryan, it's easy to be hyper-critical about every aspect of his play, which is unfair. Anyhow, you couldn't call him a non-scorer, and although it would be lovely if he could finish like Jimmy Greaves or Denis Law, it would be unrealistic to expect it.

What's so delightful is that, despite all he's achieved, even in his thirties Ryan Giggs still seems to retain the hunger to win more. Long may he continue to grace Manchester United's left wing.

252. NEIL WHITWORTH

OTHER CLUBS:
WIGAN ATHLETIC 89/90 (2, 0);
PRESTON NORTH END ON LOAN 91/2 (6, 0);
BARNSLEY ON LOAN 91/2 (11, 0);
ROTHERHAM UNITED ON LOAN 93/4 (8, 1);
BLACKPOOL ON LOAN 93/4 (3, 0); KILMARNOCK 94/5-97/8 (76, 3);
WIGAN ATHLETIC 97/8 (4, 0); HULL CITY 98/9-99/00 (19, 2);
EXETER CITY 00/01-02/03 (57, 1).

NEIL WHITWORTH		
COMP.	APPS	GLS
LEAGUE	1	0
TOTAL	1	0

BORN	WIGAN 12TH APRIL 1972
POSITION	CENTRAL DEFENDER
JOINED UNITED	JULY 1990 FROM WIGAN - £45,000
UNITED DEBUT & FAREWELL	SOUTHAMPTON (A) DIV. 1 - 13/03/1991
LEFT UNITED FOR	KILMARNOCK SEPT. 1994 - £265,000

When Neil Whitworth was in his first spell at Wigan, he was given rave reviews by John Benson, a man whose judgement I respect. I think Alex Ferguson was extremely keen on him, too, keen enough to take him after only a couple of League outings. The kid had something about him.

In the event, it didn't work out for the young centre-half at Old Trafford, but it's clear by the size of the fee United received when he left that, even at that point, there were expectations of him.

Unfortunately, later on the lad struggled badly with both injury and illness, and never played that many games for anybody.

253. PAUL WRATTEN

OTHER CLUBS:
HARTLEPOOL UNITED 92/3-93/4 (57, 1).

PAUL WRATTEN		
COMP.	APPS	GLS
LEAGUE	0 (2)	0
TOTAL	0 (2)	0

BORN	MIDDLESBROUGH 29TH NOVEMBER 1970
POSITION	MIDFIELDER
JOINED UNITED	JUNE 1987 FROM JUNIOR FOOTBALL
UNITED DEBUT	WIMBLEDON (H) DIV. 1 - 02/04/1991
UNITED FAREWELL	CRYSTAL PALACE (A) DIV. 1 - 11/05/91
LEFT UNITED FOR	HARTLEPOOL UNITED MAY 1992

Alex Ferguson had a particular liking for Paul Wratten, thought he was a hell of a talent. But the promising midfielder sustained a terrible knee injury, which ruined his prospects with Manchester United before his career had a chance to get off the ground.

I suffered similarly myself, so I always feel for these young men. Sadly, we were never to see what Paul might have achieved had his gifts been able to reach full bloom.

BORN	KIROVOGRAD, UKRAINE 23RD JANUARY 1969
POSITION	WINGER
JOINED UNITED	MAY 1991 FROM SHAKHTYOR DONETSK - £1M
UNITED DEBUT	CRYSTAL PALACE (A) DIV. 1 - 11/05/1991
UNITED HONOURS	PREMIERSHIP 1992/3, 1993/4 FA CUP 1993/4 LEAGUE CUP 1991/2
UNITED FAREWELL	ARSENAL (H) PREM. - 22/03/1995
LEFT UNITED FOR	EVERTON AUGUST 1995 - £5.5M

ANDREI KANCHELSKIS		
COMP.	APPS	GLS
LEAGUE	96 (27)	28
FAC	11 (1)	4
LC	15 (1)	3
EUROPE	7	1
OTHERS	3	0
TOTAL	132 (29)	36

254. ANDREI KANCHELSKIS

OTHER HONOURS:
23 USSR/CIS caps 1989-92;
36 RUSSIA caps 1993-98.

OTHER CLUBS:
DYNAMO KIEV 88-89 (22, 1);
SHAKHTYOR DONETSK 90-91 (21, 3), BOTH USSR;
EVERTON 95/6-96/7 (52, 20);
FIORENTINA, ITALY, 96/7-97/8 (26, 2);
GLASGOW RANGERS 98/9-01/02 (71, 11);
MANCHESTER CITY ON LOAN 00/01 (10, 0); SOUTHAMPTON 02/03 (1, 0);
AL HALIL, SAUDI ARABIA, 02/03; DYNAMO MOSCOW 03/04;
SATURN RAMENSKOYE, RUSSIA, 04/05.

A ndrei Kanchelskis was a flying machine and I loved him to pieces. I was never quite sure that he knew where he was going, but his pace was breathtaking and he was a pleasure to watch. On his day it seemed that nobody could stop him.

He was a proper winger, not a wide midfielder as they call them now, and he could do everything I expected of a winger. That meant going past defenders on the outside and slinging balls across, sometimes cutting inside to use his less-favoured left peg, which actually wasn't much less effective than his devastating right. In fact, he was as dangerous in the centre as he was at the byline, and he could finish explosively, too, which completed the package.

Yet for all his assets, Andrei wasn't a regular throughout his sojourn at Old Trafford, making fewer than 100 League starts while winning four major honours and scoring plenty of goals for an outside-right.

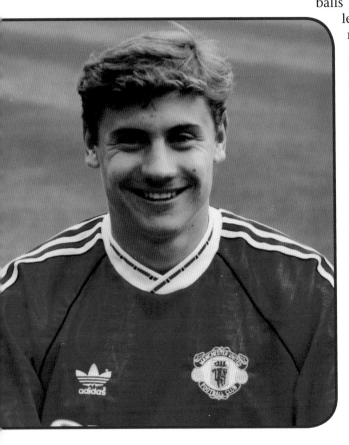

Should he have played more games? Of course, Ryan Giggs and Lee Sharpe were on the scene, which made for the most demanding competition for places imaginable. But they were both left-siders while Andrei operated on the right so he should have had a decided advantage, and when I look at his goals-to-games ratio, I can only conclude that he deserved to play more frequently than he did.

He meshed ideally with Mark Hughes and Eric Cantona, who were both adept at holding the ball before releasing it to the racing Kanchelskis at the ideal moment. With either

Giggs or Sharpe on the other flank, it was an ideal situation, an incredibly potent attack.

For all that, I could imagine that Andrei could drive his manager daft, because some of his decisions about whether to cross, shoot or go past the defender left a lot to be desired. Even so, most opponents would have hated facing him.

I don't think we'll ever know the full story of why he left United at the peak of his powers when he was only 26. We know that he disagreed with Alex Ferguson when he wasn't picked on occasions, so probably that was a major factor, certainly more believable than lurid tabloid tales that he was being targeted by the Russian underworld.

United received a huge fee when Andrei went to Everton, for whom he scored 20 times in 52 League games, a phenomenal tally for a flankman. But then he began wandering from club to club, which was a shame and a waste.

Undoubtedly a lot of supporters were dismayed by his exit, but then United won the double. That's a characteristic of the manager. He always seems to ram your opinions down your throat by the results his teams produce.

Still, it is undeniable that Andrei was a massive asset to the English game, always offering the prospect of thrills and excitement, which is something you cannot say truthfully about too many modern players.

For me the bottom line was that, although he drove me bonkers at times, what he served up was sheer enjoyment, not least because he always seemed to play with a smile on his face.

Andrei had grown up in tough circumstances in the Ukraine, and it must have been unbelievable for him to embrace such a high standard of living through playing a game. He managed to communicate his evident joy at his good fortune and, in doing so, he created joy for the rest of us.

'The bottom line was that, although he drove me bonkers at times, what he served up was sheer enjoyment.'

BORN	GLADSAXE, DENMARK 18TH NOVEMBER 1963
POSITION	GOALKEEPER
JOINED UNITED	AUGUST 1991 FROM BRONDBY, DENMARK £750,000
UNITED DEBUT	NOTTS COUNTY (H) DIV. 1 - 17/08/1991
UNITED HONOURS	EUROPEAN CUP 1998/9 PREMIERSHIP 1992/3, 1993/4, 1995/6, 1996/7, 1998/9 FA CUP 1993/4, 1995/6, 1998/9 LEAGUE CUP 1991/2
UNITED FAREWELL	BAYERN MUNICH (BARCELONA) EC - 26/05/1999
LEFT UNITED FOR	SPORTING LISBON JUNE 1999

PETER SCHMEICHEL		
COMP.	APPS	GLS
LEAGUE	292	0
FAC	41	0
LC	17	0
EUROPE	42	1
OTHERS	6	0
TOTAL	398	1

255. PETER SCHMEICHEL

HONOURS:
129 DENMARK CAPS 1987-2001.
OTHER CLUBS:
GLADSAXE-HERO, HVIDOVRE, BRONDBY, ALL DENMARK;
SPORTING LISBON, PORTUGAL, 99/00-00/01;
ASTON VILLA 01/02 (29, 1);
MANCHESTER CITY 02/03 (29, 0).

In the modern game there haven't been many great 'keepers – principally, I'd say, because of the silly light ball that's now in vogue – but Peter Schmeichel bucked the trend. Indisputably he was the pick of his era, and he did a stupendous job for Manchester United.

The daft thing is that, magnificent though his United record is, it could have been even more fabulous. I can't believe that he never regretted his decision to leave for Sporting Lisbon because he didn't want the severity of an English campaign. He as good as indicated that he had made a mistake by coming back to play for Aston Villa and Manchester City. What was the point of all that?

How much the club really knew about Schmeichel when they signed him from Denmark, I wouldn't know. Certainly he was an unknown quantity to the vast majority of supporters, and he took a while to settle into the English game, where there were far more crosses to deal with than he was accustomed to. Soon enough, though, he was coping, and before long he was going from strength to strength.

Peter's way was to impose his presence on the people around him, and I must say that he always came over to me as an arrogant individual, though perhaps that was his way of building up his confidence and dealing with the pressure.

His defenders were always in the wrong, he was always right, nothing was ever his fault. In truth, his lambastings didn't seem to bother Brucie, Pally, Denis Irwin and company unduly, but that's because of the way they were. I don't think he'd have got away with it for a minute with Roy Keane or Bryan Robson on a regular basis.

Schmeichel could point to phenomenal achievements, fair enough, but there were times I believe he got carried away with himself, such as when he made his stupid comment to the effect that his United side would have beaten the 1968 European Cup winners by ten goals.

Denis Law answered him quite succinctly by saying: 'So you might, but we're all in our sixties now.' That was the way to brush aside such an inane remark, with total contempt. Schmeichel was five years of age when that team won the European Cup, so what the hell would he know about them? That incident epitomised him to me. He had that all-embracing arrogance and thought processes which trumpeted: 'I'm the best.'

Possibly that's what helped him to be the best, but there have been many great 'keepers before him, such as Gordon Banks, who didn't have that sort of attitude, so was it necessary?

All that to one side, I would never deny that Peter was a wonderful goalkeeper. He always stood up and made himself a formidable barrier. He didn't give attackers easy options, he managed to spread himself, sometimes even in mid-air.

How does he compare with the greats of the past? Most people would call him better than Harry Gregg, but if Harry had been able to play the majority of his games in the side which was devastated at Munich, then the judgement might have been different.

In United terms I consider Reg Allen to be as good as anybody we've had between the posts, but I'm in the minority because not everybody has seen him. Let's just say Peter joins Reg, Greggy and Alex Stepney as superb 'keepers for United down the years.

The modern people will say that Schmeichel was easily the best, and they might be right. For somebody to be as good as him in today's game, complete with the ridiculous blowaway ball, proves his worth beyond question.

'For somebody to be as good as him in today's game, complete with the ridiculous blowaway ball, proves his worth beyond question.'

BORN	WEST HAM, LONDON 4TH APRIL 1964
POSITION	DEFENDER
JOINED UNITED	AUGUST 1991 FROM QPR - £1.7M
UNITED DEBUT	NOTTS COUNTY (H) DIV. 1 - 17/08/1991
UNITED HONOURS	PREMIERSHIP 1992/3, 1993/4 FA CUP 1993/4 LEAGUE CUP 1991/2
UNITED FAREWELL	READING (A) FAC - 27/01/1996
LEFT UNITED FOR	DERBY CO. - JUNE 1996

PAUL PARKER		
COMP.	APPS	GLS
LEAGUE	100 (5)	1
FAC	14 (1)	1
LC	15	0
EUROPE	7 (3)	0
OTHERS	1	0
TOTAL	137 (9)	2

256. PAUL PARKER

OTHER HONOURS:

19 ENGLAND CAPS 1989-94.

OTHER CLUBS:

FULHAM 80/1-86/7 (153, 2);
QUEEN'S PARK RANGERS 87/8-90/1 (125, 1);
DERBY COUNTY 96/7 (4, 0);
SHEFFIELD UNITED 96/7 (10, 0);
FULHAM 96/7 (3, 0); CHELSEA 96/7 (3, 0).

Jimmy Murphy always told me that Paul Parker was as accomplished a man-for-man marker as he'd ever seen, though the lad didn't often play that role for Manchester United, spending most of his Old Trafford days as a right-back.

I always believed that Paul had spent too long with Fulham and Queen's Park Rangers, virtually ten years in total, before joining United. That was a great shame because I think those London clubs saw the very best years of his career. That was when he won his England caps, when he was absolutely at the top of his game and free from niggling injuries.

I never thought he was quite as authoritative with United as he had been during that England prime and I only wish he had arrived at Old Trafford five years earlier. It might have stopped him from picking up a few bad footballing habits.

Paul was as quick as lightning, but he didn't have such impressive feet as, say, Denis Irwin. Playing alongside the centre-half, or as an out-and-out sweeper as he did frequently for QPR, his speed suited him admirably.

With Paul's pace being so all-important, his overall effectiveness declined when he was no longer the quickest following a few injuries. For instance, his lack of height and ordinary ability on the ball began to be more noticeable.

By the time he came back to anything like his best shape, the two Nevilles had appeared on the scene and life was always going to be more difficult for him.

If Paul had been fully fit when he left United, he might have made more impact elsewhere. As it was he spent time at four clubs in one season, which is astonishing. Maybe his desire had evaporated a little bit, having won so much in Alex Ferguson's team.

Paul is a delightful character, a very relaxed young man who has been to a couple of Former Players Association events, and he would be welcome at more in the future.

257. IAN WILKINSON

OTHER CLUBS:
CREWE ALEXANDRA 93/4 (3, 0).

IAN WILKINSON		
COMP.	APPS	GLS
LC	1	0
TOTAL	1	0

BORN	WARRINGTON 2ND JULY 1973
POSITION	GOALKEEPER
JOINED UNITED	JUNE 1989 FROM JUNIOR FOOTBALL
UNITED DEBUT & FAREWELL	CAMBRIDGE UNITED (A) LC - 09/10/1991
LEFT UNITED FOR	CREWE ALEXANDRA OCTOBER 1993

Like so many Manchester United reserves, Ian Wilkinson was given his sole first-team opportunity in a League Cup tie against opposition from a lower division, and it didn't tell us an awful lot about him.

But with Peter Schmeichel, Les Sealey and Gary Walsh all looming large at the club, I don't think he was likely to get much of a look-in at Old Trafford and I wasn't surprised when he was released to join Crewe. Unfortunately, not long after moving to Gresty Road, Ian was forced to retire following an eye injury.

258. DION DUBLIN

OTHER HONOURS:
4 ENGLAND CAPS 1998.

OTHER CLUBS:
CAMBRIDGE UNITED 88/9-91/2 (156, 53);
COVENTRY CITY 94/5-98/9 (146, 60);
ASTON VILLA 98/9-03/04 (155, 47);
MILLWALL ON LOAN 01/02 (4, 2);
LEICESTER CITY 04/05- (37, 5).

DION DUBLIN		
COMP.	APPS	GLS
LEAGUE	4 (8)	2
FAC	1 (1)	0
LC	1 (1)	1
EUROPE	0 (1)	0
TOTAL	6 (11)	3

BORN	LEICESTER 22ND APRIL 1969
POSITION	STRIKER
JOINED UNITED	AUGUST 1992 FROM CAMRIDGE UNITED - £1.1M
UNITED DEBUT	SHEFFIELD UNITED (A) PREM. - 15/08/1992
UNITED HONOURS	PREMIERSHIP 1992/3
UNITED FAREWELL	COVENTRY CITY (H) PREM. - 08/05/1994
LEFT UNITED FOR	COVENTRY CITY SEPTEMBER 1994 - £2M

The purchase of Dion Dublin surprised me, though it amazed me even more that the club doubled their money when they sold the big, strapping striker to Coventry City. To me, quite simply, he never appeared at ease in his role as spearhead of the Manchester United attack.

To be fair to Dion, apparently a lovely person and a talented jazz saxophonist, he did well to revive his career after suffering a broken leg and terrible ligament damage against Crystal Palace in only his third full game for United.

Later he looked a much more effective performer at Coventry and Villa, which suggests that maybe the stage was simply too big for him at Old Trafford, as has proved to be the case for so many players down the decades.

As he approached the veteran stage, Dion played frequently as a central defender, and did pretty well. He can look back on a fulfilling career in the game.

BORN	BURY
	18TH FEBRUARY 1975
POSITION	FULL-BACK
JOINED UNITED	JULY 1991 FROM
	JUNIOR FOOTBALL
UNITED DEBUT	TORPEDO MOSCOW (H)
	UEFA - 16/09/1992
UNITED HONOURS	EUROPEAN CUP 1998/9
	PREMIERSHIP
	1995/6, 1996/7,
	1998/9, 1999/2000,
	2000/1, 2002/3
	FA CUP 1995/6,
	1998/9, 2003/4

GARY NEVILLE		
COMP.	APPS	GLS
LEAGUE	301 (14)	5
FAC	36 (2)	0
LC	11 (1)	0
EUROPE	91 (5)	2
OTHERS	8 (1)	0
TOTAL	447 (23)	7

259. GARY NEVILLE

OTHER HONOURS:
76 ENGLAND CAPS 1995-.

What a staggering career Gary Neville is having. Only 30 years old, he has played well in excess of 400 games for Manchester United, he can point to a list of major honours as long as a giant's arm and he has collected more than 70 England caps.

In the youth team he played at centre-half alongside Chris Casper and, together with five more members of that famous intake, he has made a magnificent contribution to the club's modern history. If you added up the games and the honours totalled by Messrs Giggs, Scholes, Beckham, Butt and the two Nevilles, it makes a powerful case for United's youth system.

Gary isn't a Goliath of a man but whenever I've seen him at centre-half, he's always looked more than useful in the role. Maybe he's the exception that proves my rule that decent central defenders don't often make effective full-backs.

But it's at right-back where he has made his name and, although he has had his critics, especially but not exclusively in the south of the country, invariably he has had the last laugh.

To that role he has brought single-minded commitment, unswerving determination and the courage to throw himself into the path of anything that poses the remotest threat to the United goal.

For many years he played directly behind his mate, David Beckham, and the two of them built up an understanding which helped to make light of Gary's natural limitations when it comes to distribution and the delivery of crosses.

In 2003/04, with David having departed to Spain, Neville Senior did not always look so comfortable, and it remains to be seen how smoothly he might mesh with Cristiano Ronaldo, Ole Gunnar Solskjaer or whoever he might link up with in the medium or long term.

Whatever else can be said of Gary Neville, there is no doubt that he's got United in his bones and few people have displayed more passion in the cause. Sometimes, I've got to say, I think he can be unnecessarily strident, but I suppose that is part of his make-up and is unlikely to change.

What speaks more tellingly than anything else about his various qualities is the fact that Alex Ferguson has retained faith with him for more than a decade, and that showed not the slightest sign of wavering in 2005. Given his renowned resilience and durability, Gary Neville may be around for some time to come.

260. DAVID BECKHAM

OTHER HONOURS:
81 ENGLAND CAPS 1996-.

OTHER CLUBS:
PRESTON NORTH END ON LOAN 94/5 (5, 2); REAL MADRID 03/04- (61, 7).

DAVID BECKHAM		
COMP.	APPS	GLS
LEAGUE	237 (28)	62
FAC	22 (2)	6
LC	10 (2)	1
EUROPE	79 (5)	15
OTHERS	8 (2)	1
TOTAL	356 (39)	85

BORN	LEYTONSTONE, LONDON 2ND MAY 1975
POSITION	MIDFIELDER
JOINED UNITED	JULY 1991 FROM JUNIOR FOOTBALL
UNITED DEBUT	BRIGHTON (A) LC - 23/09/1992
UNITED HONOURS	EUROPEAN CUP 1998/9 PREMIERSHIP 1995/6, 1996/7, 1998/9, 1999/00, 2000/1, 2002/3 FA CUP 1995/6, 1998/9
UNITED FAREWELL	EVERTON (A) PREM. - 11/05/2003
LEFT UNITED FOR	REAL MADRID JULY 2003 - £25M

I always find it hard to talk about David Beckham because it's become extraordinarily difficult to separate the footballer from the media plaything. He's a legend in his own lifetime, possibly through no fault of his own.

David received his big chance when Andrei Kanchelskis was transferred to Everton in the summer of 1995, and he seized it for all he was worth, helping United to win the League and FA Cup double in his first full season.

Then, during the following autumn, his life changed forever on the sunny afternoon at Selhurst Park when he scored a goal from his own half against Wimbledon and the celebrity bandwagon began to roll with a vengeance.

I find the whole Beckham thing slightly bewildering. I'll always be sceptical about his exalted position in football because I can't remove this question from my mind: how much was it the result of his ability to play, and how much the result of his wife's showbiz circus.

I suppose it was a combination of the two factors, but I'm convinced that the whole crazy Posh Spice syndrome was the dominant consideration. I think the people around her recognised at an early stage what they had in Beckham, and I'm afraid he proved susceptible to all the razzmatazz.

But let's try to take him in isolation as a footballer, which I find far more palatable. They call him a midfielder, but in fact for Manchester United he was an outside-right, no more and no less.

Did he go past full-backs? Virtually never. Did he have many tricks? No. Did he have an exceptional body-swerve? Again no.

Was he clever at cutting inside and clipping a ball back with his left peg? No. Did he work hard? Certainly; nobody could reasonably accuse him of giving less than 100 per-cent. Could he cross the ball? Yes, brilliantly at times, but as anybody who has played up front will tell you, it's far easier to sling the ball across than to put it in the back of the net.

As I mentioned when talking about Denis Irwin, crossing on the run is an art form, but most of David's best deliveries were made when the ball was stationary. Either that or they came from the middle third, where they are far less likely to cause damage than if released from near the byline.

Can he strike a dead ball with accuracy and power? Of course he can; he has scored memorable goals to prove it, although his actual percentage of goals from free-kicks was far lower than people might imagine.

What about his all-round passing? It's fine, but unquestionably some way behind that of his fellow youth-team graduate, Paul Scholes.

But don't get me wrong, David Beckham is a good player. But a world-class performer? Not in my book. Given the choice, I would go for Steve Coppell on my right wing every time. Week-in and week-out, he did a fantastic job for United – and his hairdo never changed!

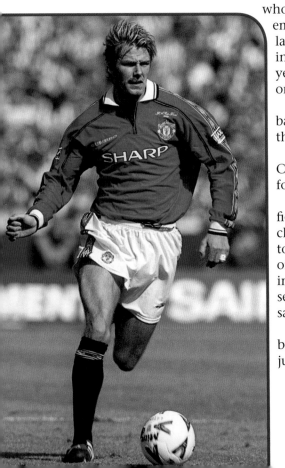

I would think that David Beckham is a very nice young man, who hasn't, in recent years, been allowed to be. Given his eminence, it might seem silly to say that some people are laughing at him, but I think some of his peers must be doing just that. Certainly some of the great players of yester-year must look at him and think: 'What the hell's going on?'

I just hope he's not truly synonymous with what football has become. If he is, then God help football! I like to think there's still more to the game than image.

In Manchester United terms, he was by no means an Eric Cantona; he wasn't a catalyst for transforming the club's fortunes.

In his first season at Real Madrid, playing in central midfield, he enjoyed a certain amount of early success, but the club had a poor season by their standards, falling away towards the end, and I don't know if he was the root cause of that. While he was adamant that he would not be leaving after a short stay at the Bernabeu, the love affair seemed to be waning slightly in 2005, though for his own sake I hope it isn't.

I've only been in his company a couple of times, and he has been delightfully courteous. I've no axe to grind with him. I just get totally confused with the whole image business and his love affair with the limelight. How has he allowed all things non-football to overtake his football?

I just wish the media would face reality and admit that, compared to the likes of Paul Scholes, Roy Keane and Ryan Giggs, David Beckham isn't quite the talking horse they have made him out to be.

261. NICKY BUTT

OTHER HONOURS:
39 ENGLAND CAPS 1997-.

OTHER CLUBS:
NEWCASTLE UNITED 04/05- (18, 1).

NICKY BUTT		
COMP.	APPS	GLS
LEAGUE	210 (60)	21
FAC	23 (6)	1
LC	7 (1)	0
EUROPE	58 (13)	2
OTHERS	9	2
TOTAL	307 (80)	26

BORN	MANCHESTER 21ST JANUARY 1975
POSITION	MIDFIELDER
JOINED UNITED	JULY 1991 FROM JUNIOR FOOTBALL
UNITED DEBUT	OLDHAM ATHLETIC (H) PREM. - 21/11/1992
UNITED HONOURS	EUROPEAN CUP 1998/9 PREMIERSHIP 1995/6, 1996/7, 1998/9, 1999/00, 2000/1, 2002/3 FA CUP 1995/6, 2003/4
UNITED FAREWELL	MILLWALL (MILLENIUM STADIUM) FAC - 22/05/2004
LEFT UNITED FOR	NEWCASTLE UNITED AUGUST 2004 - £2.5M

Nicky Butt underwent a radical change, and it did not become him. When Nicky was first in the United side he epitomised to me a young lad from north Manchester. He'd put his foot in, all muck and nettles. 'They shall not pass' was his motto, and when he won the ball he would give it, simply and efficiently, to someone who could play. In that vein, I think he performed a wonderful service for Manchester United.

But in 2003/04 – and I hope I'm wrong but it's a distinct impression – it seemed that basic approach was no longer good enough for him. Now he wanted to embellish it. To use a phrase much favoured by Matt Busby and Jimmy Murphy in the old days, he wanted to get mixed up with the players.

There is a role in the game for every kind of footballer. There's room for the Giggs', room for the Beckhams, room for the Scholes', and also there's room for the Nicky Butts and the Gary Nevilles, people who should keep it simple.

But the one thing that bothers me is if the Butts and the Nevilles forget why they are effective, and try to play like the Giggs', the Beckhams and the Scholes'.

In Nicky's case, not only was he trying to emulate more gifted colleagues, it appeared that he

was not even moving around the pitch at his customary speed. Where he used to be in and biting at anything that moved – and he was very, very good at that – he had become something of a stroller.

The one thing nobody, from any walk of life, should do is attempt to be something they're not. He needs to be the destructive force first; then, and only if time allows, he can try his hand at being creative. If he loses what he's best at, it would be a great shame, because he has already proven his worth for United and England.

I think the summer of 2004 was the time for Nicky to get away from Manchester United, and I am pleased for him that he secured his move to Newcastle.

Sometimes you can be part of a set-up for too long, and you need a change. It was bad enough for him when he was third choice behind Keane and Scholes, but then Phil Neville emerged as a midfielder, and also there were Eric Djemba-Djemba, Darren Fletcher and Kleberson to worry about. Add it all up and that was far too much competition for Nicky Butt.

BORN	CAILLOLS, NR. MARSEILLES 24TH MAY 1966
POSITION	FORWARD
JOINED UNITED	NOVEMBER 1992 FROM LEEDS UNITED - £1.2M
UNITED DEBUT	MANCHESTER CITY (H) PREM. - 06/12/1992
UNITED HONOURS	PREMIERSHIP 1992/3, 1993/4, 1995/6, 1996/7 FA CUP 1993/4, 1995/6
UNITED FAREWELL	WEST HAM UNITED (H) PREM. - 11/05/1997
RETIRED	MAY 1997

ERIC CANTONA		
COMP.	APPS	GLS
LEAGUE	142 (1)	64
FAC	17	10
LC	6	1
EUROPE	16	5
OTHERS	3	2
TOTAL	184 (1)	82

262. ERIC CANTONA

OTHER HONOURS:
45 FRANCE CAPS 1987-95.
PFA FOOTBALLER OF THE YEAR 1994;
FWA FOOTBALLER OF THE YEAR 1996.

OTHER CLUBS:
AUXERRE 83/4-85/6 (13, 2);
MARTIGUES 85/6 (0, 0);
AUXERRE 86/7-87/8 (68, 21);
MARSEILLES 88/9 (22, 5);
BORDEAUX ON LOAN 88/9 (11, 6);
MONTPELLIER 89/90 (33, 10); MARSEILLES 90/1 (18, 8);
NÎMES 91/2 (17, 2), ALL FRANCE; LEEDS UNITED 91/2-92/3 (28, 9).

If ever a man was a catalyst for the emergence of a great football side, then it was Eric Cantona with Manchester United. He's not the best player the club has ever had, and he didn't make the most appearances or score the most goals. But the day he walked in, something clicked, and United have never been the same since.

Why? Perhaps Eric thought it was about time he started to show people exactly what he could do after quite a few years of comparative under-achievement.

His value to the young players was incalculable, you couldn't put a price on it. They watched him and saw that when a training session finished, Eric didn't come in for a shower. He'd get a ball out and he would practice his skills, and that encouraged them to adopt a similar approach.

In fact, we're talking not only about the kids who were coming through around the time of his arrival, the likes of Scholes and Beckham, but even established international stars like Mark Hughes will admit to having learned plenty from the Cantona method.

Before his sojourn at Old Trafford, Eric's record is bizarre for such a colossal talent. He played for seven French clubs without ever settling, and there was a brief stay at Leeds, whom he helped to lift the League title at United's expense.

The frightening thing is that in that eight-year spell, between the ages of 18 and 26, he played fewer than 200 League games at a time when his great gifts should have been gracing the football world.

It all changed for Eric when United signed him on a fluke. Leeds rang the chairman, Martin Edwards, to ask about Denis Irwin, the conversation turned to the Frenchman, and the rest is glorious history.

I have monitored Old Trafford affairs practically all my life, and kept a close eye on all that's been happening in the wider world of English football. But I can confidently say that never in my experience has one man's influence on a club been more far-reaching than Eric Cantona's on Manchester United.

Eric and the Red Devils seemed to have a marriage that was made in heaven. It was something he had never known before, and his turbulent relationships with many of his former employers are well documented.

Coup de grace: Eric Cantona supplies an uplifting end to a disappointing game as he volleys a magnificent late winner against Liverpool in the 1996 FA Cup Final.

Alex Ferguson's cap is not exactly short of feathers, but Eric represents the finest and most luxuriant of them all. He was able to make the most of this hitherto tormented genius where other managers had failed conspicuously to get him to use his obvious gifts in the right direction. It might have had something to do with the surroundings. He might have looked at our young men, like Scholes and company, and thought to himself: 'I can lead these children into the Promised Land.'

What did Eric bring to the team that had been missing before? A certainty of his own worth, a self-confidence that verged on arrogance, and a touch of inspiration. There was no single secret, no magic potion; he could play the game, it was as simple as that.

Unusually for a great player – and I use that adjective advisedly – he was upright; there was no crouching for Cantona. His awareness, his vision, his control, his chest-work, his heading ability, his finishing with either foot, his huge commanding presence . . . they were all massive factors in his success.

People wonder about what might have happened had he arrived at United five years earlier, but the fact is he might have brought nothing. He might still have been immersed in his petulant period and we might never have seen the best of him.

He was just a freak of nature for Manchester United. Everything about him was right for us at the time. It was amazing that Leeds let him go, but perhaps Howard Wilkinson couldn't handle him, in the same way that Gerard Houllier couldn't cope with him in the French set-up. It's strange that both of those managers were schoolteachers, and as soon as he got down to the nitty-gritty with a dyed-in-the-wool football man he thrived.

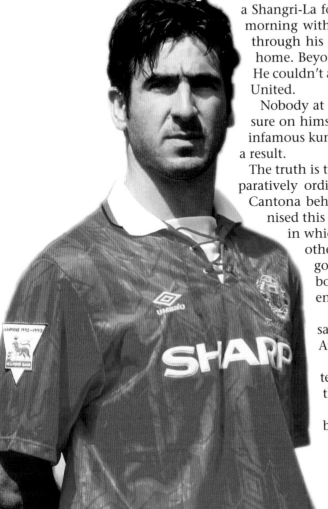

Alex saw very quickly that he had something special and he treated the Frenchman as a grown-up. Manchester United was a Shangri-La for Eric, a place where he could wake up in the morning with a smile on his face, he could still be smiling through his day's work, and still be smiling when he went home. Beyond that, he was appreciated, and he was loved. He couldn't ask for any more, and neither could Manchester United.

Nobody at Old Trafford put pressure on him. He put pressure on himself occasionally, such as when he delivered his infamous kung-fu kick at Selhurst Park and was suspended as a result.

The truth is that until the arrival of Eric, United were a comparatively ordinary side. During his tenure at Old Trafford, Cantona behaved and performed like a genius. Alex recognised this and made sure that he had the right conditions in which to flourish. He treated him differently to the others because that was what was required for the good of the club. He gave them something nobody else had. Eric *was* different. Vive la Différence!

He took United by the scruff of the neck and said: 'Come on, let's go out and enjoy ourselves.' And didn't they just.

Why didn't he do more in Europe? Perhaps the team as a whole wasn't good enough, simple as that. Why single out Cantona as a specific culprit?

In the end, he packed in when he was only 31 because, I think, he was fed up. He'd had enough of that. He's a very complex character and for us to try and rationalise his decisions would send us to the funny farm.

Suffice it to say that his impact was colossal. Why, my son even named his cat after him!

263. KEITH GILLESPIE

OTHER HONOURS:
60 NORTHERN IRELAND CAPS 1994-.

OTHER CLUBS:
WIGAN ATHLETIC ON LOAN 93/4 (8, 4);
NEWCASTLE UNITED 94/5-98/9 (113, 11);
BLACKBURN ROVERS 98/9-02/03 (113, 5);
WIGAN ATHLETIC ON LOAN 00/01 (13, 4);
LEICESTER CITY 03/04-04/05 (42, 2).

KEITH GILLESPIE		
COMP.	APPS	GLS
LEAGUE	3 (6)	1
FAC	1 (1)	1
LC	3	0
TOTAL	7 (7)	2

BORN	LARNE, NORTHERN IRELAND 18TH FEBRUARY 1975
POSITION	WINGER
JOINED UNITED	JULY 1991 FROM IRISH JUNIOR FOOTBALL
UNITED DEBUT	BURY (H) FAC - 05/01/1993
UNITED FAREWELL	COVENTRY CITY (H) PREM. - 03/01/1995
LEFT UNITED FOR	NEWCASTLE UNITED JAN 1995 VALUED AT £1M IN PART EXCHANGE FOR ANDY COLE

I don't think anyone ever named a cat after Keith Gillespie, but they might have done following his debut against Bury, in which he was superb. He ran the Shakers' defence daft that night, going past players seemingly at will and causing havoc.

Of course, by then one of the worst things in the football world was happening to him. Because he was a winger from Northern Ireland and playing for Manchester United, he had to put up with a whole raft of fatuous comparisons with George Best.

It was no consolation to Keith, but he was only the latest in a long line of lads to suffer and it makes me mad. The people who hand out these crazy tags have never played the game, and just don't appreciate how superb a player would need to be to be compared to Best.

After his tormenting of Bury, even more was expected of him, and it's fair to say that, given his abundant ability, he has under-achieved.

It seemed that Keith had a brief go in the first team and then departed before we could really assess what he could do. I guess the big problem for him was the presence of Andrei Kanchelskis, although still the Irishman seemed a good bet for the future.

But the manager decided he could do without him, albeit reluctantly, and included him in the package to Newcastle when he signed Andy Cole. Keith impressed on Tyneside for a time, but then he had some problems off the pitch, and eventually he moved on, never quite living up to that early potential.

Perhaps if he'd stayed at Old Trafford he might have done more, and it's ironic to reflect that only a few months after his departure, Kanchelskis had gone, too. But I'd guess that Keith

had precious little choice in the matter.

Later he might have cast an envious eye backwards, and probably so did Sir Alex. Had the lad stayed, he might have had a run in the side with Eric, and he'd have been a better player for the experience.

It's very difficult for any youngster to leave United and succeed, because the moment he walks out of the Old Trafford door, with all due respect to other clubs, he is on his way down.

BORN	CORK, ROI 10TH AUGUST 1971
POSITION	MIDFIELDER
JOINED UNITED	JULY 1993 FROM NOTTINGHAM F. - £3.75M
UNITED DEBUT	ARSENAL (WEMBLEY) CS - 07/08/1993
UNITED HONOURS	PREMIERSHIP 1993/4, 1995/6, 1996/7, 1998/9, 1999/00, 2000/1, 2002/3 FA CUP 1993/4, 1995/6, 1998/9, 2003/4

ROY KEANE		
COMP.	APPS	GLS
LEAGUE	305 (16)	33
FAC	44 (2)	2
LC	12 (2)	0
EUROPE	80 (1)	14
OTHERS	12	2
TOTAL	453 (21)	51

264. ROY KEANE

OTHER HONOURS:
65 REPUBLIC OF IRELAND CAPS 1991-.
PFA FOOTBALLER OF THE YEAR 2000.
FWA FOOTBALLER OF THE YEAR 2000

OTHER CLUBS:
NOTTINGHAM FOREST 90/1-92/3 (114, 22).

Roy Keane stands as one of the finest, most colossally influential footballers Manchester United, or anyone else, have had since the war. Like all the genuine greats, he was possessed by an almost frighteningly fierce, all-consuming will to win, and there was nothing he couldn't do.

Like Bryan Robson, with whom the Irishman overlapped all too briefly at Old Trafford, Roy was a box-to-box player, compellingly effective in all areas of the pitch. You don't see many like him, and when you do you have to embrace them because their value to the team is overwhelming.

Arguably he was the most telling factor in United's continued success after Bryan left. Taking over Robbo's inspirational mantle, he marauded here, there and everywhere like an ungovernable force of nature, putting his foot in, winning the headers, throwing his body in front of anything that threatened his team's goal, passing the ball superbly, handing out the bollockings where necessary, generally leading by example.

The terrifying question in the summer of 2005 was: how do you replace such a man? It seemed that Roy was going to be good for at least another season, but what about beyond that? The need could hardly have been more pressing and there didn't seem to be anyone of remotely similar stature on the club's books, which is hardly surprising.

The strength of Keane's character was unbelievable. For example, when United played Juventus in the semi-final second leg of the European Cup in 1999, United went two down early on, but even though Roy was never going to be able to play in the final because of an impending suspension, it was he who pulled them back into contention with a magnificent headed goal, and it was he who drove them on to win the match.

Where a lesser individual might have sulked, he was utterly indomitable, and it was one of the few occasions it would be fair to call a single player indispensable. He just would not countenance the thought of losing, even though he was doomed to miss out on the big day himself, and he lifted United by their bootlaces, playing as though it was going to be his last game ever.

People with that sort of mentality are thin on the ground, and they are priceless. For instance, Paul Gascoigne found himself in a similar situation when playing for England in the 1990 World Cup Finals, and how did he react? He cried!

If there has been a flaw in the Keane contribution down the years it has been his temperamental excesses. Maybe that's where you can draw a line between Roy and Robbo, who wasn't prone to such lapses. I believe the Irishman has done himself less than justice with some of his outbursts, but that's the nature of the man and there's not a great deal you can do about it if you want him at your club.

That's the way Roy is built, so that he is capable, for example, of the controversial and unsavoury business with Alfie Haaland of Manchester City. In no way can I begin to condone what he did to Haaland.

But I suppose one tends to wear blinkers and say: 'We need the best of Roy Keane so we'll have to take the baggage that goes with it.' I don't think you'd find too many Manchester United fans who didn't bless the day he signed for their club.

When he arrived at Old Trafford, I couldn't have been more delighted. I always thought he was ten times the player Paul Ince was, for example. It seemed possible to me that he could give us what we were losing with the impending retirement of Robbo.

Is Roy Keane management material? Is he another Alex Ferguson waiting to blossom? What a fascinating thought! I'd have said, initially, that I can't believe he will ever become a boss. But more recently he has muttered about management possibly being on his agenda, so we'd better keep an eye on the situation.

'If there has been a flaw in the Keane contribution down the years it has been his temperamental excesses. Maybe that's where you can draw a line between Roy and Robbo, who wasn't prone to such lapses.'

BORN	Bury
	21st April 1975
POSITION	Winger
JOINED UNITED	July 1991 from
	junior football
UNITED DEBUT	West Ham United (A)
	Prem. - 26/02/1994
UNITED FAREWELL	Liverpool (H)
	Prem. - 10/04/1998
LEFT UNITED FOR	Huddersfield Town
	July 1998

BEN THORNLEY		
COMP.	APPS	GLS
LEAGUE	1 (8)	0
FAC	2	0
LC	3	0
TOTAL	6 (8)	0

265. BEN THORNLEY

OTHER CLUBS:
STOCKPORT COUNTY ON LOAN 95/6 (10, 0);
HUDDERSFIELD TOWN ON LOAN 95/6 (12, 2);
HUDDERSFIELD TOWN 98/9-00/01 (99, 5);
ABERDEEN 01/02-02/03 (30, 3);
BLACKPOOL 02/03 (12, 0); BURY 03/04 (5, 0).

As a kid Ben Thornley played with the Neville lads and the coaches believed that he was going to be more than useful as a left winger who would score a few goals.

But just as his big chance appeared to be in the offing – apparently Alex Ferguson intended to select him for the next first-team match – he picked up an horrendous injury from Blackburn's Nicky Marker in a reserve game, and although he recovered to continue his career, he was never the same force again. As I know to my cost, it's the hardest thing in the world for a kid to suffer a bad one and get over it fully.

At junior level, where often he lined up at outside-left with Ryan Giggs playing inside him, Ben had been quick and direct, always wanting to attack his full-back, but when he returned to something approaching fitness he was forced to change his style radically. Sadly, he had lost that initial explosion of pace that took him away from defenders, and he had to become more circumspect.

At that point his prospects at United hardly seemed bright with Giggs and Lee Sharpe ahead of him, and it must have been excruciating for poor Ben to watch his mates – the Nevilles, Scholesy and the rest – doing so well, while he faced a future in the lower divisions.

BORN	Glasgow
	22nd August 1973
POSITION	Forward
JOINED UNITED	July 1989 from
	junior football
UNITED DEBUT	Coventry City (H)
& FAREWELL	Prem. - 08/05/1994
LEFT UNITED FOR	Kilmarnock - Sept. 1994

COLIN McKEE		
COMP.	APPS	GLS
LEAGUE	1	0
TOTAL	1	0

266. COLIN McKEE

OTHER CLUBS:
BURY ON LOAN 92/3 (2, 0);
KILMARNOCK 94/5-97/8 (76, 11);
FALKIRK 98/9 (4, 0).

It was 'hello' and 'goodbye' for Colin McKee as Manchester United were presented with the 1994 Premiership trophy in the spring sunshine at Old Trafford. The tall, hard-running frontman, who had been prominent as United won the FA Youth Cup in 1992, made his sole senior start for the club that day, but by autumn he was on his way back to his native Scotland, judged as not up to standard for the English top division.

267. DAVID MAY

OTHER CLUBS:
BLACKBURN ROVERS 88/9-93/4 (123, 3);
HUDDERSFIELD TOWN ON LOAN 99/00 (1, 0);
BURNLEY 03/04 (35, 4).

DAVID MAY		
COMP.	APPS	GLS
LEAGUE	68 (17)	6
FAC	6	0
LC	9	1
EUROPE	13 (2)	1
OTHERS	2 (1)	0
TOTAL	98 (20)	8

BORN	OLDHAM 26TH JUNE 1970
POSITION	DEFENDER
JOINED UNITED	JULY 1994 FROM BLACKBURN R. - £1.2M
UNITED DEBUT	BLACKBURN ROVERS (WEMBLEY) CS - 14/08/1994
UNITED HONOURS	PREMIERSHIP 1995/6, 1996/7 FA CUP 1995/6, 1998/9
UNITED FAREWELL	BURNLEY (A) LC - 03/12/2002
LEFT UNITED FOR	BURNLEY - JUNE 2003

It was a major surprise to me when Alex Ferguson signed David May from Blackburn Rovers. I never thought he was anything like good enough for Manchester United.

When pressed into duty as a full-back, he suffered some painful runarounds, notably against Gothenburg in the Champions League when he was tormented by Jesper Blomqvist, but I never thought he dominated as a central defender either. Certainly he never inspired any confidence in me.

Steve Bruce was blazing when he was left out of the team for the 1996 FA Cup Final in favour of David May, and I could sympathise with his view. Somehow, May never even looked like a footballer. To me his legs always seemed unnaturally short for his body, and he didn't appear mobile enough to defend against some of the pacier attackers.

For all that, he pocketed four major honours during his time at Old Trafford, and I believe he was fortunate in that United suffered injuries to centre-halves. Brucie and Pally hadn't missed games for ages, then they both experienced back problems and May was on the spot to benefit. Nothing against David personally, and he was probably up to scratch for Blackburn. But United? No way.

CENTRE OF ATTENTION: David May – he's the blond lad with his left hand on the trophy – was the life and soul of the celebration party when United won the European Cup in 1999. He wasn't quite as prominent during the game, which he spent on the bench.

BORN	NOTTINGHAM 15TH NOVEMBER 1974
POSITION	FULL-BACK
JOINED UNITED	JULY 1991 FROM JUNIOR FOOTBALL
UNITED DEBUT	PORT VALE (A) LC - 21/09/1994
UNITED FAREWELL	LEICESTER CITY (A) LC - 27/11/1996
LEFT UNITED FOR	EVERTON JAN 1998 - £400,000

JOHN O'KANE

COMP.	APPS	GLS
LEAGUE	1 (1)	0
FAC	1	0
LC	2 (1)	0
EUROPE	1	0
TOTAL	5 (2)	0

268. JOHN O'KANE

OTHER CLUBS:
BURY ON LOAN 96/7 (13, 3);
BRADFORD CITY ON LOAN 97/8 (7, 0);
EVERTON 97/8-98/9 (14, 0);
BURNLEY ON LOAN 98/9 (8, 0);
BOLTON WANDERERS 99/00-00/01 (38, 2);
BLACKPOOL 01/02-02/03 (52, 4).

John O'Kane was a highly promising member of the famous youth team, a lad with every scrap of ability needed to make the grade. But perhaps he lacked that little bit of drive, determination, dedication, call it what you will, which makes the difference between going all the way and falling by the wayside. The game appeared to come fairly easy to John, who could play at full-back or on the right side of midfield. He had pace, he knew what to do with the ball and he always seemed to have the time to do it.

Having not made it at Old Trafford, he wasn't exactly on the scrapheap when he fetched up at Everton, which represented a tremendous second chance. Duly he made the first team under Howard Kendall, who had paid £400,000 for him, then later he broke through for Sam Allardyce at Bolton.

Okay, Everton were in disarray at the time, in ongoing decline, but Bolton were on the way up so there was every chance for a lad with his talent if he was sufficiently focused. I know boys who would give their right arms for the opportunities that fell to John O'Kane, but he never made the most of them. Had he come through at United, then what might have happened to Gary Neville? Unquestionably John was more of a natural footballer than Gary, more comfortable on the ball, but in terms of application it was no contest. Whatever anyone says about the older Neville, no one could ever question his application.

TWO WHO MISSED THE OLD TRAFFORD BOAT: John O'Kane (left) celebrates FA Youth Cup glory in 1992. The boy with him, who never made it into the first team, is Robbie Savage.

269. SIMON DAVIES

OTHER HONOURS:
1 WALES CAP 1996.

OTHER CLUBS:
EXETER CITY ON LOAN 93/4 (6, 1);
HUDDERSFIELD TOWN ON LOAN 96/7 (3, 0);
LUTON TOWN 97/8-98/9 (22, 1);
MACCLESFIELD TOWN 98/9-99/00 (48, 3);
ROCHDALE 00/01 (12, 1).

SIMON DAVIES		
COMP.	APPS	GLS
LEAGUE	4 (7)	0
LC	3 (2)	0
EUROPE	3 (1)	1
TOTAL	10 (10)	1

BORN	MIDDLEWICH, CHESHIRE 23RD APRIL 1974
POSITION	MIDFIELDER
JOINED UNITED	JULY 1990 FROM JUNIOR FOOTBALL
UNITED DEBUT	PORT VALE (A) LC - 21/09/1994
UNITED FAREWELL	LEICESTER CITY (A) LC - 27/11/1996
LEFT UNITED FOR	LUTON TOWN AUG. 1997 - £150,000

There were those among the United coaching staff who believed Simon Davies would advance a lot further in the game than he was ultimately to manage.

Yet another member of the ultra-productive 1992 FA Youth Cup-winning side, Simon was a lanky, left-sided midfielder with plenty of skill, and he made a bit of a splash by scoring a neat goal against Galatasaray at Old Trafford. In the end, though, he did no more than lurk around the edges of the first team, which was understandable, maybe, with his fellow Welsh international Ryan Giggs so entrenched on the scene and so clearly in a different class.

At the very least, however, I'd have thought Simon would have made a career in the lower divisions, but it wasn't to be and he moved into non-League football while still in his mid-twenties.

270. PAUL SCHOLES

OTHER HONOURS:
66 ENGLAND CAPS 1997-2004.

PAUL SCHOLES		
COMP.	APPS	GLS
LEAGUE	259 (62)	87
FAC	23 (9)	12
LC	11 (5)	8
EUROPE	74 (11)	21
OTHERS	10	0
TOTAL	377 (87)	128

BORN	SALFORD 16TH NOVEMBER 1974
POSITION	MIDFIELDER OR FORWARD
JOINED UNITED	JULY 1991 FROM JUNIOR FOOTBALL
UNITED DEBUT	PORT VALE (A) LC - 21/09/1994
UNITED HONOURS	PREMIERSHIP 1995/6, 1996/7, 1998/9, 1999/00, 2000/1, 2002/3 FA CUP 1995/6, 1998/9, 2003/4

What a rare joy it is to watch such a complete craftsman as Paul Scholes plying his trade. He was born to play football, and is as fine an exponent of the dear old game as Manchester United have had on their books in the last 20 years and more. Certainly for my money, he's on a different plane – an altogether more celestial one – to most of the so-called superstars I get so sick of hearing about.

For example, people talk in such glowing terms of David Beckham, who hasn't shown me that he's fit to lace Scholesy's boots. If only David was as good as Paul, then he could boast and he could wear his hair in 83 different styles, and I wouldn't mind a bit.

Paul Scholes is a star who, for many years, didn't get even a tiny percentage of the credit he deserved. That's always likely to happen because most of the people who write about the game don't have a clue.

They might know that Beckham can cross a ball, and that he's married to Posh Spice; they understand that Gazza is a clown; but when it comes to the nuts and bolts of the game, they are ignorant.

They want cubby-holes for everyone, and there wasn't a convenient one for Paul. Another such case was Johnny Morris. He was always overshadowed, too. That seems to be the way of the world.

WOEFULLY UNLUCKY: he didn't play in the European Cup Final, but Paul Scholes richly deserved his moment of glee with the coveted trophy.

But people on the inside of football know that Scholes is a thoroughbred. I have heard respected opponents, such as Patrick Vieira, asked to pick out a top operator, and infallibly they choose Scholes. Does that not tell people anything?

Paul is happy to be a footballer, he doesn't aspire to anything else, and I like practically everything about him. He's got supreme vision, he's blessed with wonderful feet, he passes like a dream, and although he's only a little lad, he's terrific in the air.

Crucially, too, he scores goals for fun, being a wonderful striker of the ball and a fantastic timer of forward runs who knows exactly when to arrive in the box. That's a skill that can never be taught – either it's in you or it's not. If the Lord above didn't put it in, then no coach ever will.

On top of all that, Paul loves playing and is as honest as the day is long. If I had to put my finger on one defect, I would say his tackling can be a little bit reckless, but nobody on this earth is perfect.

Perhaps it's been a problem to him that apparently he finds the game so easy. He can be played behind the front two, or as an out-and-out striker, or as a central midfielder, or as a wide man either on the right or left. You could put him anywhere and he would be excellent.

As a result, he might have suffered a bit for his versatility instead of being allowed to specialise. Personally I would use him as a central midfielder who gets forward more than he stays back, and I would never even ponder the possibility of wasting him on the wing. The bottom line, though, is that as long as I could have Scholesy in my side, I'd be happy.

He's such a magnificent technician, who has scored some of the most memorable United goals of the modern era. One that sticks in my mind is the volley direct from a Beckham corner at Bradford on the way to yet another League title. Very few players could have put that one away, but he made it look simplicity itself.

Despite being such a quiet, self-effacing fellow who has to look after his asthma, Paul can be a bit fiery at times, and although he's about half the size of an average thimble he can hardly be missed with his ginger hair, so there's never any chance that he'll get away with a misdemeanour.

In 2005, he remained a massively influential player, who still had plenty to give. But when the time does come for him to step aside, he will be as hard to replace as Robson, or Cantona, or Keane. For the club's sake, I hope he has another four or five years in him at the top level. It's unthinkable that he should go earlier, because they never look the same side without him. He offers an added dimension, as did Cantona in his time, but Beckham didn't because he lacked the subtlety of the other two.

Scholesy plays the surprising little balls around the corner, nicks them into people in unexpected positions with unerring instinct, and the day he stops doing that in a Manchester United shirt will be a tremendously sad one for all who espouse the Old Trafford cause.

He surprised a lot of observers when he announced his retirement from the international scene. Why did he do it? Was it that he prefers home and family to fame and fortune? Or was he fed up with being played here, there and everywhere by Sven-Goran Eriksson? I think the former and I base that on the fact that away from the game, he's a gem of a lad. When he got his first car from Manchester United, he went back to Danny McGregor, the commercial manager, and said he needed to swap his new motor. Danny was surprised, to put it mildly, because the car was a snappy little sporty number, one that most boys would give their eye-teeth for.

When asked what the problem was, Paul replied that it was too much of a squash for his mum; she couldn't get into it comfortably! Now here's a top-class footballer who has just been handed the keys to a highly desirable set of wheels and what's he thinking about? His mum. The girl he's married, who was his boyhood sweetheart, is a very lucky lass. Any lad who treats his mother so well is always going to look after his wife and kids – and nothing's more important than that, not even football.

> 'For the club's sake, I hope he has another four or five years in him at the top level. It's unthinkable that he should go earlier, because they never look the same side without him. He offers an added dimension, as did Cantona in his time.'

BORN	BURNLEY 28TH APRIL 1975
POSITION	CENTRAL DEFENDER
JOINED UNITED	JULY 1991 FROM JUNIOR FOOTBALL
UNITED DEBUT	PORT VALE (H) LC - 05/10/1994
UNITED FAREWELL	WIMBLEDON (H) FAC - 25/01/1997
LEFT UNITED FOR	READING NOV. 1998 - £300,000

CHRIS CASPER		
COMP.	APPS	GLS
LEAGUE	0 (2)	0
FAC	1	0
LC	3	0
EUROPE	0 (1)	0
TOTAL	4 (3)	0

271. CHRIS CASPER

OTHER CLUBS:
BOURNEMOUTH ON LOAN 95/6 (16, 1);
SWINDON TOWN ON LOAN 97/8 (9, 1);
READING 98/9-99/00 (47, 0).

It was my impression that Chris Casper was a tad short, and maybe lacked a little physical presence, to become a central defender at the highest level.

It didn't matter in Manchester United's successful 1992 youth team, in which neither Chris nor his fellow centre-half Gary Neville were giants, because neither were most of their opponents.

Chris was a smooth, cultured footballer, but when a lad gets into that big, ugly world of the Premiership, he has to have something extra, a certain edge that enables him to survive and flourish, and perhaps he wasn't quite ruthless enough.

Possibly he found the game easier as a kid, playing in a good side and coming from a footballing family, his father being the accomplished long-serving Burnley striker Frank Casper.

Like all lads in that situation, he carried a large burden of expectation. No matter how positive the influences around them, such circumstances can overwhelm them because they have to please too many people.

Alex Ferguson gave Chris a handful of chances to show what he could do, but he never looked to me as if he would become a first-team regular.

Tragically for the lad, while playing for Reading against Cardiff he sustained an injury which ultimately finished his career prematurely. At least he received a sizeable pay-out in compensation, but no amount of money could really make up for what he had lost.

BORN	WATFORD 10TH DECEMBER 1975
POSITION	STRIKER
JOINED UNITED	JUNE 1994 FROM BRADFORD C. - £100,000
UNITED DEBUT	PORT VALE (H) LC - 05/10/1994
UNITED FAREWELL	NEWCASTLE UNITED (A) LC - 26/10/1994
LEFT UNITED FOR	MACCLESFIELD TOWN JUNE 1998

GRAEME TOMLINSON		
COMP.	APPS	GLS
LEAGUE	0 (2)	0
TOTAL	0 (2)	0

272. GRAEME TOMLINSON

OTHER CLUBS:
BRADFORD CITY 93/4 (17, 6);
LUTON TOWN ON LOAN 95/6 (7, 0);
BOURNEMOUTH ON LOAN 97/8 (8, 1); MILLWALL ON LOAN 97/8 (3, 1);
MACCLESFIELD TOWN 98/9-99/00 (46, 6); EXETER CITY 00/01-01/02 (56, 6).

United paid a lot of money for Graeme Tomlinson as an unproven kid, but he had the rotten luck to suffer a debilitating injury in the early part of his Old Trafford tenure.

Because of that fee, it might be that too much was expected too soon from the boy. Of course, the money was nothing to do with him and he should have been judged as the youngster he was. In the end, his career petered out rather anti-climactically in the lower divisions.

273. KEVIN PILKINGTON

OTHER CLUBS:
ROCHDALE ON LOAN 95/6 (6, 0);
ROTHERHAM UNITED ON LOAN 96/7 (17, 0);
PORT VALE 98/9-99/00 (23, 0);
MANSFIELD TOWN 00/01-04/05 (167, 0)
NOTTS COUNTY 05/06-.

KEVIN PILKINGTON		
COMP.	APPS	GLS
LEAGUE	4 (2)	0
FAC	1	0
LC	1	0
TOTAL	6 (2)	0

BORN	HITCHIN, HERTFORDSHIRE 8TH MARCH 1974
POSITION	GOALKEEPER
JOINED UNITED	JULY 1992 FROM JUNIOR FOOTBALL
UNITED DEBUT	CRYSTAL PALACE (H) PREM. - 19/11/1994
UNITED FAREWELL	COVENTRY CITY (A) PREM. - 28/12/1997
LEFT UNITED FOR	PORT VALE - JUNE 1998

Kevin Pilkington was engulfed by the gigantic shadow of Peter Schmeichel as he grew up at Old Trafford, but the coaches were always impressed by his quality and had genuine hopes of him.

In truth, he had scant chance at United and I'm delighted that he went on to forge a niche at Mansfield, becoming captain in 2003/04 and leading Keith Curle's team to the Third Division play-off final. Kevin's experience shows that, given a level head and the determination to continue working hard, there can be life after Manchester United in the lower leagues.

274. ANDY COLE

OTHER HONOURS:
15 ENGLAND CAPS 1995-2001.

OTHER CLUBS:
ARSENAL 90/1 (1, 0);
FULHAM ON LOAN 91/2 (13, 3);
BRISTOL CITY 91/2-92/3 (41, 20);
NEWCASTLE UNITED 92/3-94/5 (70, 55);
BLACKBURN ROVERS 01/02-03/04 (83, 27);
FULHAM 04/05- (31, 12).

ANDY COLE		
COMP.	APPS	GLS
LEAGUE	161 (34)	93
FAC	19 (2)	9
LC	2	0
EUROPE	43 (7)	19
OTHERS	6 (1)	0
TOTAL	231 (44)	121

BORN	NOTTINGHAM 15TH OCTOBER 1971
POSITION	STRIKER
JOINED UNITED	JANUARY 1995 FROM NEWCASTLE UNITED £6M PLUS KEITH GILLESPIE
UNITED DEBUT	BLACKBURN ROVERS (H) PREM. - 22/01/1995
UNITED HONOURS	EUROPEAN CUP 1998/9 PREMIERSHIP 1995/6, 1996/7, 1998/9, 1999/00, 2000/1 FA CUP 1995/6, 1998/9
UNITED FAREWELL	WEST HAM UNITED (H) PREM. - 08/12/2001
LEFT UNITED FOR	BLACKBURN ROVERS DEC. 2001 - £8M

Pull him to pieces how you will – and plenty of people have done just that – but you can never take away from Andy Cole the fact that he was a fantastic goal-scorer, one of the most effective out-and-out marksmen in European football over the last ten to 15 years.

Yet there was a period in his early days when it seemed as though he might not make it. George Graham didn't fancy him at Arsenal, evidently preferring Kevin Campbell, but then he rebuilt his career at Bristol City before catching fire at Newcastle.

Cole's record at St James' Park was so persuasive that Alex

Ferguson was determined to get him, even at the price of letting the promising Keith Gillespie leave Old Trafford before he had reached his prime.

United paid a record fee to land Andy, but no one can ever say that Alex did badly out of the deal. Indeed, six years later, after winning the European Cup and just about every other trophy that was available with Cole as his main striker, he sold him to Blackburn for a substantial profit.

Right from the start, though, the boy had to take plenty of stick. He failed to take a good opportunity in his debut against Blackburn, then at the end of his first season he missed three inviting chances in the final match against West Ham. If one of them had gone in then United would have retained their Championship. Maybe it was unfair to blame him, but some did, and his popularity never completely recovered from that.

Andy was different to any player at the club for a very long time in that, certainly at first, he was strictly a goal-scorer and little else. However, his overall game, joining in the approach play and bringing others into moves, improved out of all recognition during his stay at Old Trafford. He played with some very fine players, such as Eric Cantona and Paul Scholes, and, to his credit, he learned plenty from them.

His detractors will point out that he was part of an exceptionally fine side which created a lot of chances, so he was bound to fill his boots, but that's unjust. Nobody could average better than a goal every two games while helping to secure eight major honours and not be a very high-class operator.

One goal he scored, with an exquisite chip from 25 yards at home to Everton, mirrored a famous one by Eric Cantona against Sunderland, which had been lionised by the pundits.

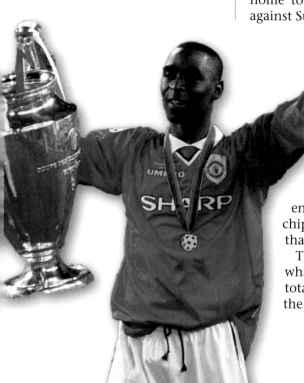

They went mad over Eric's effort, which was indeed magnificent, while Cole's got no more than routine praise, which didn't seem particularly fair.

Even after leaving United, aged 30, he was far from finished, helping Blackburn to lift the League Cup in his first campaign, thus completing his collection of honours.

Yet as brilliant as his record was, he was never taken fully to the fans' hearts. He seemed to have a certain chip on his shoulder, and his demeanour rarely suggested that he was enjoying the game.

Then there was his demand that he be called Andrew; what was that all about? It came across as a pathetic, totally unnecessary affectation of grandeur. See it from the point of view of a factory worker who grafts hard all week, then pays £30 for his ticket to watch United on Saturday – he'll be the one to decide what he calls the centre-forward. Whether it's Charlie Cole or Nat King Cole, that's up to him because he's paying his wages.

What Cole was thinking of I don't know. Do some of these players forget where they came from? Every night they should get down on their knees and thank God that they've been so lucky to be making such a fabulous living out of football. They make me tired.

---

275. PHIL NEVILLE

OTHER HONOURS:
52 ENGLAND CAPS 1996-.

PHIL NEVILLE		
COMP.	APPS	GLS
LEAGUE	210 (53)	5
FAC	25 (6)	1
LC	16 (1)	0
EUROPE	43 (22)	2
OTHERS	7 (3)	0
TOTAL	301 (85)	8

BORN	BURY 21ST JANUARY 1977
POSITION	FULL-BACK, MIDFIELDER
JOINED UNITED	JULY 1993 FROM JUNIOR FOOTBALL
UNITED DEBUT	WREXHAM (H) FAC - 28/01/1995
UNITED HON-OURS	PREMIERSHIP 1995/6, 1996/7, 1998/9, 1999/00, 2000/1, 2002/3 FA CUP 1995/6, 1998/9

When he was a youngster, I always felt that Phil was the more talented of the two Neville brothers, and nothing has happened since to change my opinion. Back in 1997 he had the world at his feet, but then he contracted glandular fever and when he came back from the illness, he wasn't the same force. In fact, his performances deteriorated so markedly that, for a long time, I was sure that he was on his way out of Old Trafford.

Something had disappeared from his game, he had lost some vital spark which had made him one of the most promising young full-backs in the country, and everybody who cared about United was demoralised, both for the club and for the lad himself.

Then amazingly, halfway through the 2002/03 campaign, Sir Alex played Phil in midfield and it was as though he had been born again as a ball-winner. I can recall one towering performance at home to Arsenal when he shut Patrick Vieira out of the game. Perhaps that was the day it all came together for him in his new role.

Phil was a revelation, kicking people for fun. You would never accuse Vieira of being afraid of anybody, but in that game, after a while, he was notable mainly for his absence from the heat of battle.

At this point, I'm sure Vieira would agree, Phil appeared to have recovered totally from the effects of glandular fever and seemed to have carved out a fresh niche for himself.

Since then, though, mainly due to injuries, sometimes he has returned to left-back, where he is competent without being outstanding. He gets by in the berth despite being right-sided – though with a far more accomplished left peg than his brother – but I've no complaint about that. United have never had a problem with right-siders at left-back.

That's all very well, extremely useful to Sir Alex, but I just hope the manager doesn't forget the admirable job Phil has done in midfield, where he's found his most effective position.

Obviously if Keane and Scholes are fit you would hope they'd play as the central pairing, but certainly in 2004 I preferred Phil to Nicky Butt as a capable deputy. The younger Neville was doing what Nicky used to do before he stopped putting his foot in and started strolling. You might call it his England complex.

With Roy being at the wrong end of his career, he's going to miss a lot of games in the future, so there's a considerable opportunity for Phil. Also it might be a tempting option to give Keane an hour, then call Neville from the bench.

Like so many others, Phil has probably been a victim of his own versatility down the years, and he might have prospered even more in his career had he been allowed to develop on his natural side, as a right-back.

BORN	MARSTON GREEN, WARKS. 5TH AUGUST 1976
POSITION	WINGER
JOINED UNITED	JULY 1992 FROM JUNIOR FOOTBALL
UNITED DEBUT	BOLTON WANDERERS (H) PREM. - 16/09/1995
UNITED FAREWELL	LEICESTER CITY (A) LC - 27/11/1996
LEFT UNITED FOR	MANCHESTER CITY APRIL 1999 - £600,000 AFTER INTIAL LOAN PERIOD

276. TERRY COOKE

TERRY COOKE		
COMP.	APPS	GLS
LEAGUE	1 (3)	0
LC	1 (2)	1
EUROPE	0 (1)	0
TOTAL	2 (6)	1

OTHER CLUBS:
SUNDERLAND ON LOAN 95/6 (6, 0);
BIRMINGHAM CITY ON LOAN 96/7 (4, 0);
WREXHAM ON LOAN 98/9 (10, 0);
MANCHESTER CITY 98/9-99/00 (34, 7);
WIGAN ATHLETIC ON LOAN 99/00 (10, 1);
SHEFFIELD WEDNESDAY ON LOAN 00/01 (17, 1);
GRIMSBY TOWN 01/02-02/03 (28, 1);
SHEFFIELD WEDNESDAY 03/04 (23, 2).

When Terry Cooke made his debut for United at home to Bolton, I got a little bit excited. He had pace, he nipped past defenders at will and he crossed the ball – basically that's all I require of a winger, and the boy did it in spades.

Some idiot in the newspaper even compared him to Maradona, which won't have helped him a lot because people just laughed at it, and that was a shame because Terry's display had merited a lot better than that. It deserved to be taken seriously.

But later he had rotten luck with injuries, United seemed intent on loaning him to virtually every other club in the

League and somewhere along the line his career lost its momentum.

He had one terrific spell on loan with City, but that fizzled out, and I had hoped that he might manage to get back on track at Sheffield Wednesday, with whom he was showing bright form in the spring of 2004.

277. PAT McGIBBON

OTHER HONOURS:
7 NORTHERN IRELAND CAPS 1995-.

OTHER CLUBS:
PORTADOWN; SWANSEA CITY ON LOAN 96/7 (1, 0); WIGAN ATHLETIC 96/7-01/02 (173, 11); SCUNTHORPE UNITED ON LOAN 01/02 (6, 1); TRANMERE ROVERS 02/03 (4, 0).

PAT McGIBBON		
COMP.	APPS	GLS
LC	1	0
TOTAL	1	0

BORN	LURGAN, NORTHERN IRELAND 6TH SEPTEMBER 1973
POSITION	CENTRAL DEFENDER
JOINED UNITED	AUGUST 1992 FROM PORTADOWN, N.I., £100,000
UNITED DEBUT & FAREWELL	YORK CITY (H) LC - 20/09/1995
LEFT UNITED FOR	WIGAN ATHLETIC MARCH 1997 - £250,000

Pat McGibbon has the dubious distinction of being sent off in the only game he ever played for Manchester United.

But he's a Northern Ireland international, and he earned United £250,000 when he went to Wigan, so the boy must have had something about him. Clearly not enough, though, to elbow aside Gary Pallister, Ronny Johnsen, or even David May.

278. WILLIAM PRUNIER

OTHER HONOURS:
FRANCE CAPS.

OTHER CLUBS:
AUXERRE 84/5-92/3 (221, 20); MARSEILLE 93/4 (35, 4); BORDEAUX 94/5 (20, 0), ALL FRANCE; FC COPENHAGEN, DENMARK; MONTPELLIER, FRANCE; NAPOLI, ITALY; COURTRAI, BELGIUM; TOULOUSE, FRANCE, 99/00-01/02.

WILLIAM PRUNIER		
COMP.	APPS	GLS
LEAGUE	2	0
TOTAL	2	0

BORN	MONTREUIL, FRANCE 14TH AUGUST 1967
POSITION	CENTRAL DEFENDER
JOINED UNITED	DECEMBER 1995 ON LOAN FROM BORDEAUX, FRANCE
UNITED DEBUT	QPR (H) PREM. - 30/12/1995
UNITED FAREWELL	TOTTENHAM H. (A) PREM. - 01/01/1996
LEFT UNITED FOR	RETURNED TO BORDEAUX JANUARY 1996

William Prunier, Eric Cantona's mate, experienced vividly contrasting fortunes on his only two outings for United. First he did extremely well as a footballing centre-half against QPR, but then he was disastrous in a heavy defeat at Tottenham, seeming to have no idea at all.

Obviously he had impressed during his eight years with Auxerre, but I'd suggest he was reaching the end of his tether by the time he got to Old Trafford, and he wasn't prepared for the pace of the Premiership. I have to doubt whether he would ever have played for United but for the Cantona connection.

BORN	AMSTERDAM 9TH FEBRUARY 1974
POSITION	FORWARD
JOINED UNITED	AUGUST 1996 FROM BARCELONA - £800,000
UNITED DEBUT	NEWCASTLE UNITED (WEMBLEY) CS - 11/08/1996
UNITED HONOURS	PREMIERSHIP 1996/7
UNITED FAREWELL	ASTON VILLA (A) PREM. - 14/05/2000
LEFT UNITED FOR	ALAVES, SPAIN - JUNE 2000

JORDI CRUYFF

COMP.	APPS	GLS
LEAGUE	15 (19)	8
FAC	0 (1)	0
LC	5	0
EUROPE	4 (7)	0
OTHERS	2 (5)	0
TOTAL	26 (32)	8

279. JORDI CRUYFF

OTHER HONOURS:
HOLLAND CAPS.

OTHER CLUBS:
BARCELONA 94/5-95/6 (41, 11);
CELTA VIGO ON LOAN 98/9 (8, 2);
ALAVES 00/01-02/03 (56, 4);
ESPANYOL 03/04- (30, 3), ALL SPAIN.

If Jordi Cruyff had been born with another surname, he'd have been lucky to get a game with anyone at the top level. I don't mean to sound cruel and dismissive, but I think it's the truth.

Jordi was one of five foreigners who arrived at Old Trafford in the summer of 1996 – offering a telling pointer on the club's future transfer policy – and I'd say he made less impact than any of the others. In fact, he must qualify as one of the worst signings Alex Ferguson ever made.

Bathed in publicity because of his father, the great Johan, the young man enjoyed a few outings for Holland during the Euro '96 tournament in England, and I can only presume that he impressed the United manager, but he left me cold. That didn't change after he was transferred to United and it's difficult to remember him ever doing anything of note.

Of course, if we say that Chris Casper was labouring under the burden of a high-achieving father, then how much heavier was poor Jordi's load.

I've seen worse footballers, but when United pay a substantial fee you expect the newcomer to be a little bit special. He showed me nothing, whether he played up front or wide in midfield.

The Jordi Cruyff equation just didn't add up. He cost £800,000, he spent four years at Old Trafford and he started only 15 League games. What was the point?

280. KAREL POBORSKY

OTHER HONOURS:
103 Czech Republic caps 1994-.

OTHER CLUBS:
Ceske Budejovice 91/2-93/4 (82, 15);
Viktoria Zizkov 94/5 (27, 10);
Slavia Prague 95/6 (26, 11), all Czech Republic;
Benfica, Portugal, 97/8-00/01;
Lazio, Italy, 00/01-01/02 (28, 4);
Sparta Prague, Czech Republic, 02/03-.

KAREL POBORSKY		
Comp.	Apps	Gls
League	18 (14)	5
FAC	2	0
LC	3	1
Europe	5 (5)	0
Others	0 (1)	0
Total	28 (20)	6

Born	Jindinchuv-Hradec, Czech. 30th March 1972
Position	Winger
Joined United	August 1996 from Slavia Prague - £3.5m
United Debut	Newcastle United (Wembley) CS - 11/08/1996
United Honours	Premiership 1996/7
United Farewell	Everton (H) Prem. - 26/12/1997
Left United for	Benfica Dec. 1997 - £2m

Karel Poborsky played his best game of the Euro '96 tournament at Old Trafford, which must have gone a long way towards securing his transfer to Manchester United. In fairness, he looked a player during those championships, certainly a cut above Cruyff, and there was stringent competition for his signature from Liverpool.

But when he came to United he didn't seem to do what he'd done for the Czech Republic, for whom he has gone on to make a century of appearances and become that country's most capped player at the time of writing. They deployed him strictly as a winger, and I don't think we did. We seemed to use him more as a roaming player up front, and I don't think it suited him.

Certainly Karel never hugged the touchline, or seemed comfortable in the role he was given. He never looked like being the long-term replacement for Andrei Kanchelskis, which I understood was the original intention, though I suppose his opportunities were restricted by the development of David Beckham.

Since leaving United he hasn't done badly, particularly at Lazio. I watched him in one match and had to blink to make sure who I was watching. He was flying past defenders all over the place and I could only wonder why he had never done that for United. Then he had me scratching my head again during Euro 2004, in which he was extremely impressive.

I'm still convinced that coming to Old Trafford frightens the life out of many people, and I reckon he must have been one of them. He was struggling with the language, too, which must be a nightmare for a young footballer. How do you ask for a pass? That's why I can't understand why we sign so many foreigners.

It'll soon reach the stage where an Englishman needs a passport to get a game in the Premiership. Maybe the instant success of Jon Stead, following his move from Huddersfield to Blackburn in 2004, will make a few more top managers turn their attention to British lads.

BORN	Sandefjord, Norway 10th June 1969
POSITION	Central Defender
JOINED UNITED	July 1996 from Besiktas, Turkey - £1.5m
UNITED DEBUT	Wimbledon (A) Prem. - 17/08/1996
UNITED HONOURS	European Cup 1998/9 Premiership 1996/7, 1998/9, 2000/1 FA Cup 1998/9
UNITED FAREWELL	Bayer Leverkusen (A) CL - 30/04/2002
LEFT UNITED FOR	Aston Villa - June 2002

RONNY JOHNSEN		
COMP.	APPS	GLS
LEAGUE	85 (14)	7
FAC	8 (2)	1
LC	3	0
EUROPE	32 (3)	0
OTHERS	3	1
TOTAL	131 (19)	9

281. RONNY JOHNSEN

OTHER HONOURS:
61 Norway caps 1991-.

OTHER CLUBS:
Tonsberg 91-92; Lyn Oslo 92-93 (31, 7); Lillestrom 94-95 (23, 4), all Norway; Besiktas, Turkey, 95/6 (22, 1); Aston Villa 02/03-03/04 (49, 1). Newcastle United 04/05 (3, 0).

Ronny Johnsen was nicknamed 'Icepack' because he spent so much time on the treatment table, and plenty of people were dismissive about him, mocking his injury record.

But they were mistaken. Ronny was a vastly underrated performer, who acquitted himself splendidly for Manchester United, and but for his fitness problems I'd imagine he would still have been playing for the club in 2005.

At the time of his recruitment, hardly anyone had heard of him – which was scarcely surprising as he was a Norwegian playing in Turkey – and he never became a star in the accepted sense of the word.

I thought Ronny was a terrific central defender, but I'm told that he started off at centre-forward as a kid, scoring plenty of goals, and I can well believe it. He was always quick and useful in the air, he had a bit of stature about him and he could pass the ball.

THREE AMIGOS: Ole Gunnar Solskjaer (left), Ronny Johnsen (centre) and Teddy Sheringham on their night of nights.

His only flaw was that he was prone to injuries. It's amazing to think that someone who won the treble and two other League titles during his stay at United averaged barely 20 starts a season.

During his final comeback for the club, after he had been written off for the umpteenth time, he performed extremely impressively, only to break down yet again. Then, after he left United, the same pattern continued at Aston Villa.

Some unkind critics reckoned that his difficulties were in his mind, but I can't believe that it was all mental, or that a player of so much ability preferred being on the sidelines to playing. I have to conclude that there were genuine physical problems.

Whatever, when you compare him to certain other defenders of his era – David May, for instance – he was in a different class, and it's a shame that he could not prolong his days at Old Trafford.

Ronny could look the part in midfield, too, because he had quick feet and was a tremendous all-round footballer. If only he'd had a little more luck.

282. OLE GUNNAR SOLSKJAER

OTHER HONOURS:
62 NORWAY CAPS 1995-.

OTHER CLUBS:
FK CLAUSENENGEN 89/90-94/5;
MOLDE 95/6, BOTH NORWAY.

OLE GUNNAR SOLSKJAER		
COMP.	APPS	GLS
LEAGUE	142 (71)	84
FAC	10 (12)	6
LC	7 (3)	6
EUROPE	34 (41)	19
OTHERS	6 (3)	0
TOTAL	199 (130)	115

BORN	KRISTIANSUND, NORWAY 26TH FEBRUARY 1973
POSITION	STRIKER OR MIDFIELDER
JOINED UNITED	JULY 1996 FROM MOLDE, NORWAY - £1.5M
UNITED DEBUT	BLACKBURN ROVERS (H) PREM. - 25/08/1996
UNITED HONOURS	EUROPEAN CUP 1998/9 PREMIERSHIP 1996/7, 1998/9, 1999/00, 2000/1, 2002/3 FA CUP 1998/9, 2003/4

No one had heard of Ole Gunnar Solskjaer when he was signed from Molde for £1.5 million in the summer of 1996, and Alex Ferguson introduced him as one for the future.

A few weeks later the audacious 23-year-old was taking the Premiership by storm and Alex could congratulate himself on pulling off the steal of a lifetime. It must have felt like winning the pools.

Everything about Ole is right to be a professional footballer. He wants to play, he loves his work and he scores lots and lots of goals. His feet are firmly attached to the ground, he trains for the joy of it and if you asked him to play inside-out or left-outside he'd be happy to oblige.

He's happily married, he's got his kids and he doesn't need anything else. I would doubt whether he's ever given his manager even the slightest flicker of a problem.

I suppose I'm a tiny bit biased because my grandson, Ben, absolutely worships him, and when I took the little lad to have his picture taken with his hero, Ole was wonderful, chatting freely about football and about his own family. It was as if the pair of them were old friends, and it's something Ben will remember all his life.

Solskjaer can play a bit, too. He's terrific with both feet, he's good in the air, he's quick, he's explosive, and invariably he gets in a strike at goal given the slightest hint of an opening. When he plays wide on the right he

FANTASY BECOMES REALITY:
Ole Gunnar Solskjaer turns away after completing United's late, late comeback in the 1999 European Cup Final against Bayern Munich in Barcelona.

crosses the ball beautifully; sometimes hard and low, sometimes chipped to the far post, his variation is superb. He's just one hell of a player.

When you consider that he's been a substitute for most of his career, his record is truly formidable, and his goals-for-games ratio will stand comparison with most.

Solskjaer has been a central figure in some of United's most important games, notably scoring the winner in the 1999 European Cup Final against Bayern Munich, and I won't forget the day he rose from the bench to hit four past Nottingham Forest in the space of 11 minutes. Ron Atkinson, then the Forest boss, summed up nicely afterwards when he admitted: 'I was just glad the feller turned up late or we might have had a cricket score!'

At one point there was talk of a move to Tottenham, to which my grandson reacted by saying that he would never support United again if that happened. I couldn't understand that business. Why we would ever dream of parting with a player of that calibre is beyond belief.

When many fans blamed the absence of Beckham for United's disappointments in 2003/04, they were utterly wrong. The biggest miss was Solskjaer, who spent most of the campaign sidelined by injury. People forget that at the climax of 2002/03, when United sneaked up on Arsenal to regain the League title, Solskjaer had displaced Beckham and did a superb job.

'When many fans blamed the absence of Beckham for United's disappointments in 2003/04, they were utterly wrong. The biggest miss was Solskjaer, who spent most of the campaign sidelined by injury.'

It didn't surprise me because he gave us what Beckham never could, and that was pace. The Norwegian could go past defenders, hurt them in the final third in a manner of which Beckham wasn't capable.

Also Ole posed far more of a goal threat, particularly when balls came in from the left, so that he could go in and meet the headers.

In Ruud van Nistelrooy's first season at Old Trafford, 2001/02, Ole played alongside him and they looked a fantastic pair, complementing each other ideally. But they never lasted as a partnership. Perhaps the manager found the equable Solskjaer too easy to move around, but that was bad news for the Dutchman.

Certainly in 2003/04 Ruud looked as if he needed somebody like Ole alongside him to take some of the strain and to work off. You've got to share the workload, you can't have one fellow doing all the chasing, and the Norwegian is such a willing workhorse.

Ole Gunnar Solskjaer would always be in my

team, either alongside the centre-forward or wide on the right. He's a credit to himself and to the game, and he's done Manchester United proud. His enforced absence in 2004/05, with a career-threatening knee injury, was devastating for the club at a time when his experience and expertise were sorely needed.

283. RAIMOND VAN DER GOUW

OTHER CLUBS:
GO AHEAD EAGLES 85/6-87/8; VITESSE ARNHEM 88/9-95/6, BOTH HOLLAND.

RAIMOND VAN DER GOUW		
COMP.	APPS	GLS
LEAGUE	26 (11)	0
FAC	1	0
LC	8 (1)	0
EUROPE	11	0
OTHERS	2	0
TOTAL	48 (12)	0

BORN	OLDENZAAL, HOLLAND 24TH MARCH 1963
POSITION	GOALKEEPER
JOINED UNITED	JULY 1996 FROM VITESSE ARNHEM
UNITED DEBUT	ASTON VILLA (A) PREM. - 21/09/1996
UNITED HONOURS	PREMIERSHIP 1999/00, 2000/1
UNITED FAREWELL	CHARLTON ATH. (H) PREM. - 11/05/2002
LEFT UNITED FOR	WEST HAM UNITED JUNE 2002

Raimond van der Gorgeous – as some of the office girls at Old Trafford used to refer to the tall, dark, handsome Dutchman – deserved far more credit than he ever received after arriving as understudy goalkeeper to Peter Schmeichel.

He proved to be an exceedingly safe pair of hands, ideal for the job he was signed to do, and after Schmeichel was replaced by Mark Bosnich, Raimond got into the team on merit when the Australian suffered various upsets.

I admit I was surprised by the recruitment of a thirtysomething, thinking that the club might have opted for someone younger, but van der Gouw had looked after himself well and he never let United down in any situation.

Eventually he replaced Jack Warner, the stalwart Welsh international, as the oldest man to make the first team since the Second World War, and even after that he was fit enough to join West Ham, although he never played a League game for them.

Raimond must look back on his time at Old Trafford as a memorable period of his life. When you leave Vitesse Arnhem at the age of 33, you can hardly expect six years with Manchester United, but that's what he got and he acquitted himself admirably, playing an active part in the squad and picking up two Championship medals. Well done to him.

BORN	SALFORD
	4TH DECEMBER 1975
POSITION	MIDFIELDER
JOINED UNITED	JULY 1992 FROM
	JUNIOR FOOTBALL
UNITED DEBUT	SWINDON TOWN (H)
	LC - 23/10/1996
UNITED FAREWELL	LEICESTER CITY (A)
	LC - 27/11/1996
LEFT UNITED FOR	PRESTON N.E.
	AUG. 1997 - £500,000

MICHAEL APPLETON		
COMP.	APPS	GLS
LC	1 (1)	0
TOTAL	1 (1)	0

284. MICHAEL APPLETON

OTHER CLUBS:
LINCOLN CITY ON LOAN 95/6 (4, 0);
GRIMSBY TOWN ON LOAN 96/7 (10, 3);
PRESTON NORTH END 97/8-00/01 (115, 12);
WEST BROMWICH ALBION 00/01-01/02 (33, 0).

Michael Appleton was a local lad who grafted hard and unpretentiously in midfield, and though he wasn't quite good enough for Manchester United, he was clearly rated highly in the game because the club picked up a substantial fee when they transferred him to Preston.

He enjoyed three productive years at Deepdale, then matured further with West Bromwich Albion before a crippling injury put him out of the game. Even today, with all the wonders of modern medical science, there are still players who lose their livelihood before their time, and Michael was unlucky enough to be one of them.

BORN	MANCHESTER
	7TH JULY 1977
POSITION	FULL-BACK
JOINED UNITED	JULY 1993 FROM
	JUNIOR FOOTBALL
UNITED DEBUT	MIDDLESBROUGH (A)
	PREM. - 23/11/1996
UNITED FAREWELL	ARSENAL (A)
	LC - 05/11/2002
LEFT UNITED FOR	OLDHAM ATH. - FEB. 2002

MICHAEL CLEGG		
COMP.	APPS	GLS
LEAGUE	4 (5)	0
FAC	3 (1)	0
LC	7 (1)	0
EUROPE	1 (2)	0
TOTAL	15 (9)	0

285. MICHAEL CLEGG

OTHER CLUBS:
IPSWICH TOWN ON LOAN 99/00 (3, 0);
WIGAN ATHLETIC ON LOAN 99/00 (6, 0);
OLDHAM ATHLETIC 01/02- 03/04 (46, 0).

They say it's better to be born lucky than to be born good-looking, and I wouldn't argue with that sentiment. Nor, I imagine, would Michael Clegg, whom I believed had a genuine chance of a long career with United.

He was an efficient, uncomplicated full-back with no airs and graces, he would put his foot in when he had to, he was quick, and he never looked out of place in his handful of outings with the first team.

But in the end, Dame Fortune did not smile on the lad. So often in football, success is dependent on being in the right place at the right time, and getting the right opportunity. Then, when the team is winning, nobody wants to make a change.

But Clegg never got the breaks while the Nevilles, for example, had them all. Indeed, I've got to say that, looking at Michael in his early senior appearances and looking at Gary Neville when he was breaking through, I wouldn't have known the difference.

Michael spent nine years at Old Trafford, working very hard

and making the utmost of what he had, surprising a few people who thought some of his contemporaries were blessed with more natural ability. I was absolutely amazed when United let him go without a fee.

286. TEDDY SHERINGHAM

OTHER HONOURS:
51 ENGLAND CAPS 1993-2002.
PFA FOOTBALLER OF THE YEAR 2001;
FWA FOOTBALLER OF THE YEAR 2001.

OTHER CLUBS:
MILLWALL 83/4-90/1 (220, 93);
ALDERSHOT ON LOAN 84/5 (5, 0);
NOTTINGHAM FOREST 91/2-92/3 (42, 14);
TOTTENHAM HOTSPUR 92/3-96/7 (166, 76) AND 01/02-02/03 (70, 22);
PORTSMOUTH 03/04 (32, 8); WEST HAM UNITED 04/05- (33, 20).

TEDDY SHERINGHAM		
COMP.	APPS	GLS
LEAGUE	73 (31)	31
FAC	4 (5)	5
LC	1	1
EUROPE	20 (11)	9
OTHERS	4 (4)	0
TOTAL	102 (51)	46

BORN	HIGHAMS PARK, LONDON 2ND APRIL 1966
POSITION	FORWARD
JOINED UNITED	JULY 1997 FROM TOTTENHAM H. - £3.5M
UNITED DEBUT	CHELSEA (WEMBLEY) CS - 03/08/1997
UNITED HONOURS	EUROPEAN CUP 1998/9 PREMIERSHIP 1998/9, 1999/00, 2000/1 FA CUP 1998/9
UNITED FAREWELL	TOTTENHAM HOTSPUR (A) PREM. - 19/05/2001
LEFT UNITED FOR	TOTTENHAM H - JUNE 2001

Teddy Sheringham arrived at United immediately after the departure of Eric Cantona and there was no shortage of garbage written about the Londoner being a straight replacement for the Frenchman. Of course, Teddy was never going to fill Eric's boots. Nobody could.

When his early performances left a lot to be desired, and he looked decidedly ponderous, it seemed to me odds-on that he would prove a poor purchase, especially as he was 31 when United bought him from Spurs, whose fans were soon taunting him that his big move hadn't produced any medals.

For all his obvious all-round ability, Teddy had never been the quickest, but good players make up for lack of physical speed with what's between their ears. In his case, I was appalled to note, he seemed a yard slow in his thinking. Talk about slow, he was virtually static, and it looked for all the world as if the place was too big for him.

Also, although he could distribute the ball accurately, Teddy used to annoy me with his passing technique. He used to remind me a bit of a young Bobby Charlton, thinking he had to pose so that people would know what he'd done, and if the pass didn't reach its intended destination, he would throw his arms up into the air.

Jimmy Murphy used to tell Bobby: 'You don't have to do that. We all know when you've hit a bad 'un. Just get on with the bloody game.' Bobby was only a kid at the

HE WON THE LOT: Teddy Sheringham is almost submerged with silverware after another tolerably successful season with United.

'He had tidy feet, he was tremendous in the air, he was clever with his chest and he could always find space ... most tellingly of all, he scored some very fine goals, again like Eric.'

time and soon he put it behind him, but I was surprised to see Sheringham doing it as an established England international.

Happily, after a nightmare first season, it all came good for Teddy with a spectacular rush. In the end it was, after all, what he had between his ears which got him out of trouble and the Tottenham supporters had to sing a different tune.

Teddy's second year transformed everything as he played an integral part in winning the treble, including important goals in both cup finals, first against Newcastle and then, so devastatingly, against Bayern Munich. The critics regarded that as a storybook swansong, but afterwards he continued from strength to strength until he was rewarded with both major Footballer of the Year awards in 2001.

Though Teddy was never another Cantona, he was similar to Eric in that he never did things in a hurry. He had tidy feet, he was tremendous in the air, he was clever with his chest and he could always find space, all like Eric. Most tellingly of all, he scored some very fine goals, again like Eric. Indeed, his goal tally at all his clubs bears comparison with most, and in 2004/05 he was still doing a fine job for Alan Pardew at West Ham.

I couldn't have been more delighted to have been proven wrong in my first assessment of Teddy, who eventually revealed to the United fans the qualities which had earned him a half-century of England caps and the gratitude of Alan Shearer, who never played better for his country than when Sheringham was at his side. When he finally departed Old Trafford, Teddy could look back on the most magical of times, which he could have extended by accepting Sir Alex's offer of an extra year. However, I wasn't surprised when he refused, because he wouldn't have been first choice and I don't think he was the sort who would have opted for a comfortable berth on the bench.

BORN	EIDSWELL, NORWAY 1ST SEPTEMBER 1969
POSITION	CENTRAL DEFENDER
JOINED UNITED	AUGUST 1997 FROM BLACKBURN ROVERS - £5M
UNITED DEBUT	SOUTHAMPTON (H) PREM. - 13/08/1997
UNITED HONOURS	PREMIERSHIP 1998/9, 1999/00
UNITED FAREWELL	WEST HAM UTD (A) PREM. - 26/08/2000
LEFT UNITED FOR	BLACKBURN ROVERS SEPT. 2000 - £1.75M AFTER INITIAL LOAN PERIOD

HENNING BERG		
COMP.	APPS	GLS
LEAGUE	49 (17)	2
FAC	7	0
LC	3	0
EUROPE	19 (4)	1
OTHERS	3 (1)	0
TOTAL	81 (22)	3

287. HENNING BERG

OTHER HONOURS:
100 NORWAY CAPS 1992-2004.

OTHER CLUBS:
KFUM OSLO, VALERENGEN, LILLESTROM, all NORWAY; BLACKBURN ROVERS 92/3-97/8 (159, 4) AND 00/01-02/3 (91, 3); GLASGOW RANGERS 03/04 (21, 0).

I was more than a little perplexed by the signing of Henning Berg, not because there was anything wrong with him but because we were paying £5 million for an extra defender who wasn't exactly in the first flush of youth.

That said, he was always a very neat and competent performer with a useful turn of speed and he did well for United, helping to win two League Championships and playing his part on the European Cup trail.

Certainly he was in a totally different category to David May, another former Blackburn man and a rival for a central defensive berth. The Norwegian, who eventually compiled a century of international caps, was a far more accomplished footballer in every way.

Much as it surprised me when Henning came, it astonished me even more when he went. Once we'd got him, and he'd proved himself at the required level, then I wondered why we didn't keep him.

You need a bit of experience around, and you never know who's going to fall prey to injury. Probably the case of Berg was similar to Teddy Sheringham's, in that he didn't fancy the prospect of being a reserve, having reached a stage of his career when he needed to be playing as much as possible.

Ironically, United might have saved themselves the original hefty purchase price by signing Henning for nothing when he was a youngster, but that opportunity passed them by.

288. JOHN CURTIS

OTHER CLUBS:
BARNSLEY ON LOAN 99/00 (28, 2);
BLACKBURN ROVERS 00/01-02/03 (61, 0);
SHEFFIELD UNITED ON LOAN 02/03 (13, 0);
LEICESTER CITY 03/04 (15, 0);
PORTSMOUTH 03/04- 04/05 (7, 0).
PRESTON NORTH END ON LOAN 04/05 (12, 0)
NOTTINGHAM FOREST 04/05- (11, 0).

JOHN CURTIS		
COMP.	APPS	GLS
LEAGUE	4 (9)	0
LC	5	0
OTHERS	0 (1)	0
TOTAL	9 (10)	0

BORN	NUNEATON, WARWICKSHIRE 3RD SEPTEMBER 1978
POSITION	DEFENDER
JOINED UNITED	JULY 1995 FROM JUNIOR FOOTBALL
UNITED DEBUT	IPSWICH TOWN (A) LC - 14/10/1997
UNITED FAREWELL	ASTON VILLA (A) LC - 13/10/1999
LEFT UNITED FOR	BLACKBURN ROVERS MAY 2000 - £2.25M

John Curtis had to contend with a load of hysterical hype as a youngster, being the centre-half for England Schoolboys and hailing from Nuneaton in the Midlands. That was Duncan Edwards territory and the inevitable mindless comparisons cropped up, which didn't help the lad one bit.

John was well-built for a boy but he never grew a lot bigger as a man, so he struggled in the central role as he became a senior player and moved to right-back while still at early stage of his development.

Duly he graduated to the fringe of the first team, giving one or two efficient displays, showcasing his speed, neat distribution and strength in the air. But then Marc Overmars ran him silly when Arsenal won at Old Trafford to turn the title race on its head in the spring of 1998. He had to be substituted that day, an extremely distressing experience for the lad, and I felt sorry for him. Perhaps not surprisingly after that, John slipped out of the United reckoning, and although he's an honest professional, it would seem he lacks something because he failed to settle at either Blackburn or Leicester.

I hope he finds a longer-term niche at Nottingham Forest, so that he can develop and re-establish the impetus of what was once a richly promising career.

289. PHIL MULRYNE

Born	Belfast 1st January 1978
Position	Midfielder
Joined United	July 1994 from junior football
United Debut	Ipswich Town (A) LC - 14/10/1997
United Farewell	Nottingham Forest (H) LC - 11/11/1998
Left United for	Norwich City March 1999 - £500,000

Phil Mulryne		
Comp.	Apps	Gls
League	1	0
LC	3	0
Total	4	0

Other Honours:
25 Northern Ireland caps 1997-.

Other clubs:
Norwich City 98/9- (161, 18).

P hil Mulryne was another who appeared to have the ability to make the grade, but who never managed to break through at Old Trafford.

Having a successful side does wonders for a club, but I'm not sure it does too much for the young players coming through. If the team becomes a virtual fixture over a five-year period, what chance is there for the kids to get in?

Virtually none, is the crushing answer, so lads who would normally have a chance, the likes of Mulryne, tend to get kicked into touch early on. He had skill, brains and a powerful shot, but with the likes of Nicky Butt taking up the midfield berths on the bench, realistically he didn't have a prayer.

Happily for him, he has done pretty well at Norwich and earned the chance to test himself at Premiership level in 2004/05.

290. ERIK NEVLAND

Born	Stavanger, Norway 10th November 1977
Position	Striker
Joined United	July 1997 from Viking Stavanger
United Debut	Ipswich Town (A) LC - 14/10/1997
United Farewell	Bury (H) LC - 28/10/1998
Left United for	Viking Stavanger December 1999

Erik Nevland		
Comp.	Apps	Gls
League	0 (1)	0
FAC	2	0
LC	0 (2)	1
Total	2 (3)	1

Other Honours:
Norway caps.

Other clubs:
Viking Stavanger, Norway, 95/6-96/7;
IFK Gothenburg, Sweden, on loan 98/9;
Viking Stavanger 99/00-.

S triker Erik Nevland arrived at Old Trafford carrying high expectations, but he was gone in the blink of an eye. United took him when he was 20, so he should have had a fair bit going for him, unlike kids who come at the age of 15, still having to learn to be an adult as well as a footballer.

All too soon he was dispatched back to Scandinavia, initially on loan, and nobody's heard much of him ever since. I suppose we're being greedy, expecting to return to Norway and find another Ole Gunnar Solskjaer. That's just unrealistic.

291. RONNIE WALLWORK

OTHER CLUBS:
CARLISLE UNITED ON LOAN 97/8 (10, 1);
STOCKPORT COUNTY ON LOAN 97/8 (7, 0);
ROYAL ANTWERP, BELGIUM, ON LOAN 98/9;
WEST BROMWICH ALBION 02/03- (52, 1);
BRADFORD CITY ON LOAN 03/04 (7, 4).

RONNIE WALLWORK		
COMP.	APPS	GLS
LEAGUE	4 (15)	0
FAC	1 (1)	0
LC	4 (1)	0
EUROPE	0 (1)	0
OTHERS	1	0
TOTAL	10 (18)	0

BORN	MANCHESTER 10TH SEPTEMBER 1977
POSITION	DEFENDER OR MIDFIELDER
JOINED UNITED	JULY 1994 FROM JUNIOR FOOTBALL
UNITED DEBUT	BARNSLEY (H) PREM. - 25/10/1997
UNITED HONOURS	PREMIERSHIP 2000/1
UNITED FAREWELL	MIDDLESBROUGH (A) FAC - 26/01/2002
LEFT UNITED FOR	WEST BROMWICH ALBION JUNE 2002

Ronnie Wallwork was associated with Manchester United from childhood, and there was a time when it seemed he might extend the arrangement deep into his adult days, but in the end he didn't make the Old Trafford cut. He started as a central defender, but he wasn't the biggest, and later I liked what I saw as a defensive midfielder, fetching and carrying and propping people up. He was nothing spectacular, but was tidy on the ball, worked diligently and seemed the sort of lad who would run through a rockface for his team.

In the old days players like Ronnie might have had more of a prolonged opportunity if they had done quite well in a handful of games, well enough in his case to earn a Championship medal in 2000/01. But that doesn't often happen now, with so many high-profile players on astronomical wages, and eventually he was squeezed out of contention. Still, having gained invaluable knowhow at United, West Bromwich Albion looked like an ideal move, and following the arrival of Bryan Robson as manager, the lad began to prove his true worth.

Ronnie showed resilience in bouncing back from a bad experience while on loan at Royal Antwerp, where they talked of suspending him for life following an alleged assault on a referee, and I hope he manages to mould a worthwhile career somewhere near the right end of the professional scale.

292. MICHAEL TWISS

OTHER CLUBS:
SHEFFIELD UNITED ON LOAN 98/9 (12, 1);
PORT VALE 00/01 (18, 2).

MICHAEL TWISS		
COMP.	APPS	GLS
FAC	0 (1)	0
LC	1	0
TOTAL	1 (1)	0

BORN	SALFORD 26TH DECEMBER 1977
POSITION	UTILITY MAN
JOINED UNITED	JULY 1994 FROM JUNIOR FOOTBALL
UNITED DEBUT	BARNSLEY (A) FAC - 25/02/1998
UNITED FAREWELL	ASTON VILLA (A) LC - 13/10/1999
LEFT UNITED FOR	PORT VALE - JUNE 2000

The versatile Michael Twiss was yet another outstanding local prospect who couldn't force his way into the United reckoning despite spending six years on the club's books. I suppose the fact that he could play practically anywhere might have been his principal problem, as being moved from pillar to post is not ideal for a youngster.

In his middle twenties Michael was playing non-League football, which rather puzzled me. Even if he didn't make it at Old Trafford, I would have expected more for him than that.

BORN	MANCHESTER 16TH MARCH 1979
POSITION	CENTRAL DEFENDER
JOINED UNITED	JULY 1996 FROM JUNIOR FOOTBALL
UNITED DEBUT	LEEDS UNITED (H) PREM. - 04/05/1998
UNITED HONOURS	PREMIERSHIP 1998/9, 2000/1, 2002/3 FA CUP 2003/4

293. WESLEY BROWN

OTHER HONOURS:
9 ENGLAND CAPS 1999-.

WESLEY BROWN		
COMP.	APPS	GLS
LEAGUE	107 (14)	1
FAC	15 (2)	0
LC	9 (1)	0
EUROPE	31 (6)	1
TOTAL	162 (23)	2

Wesley Brown is a favourite of mine and, although he has known horrendously difficult times with injury and been peppered with fusillades of undeserved flak for the occasional error, I have never doubted for a second that he has the capacity to become one of the outstanding international players of the next seven or eight years.

I was doing a lunchtime interview with the journalist David Meek on MUTV a good few years ago, and he asked me what I thought of Wes. I replied that he'd play for England before he was 21; and, by God, so he did.

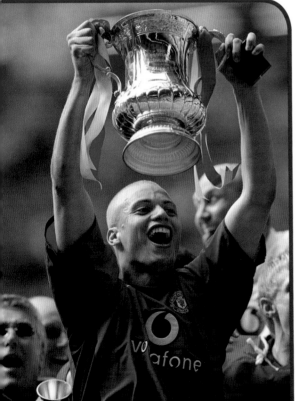

But if ever a lad has been crucified by a savage succession of injuries, at least two of which could easily have ended his career, then it's the tall young Mancunian. It speaks volumes for him that he's come back each time, ultimately looking as tremendous a defender as ever.

His gifts screamed at me from the first moment I laid eyes on him in his teens. He was never rough because that's simply not his style, and although he was a bit raw, it was abundantly clear to me that he was blessed, both with glorious talent and a perfect physique for playing the game.

Even at that stage, his touch with both feet was impeccable, he was terrific in the air, he moved like greased lightning and he never got rattled.

If any further evidence were needed of his exceptional ability, I'd point out that he is one of the few natural centre-halves I have known to excel as a full-back, too. In short, he's got everything needed to become a superstar. I just hope and pray that the gruesome fortune which has threatened to halt him in his tracks is now behind him for good.

I agreed with Sir Alex Ferguson that it would have been wrong to take Wes to Portugal for Euro 2004 because a lot would have been expected of him and I think it did him more good to rest on a beach to complete his recuperation from his latest fitness problem. He's got a lifetime to play for his country, after all.

Of course, he's been vilified for the odd mistake, but I believe you'd be hard pushed to find a better central defender in the whole of the Premiership. Rio Ferdinand? Sol Campbell? John Terry? Give me Wes Brown every time.

But football is such that a centre-forward can miss five easy chances and then score one, and he's a hero. A centre-half can make one bad tackle and he's branded a clown. There's no justice, but that's the way it is.

Despite the numerous brickbats, I have never lost faith in Wes because his sort of ability does not go away. He always wants to play football. Sometimes, I admit, you look at him and Rio, both of whom like to stroke the ball around, and you wonder who's going to kick it into Row Z occasionally, when it needs doing.

On balance, though, I can live with that because Wes is a supreme talent and with average good fortune – and he's had little but the rotten variety so far – he can become one of the game's immortals.

Happily, I have every reason to believe that both his feet are adhering firmly to the ground, and that there is no danger of him being carried away with his own importance. Like all young men, he probably needs a rollicking from the manager every now and again, but I think he has the common sense to understand that anything after Manchester United would be an anti-climax.

It was a pleasure when my MUTV prediction on the boy's international future proved to be correct, and I can't wait to monitor the next stage of his career. God speed, Wes.

294. DANNY HIGGINBOTHAM

OTHER CLUBS:
ROYAL ANTWERP, BELGIUM, ON LOAN 98/9; DERBY COUNTY 00/01-02/03 (86, 3); SOUTHAMPTON 02/03- (57, 1).

DANNY HIGGINBOTHAM		
COMP.	APPS	GLS
LEAGUE	2 (2)	0
LC	1	0
EUROPE	0 (1)	0
OTHERS	1	0
TOTAL	4 (3)	0

BORN	MANCHESTER 29TH DECEMBER 1978
POSITION	FULL-BACK
JOINED UNITED	JULY 1995 FROM JUNIOR FOOTBALL
UNITED DEBUT	BARNSLEY (A) PREM. - 10/05/1998
UNITED FAREWELL	ASTION VILLA (A) PREM. - 14/05/2000
LEFT UNITED FOR	DERBY COUNTY JULY 2000 - £2M

I was a bit surprised that Danny Higginbotham was allowed to leave United. I know £2 million seemed a lot of money for a youngster, but that may not appear to be the case if he continues to develop.

Danny can play at left-back or in central defence, looks comfortable in both roles, and he has a useful turn of speed.

He did a decent job for Derby County in difficult circumstances, because they were always struggling during his time at the club, but he impressed Gordon Strachan enough to win a move to Southampton, where he has continued to excel.

Danny has applied himself exceptionally well to consolidate at the top level, and certainly in the spring of 2004 he would have been extremely useful to have in United's squad.

I'm pleased for the lad, who showed a lot of character to regain his momentum after he was involved in the same scrape as Ronnie Wallwork during their time together in Antwerp.

BORN	KAMPEN, HOLLAND 17TH JULY 1972
POSITION	CENTRAL DEFENDER
JOINED UNITED	JULY 1998 FROM PSV EINDHOVEN - £10.75M
UNITED DEBUT	ARSENAL (WEMBLEY) CS - 09/08/1998
UNITED HONOURS	EUROPEAN CUP 1998/9 PREMIERSHIP 1998/9, 1999/00, 2000/1 FA CUP 1998/9
UNITED FAREWELL	FULHAM (H) PREM. - 19/08/2001
LEFT UNITED FOR	LAZIO, ITALY AUGUST 2001 - £16.5M

JAAP STAM		
COMP.	APPS	GLS
LEAGUE	79	1
FAC	7 (1)	0
EUROPE	32	0
OTHERS	7 (1)	0
TOTAL	125 (2)	1

295. JAAP STAM

OTHER HONOURS:
67 HOLLAND CAPS 1996-.

OTHER CLUBS:
FC ZWOLLE 92/3 (32, 1);
CAMBUUR LEEUWARDEN 93/4-94/5 (66, 3);
WILLEM II 95/6 (19, 1);
PSV EINDHOVEN 95/6-97/8 (81, 11), ALL HOLLAND;
LAZIO, ITALY, 01/02-03/04 (38, 1);
AC MILAN 04/05-.

Jaap Stam was a big, big signing for United, but an even bigger departure. I think we'll go to our graves wondering about the rights and wrongs of that. When he arrived from PSV he didn't have the greatest of starts. Nicolas Anelka gave him a runaround in the Charity Shield and for six or eight games he looked ordinary in the extreme. But then he settled down to become one of the most influential players at the club.

Johan Cruyff described him at the time of his move as the best defender on the planet, and pretty soon you could understand why, as he played a colossal part in United winning the treble during his first season at Old Trafford. Then they won two more titles immediately afterwards, totally dominating the domestic scene, and it was difficult to imagine a more solid performer.

Although it would be stupid to say that Jaap was the sole reason that United won three Championships on the trot, it would be even more daft to contend that he was less than effective. The Dutchman's greatest strength was his strength, and attackers just seemed to bounce off him. He was dominant in the air and he had pace, too, which is a pretty decent combination for a centre-half.

'No matter what anyone says in retrospect, Jaap was magnificent for Manchester United and selling him was a strange decision.'

Beyond that, he had a commanding presence about him, an aura of power that was bigger than his actual stature. With that stern, unsmiling face under his shaven head, he conveyed an impression that he could withstand anything.

It was as though he was impregnable, and if you dreamed up an Identikit picture of the perfect defender, it would come out looking not unlike Jaap Stam.

But suddenly he was on his bike and I find the circumstances of his transfer to Lazio utterly bewildering. True he suffered a serious Achilles injury during his time at United, but we had just completed our League hat-trick when he left, so in terms of team performances it didn't affect us too much.

One reason advanced by the manager to explain his sale was that he wasn't enough of a teacher for youngsters like Wes Brown, but I didn't buy that for a second.

Based on his form during his three seasons at the club, you would have been happy to field Jaap in any United side since the war. Pally and Brucie were a majestic partnership, but who's to say that Stam and Brown or Silvestre would not have equalled it, at least.

No matter what anyone says in retrospect, Jaap was magnificent for Manchester United and selling him was a strange decision. I know there was some controversy over his book, but I don't think it contained anything too earth-shattering, so I don't believe the answer lies there.

The player had just been given a new contract and had just moved into a new house. He was preparing for a long stay, so what happened? The manager knows his reasons, but he's not revealing them to us. The only question that truly matters is this. After the deal was done, were United stronger or weaker? I'm afraid to say that the clear answer is weaker.

BORN	CANAAN, TOBAGO 3RD NOVEMBER 1971
POSITION	STRIKER
JOINED UNITED	AUGUST 1998 FROM ASTON VILLA - £12.6M
UNITED DEBUT	WEST HAM UNITED (A) PREM. - 22/08/1998
UNITED HONOURS	EUROPEAN CUP 1998/9, PREMIERSHIP 1998/9, 1999/00, 2000/1 FA CUP 1998/9
UNITED FAREWELL	MIDDLESBROUGH (A) FAC - 26/01/2002
LEFT UNITED FOR	BLACKBURN ROVERS JULY 2002 - £2M

DWIGHT YORKE		
COMP.	APPS	GLS
LEAGUE	80 (16)	48
FAC	6 (5)	3
LC	3	2
EUROPE	28 (8)	11
OTHERS	3 (3)	2
TOTAL	120 (32)	66

296. DWIGHT YORKE

OTHER HONOURS:
TRINIDAD AND TOBAGO CAPS.
OTHER CLUBS:
ASTON VILLA 89/90-98/9 (231, 75);
BLACKBURN ROVERS 02/03-04/05 (60, 12);
BIRMINGHAM CITY 04/05 (13, 2);
SYDNEY FC 05-.

It's fair to say that when Dwight Yorke arrived at Old Trafford, he wasn't the striker most United fans had been craving. They had set their hearts on Patrick Kluivert, or some such superstar, and there was a generally scathing reaction to the signing.

Certainly it was felt that £12.6 million was a hell of a lot of money for Dwight, but he settled in quickly, played a massive part in winning the treble, picked up two more title medals in consecutive years, so who could argue with the manager's judgement?

Yorke's scoring record of around a goal every two games was phenomenal at the top level, yet pretty soon, just like Jaap, he was out of the door. So once again we're left to ask: what went wrong? We can only assume that he wasn't toeing the line the way Alex Ferguson expected.

If that was the case then it's the old story: if there's a battle between manager and player, then the manager will always win. Alex seems to have had plenty of those conflicts since joining United, maybe more than Matt Busby had, maybe not. Alex has to contend with a constant media circus, and what it doesn't know then it makes up, so we may never know the truth.

Perhaps Yorke's well-documented difficulties away from the game had an effect on his performances, and I feel it is wrong that footballers should have no privacy. When I saw that the model Naomi Campbell had sued over intrusion into her life, it prompted the thought that Dwight might have been a candidate to do the same thing. Footballers live in goldfish bowls and I feel a bit sorry for them. I know some of them encourage it, but as a group, maybe they deserve a bit better.

I admit that I doubted the wisdom of signing Dwight Yorke because I never thought he was such a prolific goal-scorer. But surrounded by better players than he was used to at Villa, he proved me wrong rather comprehensively.

When he went United dropped £10 million, which is a lot of

dough over three years or so, but when you take all the trophies into account you could say the lad had given impeccable value for money.

During Dwight's stay, United had four front-line strikers who complemented each other ideally. He dovetailed particularly neatly with Andy Cole, who was more single-minded when it came to scoring goals, while Dwight appeared happy to be part of a team, perhaps because he had played in midfield for Villa and was an accomplished all-round footballer.

He was useful in the air despite not being the biggest, he was neat in possession, and although he wasn't the quickest, he knew enough about the game to make space.

In the cold, hard light of day, no matter what the unhappy circumstances of his departure, Dwight Yorke was a success for Manchester United and, whatever else, his seemingly ever-present grin was a welcome tonic in these oh-so-serious sporting times.

297. JESPER BLOMQVIST

OTHER HONOURS:
SWEDEN CAPS.

OTHER CLUBS:
TAVELSJO IK, SWEDEN; UMEA, SWEDEN;
IFK GOTHENBURG, SWEDEN, 92/3-96/7 (71, 18);
AC MILAN, ITALY, 96/7 (20, 1);
PARMA, ITALY, 97/8 (28, 1);
EVERTON 01/02 (15, 1);
CHARLTON ATHLETIC 02/03 (3, 0); DJURGARDEN, SWEDEN, 03/04-.

JESPER BLOMQVIST		
COMP.	APPS	GLS
LEAGUE	20 (5)	1
FAC	3 (2)	0
LC	0 (1)	0
EUROPE	6 (1)	0
TOTAL	29 (9)	1

BORN	TAVELSJO, SWEDEN 5TH FEBRUARY 1974
POSITION	WINGER
JOINED UNITED	JULY 1998 FROM PARMA, ITALY - £4.4M
UNITED DEBUT	CHARLTON ATHLETIC (H) PREM. - 09/09/1998
UNITED HONOURS	EUROPEAN CUP 1998/9 PREMIERSHIP 1998/9
UNITED FAREWELL	BAYERN MUNICH (BARCELONA) EC - 26/05/1999
LEFT UNITED FOR	EVERTON - NOVEMBER 2001

Jesper Blomqvist never seemed anything special to me, being too lightweight for the English game and cursed with serial injuries. Wherever he has been, he has never made many appearances, and that would make me think there's something wrong with him.

It's said the Swede moved to Old Trafford on the back of one great game for Gothenburg when they murdered United and he gave his marker, David May, a particularly torrid time. I suppose that after such a performance, if Alex Ferguson was looking for a winger, then it might have seemed that Jesper was worth a punt.

It was a major transfer, because Blomqvist was a respected international who cost £4.5 million, yet fundamentally he never amounted to more than extremely expensive cover for Ryan Giggs.

Still, he finished up with a European Cup winner's medal, playing on the left in the final against Bayern Munich, with Giggs on the right and Beckham in the middle due to the una-

vailability of Scholes and Keane.

Jesper wasn't a goal-scorer, he carried no threat at all, managing to hit the target only once for the club, and although he had skill, he was too easy to brush off the ball. He never emerged from Giggs' shadow, and it never seemed remotely likely that he would.

In the end he spent three years with the club, but only seven months of that was around the team, because he was injured when he arrived and for the better part of his entire stay.

Clearly we never saw the best of Jesper Blomqvist, but I can't help wondering if we missed very much.

BORN	SCUNTHORPE 9TH FEBRUARY 1979
POSITION	MIDFIELDER
JOINED UNITED	JULY 1995 FROM JUNIOR FOOTBALL
UNITED DEBUT	BRONDBY (A) CL - 21/10/1998
UNITED FAREWELL	WATFORD (A) PREM. - 29/04/2000
LEFT UNITED FOR	MIDDLESBROUGH AUGUST 2001 - £1.5M

MARK WILSON		
COMP.	APPS	GLS
LEAGUE	1 (2)	0
LC	2	0
EUROPE	2 (2)	0
OTHERS	1	0
TOTAL	6 (4)	0

298. MARK WILSON

OTHER CLUBS:
WREXHAM ON LOAN 97/8 (13, 4);
MIDDLESBROUGH 01/02-04/05 (16, 0);
STOKE CITY ON LOAN 02/03 (4, 0);
SWANSEA CITY ON LOAN 03/04 (12, 2);
SHEFFIELD WEDNESDAY ON LOAN 03/04 (3, 0).
DONCASTER ROVERS ON LOAN 04/05 (3, 0)
LIVINGSTON ON LOAN 04/05 (5, 0);
DALLAS BURN, USA 05-.

Mark Wilson represents an unbelievable piece of business on United's part. He barely played for the first team yet the club pocketed £1.5 million when he went to Middlesbrough, where he has made only limited impact. He was a tall, upright midfielder, but he looked totally ordinary to me. He's another one who has been plagued with injuries, so perhaps I shouldn't be too harsh.

BORN	SCARBOROUGH 2ND JANUARY 1978
POSITION	MIDFIELDER
JOINED UNITED	MARCH 1998 FROM YORK CITY - £350,000+
UNITED DEBUT	BURY (H) LC - 28/10/1998
UNITED FAREWELL	LEICESTER CITY (H) PREM. - 17/03/2001
LEFT UNITED FOR	MIDDLESBROUGH AUGUST 2001 - £2M

JONATHAN GREENING		
COMP.	APPS	GLS
LEAGUE	4 (10)	0
FAC	0 (1)	0
LC	6	0
EUROPE	2 (2)	0
OTHERS	1 (1)	0
TOTAL	13 (14)	0

299. JONATHAN GREENING

OTHER CLUBS:
YORK CITY 96/7-97/8 (25, 2);
MIDDLESBROUGH 01/02-03/04 (99, 4);
WEST BROMWICH ALBION 04/05- (34, 0).

Obviously Steve McClaren, as Sir Alex Ferguson's former number-two, was using his insider information to sign both Jonathan Greening and Mark Wilson for Middlesbrough, but I'm not convinced that he did his new employers any particular favours. If he'd taken the pair of them on free transfers, I'd have said that's not bad business, but I thought

'Boro paid through the nose.

In fairness, Greening did better than Wilson at the Riverside, and subsequently he earned praise at West Bromwich, but I don't think he's a top-quality Premiership player.

He was used by 'Boro and Albion exclusively as a midfielder, but when he joined United from York it was as a striker, and it always appeared to me that he had an inflated idea of his own ability.

He never managed to break through, he never scored a goal, and for somebody signed as a forward player, that's got to be a disappointment considering he made 27 appearances, about half of which were as a substitute.

Some saw Greening as David Beckham's deputy on the right side of midfield, but I never saw him as that. He had a bit of skill but he always gave me the impression that he thought he was a player, while never succeeding in convincing me he was.

I wasn't surprised when he left, but I must admit to raising an eyebrow at the size of his fee. From Manchester United's point of view, that was one magnificent deal.

300. ALEX NOTMAN

OTHER CLUBS:
ABERDEEN ON LOAN 98/9 (2, 0);
SHEFFIELD UNITED ON LOAN 99/00 (10, 3);
NORWICH CITY 00/01-03/04 (54, 1).

ALEX NOTMAN		
COMP.	APPS	GLS
LC	0 (1)	0
TOTAL	0 (1)	0

BORN	EDINBURGH 10TH DECEMBER 1979
POSITION	STRIKER
JOINED UNITED	DECEMBER 1995 FROM JUNIOR FOOTBALL
UNITED DEBUT & FAREWELL	TOTTENHAM HOTSPUR (A) LC - 02/12/1998
LEFT UNITED FOR	NORWICH CITY NOV. 2000 - £250,000

Alex Notman was a tiny Scottish striker who made no impact at senior level for Manchester United, principally because he was an out-and-out front-runner with no stature at all. Later, with Norwich City, he moved back to midfield before suffering a career-ending injury, for which he has my heartfelt sympathy. I know how it feels.

301. NICK CULKIN

OTHER CLUBS:
HULL CITY ON LOAN 99/00 (4, 0);
BRISTOL ROVERS ON LOAN 00/01 (45, 0);
LIVINGSTON ON LOAN 01/02 (21, 0);
QUEEN'S PARK RANGERS 02/03-03/04 (22, 0)

NICK CULKIN		
COMP.	APPS	GLS
LEAGUE	0 (1)	0
TOTAL	0 (1)	0

BORN	YORK 6TH JULY 1978
POSITION	GOALKEEPER
JOINED UNITED	SEPTEMBER 1995 FROM YORK CITY - £250,000
UNITED DEBUT & FAREWELL	ARSENAL (A) PREM. - 22/08/1999
LEFT UNITED FOR	QUEEN'S PARK RANGERS JULY 2002

Nick Culkin had the shortest first-team career of them all. When Rai van der Gouw took a knock against Arsenal, Nick was called on and he wasn't part of the action for more than ten seconds. All he was required to do was take the free-kick awarded after the Dutchman's injury.

Like Jonathan Greening, he was only a kid when he arrived

from York for a sizeable fee. He did well for a season on loan at Bristol Rovers and then impressed during a similar arrangement at Livingston before leaving United as a curious footnote in the club's history.

BORN	CAPE TOWN, SOUTH AFRICA 21ST MAY 1977
POSITION	MIDFIELDER/FULL-BACK
JOINED UNITED	AUGUST 1999 FROM ATLETICO MADRID - £2M
UNITED DEBUT	NEWCASTLE UNITED (H) PREM. - 30/08/1999

QUINTON FORTUNE		
COMP.	APPS	GLS
LEAGUE	53 (23)	5
FAC	8 (1)	1
LC	8	0
EUROPE	16 (12)	2
OTHERS	3 (2)	2
TOTAL	88 (38)	10

302. QUINTON FORTUNE

OTHER HONOURS:
47 SOUTH AFRICA CAPS 1996-.

OTHER CLUBS:
MALLORCA, SPAIN, 95/6 (8, 1);
ATLETICO MADRID, SPAIN, 95/6-98/9 (7,0).

Quinton Fortune is not my idea of a Manchester United footballer. I've seen him at full-back, I've seen him in central midfield and I've seen him wide on the left, and I've yet to be convinced of his ability to fill any of those roles.

I don't think Quinton is suited to left-back because he doesn't see what's happening around him. Certainly I don't see him worrying Ryan Giggs for his position on the left, and if they're looking for a yard-dog in the centre of midfield – though why they should need one, given the players at their disposal, I do not know – then I would have thought they could do better than the South African.

If you say the lad's worth a place in the squad because he can fill in anywhere down the left-hand side if there's an emergency, then I wouldn't argue, but he's not got the quality to become a regular.

BORN	PALERMO, ITALY 18TH FEBRUARY 1970
POSITION	GOALKEEPER
JOINED UNITED	AUGUST 1999 FROM VENEZIA, ITALY - £4.5M
UNITED DEBUT	LIVERPOOL (A) PREM. - 11/09/1999
UNITED FAREWELL	CHELSEA (A) PREM. - 03/10/1999
LEFT UNITED FOR	REGGINA INITIALLY ON LOAN

MASSIMO TAIBI		
COMP.	APPS	GLS
LEAGUE	4	0
TOTAL	4	0

303. MASSIMO TAIBI

OTHER CLUBS:
LICATA, AC MILAN (TWICE), COMO CALCIO,
PIACENZA, VENEZIA, REGGINA, ALL ITALY.

Massimo Taibi was voted man of the match for his debut against Liverpool, despite making one error which cost a goal, and I see the bottle of champagne which he received for that performance every time I walk through the doors of Marcello's excellent restaurant in Hale Barns, which the Italian goalkeeper used to frequent on a regular basis. Unfortunately, it's about the only agreeable association lingering in my mind from Massimo's stint in Manchester.

When you think that he cost £4.5 million, that he was with the club only a year, during which he played four games, and that when he left, United never got two bob for him, I would say that he was not one of the finest buys in Old Trafford history.

If you pay that sort of money for a player then you've got to know something about him. Obviously he'd been watched, but what they saw in him was beyond me. The manager can't be expected to scout every player he signs, but I would think he wanted to ask some pointed questions of the person who recommended him. You have to rely on your staff, and the purchase of Taibi has to be one of the worst decisions made at Old Trafford for a long time.

Apart from that Liverpool game, where he had a fair bit of luck going for him, he never looked the part. I won't dwell on his howler against Southampton, because that was a one-off which could happen to anybody; it was his overall play that I didn't like.

Our old trainer Tom Curry used to say of a dodgy 'keeper that if there was a barrel-load of hay going across, he wouldn't have got a handful, and that's how I felt about the Italian.

He wasn't a young lad with scope for improvement. He'd been around long enough for our scouts to find out what he was really like. However you look at it, Mr Taibi was a huge mistake.

304. MIKAEL SILVESTRE

OTHER HONOURS:
36 FRANCE CAPS 2001-.

OTHER CLUBS:
RENNES, FRANCE, 95/6-97/8 (49, 0);
INTERNAZIONALE OF MILAN 98/9 (18, 1).

MIKAEL SILVESTRE		
COMP.	APPS	GLS
LEAGUE	186 (13)	4
FAC	13 (2)	1
LC	7	0
EUROPE	51 (7)	2
OTHERS	7	1
TOTAL	264 (22)	8

BORN	CHAMBRAY-LES-TOURS, FRANCE 9TH AUGUST 1977
POSITION	DEFENDER
JOINED UNITED	SEPTEMBER 1999 FROM INTERNAZIONALE - £4M
UNITED DEBUT	LIVERPOOL (A) PREM. - 11/09/1999
UNITED HONOURS	PREMIERSHIP 1999/00 2000/01, 2002/03 FA CUP 2003/04

Liverpool manager Gerard Houllier wanted to sign Mikael Silvestre from Inter Milan as a left-back, but the player saw himself as a centre-half, which was a major factor in his choosing Old Trafford over Anfield.

The irony was that, for a long time after the transfer, he was deployed as United's left-back, which I have never believed to be his best position. I have to agree heartily with Mikael on that one.

If he was going to be in my team, he would have to be in central defence or, possibly, wide on the left, where he has never been tried by Sir Alex.

It's fair to say that since moving to centre-half, he has improved virtually with every game he has played, so much so that he broke into the French side on a regular basis. At this stage, he looks a fine investment for £4 million, and his success takes some of the pain away from the failure of Taibi, who made his United entrance on the same day.

Mikael's most impressive asset is his incredible pace, he's improved upstairs and he's always been more than decent with his left peg. If I had to be hyper-critical I'd like him to work on his right side, though probably that's unfair. After all, no one would expect Steve Davis to play snooker right- and left-handed, so why should footballers be treated any differently?

By the end of the 2003/04 season, the Frenchman had become a hugely important part of Manchester United's team. But one year on, rightly or wrongly, Rio Ferdinand had returned to become the first-choice centre-half, while Wes Brown and Mikael were sharing the other central role. With speculation over yet another new signing, at the time of writing it was diffcult to perceive how things would settle down.

Whatever else, I hope Mikael is not returned to the left-back berth, because I don't think he's worth his place there, and anyway it would seem an unlikely move by Sir Alex following the success of Gabriel Heinze.

However, what the situation does offer is an opportunity to use three very quick and talented central defenders as a back three. Fergie has always played 4-4-2, but it would be an interesting experiment.

Every now and again Silvestre can open a game out with a raking, long-distance pass, although only left to right, and, rather perversely, it is his very comfort on the ball which bothers me when he is on the left of a back four.

Particularly in his early United days, he worried me by looking a bit casual in possession, you might even call it dozy, and there's less chance of that mattering if he's playing with the ball coming on to him in the central position.

He likes to take a touch, he wants to play, just like Brown, Ferdinand and John O'Shea. They're all footballers, and they don't have the instinct of, say, a Jaap Stam for pure defending. Whether United will come to regret that, we shall find out in due course.

305. JOHN O'SHEA

OTHER HONOURS:
24 REPUBLIC OF IRELAND CAPS 2001-.

OTHER CLUBS:
BOURNEMOUTH ON LOAN 99/00 (10, 1);
ROYAL ANTWERP, BELGIUM, ON LOAN 00/01.

JOHN O'SHEA		
COMP.	APPS	GLS
LEAGUE	78 (19)	4
FAC	10 (1)	1
LC	13	0
EUROPE	23 (8)	0
OTHERS	1 (1)	0
TOTAL	125 (29)	5

BORN	WATERFORD, ROI. 30TH APRIL 1981
POSITION	DEFENDER
JOINED UNITED	AUGUST 1998 FROM IRISH JUNIOR FOOTBALL
UNITED DEBUT	ASTON VILLA (A) LC - 13/10/1999
UNITED HONOURS	PREMIERSHIP 2002/03 FA CUP 2003/04

John O'Shea is a lovely, delightfully modest young man and I'm pleased for him that he's fared so exceptionally well in his fledgling Manchester United career, but if I had to criticise him, I'd say that he's just a little too gentle with some of his opponents.

Why doesn't he kick one or two of them, let them know he's around? A little nastiness is all part of defending, no matter how you like to dress it up.

When John played in the reserves, people talked him up as a centre-half, and he was un-deniably impressive in that role when offered a few senior starts. But his chances were al-ways going to be limited, with the likes of Brown, Ferdinand and company around the club, so it was gratifying when he emerged excitingly at left-back.

John plays on the left off his right foot, something that has occurred successfully over many years at United, going all the way back to John Aston and Roger Byrne. If the Irishman finishes up half as accomplished an operator as either of them, then no one at Old Trafford will be complaining.

Against a background of the team as a whole struggling defensively, John wasn't quite as consistent in his second full season as in his first. But there were a lot of changes at the back and in midfield, and it's a fact that people defend more effectively when the side is settled.

He's a big, tall lad who covers a deceptive amount of ground with his long strides, and although he's not the quickest, that will cause him less problems on the flank than in the centre. He's terrific on the ball and has proved immensely useful as an attacking out-let, notably so at St James' Park in the spring

of 2003, when he ran Newcastle ragged, even pulling off one outrageous nutmeg.

John's naturally gifted at going forward, and he doesn't get fazed if he finds himself in the opponents' penalty area, having the composure and the presence of mind to do the right thing.

Unless he's exceedingly unlucky, I think he can look forward to a lengthy and productive stay at United, possibly finishing up at right-back, on his natural side, though there are other options.

Against Burnley in the League Cup during 2002/03, he played in central midfield and showed he had enough talent to carry off that role, and he scored with an exquisite chip at Highbury in February 2005. For all that, I'm not sure if he could get backwards and forwards quickly enough in that advanced position. As a defender you tend to be facing the ball and midfield might find him out a bit, but who knows?

I just hope that Manchester United don't treat John O'Shea lightly and allow him to be submerged by costly imports. That would be a shameful waste.

306. RICHARD WELLENS

OTHER CLUBS:
BLACKPOOL 99/00-04/05 (188, 16);
OLDHAM ATHLETIC 05/06-.

RICHARD WELLENS		
COMP.	APPS	GLS
LC	0 (1)	0
TOTAL	0 (1)	0

BORN	MANCHESTER 26TH MARCH 1980
POSITION	MIDFIELDER
JOINED UNITED	JULY 1996 FROM JUNIOR FOOTBALL
UNITED DEBUT & FAREWELL	ASTON VILLA (A) LC - 13/10/1999
LEFT UNITED FOR	BLACKPOOL - MARCH 2000

Richard Wellens barely made a ripple on the Old Trafford pond, taking the now-traditional League Cup route to his sole senior start. The boy had plenty going for him as an all-round midfielder, though, as he has proved by thriving with Blackpool and being voted into the PFA's Second Division team of the year in 2003/04.

307. LUKE CHADWICK

OTHER CLUBS:
ROYAL ANTWERP, BELGIUM, ON LOAN 99/00 AND 00/01;
READING ON LOAN 02/03 (15, 1);
BURNLEY ON LOAN 03/04 (36, 5).
WEST HAM UNITED 04/05- (32, 1).

LUKE CHADWICK		
COMP.	APPS	GLS
LEAGUE	11 (14)	2
FAC	1 (2)	0
LC	5	0
EUROPE	1 (5)	0
TOTAL	18 (21)	2

BORN	CAMBRIDGE 18TH NOVEMBER 1980
POSITION	WINGER
JOINED UNITED	JUNE 1997 FROM JUNIOR FOOTBALL
UNITED DEBUT	ASTON VILLA (A) LC - 13/10/1999
UNITED HONOURS	PREMIERSHIP 2000/01
UNITED FAREWELL	BURNLEY (A) LC - 03/12/2002
LEFT UNITED FOR	WEST HAM UNITED AUGUST 2004

I would imagine that Luke Chadwick could drive a manager to drink. He goes this way, he goes that way, he can beat people, and there was a little period when he didn't do badly. In fact, for a short time, you could say he looked exciting.

Yet for all that, he didn't follow through by making a lasting impact, and I never thought he was going to be a United player in the long term. He seemed a little bit too much like an ungainly, out-of-control puppet, tall and gangly and awkward, his arms and legs not appearing to move in unison.

Luke had pace, and a trick or two to go past his markers, and there is no doubt that he embarrassed a few high-quality defenders. But I was always worried about his end-product because only rarely did he lift his head to have a look about him. Usually he lacked the composure to make the most of his undoubted natural talent, which was a shame.

If I was a full-back facing Luke Chadwick I'd stand inside and show him down the line, and I think that more often than not he would run the ball out of play himself. A winger at the top level, no matter how gifted he might be, has got to have rather more than that.

He joined West Ham in the summer of 2004 and needed to make a major impact at Upton Park.

308. DAVID HEALY

OTHER HONOURS:
41 NORTHERN IRELAND CAPS 2000-.

OTHER CLUBS:
PORT VALE ON LOAN 99/00 (16, 3);
PRESTON NORTH END 00/01-04/05 (139, 44);
NORWICH CITY ON LOAN 02/03 (13, 2);
LEEDS UNITED 04/05- (28, 7).

DAVID HEALY		
COMP.	APPS	GLS
LEAGUE	0 (1)	0
LC	0 (2)	0
TOTAL	0 (3)	0

BORN	DOWNPATRICK, N IRELAND 5TH AUGUST 1979
POSITION	STRIKER
JOINED UNITED	JULY 1996 FROM IRISH JUNIOR FOOTBALL
UNITED DEBUT	ASTON VILLA (A) LC - 13/10/1999
UNITED FAREWELL	IPSWICH TOWN (H) PREM. - 23/12/2000
LEFT UNITED FOR	PRESTON NORTH END DECEMBER 2000 - £1.5M

There were great expectations for David Healy, with some people at Old Trafford reckoning that he might save United millions by making it unnecessary to sign a new striker.

Like so many kids today, he made his debut in the League Cup, but the manager never had enough confidence in him to give him a run in the Premiership, instead cashing in to the tune of £1.5 million by selling him to Preston.

Initially David, a natural finisher, did exceptionally well at Deepdale, and some pundits thought the club might come to regret his sale, that all his potential was going to come back to haunt us.

I suppose it's conceivable that such a thing may yet happen, because he was still in his mid-twenties in 2004, the year he became the top scorer in Northern Ireland's history by notching his 14th international goal. However, the indications were that he'd found his level in the First Division and I'll be surprised if he rises above it.

I find it fascinating, though, to reflect on who makes the crucial decision that a lad like David is not actually the next

Ruud van Nistelrooy? Is it the Boss, or the coaches in the reserve teams? Are we sometimes making decisions a bit early? David, who was first capped in his teens, was still only 21 when he left and I reckon it's a major flaw in the method of big clubs that they allow youngsters to leave so early.

I think back to the 1950s and Roger Byrne, a late developer who would never have been heard of under the current system. I suppose it reflects modern society in general, in that everybody wants everything yesterday. Therefore, if one wave of kids haven't done it in two years, there's always another wave on the way.

Robbie Savage was rejected by United as a boy but went on to make the grade for Leicester and Birmingham; Neil Lennon was turned away by Manchester City, then starred for Leicester and Celtic. Food for thought.

309. PAUL RACHUBKA

BORN	SAN LUIS OBISPO, USA 21ST MAY 1981
POSITION	GOALKEEPER
JOINED UNITED	JUNE 1997 FROM JUNIOR FOOTBALL
UNITED DEBUT	SOUTH MELBOURNE RIO DE JANEIRO, CLUB WORLD CHAMPIONSHIP 11/01/2000
UNITED FAREWELL	LEICESTER CITY (H) PREM. - 17/03/2001
LEFT UNITED FOR	CHARLTON ATH MAY 2002

PAUL RACHUBKA		
COMP.	APPS	GLS
LEAGUE	1	0
LC	0 (1)	0
OTHERS	0 (1)	0
TOTAL	1 (2)	0

OTHER CLUBS:
OLDHAM ATHLETIC ON LOAN 01/02 (16, 0); ;
HUDDERSFIELD TOWN ON LOAN 03/04 (13, 0);
MILTON KEYNES DONS ON LOAN 04/05 (4, 0);
NORTHAMPTON TOWN ON LOAN 04/05 (10, 0);
HUDDERSFIELD TOWN 04/05- (29, 0).

We never saw enough of the young American Paul Rachubka to find out what he was made of. Certainly he did nothing wrong in his handful of senior outings, with a clean sheet on his only Premiership start, at home to Leicester, being the highlight. After leaving Old Trafford, he failed to make an early breakthrough for Charlton, but enjoyed a fruitful spell on loan at Huddersfield, helping them rise to Division Two via the play-offs in 2003/04. Then he enlisted with Milton Keynes Dons, the club formerly known as Wimbledon, before returning to the Terriers.

310. FABIEN BARTHEZ

OTHER HONOURS:
75 FRANCE CAPS 1994-.

OTHER CLUBS:
TOULOUSE 91/2 (26, 0);
MARSEILLES 92/3-94/5 (106, 0);
MONACO 95/6-99/00 (143, 0);
MARSEILLES INITIALLY ON LOAN 03/04-.

FABIEN BARTHEZ		
COMP.	APPS	GLS
LEAGUE	92	0
FAC	4	0
LC	4	0
EUROPE	37	0
OTHERS	2	0
TOTAL	139	0

BORN	LAVELANET, FRANCE 28TH JUNE 1971
POSITION	GOALKEEPER
JOINED UNITED	MAY 2000 FROM MONACO - £7.8M
UNITED DEBUT	CHELSEA - WEMBLEY CS - 13/08/2000
UNITED HONOURS	PREMIERSHIP 2000/01, 2002/03
UNITED FAREWELL	REAL MADRID (H) EC - 23/04/2003
LEFT UNITED FOR	MARSEILLES - OCT 2003

When Fabien Barthez arrived at Old Trafford, he would have been a lot of people's idea of the best goalkeeper in the world, so signing him was greeted as something of a coup.

That was understandable because he was the French national 'keeper who had won the world and European international championships, and he had picked up a European Cup winner's medal while doing the club rounds in France.

Clearly he was a top man, and with United he looked the part from the very beginning, playing terrifically on the way to the title in his first English season.

I know he dropped a few rickets after that, most memorably at Arsenal where his errors cost a couple of goals, but that sort of thing happens to all 'keepers at one time or another. It's inevitable. Outfield players don't shine every time they take the field, so why should goalkeepers?

Critics moaned about him dribbling the ball out of his area and the crazy chances he took, but he'd always done that for France, so it should have come as no surprise that he was a showman. If United didn't want that sort of thing, then there was no point in buying Fabien Barthez. He was always going to be an extrovert.

Since leaving Manchester, has he proved Sir Alex Ferguson, who presumably considered him to be a spent force, right or wrong? Well, he went to Marseilles and reached the final of the UEFA Cup in his first half-season, and no one could accuse him of being responsible for France's unexpectedly early exit from Euro 2004. No way did he look any less of a performer than when he first fetched up at Old Trafford.

I just can't work out how he went from being a world-class star and first choice at United to third, or even fourth choice in a very short space of time. It doesn't make any kind of sense. I can't believe that he isn't a better 'keeper than Roy Carroll, Ricardo Lopez, or Tim Howard.

The Frenchman was a terrific performer and that's why he was signed. Did he become a bad one, all of a sudden? No. Did he have a couple of poor games? Yes, which is the norm for any goalkeeper who was ever born. Whatever, his Old Trafford experience has done nothing to diminish his love of the game or to change the flamboyant way he approaches it.

He's not an old man in goalkeeping terms and I think he still had plenty to offer Manchester United when they let him go. He's looked after himself superbly, he's played successfully at the highest level, and he brings unparalleled experience to his work.

Now he's gone and that's just another mystery, but I'm not complaining. That's part of the joy of the game, and it helps to make the football world go round.

BORN	EDINBURGH 26TH FEBRUARY 1981
POSITION	MIDFIELDER
JOINED UNITED	JUNE 1997 FROM JUNIOR FOOTBALL
UNITED DEBUT	WATFORD (A) LC - 31/10/2000
UNITED FAREWELL	DEPORTIVO LA CORUNA (A) EC - 18/03/2003
LEFT UNITED FOR	HIBERNIAN - JUNE 2005

MICHAEL STEWART		
COMP.	APPS	GLS
LEAGUE	5 (2)	0
FAC	0 (1)	0
LC	2 (2)	0
EUROPE	0 (2)	0
TOTAL	7 (7)	0

311. MICHAEL STEWART

OTHER HONOURS:
3 SCOTLAND CAPS 2002-.

OTHER CLUBS:
ROYAL ANTWERP, BELGIUM, ON LOAN 99/00;
NOTTINGHAM FOREST ON LOAN 03/04 (13, 0);
HEART OF MIDLOTHIAN ON LOAN 04/05 (17, 0);
HIBERNIAN 05/06-.

The Manchester United coaching staff thought very highly of Michael Stewart, a ginger-haired midfielder with fire in his belly, and he won three Scotland caps at an early age.

Maybe he was a tad too keen with his tackling at times, but he always impressed me by his all-round game, doing the simple things well, winning the ball and passing it on.

In fact, he reminded me of a young Nicky Butt, showing that he wasn't going to be an easy ride for anybody, and I expected him to be knocking on the door of the first team in the not-too-distant future.

He did well on loan at Antwerp before settling back into life at Old Trafford, then I thought his loan to Nottingham Forest would do him the world of good, playing first-team football at a decent level rather than sticking too long in the reserves.

He started competently at the City Ground but Forest were having a difficult time, he lost his place and the management changed. After that, having celebrated his 23rd birthday,

Michael found himself further down in United's pecking order than at any time since his breakthrough. A fresh start was imperative, and after a season long loan to Hearts, he accepted a permanent move across Edinburgh to Hibs.

312. DANNY WEBBER

OTHER CLUBS:
PORT VALE ON LOAN 01/02 (4, 0);
WATFORD ON LOAN 01/02-02/03 (17, 4);
WATFORD 03/04-04/05 (55, 17).
SHEFFIELD UNITED ON LOAN 04/05- (7, 3).

DANNY WEBBER		
COMP.	APPS	GLS
LC	1 (1)	0
EUROPE	0 (1)	0
TOTAL	1 (2)	0

BORN	MANCHESTER 28TH DECEMBER 1981
POSITION	STRIKER
JOINED UNITED	JULY 1998 FROM JUNIOR FOOTBALL
UNITED DEBUT	SUNDERLAND (A) LC - 28/11/2000
UNITED FAREWELL	DEPORTIVO LA CORUNA (A) EC - 18/03/2003
LEFT UNITED FOR	WATFORD - JULY 2003

I liked the look of Danny Webber. He was quick enough to catch pigeons, he was a neat finisher and comfortable in possession, all in all a very useful package. But it's extremely difficult for a young striker to achieve a lasting impact at United – in fact, no one has done so since Mark Hughes – so Danny went to Watford, where he started well before suffering injury.

313. ANDY GORAM

OTHER HONOURS:
43 SCOTLAND CAPS 1985-1998.

OTHER CLUBS:
OLDHAM ATHLETIC 81/2-97/8 (195, 0);
HIBERNIAN 87/8-90/1 (138, 1);
GLASGOW RANGERS 91/2-97/8 (184, 0); NOTTS COUNTY 98/9 (1, 0);
SHEFFIELD UNITED 98/9 (7, 0); MOTHERWELL 98/9-00/01 (57, 0);
COVENTRY CITY 01/02 (7, 0); OLDHAM ATHLETIC 01/02 (4, 0);
QUEEN OF THE SOUTH 02/03 (19, 0).

ANDY GORAM		
COMP.	APPS	GLS
LEAGUE	2	0
TOTAL	2	0

BORN	BURY 13TH APRIL 1964
POSITION	GOALKEEPER
JOINED UNITED	MARCH 2001 FROM MOTHERWELL - £100,000
UNITED DEBUT	COVENTRY CITY (H) PREM. - 14/04/2001
UNITED FAREWELL	SOUTHAMPTON (A) PREM. - 13/05/2001
LEFT UNITED FOR	COVENTRY CITY AUGUST 2001

How on earth did Andy Goram get to United's first team at the age of 37 and looking about two stone overweight? They paid £100,000 to sign him, he played in two games and, to be brutally frank, he appeared horribly out of his depth.

Going way back, he was an extremely promising prospect as a kid at Oldham, then he progressed to a cracking career with Hibs, Rangers and Scotland, but that was not the Andy Goram we saw taking the field as United closed in on the title in the spring of 2001.

I know Barthez and van der Gouw were injuried, but the appearance of Goram between United's posts in a Premiership match was nothing short of bizarre.

BORN	BELGRADE, YUGOSLAVIA 6TH FEBRUARY 1982
POSITION	MIDFIELDER
JOINED UNITED	FEBRUARY 1999 FROM BROMMA POJKARNA - £1M
UNITED DEBUT	TOTTENHAM H. (A) PREM. - 19/05/2001
UNITED FAREWELL	ARSENAL (A) LC - 05/11/2001
LEFT UNITED FOR	RANGERS - JAN 2005

BOJAN DJORDIC		
COMP.	APPS	GLS
LEAGUE	0 (1)	0
LC	1	0
TOTAL	1 (1)	0

314. BOJAN DJORDJIC

OTHER CLUBS:
BROMMA POJKARNA, SWEDEN, 98/9;
SHEFFIELD WEDNESDAY ON LOAN 01/02 (5, 0);
AGF AARHUS, DENMARK, ON LOAN 02/03;
RED STAR BELGRADE ON LOAN 03/04,
RANGERS 04/05 (4, 0); PLYMOUTH ARGYLE 05/06-.

Bojan Djordjic had outstanding ability, they say, but I'd point out he had that much ability he couldn't get a game. Manchester United paid £1 million for him when he was 17 but really he has never managed to trouble the scorer.

When you've invested so much money on a kid who hasn't made the grade, and he's got a long contract, you let him go on a series of loans with the deep and passionate hope that somebody fancies him and takes him off your hands, which is exactly what Rangers did.

BORN	OSS, HOLLAND 1ST JULY 1976
POSITION	STRIKER
JOINED UNITED	MAY 2001 FROM PSV EINDHOVEN - £19M
UNITED DEBUT	LIVERPOOL MILLENNIUM STADIUM CS - 12/08/2001
UNITED HONOURS	PREMIERSHIP 2002/03 FA CUP 2003/04

RUUD VAN NISTELROOY		
COMP.	APPS	GLS
LEAGUE	109 (6)	74
FAC	9 (3)	14
LC	4	1
EUROPE	37 (2)	36
OTHERS	2	1
TOTAL	161 (11)	126

315. RUUD VAN NISTELROOY

OTHER HONOURS:
42 HOLLAND CAPS 1998-.
OTHER CLUBS:
DEN BOSCH 93/4-96/7 (69, 17);
HEERENVEEN 97/8 (31, 13);
PSV EINDHOVEN 98/9-00/01 (67, 62), ALL HOLLAND.

Not since Denis Law in his prime have Manchester United been blessed with such a prolific marksman, or a man with such an all-consuming passion for scoring goals, as Ruud van Nistelrooy.

When watching the Dutchman in action, it becomes rapidly apparent that he loves putting the ball in the net more than anything else on earth. When he hits the target, as he has incessantly since arriving at Old Trafford, becoming the club's fastest goal centurion in the process, he is ecstatic; and when he registers a blank then he's as miserable as sin.

Ruud isn't a greyhound – certainly no Thierry Henry when it comes to pace – though he's not exactly a slouch over the ground. He's strong and resilient, and he can be an awkward customer; he holds the ball up well, he's superb with his back to goal, and he's got a decent touch.

But what marks him out as special is the most golden gift in all of football, that of knocking the ball between the posts with the kind of regularity which any manager would kill for.

Like most of the great goal-scorers – Denis Law, Jimmy Greaves, Stan Pearson – Ruud rarely, if ever, finds the net from outside the penalty area, which is where he differs from Thierry Henry, who seems capable of firing them in from anywhere.

Almost invariably van Nistelrooy operates as a predator, a box player, but he's not like anyone else, he's got a style that's all his own. Certainly you could never call him a one-dimensional tap-in merchant because there's variety to his game, as he demonstrated so dramatically with his run from halfway to slot in a stupendous goal at home to Fulham in March 2003.

It's astonishing that Ruud has maintained such a high level for United after missing a whole season with a serious knee injury, the type that has wrecked many a promising career. Obviously Sir Alex Ferguson thought an awful lot of him to give him that year to recover, keeping in close contact all the while, letting the lad know that the club still wanted him.

As the 2004/05 campaign was about to kick off, people were drooling at the thought of a productive link between van Nistelrooy and Louis Saha, but some were worried that they would occupy each other's territory, despite Ruud being right-rided and Louis being a left-footer.

Certainly the Dutchman needs a partner, as any marksman does, someone who can share the load and offer alternatives, as Ole Gunnar Solskjaer did to such great effect with Ruud in his first term at Old Trafford.

Sometimes Fergie hasn't given him a co-striker, and he's done exceptionally well in the circumstances, making light of a colossal workload, chasing balls to either flank yet still managing to pop up in the middle. But if that policy were to be pursued relentlessly for any length of time, it would wear anyone down.

I hope Ruud doesn't leave United when he's in his prime, for Real Madrid or anywhere else. If it happened then most fans would be aghast, no matter who was pulled in as a replacement. They would demand to know, and understanda-

A STUDY IN SINGLE-MINDEDNESS: Ruud van Nistelrooy shields the ball from Liverpool's Sami Hyypia.

bly so, why anyone attempting to build a team to win the Champions League should tell their top striker.

That said, if I was chairman of Manchester United and somebody offered, say, £40 million, Ruud's feet wouldn't touch the deck. He'd be on his way. After all, there's no guarantee that he'll ever score 40 goals in a season again, he might fall prey to injury at any time – as happened in 2004/05 – and you ought to be able to recruit several top-quality performers with that sort of money.

But that's hypothetical, and it's far more pleasurable to debate where the lad stands in the pantheon of great strikers, present and past. Club loyalty notwithstanding, I'd have to be honest and name Henry as the best in the world as I write, though he is followed closely by van Nistelrooy; and in United terms, suffice it to say that Ruud would have been welcomed as the centre-forward in any team during my lifetime.

BORN	BUENOS AIRES, ARGENTINA 9TH MARCH 1975
POSITION	MIDFIELDER
JOINED UNITED	JULY 2001 FROM LAZIO, ITALY - £28.1M
UNITED DEBUT	FULHAM (H) PREM. - 19/08/2001
UNITED HONOURS	PREMIERSHIP 2002/03
UNITED FAREWELL	CHARLTON ATHLETIC (H) PREM. - 03/05/2003
LEFT UNITED FOR	CHELSEA AUGUST 2003 - £15M

JUAN SEBASTIAN VERON		
COMP.	APPS	GLS
LEAGUE	45 (6)	7
FAC	2	0
LC	4 (1)	0
EUROPE	24	4
TOTAL	75 (7)	11

316. JUAN SEBASTIAN VERON

OTHER HONOURS:
56 ARGENTINA CAPS 1996-.

OTHER CLUBS:
ESTUDIANTES, ARGENTINA, 93/4-95/6 (60, 7);
BOCA JUNIORS, ARGENTINA, 95/6 (17, 4);
SAMPDORIA, ITALY, 96/7-97/8 (61, 7);
PARMA, ITALY, 98/9 (26, 1);
LAZIO, ITALY, 99/00-00/01 (53, 11);
CHELSEA 03/04- (7, 1);
INTERNAZIONALE OF MILAN ON LOAN 04/05-.

Juan Sebastian Veron was signed from Lazio for £28.1 million, what I considered to be a ridiculous amount of money, not because he couldn't play – certainly he could – but because I couldn't believe that anybody could be worth that sort of cash.

He was supposed to be the one to supply the final ingredient of flair and imagination, and in ten per-cent of his games for United he was a delight. But week in and week out, he was anything but spectacular. In fact, he was downright ordinary; and I'd say that any club who pays £28.1 million is entitled to the spectacular on a regular basis.

You might say he frustrated a lot of people, but you might be closer to the truth if you said he drove them stark raving mad, and probably one of those who felt it most was Roy Keane.

Veron was a very fine international player for Argentina, but United could have signed, say Scott Parker from Charlton or Matty Holland from Ipswich, who would have done a better job in the English League.

I don't think it helped that, to some degree, Veron and Beckham were occupying similar areas of the field. I could never work out what their footballing relationship was. I'm not talking about how they got on off the pitch, but in a professional sense it appeared to me there was jealousy and/or friction between the two. They both wanted to operate in similar areas and to do similar things. For instance, they both wanted to take free-kicks.

'The Argentinian has been called the most expensive mistake in the history of English football, and there's a strong case to support that argument.'

How ironic, then, that they should both leave the club at the same time. By then, it should be stressed, Beckham had nothing to prove, unlike Veron who, in United terms, had everything to prove. Some felt that if Beckham went, then Veron should have stayed, but I believe that, deep down, Sir Alex realised that the Argentinian was not his sort of player after all. I don't think he did enough when he wasn't at the top of his game to suit the manager.

Veron didn't want to play at 100 mph. His attitude was more: 'When we get it you let us play, and when you get it we'll let you play.' But the Premiership is far too hectic and competitive for that approach. We all know he could pass like a dream, but tackling and chasing did not come naturally to him.

Van Nistelrooy cost a lot, too, but he is the striker who's going to win games for you. Veron, a midfielder, cost nearly half as much again and we didn't know exactly where we could fit him into the side. We already had a midfield of Beckham, Roy, Scholesy and Giggs, so perhaps Veron was an unnecessary disruption. Maybe at one stage the manager had visions of him replacing Beckham, but in the end he was pushed about all over the shop, even wide on the left, where he never looked at home.

The Argentinian has been called the most expensive mistake in the history of English football, and there's a strong case to support that argument. Manchester United lost £13 million on him in the space of two years, which illustrates why there can be no real justification for turning down a massive offer for anyone, Ruud van Nistelrooy included. There are so many uncertainties in the world of football, and a plc has to take its vast sums of money wherever it can.

BORN	ENNISKILLEN, N. IRELAND 30TH SEPTEMBER 1977
POSITION	GOALKEEPER
JOINED UNITED	JULY 2001 FROM WIGAN ATHLETIC - £2.5M
UNITED DEBUT	ASTON VILLA (A) PREM. - 26/08/2001
UNITED HONOURS	PREMIERSHIP 2002/03 FA CUP 2003/04
UNITED FAREWELL	ARSENAL MILLENNIUM STADIUM FAC - 21/05/2005
LEFT UNITED FOR	WEST HAM UTD - MAY 2005

ROY CARROLL		
COMP.	APPS	GLS
LEAGUE	46 (3)	0
FAC	7 (1)	0
LC	5	0
EUROPE	10	0
TOTAL	68 (4)	0

317. ROY CARROLL

OTHER HONOURS:
16 NORTHERN IRELAND CAPS 1997-.

OTHER CLUBS:
HULL CITY 95/6-96/7 (46, 0);
WIGAN ATHLETIC 97/8-00/01 (135, 0);
WEST HAM UNITED 05/06-.

It was easy to forget Roy Carroll in the summer of 2001, thanks to the multi-million-pound arrivals of Ruud van Nistelrooy and Juan Sebastian Veron. Thereafter the Irishman was patient, often when he had an opportunity he did well for United, but somehow I always had a lingering doubt.

Perhaps I'm being unfair to him, but he didn't always look the most athletic of goalkeepers to me. He seemed to have a reasonably safe pair of hands, but every time I saw him I asked the question: 'Are you all right? Are you happy performing on this huge stage? Are there not occasions when you think you shouldn't be here?' During the spring of 2004,

'He came in for two crunch games against Arsenal and performed brilliantly. But for Roy Carroll they wouldn't have reached the FA Cup Final. He was the match-winner beyond question.'

when United were going through a rough patch, he came in for two crunch games against Arsenal and performed brilliantly. But for Roy Carroll they wouldn't have reached the FA Cup Final. He was the match-winner beyond question.

So why did I worry? Perhaps it's because he started off at Hull ten years ago and worked his way to Wigan before coming to Old Trafford, which is hardly a conventional route these days. It was a great shame for Roy that he wasn't rewarded with the Millennium start his semi-final display had deserved, though at least he got on as a substitute, and his winner's medal was richly deserved. One patchy year down the line though, following much debate about a new contract and another FA Cup Final appearance, he was released to join West Ham.

318. LAURENT BLANC

OTHER HONOURS:
97 FRANCE CAPS 1989-2000.

OTHER CLUBS:
MONTPELLIER, FRANCE, 83/4-90/1 (243, 76);
NAPOLI, ITALY, 91/2 (31, 6);
NIMES, FRANCE, 92/3 (29, 1);
ST ETIENNE, FRANCE, 93/4-94/5 (70, 18);
AUXERRE, FRANCE, 95/6 (23, 2); BARCELONA, SPAIN, 96/7 (28, 1);
MARSEILLES, FRANCE, 97/8-98/9 (63, 13); INTERNAZIONALE, ITALY, 99/00-00/01 (67, 6).

LAURENT BLANC		
COMP.	APPS	GLS
LEAGUE	44 (4)	1
FAC	3	0
EUROPE	24	3
TOTAL	71 (4)	4

BORN	ALES, FRANCE 19TH NOVEMBER 1965
POSITION	CENTRAL DEFENDER
JOINED UNITED	SEPTEMBER 2001 FROM INTERNAZIONALE, ITALY
UNITED DEBUT	EVERTON (H) PREM. - 08/09/2001
UNITED HONOURS	PREMIERSHIP 2002/03
UNITED FAREWELL	EVERTON (A) PREM. - 11/05/2003
RETIRED	JUNE 2003

If ever a man should have become a Manchester United player 20 years earlier than he did, it's Laurent Blanc. He was some player in his pomp, and I'd have loved to have seen him at Old Trafford in his younger days.

I don't think there's ever been a central defender more comfortable when he was in possession. The game seemed so easy to him and he was a supreme artist in his own right.

During his stay at Old Trafford, there was no problem when the ball came to him. He was terrific in the air and had wonderful feet. But he was already 36 when he arrived so at best he was only going to be a stopgap. He was an old man, still with superb ability, but he couldn't turn and run, so sometimes, inevitably, he was exposed. What else could you expect?

Blanc's career record is quite strange for such a high-quality performer. After spending seven years with his first club, Montpellier, he went on a whistle-stop tour of Europe, rarely stopping anywhere more than a season, which is not what you expect from one of the class acts of our era. Perhaps it was for financial reasons, perhaps he liked a change of scene, but it's difficult to understand.

The manager tried to partially explain the sale of Jaap Stam by saying the Frenchman was the teacher that the Dutchman never was. If that is the case, then who am I to argue? But it puzzles me. If he was going to be a professor to Wes Brown and Mikael Silvestre, then why he didn't play more?

'He was an old man, still with superb ability, but he couldn't turn and run, so sometimes, inevitably, he was exposed. What else could you expect?'

BORN	BOLTON 28TH OCTOBER 1980
POSITION	FULL-BACK
JOINED UNITED	JUNE 1997 FROM JUNIOR FOOTBALL
UNITED DEBUT	ARSENAL (A) LC - 05/11/2001
UNITED FAREWELL	DEPORTIVO LA CORUNA (A) EC - 18/03/2003
LEFT UNITED FOR	BURNLEY - JUNE 2003

LEE ROCHE		
COMP.	APPS	GLS
LEAGUE	0 (1)	0
LC	1	0
EUROPE	1	0
TOTAL	2 (1)	0

319. LEE ROCHE

OTHER CLUBS:
WREXHAM ON LOAN 00/01 (41, 0);
BURNLEY 03/04-04/05 (54, 2);
WREXHAM 05/06-.

Lee Roche reminded me a lot of a young Gary Neville, yet while Gary survived and prospered, Lee didn't last the course. After gaining a season's worth of first-team experience with Wrexham, he helped United's reserves to win their league title in 2001/02 but was unable to take the next step at Old Trafford. Instead he joined Burnley, where he found himself in and out of the team at a difficult time for the club.

BORN	BROMSGROVE, WORCS. 6TH FEBRUARY 1982
DIED	OXFORDSHIRE 9TH AUGUST 2003
POSITION	FORWARD
JOINED UNITED	JULY 1999 FROM JUNIOR FOOTBALL
UNITED DEBUT & FAREWELL	ARSENAL (A) LC - 05/11/2001

JIMMY DAVIS		
COMP.	APPS	GLS
LC	1	0
TOTAL	1	0

320. JIMMY DAVIS

OTHER CLUBS:
SWINDON TOWN ON LOAN 02/03 (13, 2).

It was a crying shame that Jimmy Davis should have destroyed his own life in a needless car crash when he had so much to look forward to. He had played for England at junior levels, he was still on Manchester United's books and he had just been loaned to Watford for the 2003/04 season. To be honest, I barely remember him as a player, but I'm told he was immensely promising, and now he's thrown away his chance to make an impression. It's unbearably tragic.

BORN	COVENTRY 22ND OCTOBER 1982
POSITION	FORWARD
JOINED UNITED	JULY 1999 FROM JUNIOR FOOTBALL
UNITED DEBUT	ARSENAL (A) LC - 05/11/2001
UNITED FAREWELL	WBA (A) LC - 03/12/2003
LEFT UNITED FOR	BARNSLEY - JUNE 2005

DANIEL NARDIELLO		
COMP.	APPS	GLS
LC	1 (2)	0
EUROPE	0 (1)	0
TOTAL	1 (3)	0

321. DANIEL NARDIELLO

OTHER CLUBS:
SWANSEA CITY ON LOAN 03/04 (4, 0);
BARNSLEY ON LOAN 03/04-04/05 (44, 14);
BARNSLEY 05/06-.

When Daniel Nardiello was loaned to Barnsley in 2003/04 he made a bit of a splash, scoring a few goals and receiving some encouraging reviews, but it seemed extremely unlikely that he would ever make his mark back at United.

Being in his early twenties, stuck in a queue of strikers which included van Nistelrooy, Saha, Solskjaer, newcomer Alan Smith, Forlan and Bellion, even Giggs and Scholes had to be taken into account, he had no chance. Yet Daniel, whose father Donato played for Coventry and Wales in the 1970s, is a competent finisher and I believe he can flourish at a lower level, having signed a permanent deal at Oakwell in 2005.

322. DIEGO FORLAN

OTHER HONOURS:
25 URUGUAY CAPS 2002-.

OTHER CLUBS:
PENAROL, URUGUAY;
INDEPENDIENTE, ARGENTINA, 98/9-01/02 (77, 36);
VILLAREAL, SPAIN 04/05-.

DIEGO FORLAN		
COMP.	APPS	GLS
LEAGUE	23 (39)	10
FAC	2 (2)	1
LC	4 (2)	3
EUROPE	8 (14)	3
OTHERS	0 (1)	0
TOTAL	37 (58)	17

BORN	MONTEVIDEO, URUGUAY 19TH MAY 1979
POSITION	STRIKER
JOINED UNITED	JANUARY 2002 FROM INDEPENDIENTE, ARGENTINA £7.5M
UNITED DEBUT	BOLTON WANDERERS (A) PREM. - 29/01/2002
UNITED HONOURS	PREMIERSHIP 2002/03
UNITED FAREWELL	CHELSEA (A) PREM. - 15/08/2004
LEFT UNITED FOR	VILLAREAL - AUGUST 2004

Diego Forlan had his moments and, after suffering an early drought which reminded me of the trials and tribulations of Garry Birtles, he scored some terrific goals during his stay at Old Trafford. But overall he did not possess the quality expected of a Manchester United striker.

I always had a bee in my bonnet about him. Did United sign him because we thought so much of him that we wanted him, or did we sign him because we didn't want Steve McClaren, formerly the number-two to Sir Alex Ferguson, to have him at Middlesbrough?

Whatever the reason, I'd love to know which member of the United staff thought he was worth £7.5 million. At that price, he should have been the finished article, and he wasn't anywhere near it.

Not that Diego is a terrible player. For instance, he's got two very good feet and he isn't slow. In fact, I would have liked to have seen him played wide over a period of time, say six or seven games, because his skill and pace might have come into their own on the flank.

In his favour, too, he was always ready to have a pot at goal, and that paid off a few times, but he didn't do it often enough. If he had then the manager wouldn't have bought Louis Saha.

On the debit side, I think he was lazy when he didn't have the ball. Here was a young man trying to make his way in a foreign country, so you'd have expected him to put himself about, but I didn't see him doing it. In the end, to be brutally honest, it all boils down to the fact that he wasn't good enough.

Diego was very popular with the other players, and he's a lovely lad who knows what his duties are away from the pitch, such as visiting schools and hospitals. But none of that can disguise the fact that he didn't do what he was signed to do.

He might fare better in a country with a Latin culture, so perhaps the transfer to Villarreal will be exactly the right move for him. I worry about South Americans in England. Apart from Ossie Ardiles, until Gilberto Silva and Edu bedded in at Arsenal, I can't think of another who has thrived over here in the long term.

Considering that, perhaps we shouldn't be surprised by the travails of Diego. But it does beg the massive question: in the face of such overwhelming evidence, why have Manchester United spent upwards of £40 million on Veron, Forlan and Kleberson?

Postscript: *Diego's first season in Spain, during which he scored 25 times for Villarreal and shared the European Golden Boot award with Thierry Henry, suggests that his migration to sunnier climes was, indeed, a wise one.*

BORN	PECKHAM, LONDON
	7TH NOVEMBER 1978
POSITION	CENTRAL DEFENDER
JOINED UNITED	JULY 2002 FROM
	LEEDS UNITED - £30M
UNITED DEBUT	ZALAEGERSZEG (H)
	CLQ - 27/08/2002
UNITED HONOURS	PREMIERSHIP 2002/03

323. RIO FERDINAND

RIO FERDINAND		
COMP.	APPS	GLS
LEAGUE	78 (1)	0
FAC	8	0
LC	5	0
EUROPE	22	0
OTHERS	1	0
TOTAL	114 (1)	0

OTHER HONOURS:
38 ENGLAND CAPS 1997-.

OTHER CLUBS:
WEST HAM UNITED 95/6-00/01 (127, 2);
BOURNEMOUTH ON LOAN 96/7 (10, 0);
LEEDS UNITED 00/01-01/02 (54, 2).

I remember saying to Manchester United chairman Martin Edwards, as we shared a meal in the Old Trafford grill room one day in the late 1990s, that Rio Ferdinand was one of the best young footballing centre-halves in the country, and that it would be worth writing a cheque for £7 million or £8 million to sign him from West Ham.

Rio was always sweet on the ball and I expected that he would develop as a pure defender, that he would come to know the difference between right and wrong in a footballing sense. Quite simply, there are times when you pull it down and play, and times when you have to kick it into Row Z.

His big problem, which persisted for a long time even after his eventual £30 million move to Old Trafford, was that when he should have been whacking it clear, he was still trying to play pretty football. It seemed he didn't realise that he hadn't always got time to be putting his foot on the ball.

To be fair, he was magnificent in the 2002 World Cup Finals

and I think that speaks volumes for the difference between our Premiership and the type of game that is played by other countries. They tend to favour a fluent build-up, keeping the ball on the ground, an approach which gives Rio time to play, to bring the ball out, to make decisions. But in the hurly-burly of our domestic competition, with tackles flying in left, right and centre and the action roaring by at 100 mph, there is no such luxury.

Rio's positioning could be questionable, too, when crosses came in. He tended to be a watcher instead of anticipating where the ball was going to end up.

In many ways he reminded me of Paul McGrath in his early days. At first Paul clearly felt it was too crude to just hammer the ball to safety; he always wanted it to look nice; his instinct was always to play. Rio's approach is the same, but sometimes that does not tie in with the practicalities of defending.

Certainly, for a season and more after joining United, I thought he was a disappointment, in that he did not make his vast ability count fully. He left a fair bit to be desired.

But happily, in the weeks before his suspension over the farcical drugs-test controversy, it was as though some penny had dropped. Suddenly he looked like the shining star, playing as everyone imagined he could all along, and he was sorely missed when he was gone.

I have always believed that players with real talent can be taught the straightforward things. What's much more difficult is transforming crude players into class acts. There is no questioning Rio's colossal ability, so it should be possible for him to become the vast asset to Manchester United which we always believed he could be, but first he must learn to defend reliably over a sustained period.

In passing, too, I have to say that in view of the way the club stood by him during his eight-month ban, the protracted deliberation over his new contract in the spring of 2005 was more than a tad perplexing. The taste it leaves in the mouth is not a pleasant one.

BORN	MADRID, SPAIN 31ST DECEMBER 1971
POSITION	GOALKEEPER
JOINED UNITED	AUGUST 2002 FROM REAL VALLADOLID - £1.5M
UNITED DEBUT	MACCABI HAIFA (H) CL - 18/09/2002
UNITED FAREWELL	CHELSEA (A) PREM. - 15/08/2004
LEFT UNITED FOR	OSASUNA, SPAIN JUNE 2005

RICARDO LOPEZ		
COMP.	APPS	GLS
LEAGUE	0 (1)	0
EUROPE	3 (1)	0
TOTAL	3 (2)	0

324. RICARDO LOPEZ

OTHER HONOURS:
1 SPAIN CAP.

OTHER CLUBS:
ATLETICO MADRID, 94/5-97/8 (1, 0);
REAL VALLADOLID 98/9-01/02 (53, 0),
BOTH SPAIN; RACING SANTANDER, SPAIN, ON LOAN 03/04.

How in the name of God did Manchester United pay £1.5 million for Ricardo Lopez? I have absolutely no idea, not the tiniest clue.

He was 30 when he was brought to Old Trafford and then he barely appeared in the first team, instead being released on loan to Santander. When he was picked, he looked distinctly erratic, hardly the type to spread confidence throughout the defence, so the mystery deepened. He's played international football, once, though it's difficult to understand why. I find the entire Ricardo episode unbelievable.

BORN	MANCHESTER 19TH OCTOBER 1982
POSITION	MIDFIELDER
JOINED UNITED	JULY 1999 FROM JUNIOR FOOTBALL
UNITED DEBUT	MACCABI HAIFA (H) CL - 18/09/2002
UNITED FAREWELL	NORTHAMPTON TOWN (A) FAC - 25/01/2004
LEFT UNITED FOR	LEEDS UNITED - JULY 2004

DANNY PUGH		
COMP.	APPS	GLS
LEAGUE	0 (1)	0
FAC	0 (1)	0
LC	2	0
EUROPE	1 (2)	0
TOTAL	3 (4)	0

325. DANNY PUGH

OTHER CLUBS:
LEEDS UNITED 04/05 - (38, 5).

Young Danny Pugh was a tidy, left-sided midfielder who was granted a few fleeting first-team opportunities but never seemed likely to get the lengthy run in the side that his development needed.

That being the case, and as he had been at Old Trafford for nearly five years, it was probably a good move for him when he joined Leeds in May 2004, shortly after Alan Smith had moved the other way.

Danny took the eye when he started against Burnley in the League Cup during 2002/03, and I felt sorry for him because people always remember him missing three chances to score in that game. But he impressed me with his overall contribution, and at least he never hid from the ball when the luck went against him, continuing to take up the right positions.

Good luck at Elland Road, Danny.

326. KIERAN RICHARDSON

OTHER HONOURS:
2 ENGLAND CAPS 2005-.

OTHER CLUBS:
WEST BROMWICH ALBION ON LOAN 04/05 (12, 3).

KIERAN RICHARDSON		
COMP.	APPS	GLS
LEAGUE	0 (4)	0
FAC	2 (1)	0
LC	5 (1)	2
EUROPE	3 (4)	0
OTHERS	0 (1)	0
TOTAL	10 (11)	2

BORN	GREENWICH, LONDON 21ST OCTOBER 1984
POSITION	MIDFIELDER
JOINED UNITED	JULY 2001 FROM JUNIOR FOOTBALL
UNITED DEBUT	OLYMPIAKOS (A) CL - 23/10/2002

Kieran Richardson is bursting with talent, and whenever he's been promoted to the first team, he's looked all right. But at best he's third choice to Ryan Giggs and Quinton Fortune, probably fourth if you think of Ronaldo switching to the left, so what hope has the young Londoner got of forging a future for himself at Old Trafford?

I don't see the point of the club paying £2 million for an average performer like Fortune, when they've got a kid like Kieran who could do a perfectly acceptable job.

Sad to say, it would be better for the boy at this stage of his career if he left, because you only learn by playing regularly against better players. You don't learn by turning out week after week in a reserve league.

The danger is stagnation and boredom. Essentially Kieran Richardson was in limbo in 2003/04 at a crucial stage of his development when he needed to be operating at a higher standard. I'm happy for the lad that, when loaned to West bromwich during the following term, he did particularly well, impressing with his pace and skill. Given the sort of settled run in a side that has been afforded to Fortune, Kieran proved that he could still be an asset at Old Trafford.

It must be very nice being at United and, for a kid, being well paid. But does it, to some degree, diminish the ambition to be in such a comfortable position, albeit temporarily? I'm not sure it all adds up to being a good way. Not for the boys, anyway.

Postcript: *Kieran's remarkable two-goal debut for England in Chicago underlines the young man's potential and emphasises my point that he is an infinitely preferable option to Fortune at club level.*

BORN	ODENSE, DENMARK 31ST OCTOBER 1984
POSITION	FORWARD
JOINED UNITED	JULY 2001 FROM DANISH JUNIOR FOOTBALL
UNITED DEBUT	MACCABI HAIFA (A) CL - 29/10/2002

MADS TIMM		
COMP.	APPS	GLS
EUROPE	0 (1)	0
TOTAL	0 (1)	0

327. MADS TIMM

OTHER CLUBS:
ODENSE; VIKING STAVANGER ON LOAN 03/04.

I'm told that Mads Timm – who regrettably has made more headlines off the pitch than on it – is an exciting prospect who cost a lot of money, so why was he on loan to a Norwegian club at exactly the time he should have been pulling out all the stops to make the breakthrough at Old Trafford? What's the point of bringing him over from Scandinavia, only to send him back for a whole season when he's still in his teens?

BORN	EDINBURGH 1ST FEBRUARY 1984
POSITION	MIDFIELDER
JOINED UNITED	JULY 2000 FROM JUNIOR FOOTBALL
UNITED DEBUT	FC BASEL (H) CL - 12/03/2003

DARREN FLETCHER		
COMP.	APPS	GLS
LEAGUE	35 (5)	3
FAC	5 (3)	0
LC	5	0
EUROPE	8 (5)	0
OTHERS	0 (1)	0
TOTAL	53 (14)	3

328. DARREN FLETCHER

OTHER HONOURS:
13 SCOTLAND CAPS 2003-.

Darren Fletcher nearly became the youngest player in Manchester United's history. He was a 16-year-old schoolboy in his first year at Old Trafford when Sir Alex Ferguson picked him for the final game of the season at Villa Park, only for his Scottish education authority to forbid it.

Not too long afterwards he suffered a broken foot, which set him back badly, then there were other injuries, and it testifies to his strength of character as much as to his obvious ability that he has come through it all to captain his country and to shine for United at the age of 20.

Darren made his real breakthrough in 2003/04, often playing wide on the right, but I don't see that as his best position. Probably he's not got the pace to prosper on the flank, and he doesn't look comfortable there.

In fact, he's a natural central midfielder, and I trust that's where his future lies. I hope he can boss that area, but it's a bit early to judge if he can cope with such an onerous responsibility. If he can, then he might even prove to be the long-term successor to Roy Keane.

Darren played in the centre against Millwall in the FA Cup Final, but he must be tested in matches against more demanding opposition, and in the not-too-distant future. He's a tre-

mendous all-round footballer, so he's got a chance. You can't have donkeys playing in midfield, because you go nowhere, and this boy is anything but a donkey.

He needs a settled run of games in his best role, even if it's for the last half-hour of matches, playing alongside Keane or Paul Scholes. I believe that's the way to develop him, so that he learns how to play with top performers.

Darren's got the quality, so with average luck – and they all need that – he could be a Manchester United player for a considerable time.

329. MARK LYNCH

OTHER CLUBS:
ST JOHNSTONE ON LOAN 01/02 (20, 0);
SUNDERLAND 04/05 (11, 0);
HULL CITY 05/06-.

MARK LYNCH		
COMP.	APPS	GLS
EUROPE	1	0
TOTAL	1	0

BORN	MANCHESTER 2ND SEPTEMBER 1981
POSITION	DEFENDER
JOINED UNITED	JULY 1998 FROM JUNIOR FOOTBALL
UNITED DEBUT & FAREWELL	DEPORTIVO LA CORUNA (A) CL - 18/03/2003
LEFT UNITED FOR	SUNDERLAND - JULY 2004

Mark Lynch spent six years at United and broke into the senior side, but he was never granted a proper chance to become established. At best, in the summer of 2004, he seemed destined to become a permanent fixture in the reserves, so it didn't surprise me when he signed for Sunderland, where he had a decent prospect of regular first-team football.

That was a sensible decision for a lad who had proved himself to be an efficient defender and who I would expect to make a living from the game away from Old Trafford.

330. TIM HOWARD

OTHER HONOURS:
10 USA CAPS.

OTHER CLUBS:
NEW YORK/NEW JERSEY METROSTARS 98-03 (85, 0).

TIM HOWARD		
COMP.	APPS	GLS
LEAGUE	44	0
FAC	8	0
LC	5	0
EUROPE	12	0
OTHERS	2	0
TOTAL	71	0

BORN	NEW BRUNSWICK, USA 6TH MARCH 1979
POSITION	GOALKEEPER
JOINED UNITED	JULY 2003 FROM NY/NJ METROSTARS £2.3M
UNITED DEBUT	ARSENAL MILLENNIUM STADIUM CS - 10/08/2003

When Tim Howard joined Manchester United, I'd never heard of him, and the thought crossed my mind that Fabien Barthez was going to be an almighty hard act to follow for a fellow coming straight out of Micky Mouse football in the States. In those circumstances, given that he was facing proper players for the first time in his life, Tim was nothing short of magnificent in 2003/04.

Okay, he was out of the side towards the back end of the season, which might or might not have had something to do with

EARLY REWARD: Tim Howard brandishes the Community Shield after his United debut.

conceding the late goal against Porto which saw United knocked out of the European Cup. By then, after a wonderful start, he'd had a little run of minor mistakes, although nothing of any great magnitude other than that one costly blunder, and Sir Alex Ferguson can only have been delighted with his overall level of performance.

At that point it seemed that, given the breaks, Tim would be standing between Manchester United's posts for a good few years – I must admit, though, that I'd said the same about Barthez, and look what happened to him – but then the picture changed significantly during the following term. To put it kindly, that campaign was a little bit demoralising for Messrs Tim Howard and Roy Carroll both. Neither of them proved reliable, so predicting who would guard United's net in the future became rather more problematical – and that was before Carroll's departure and Edwin van der Sar's arrival.

Tim was 26 in the spring of 2005, and although probably he won't reach his peak for several more seasons, now is the time for him to consolidate his position. His next couple of years will be do-or-die, and he will have to develop in the shadow of the veteran Dutchman. Still, I like Tim's style. He stands up, which impresses me; he's athletic and recovers quickly if he does go to ground. Crucially, too, he's got a bit of a presence about him, which can be enough to make the difference between a top 'keeper and an average one.

BORN	DOUALA, CAMEROON 4TH MAY 1981
POSITION	MIDFIELDER
JOINED UNITED	JULY 2003 FROM NANTES, FRANCE - £3.5M
UNITED DEBUT	ARSENAL MILLENNIUM STADIUM CS - 10/08/2003
UNITED FAREWELL	EXETER CITY (A) FAC - 19/01/2005
LEFT UNITED FOR	ASTON VILLA JANUARY 2005 - £1.35M

ERIC DJEMBA-DJEMBA		
COMP.	APPS	GLS
LEAGUE	13 (7)	0
FAC	2 (1)	0
LC	5	1
EUROPE	6 (3)	1
OTHERS	1 (1)	0
TOTAL	27 (12)	2

331. ERIC DJEMBA-DJEMBA

OTHER HONOURS:
11 CAMEROON CAPS 2002-.

OTHER CLUBS:
NANTES, FRANCE, 01/02-02/03 (42, 1).
ASTON VILLA 04-05- (6, 0).

The first time I saw Eric Djemba-Djemba, I thought: 'He'll do for me.' He looked the part from the moment he came on as a substitute during the Community Shield against Arsenal at the Millennium Stadium.

The lad was ready to put his foot in, and although he's no giant, his physique looked strong enough to withstand the rigours of the English game. He passed the ball accurately, he wasn't afraid to take a few people on occasionally, he got himself about the field well, he supported his team-mates intelligently and he showed decent awareness.

But Eric's first campaign at Old Trafford was blighted by having to attend the African Nations Cup, which interrupted his momentum just as it was beginning to build, and then he went home to Africa because his mother was seriously ill, so effectively he hardly played for United. Certainly he never had the chance to settle so he could show what he could do.

Clearly season 2004/05 was going to be hugely important to his future at the club, a case of make or break. As it turned out, he couldn't carve a niche for himself and he ended up making a fresh start at Aston Villa, only to suffer injury soon after his transfer. I wish him better luck in the seasons ahead.

332. CRISTIANO RONALDO

OTHER HONOURS:
21 PORTUGAL CAPS 2003-.

OTHER CLUBS:
SPORTING LISBON, PORTUGAL, 02/03 (25, 3).

CRISTIANO RONALDO		
COMP.	APPS	GLS
LEAGUE	40 (22)	9
FAC	11 (1)	6
LC	3	0
EUROPE	10 (3)	0
TOTAL	64 (26)	15

BORN	FUNCHAL, MADEIRA 5TH FEBRUARY 1985
POSITION	UTILITY FORWARD
JOINED UNITED	AUGUST 2003 FROM SPORTING LISBON £12.24M
UNITED DEBUT	BOLTON WANDERERS (H) PREM. - 16/08/2003

HOT STUFF: it was a sweltering day in Cardiff, so Cristiano Ronaldo had an excuse for doffing his shirt after nodding United's opener in the 2004 FA Cup Final victory over Millwall.

Master Cristiano Ronaldo, beloved of my grandson James, who just adores all those twists and turns and stepovers. I share much of that enthusiasm, but I'm not going to weigh this extravagantly gifted young man down with unnecessarily lavish expectations at this early stage of his career.

When he came on for his debut in the last half-hour at home to Bolton on the first day of 2003/04, it was like watching a circus act. I just hope that's not how he finishes up.

He was overdoing the tricks at first, more like a show pony than a professional footballer, but he didn't know any different. I said at the time that when he gets a big, nasty full-back kicking him up the backside, he'll find out that there's easier, and more effective, ways to play the game.

Happily, by the end of his first English campaign, there were deeply encouraging signs that he was learning the lesson.

Manchester United, with all the razzmatazz attached to them, were not the easiest club for Ronaldo to join, particularly when they were not having the best of seasons, but by and large he has made satisfactory progress.

He has realised that the game is physical, and

he appears to have understood that his party pieces are worthwhile only if they take him past his marker, so he's improved as he's gone along.

Unquestionably he finished 2003/04 a far more dangerous player than he started it, culminating with a thrilling display against Millwall in the FA Cup Final which should certainly have earned him the man-of-the-match accolade. Why Sven-Goran Eriksson chose Ruud van Nistelrooy instead defies logic. Ronaldo's dribbling tends to get all the attention, and undoubtedly it can be destructive, but I'm encouraged also by his crossing. True, it leaves room for improvement, but it's impressive that he doesn't mind which foot he's using, which is extremely unusual in this day and age.

He's a tall lad, too, not bad in the air, but he doesn't punch his weight yet. He's what I'd call 6ft going on 5ft 9ins, but he nodded United in front against Millwall and he scored for Portugal with terrific headers against Greece and Holland in Euro 2004, so he's working on the right lines.

I hope sincerely that he will become a truly big player for Manchester United. They will expect no less, having paid a lot of dough for him. Of course, if you are going to take that sort of talent at 18 years old, then it doesn't come cheaply.

Does Cristiano Ronaldo excite me? I take a lot of exciting. I never get up off my seat. Let's just say I've got a pleasant feeling of anticipation . . .

BORN	URAI, BRAZIL 19TH JUNE 1979
POSITION	MIDFIELDER
JOINED UNITED	AUGUST 2003 FROM ATLETICO PARANAENSE £5.8M
UNITED DEBUT	WOLVERHAMPTON W (H) PREM. - 27/08/2003

JOSE PEREIRA KLEBERSON		
COMP.	APPS	GLS
LEAGUE	16 (4)	2
FAC	1	0
LC	4	0
EUROPE	3 (2)	0
TOTAL	24 (6)	2

333. JOSE PEREIRA KLEBERSON

OTHER HONOURS:
21 BRAZIL CAPS 2002-.

OTHER CLUBS:
NICHIKA, PSTC, BOTH BRAZIL;
ATLETICO PARANAENSE, BRAZIL, 99-03 (100, 12).

Kleberson is a Brazilian international with a World Cup winner's medal in his cabinet, but he made no impression on me either before or after his transfer to Manchester United.

I look at him, and his Brazilian team-mate Gilberto Silva at Arsenal, and they're light years apart. Gilberto does a grand job for Arsenal, steady and easy, whether as a defensive midfielder or farther forward. Edu's another Brazilian I prefer to Kleberson, who has done absolutely nothing for me and I don't think I'm on my own.

Of course, his life has undergone a dramatic change, settling in this country with a 17-year-old wife and a new child, but we come back to my overall misgivings about South Americans in English football. In general, I don't think the two go together.

It might have been seen as significant that, despite Kleberson being a World Cup winner, there was never any great competition to sign him. Leeds were in the hunt for a while, but that was it. It makes me wonder: had United watched him play a lot of games for his club, or was someone at the World Cup and thought he didn't do badly in a particular game?

Our league is particularly difficult to play in because it's physical, and Kleberson, who isn't a big lad, has not shown me that he can cope with it. I don't know what his best position would be, though I'd guess it would be central midfield. So far he's played all over the midfield, and just behind the striker, all to no great effect.

Kleberson was facing a huge second season in 2004/05, with everything to prove, and as that campaign drew to an end, it had become fairly evident that the world champion had found the Premiership a step too far. I can't see him ever being a success in our helter-skelter league.

334. DAVID BELLION

OTHER CLUBS:
CANNES, FRANCE; SUNDERLAND 01/02-02/03 (20, 1).

DAVID BELLION		
COMP.	APPS	GLS
LEAGUE	5 (19)	4
FAC	2 (1)	0
LC	5	2
EUROPE	2 (5)	2
OTHERS	1	0
TOTAL	15 (25)	8

BORN	SEVRES, FRANCE 27TH NOVEMBER 1982
POSITION	FORWARD
JOINED UNITED	JULY 2003 FROM SUNDERLAND - £2M+
UNITED DEBUT	WOLVERHAMPTON W (H) PREM. - 27/08/2003

David Bellion has speed to burn but he looks totally lacking in co-ordination and I can't find a redeeming feature about him, apart from his pace. He scored one decent goal in his first season at Old Trafford, cutting inside from the left and knocking it in with his right foot, but I would be less than astonished if that turned out to be an isolated highlight.

It's difficult to see what he could do for the team because he doesn't appear to have a footballing brain. It seems that he runs very fast in a random fashion, and though sheer pace is a priceless asset, it is not enough on its own. I hope I'm wrong, but I can't ever see the boy improving, whether he plays in a wide position or as a striker. I never like to be derogatory about footballers but I can't find anything positive to say about David Bellion.

BORN	HEMEL HEMPSTEAD, HERTS. 19TH NOVEMBER 1985
POSITION	MIDFIELDER
JOINED UNITED	JULY 2002 FROM JUNIOR FOOTBALL
UNITED DEBUT	LEEDS UNITED (A) LC - 28/10/2003

CHRIS EAGLES		
COMP.	APPS	GLS
FAC	1	0
LC	1 (4)	0
EUROPE	1 (1)	0
OTHERS	0 (1)	0
TOTAL	3 (6)	0

335. CHRIS EAGLES

OTHER CLUBS:
WATFORD ON LOAN 04/05 (13, 1);
SHEFFIELD WEDNESDAY ON LOAN 05/06-.

The word is that Chris Eagles can play. Everybody keeps on saying it, but when is it going to happen on a consistent basis, even at reserve level?

The boy was an ever-present and earned some rave reviews when United won the FA Youth Cup in 2002/03, then he showcased his skills briefly when he came on as a substitute at Leeds in the League Cup and caused a few problems. What Chris needs now is more senior opportunities, but will he get them? I am told he did well on loan at Watford in 2004/05, but there is an enormous chasm in class between the Premiership and the next level down.

BORN	CHESTER 20TH SEPTEMBER 1984
POSITION	FORWARD
JOINED UNITED	JULY 2001 FROM JUNIOR FOOTBALL
UNITED DEBUT	LEEDS UNITED (A) LC - 28/10/2003

EDDIE JOHNSON		
COMP.	APPS	GLS
LC	0 (1)	0
TOTAL	0 (1)	0

336. EDDIE JOHNSON

OTHER CLUBS:
ROYAL ANTWERP ON LOAN 03/04;
COVENTRY CITY ON LOAN 04/05 (26, 5);
CREWE ALEXANDRA ON LOAN 05/06.

During the course of compiling this book, I have complained often enough about people comparing kids with stars of the past, so I'm not going to go overboard about Eddie Johnson's similarity to the young Mark Hughes. But it's a fact that there is a resemblance: Eddie has the same solid build and, like the great Welshman, he uses his brain as well as his brawn. It surprised me that he was sent to Coventry on loan for 2004/05 because he had already had a spell away at Antwerp, and I just hope he receives the opportunity his talent deserves. Paddy Crerand, who has seen the boy play repeatedly and whose judgement I respect, advises us to watch this space.

337. PHIL BARDSLEY

PHIL BARDSLEY		
COMP.	APPS	GLS
FAC	0 (1)	0
LC	1	0
TOTAL	1 (1)	0

BORN	SALFORD 28TH JUNE 1985
POSITION	DEFENDER
JOINED UNITED	JULY 2001 FROM JUNIOR FOOTBALL
UNITED DEBUT	WBA (A) LC - 03/12/2003

Full-back Phil Bardsley made a favourable impression with his two cup outings during 2003/04, and probably he is due some chances on the bench at Premiership level. He appeared competent at all aspects of the game, and commendably level-headed, but given the competition for places at Old Trafford, it's difficult to see the boy getting the run he needs.

338. PAUL TIERNEY

OTHER CLUBS:
CREWE ALEXANDRA ON LOAN 02/03 (17, 1);
COLCHESTER UNITED ON LOAN 03/04 (2, 0).
BRADFORD CITY ON LOAN 04/05 (16, 0)
LIVINGSTON 05/06-.

PAUL TIERNEY		
COMP.	APPS	GLS
LC	1	0
TOTAL	1	0

BORN	SALFORD 15TH SEPTEMBER 1982
POSITION	DEFENDER
JOINED UNITED	JULY 1999 FROM JUNIOR FOOTBALL
UNITED DEBUT & FAREWELL	WBA (A) LC - 03/12/2003
LEFT UNITED FOR	LIVINGSTON - JUNE 2005

A local lad like Phil Bardsley, Paul Tierney looked like a tolerably efficient all-round defender but, having reached his twenties without breaking through, his chance had passed him by and he was freed. That's a sad situation for a young person striving to make his way, but in the brutal world of Premiership football, that's how it is.

339. LOUIS SAHA

OTHER HONOURS:
8 FRANCE CAPS 2004-.

OTHER CLUBS:
METZ, FRANCE, 97/8-99/00 (47, 5);
NEWCASTLE UNITED ON LOAN 98/9 (11, 1);
FULHAM 00/01-03/04 (117, 53).

LOUIS SAHA		
COMP.	APPS	GLS
LEAGUE	16 (10)	8
FAC	0 (2)	0
LC	4	1
EUROPE	1 (3)	0
TOTAL	21 (15)	9

BORN	PARIS 8TH AUGUST 1978
POSITION	FORWARD
JOINED UNITED	JANUARY 2004 FROM FULHAM - £12.8M
UNITED DEBUT	SOUTHAMPTON (H) PREM. - 31/01/2004

Considering the inevitably debilitating effects of his tediously drawn-out transfer saga, of the sort we cannot seem to avoid these days, Louis Saha did remarkably well to make such a positive immediate impact at Old Trafford.

The Frenchman, who became a full international soon after making the move, supplied a clutch of goals in short order, encouraging the thought that he and Ruud van Nistelrooy might form a partnership to strike fear into any opponent in

the years ahead.

Saha revealed touch and pace, and demonstrated that he was not bad in the air, probably better than van Nistelrooy in that department, while it became obvious that he shared with Ruud an obsession for scoring goals.

He was in his mid twenties, presumably on the threshold of his prime, and I thought he could be what United had needed for a considerable while – somebody to take some of the weight off the Dutchman's slim shoulders.

If forwards hold the ball in the attacking areas, then they're keeping the weight off their defence, offering the fellows at the back a much-needed breather, and the Saha-van Nistelrooy combination ought to have been eminently capable of that. Oh, and of scoring a few goals, too, of course.

Unfortunately injuries to both players meant that 2004/05 proved to be a non-event for the much-heralded combination. Ruud's problem lasted months rather than the anticipated weeks, and as for Louis, he seemed to pick up some sort of knock, pull or strain practically every time he took the field.

I had hoped that Sir Alex would give them a long-term opportunity to play as a pair, with Ryan Giggs and either Cristiano Ronaldo or Ole Gunnar Solskjaer – how I long to see the influential Norwegian return to full fitness – as suppliers in the wide berths. Certainly that would have provided the two front-men with plenty of ammunition. But now the landscape has been transformed by the arrival of Wayne Rooney and Alan Smith and, given the manager's cautious 5-4-1 formation of recent times, my original notion might be seen as tilting at windmills.

340. ALAN SMITH

15 ENGLAND CAPS 2001-.
OTHER CLUBS:
LEEDS UNITED 98/9-03/04 (172, 38).

Alan Smith		
COMP.	APPS	GLS
LEAGUE	22 (9)	6
FAC	0 (3)	0
LC	1 (1)	1
EUROPE	3 (2)	2
OTHERS	1	1
TOTAL	27 (15)	10

BORN	ROTHWELL, YORKSHIRE 28TH OCTOBER 1980
POSITION	FORWARD
JOINED UNITED	SUMMER 2004 FROM LEEDS UNITED - £7M
UNITED DEBUT	ARSENAL MILLENNIUM STADIUM CS - 8/08/2004

Alan Smith didn't have a bad first season for United, especially in the autumn when he was the outstanding performer in a side that was struggling to get out of the blocks, and it seemed for a while that he might pose Sir Alex a few long-term selection headaches.

But my hand-on-heart verdict at the end of his introductory Old Trafford campaign, admittedly one in which his impetus was slowed by an injury in January, is that he's not good enough to be a first-choice striker for Manchester United.

Of course, his work-rate and his devotion to fighting for the cause are superb, and all that honest endeavour carries him a long way – but not quite far enough for me. The simple nub of the matter is that he doesn't score enough goals; he didn't for Leeds and he hasn't for United.

In fairness, when Alan was at Elland Road, I was never sure what the management wanted from him. Did they see him as a spearhead – he was always excellent in the air for his size – or did they want him play off a centre-forward? Was he expected to fill wide positions, or drop deep into midfield? He seemed to fit in with whatever was required at the time, and that was to his credit. So was the way he settled in after moving to Manchester, proving responsive to his new team-mates and impressing everyone with his raw desire to play. That eagerness to be on the pitch, in the heat of the battle, is his greatest strength, and if he wasn't a professional footballer then I have no doubt he'd be throwing his all into turning out for a Sunday morning team.

I've heard some fanciful notions about the boy. One is that, because of his fighting qualities, he could be the long-term replacement for Roy Keane. No way. To hold things together in the centre of the park, it's not enough to be hard and willing. You need the incisive, imaginative brain of an old-fashioned inside-forward – you might call it nous – and I haven't seen that in Alan.

Another theory runs that he is reminiscent of Mark Hughes, but he's a million miles behind Sparky. Alan might have the same ruggedness, but Hughes was a supreme all-round player, while the lad from Leeds is merely a good one. That's the difference.

For all that, I don't want to be misinterpreted: Alan Smith is not a bad footballer and he has not been a bad buy. He cost £7 million, and if you compare that fee with, for example, Veron's £28 million, then he looks a bargain! For the future, if United are thinking of having him on the bench and bringing him on to graft, up front or in midfield in the event of an injury, then I'd say he's a fine addition to the squad; indeed, on the evidence of 20004/05 he might do a better job as a substitute than, say, Saha, who cost half as much again.

In the past Alan had a problem with his temperament, and at a club like United it's no good if players are going to lose

> *'Eagerness to be on the pitch, in the heat of the battle, is his greatest strength, and if he wasn't a professional footballer then I have no doubt he'd be throwing his all into turning out for a Sunday morning team.'*

appearances through suspensions. But happily he has worked hard to improve in that respect; the penny has dropped.

He is a lovely character, popular with the other players, and I think he likes being at Manchester United. I know he's ambitious, but as long as he remains in the first-team pool, I wouldn't be surprised if he remains happy at the club. I hope he does.

BORN	ARLINGTON HEIGHTS, CHICAGO, USA 1ST MARCH 1986
POSITION	DEFENDER
JOINED UNITED	SEPTEMBER 2003 FROM CHICAGO SOCKERS
UNITED DEBUT	ARSENAL MILLENNIUM STADIUM CS - 8/08/2004

JONATHAN SPECTOR		
COMP.	APPS	GLS
LEAGUE	2 (1)	0
FAC	1	0
LC	0 (1)	0
EUROPE	1 (1)	0
OTHERS	0 (1)	0
TOTAL	4 (4)	0

341. JONATHAN SPECTOR

OTHER CLUBS:
CHICAGO SOCKERS, USA.

I feel a bit frustrated on behalf of Jonathan Spector because he impressed me when given his senior breakthrough at the start of 2004/05, and I thought he deserved another chance before the end of the season. Essentially he's a right-sided central defender and it spoke volumes for his assurance and composure that he looked so comfortable out of position at left-back.

Of course, it hasn't been easy for the young American to become established in that role because Gabriel Heinze came in and excelled, John O'Shea is on the scene, and even Quinton Fortune has been deployed at left-back, though if Fortune is a better defender than Spector then I can plait sawdust.

Jonathan took my eye on his debut at Ewood Park. He's quick, he plays the game simply, he's neat on the ball, he's decent in the air, he doesn't flap and he's got an even temperament. An old head on young shoulders, you might say.

I just hope such a promising performer isn't allowed to vanish into oblivion. If he's given sufficient opportunity, I can see him pushing the Nevilles or O'Shea for the right-back berth, and it would be instructive to see him have a run-out in the centre of defence. Whatever, he's a welcome increase to United's options at the back. Perhaps it's just his curly hair, but he reminds me of Jimmy Nicholl – and if he does as well as Jimmy then I don't think anybody would be too disappointed.

342. LIAM MILLER

OTHER HONOURS:
9 REPUBLIC OF IRELAND CAPS 2004-.

OTHERS CLUBS:
CELTIC 99/00-03/04 (26, 2);
AARHUS, DENMARK, ON LOAN 01/02.

LIAM MILLER		
COMP.	APPS	GLS
LEAGUE	3 (5)	0
FAC	2 (2)	0
LC	2	1
EUROPE	3 (2)	0
TOTAL	10 (9)	1

BORN	CORK, ROI 13TH FEBRUARY 1981
POSITION	MIDFIELDER
JOINED UNITED	JULY 2004 FROM CELTIC
UNITED DEBUT	DINAMO BUCHAREST (A) EC - 11/08/2004

Liam Miller has been an enormous disappointment to me since his arrival at Old Trafford from Celtic Park. He had been talked up massively as a top new midfield talent and, in his first season in England, he has appeared unremarkable in every way.

Sure, he's neat and tidy enough on the ball when he's got the time, but unfortunately for him, time is a luxury not afforded to Premiership players. On his showings so far, I wonder whether he is quick enough, either mentally or physically, for the game south of the border. In fairness to him, although he had made something of an impact as a Republic of Ireland international, he had only a handful of appearances in Scottish football under his belt, and stepping up to join Manchester United must have seemed like a quantum leap.

I hope he settles down, and that what appears to be a lack of pace shows itself to be nothing more than a struggle to come to terms with the higher standard. Can he win that struggle and make the grade at Old Trafford? I have grave doubts.

343. GABRIEL HEINZE

OTHER HONOURS:
20 ARGENTINA CAPS.

OTHER CLUBS:
NEWELL'S OLD BOYS, ARGENTINA, 96/7;
VALLADOLID, SPAIN, 97/8 AND 99/00-00/01;
SPORTING LISBON, PORTUGAL, 98/9;
PARIS ST GERMAIN, FRANCE, 01/02-03/04.

GABRIEL HEINZE		
COMP.	APPS	GLS
LEAGUE	26	1
FAC	4	0
LC	2	0
EUROPE	7	0
TOTAL	39	1

BORN	CRESPO, ARGENTINA 19TH APRIL 1978
POSITION	LEFT-BACK
JOINED UNITED	JUNE 2004 FROM PARIS ST. GERMAIN - £6.9M
UNITED DEBUT	BOLTON WANDERERS (H) PREM. - 11/09/2004

Gabriel Heinze has been a breath of fresh air since his much-delayed arrival at Old Trafford, and he has proved a welcome exception to my strongly-held view that South Americans rarely do the business in the English game. Of course, he didn't come directly from his native Argentina but from Paris St Germain, and he had extensive experience of top European football, which probably made a world of difference.

After it was announced that United had signed Gabriel, it was evident that he would miss the start of our season because of the Copa America, and the situation worsened when he re-

WORTH WAITING FOR: Gabriel Heinze stopped off in Athens to pick up an Olympic gold medal with Argentina, after which he made a magnificent start to his Manchester United career.

vealed his intention of playing in the Olympic Games. There were those at Old Trafford who were livid, but it wasn't the player's fault. People don't often get the opportunity to represent their country in the Olympics, and if that was seen as a problem then the right questions should have been asked before the transfer. Moaning afterwards just made United look inadequate.

Happily, when Heinze finally got here, it was obvious straight away that it had been worth the wait. Appearing totally unfazed by all the furore which surrounds the Premiership, he scored on his debut against Bolton and, more importantly, settled in as a battle-hardened defender of the highest order.

I'm delighted to say that Gabriel is no fancy dan. He's strong and fast, he puts his foot in ferociously, he's competitive in the air, and he can play football. With his toughness, extreme left-sidedness and unquenchable enthusiasm he reminds me of Stuart Pearce. True, he plunges into the occasional rash tackle but if he makes a mistake then invariably he is quick enough to recover from it, and the United rearguard looks a lot more secure with him in it. Gabriel plays the game with a smile on his face, which is refreshing these days, and that's just another reason why the fans love him.

What amazes me about him, though, is that he is only 27 and yet already he's been based in five major footballing nations – Argentina, Spain, Portugal, France and now England. Is that because clubs keep on making money out of his transfers, or has he got serially itchy feet? I hope for United's sake that it's the former rather than the latter.

BORN	Croxteth, Liverpool 24th October 1985
POSITION	Forward
JOINED UNITED	September 2004 from Everton - £27m
UNITED DEBUT	Fenerbahce (H) EC - 28/09/2004

WAYNE ROONEY		
COMP.	APPS	GLS
LEAGUE	24 (5)	11
FAC	6	3
LC	1 (1)	0
EUROPE	6	3
TOTAL	37 (6)	17

344. WAYNE ROONEY

OTHER HONOURS:
23 England caps 2003-.

OTHER CLUBS:
Everton 02/03-03/04 (67, 15).

On the strength of his pure, utterly ravishing ability on a football field, Wayne Rooney has every opportunity in the world to become as big a player as Manchester United have ever had. When you glance at the roll-call of superlative performers to have graced Old Trafford before him, then you get some idea of my regard for the talent with which this unusual young man has been blessed.

The game suits Wayne. He's only a kid, but he's built like a man and he plays like one. He revels in the thrill of it all, he relishes the battle, there is no fear of any opposition. He loves scoring goals, his awareness is acute and there seems nothing he can't do.

Though he has his bad days, like every other footballer in history, he excels in game after game. He's one of those individuals who wants to seize control of every contest he finds himself in. Everything about him proclaims that he is in his element, the right lad in the right place at the right time.

Unwise though it might prove to be – and certainly I could never imagine myself doing this until Rooney came along – people will talk of him in the same breath as Duncan Edwards. He's mountainously built like Duncan was; he uses his body power like Duncan did; he's got the same instinct for playing, for tackling, for passing, for shooting, that Duncan had. Of course, he's got a long way to go to be another Edwards, but he's unquestionably world-class while still in his teens, so you never know.

He cost £27 million as an 18-year-old, which is staggering, but I think United were right to push the boat out for him. If you aspire to be the biggest club in the world, how can you let someone else buy the best English player available, the best young player in the country, potentially the best of all anywhere in the world.

Wayne was overwhelmingly impressive for England during Euro 2004 – they might have gone a lot further in the tournament had he not been injured – and then returned home to be faced with endless fuss over his transfer. He appeared to be unbothered by it all and enjoyed a terrific first season at United, scoring some truly sensational goals in the process.

Up to this point he has been a miracle man, and I think he could continue as a miracle man throughout most of his career. I don't think his type of talent will burn out; rather I believe it will last and he will improve, mind-boggling though that seems. People might laugh and say: 'How can he get bet-

'He's one of those individuals who wants to seize control of every contest he finds himself in. Everything about him proclaims that he is in his element, the right lad in the right place at the right time.'

ter?' But he can. For instance, he can learn to play the game more simply. Two or three years down the line he will realise that he can run ten yards and pass the ball 20, instead of running 25 and passing it five.

Then there is the question of his temperament. He's been in a few scrapes, though I wouldn't have thought he was any more of a rascal or a tearaway than Roy Keane was a decade or so ago, and the Irishman has settled down, in many ways, at least. I trust that Wayne recognises the infinite scale of his opportunity with Manchester United. He can become a multimillionaire and a national hero, all for taking part in a game which he loves so much that he would play it for nothing, on street corners with his mates, if he hadn't been born with such a golden gift.

And here's another thought. I have a sneaking feeling, and I did mention this to the manager, that one day, in the fullness of time, Wayne might conceivably be the right man to replace Keane in central midfield. He gets up and down like Roy used to, he puts his foot in like Roy used to, he's good in the air like Roy is, and he's a better finisher than Roy ever was. There will be those who say you can't afford to play him in midfield because he's needed up front, but I'm not sure about that. In 2004/05 he spent much of his time in a variety of positions – wide left, wide right, all over the place – and I think he can answer any question asked of him.

What the boy's got cannot be bought. God either gives it to you or he doesn't. If he does then you finish up as Wayne Rooney; if he doesn't then you finish up more like Mickey Rooney. God speed, son.

345. GERARD PIQUE

OTHER CLUBS:
BARCELONA.

BORN	BARCELONA 2ND FEBRUARY 1987
POSITION	DEFENDER
JOINED UNITED	SUMMER 2004 FROM BARCELONA
UNITED DEBUT	CREWE ALEXANDRA (A) LC - 26/10/2004

GERARD PIQUE		
COMP.	APPS	GLS
FAC	1	0
LC	0 (1)	0
EUROPE	0 (1)	0
TOTAL	1 (2)	0

When United signed centre-half Gerard Pique as a 17-year-old from Barcelona, the Catalans appeared to be hugely upset by his exit, which confirms my own impression that the youngster is an exceedingly promising prospect with a genuine chance of making the Premiership grade.

At this early stage of his development he appears to have all the requisites of a classy central defender. First and foremost, he is determined to win the ball, showing both bravery and a sharp sense of anticipation when he makes his tackles, and he's a tall lad who makes his height count in aerial combat. When he earns possession he can play, and it comes as no surprise to learn that Arsenal were also monitoring his progress before he left the Nou Camp. Definitely one to watch.

346. SYLVAN EBANKS-BLAKE

SYLVAN EBANKS-BLAKE		
COMP.	APPS	GLS
LC	0 (1)	0
TOTAL	0 (1)	0

BORN	CAMBRIDGE 29TH MARCH 1986
POSITION	FORWARD
JOINED UNITED	JULY 2002 FROM JUNIOR FOOTBALL
UNITED DEBUT	CREWE ALEXANDRA (A) LC - 26/10/2004

Those who coach Sylvan Ebanks-Blake speak in glowing terms of a powerful front-runner who is pacy, willing to work and eager to learn. The snag is that, as I write, the lad is 19 years old, the same age as a certain Wayne Rooney, and what with all the rest of the strikers in United's senior squad, I wonder how on earth he's going to find an opening. He's got a hell of a task on his hands if he's going to make a lasting impact.

347. GIUSEPPE ROSSI

OTHER CLUBS:
PARMA.

GIUSEPPE ROSSI		
COMP.	APPS	GLS
LC	0 (2)	0
TOTAL	0 (2)	0

BORN	CLIFTON, NEW JERSEY 1ST FEBRUARY 1987
POSITION	FORWARD
JOINED UNITED	JULY 2004 FROM PARMA, ITALY
UNITED DEBUT	CRYSTAL PALACE (H) LC - 10/11/2004

Italian under-19 international striker Giuseppe Rossi is no more than a slip of a lad, but he's oozing with natural ability. He's got quick feet, he's aware of passing options and he appears a natural to play alongside a more direct front-man. Thus, after arriving from Parma with something of a fanfare and settling quickly, he linked up effectively with Sylvan Ebanks-Blake in the reserves. But if he's going to make meaningful improvement he needs to play with top team-mates against top opponents – so who's going to step aside for Giuseppe?

I understand that clubs have got to be looking eternally for gifted kids, in the hope of finding another Rooney without spending £27 million. But with the greatest of respect to the likes of Rossi, I've been hearing stories about United signing wonder-boys for five years now, and I haven't seen one come through yet.

BORN	SOUTHPORT 4TH NOVEMBER 1984
POSITION	MIDFIELDER
JOINED UNITED	JULY 2001 FROM JUNIOR FOOTBALL
UNITED DEBUT	ARSENAL (H) LC - 1/12/2004

DAVID JONES		
COMP.	APPS	GLS
FAC	1	0
LC	0 (1)	0
TOTAL	1 (1)	0

348. DAVID JONES

I do like David Jones. I've only seen a little bit of the rookie midfielder, but he looks a player in the making. He's accomplished on the ball, he's not afraid to stick his foot in where it hurts and his passing has got a dash of imagination about it.

But David is yet another of United's little gang of League Cup men. When is he going to play in the Premiership, so we can really find out what he's made of? He desperately needs a chance to prove himself at the top level, to show he can perform alongside men while still a boy himself, if he's ever going to climb the mountain with Manchester United.

STOP PRESS

EDWIN VAN DER SAR

BORN	VOORHOUT, HOLLAND 29TH OCTOBER 1970
POSITION	GOALKEEPER
JOINED UNITED	JUNE 2005 FROM FULHAM - £2M

OTHER HONOURS:
100 HOLLAND CAPS 1995-.

OTHER CLUBS:
AJAX 90/1-97/8 (192, 1);
JUVENTUS 98/9-00/01 (100, 0);
FULHAM 01/02-04/05 (27, 0).

Edwin van der Sar was United's intended replacement for Peter Schmeichel back in 1999, but he joined Juventus instead. Since then he has racked up his century of international caps and, over the seasons, he has been an admirably competent performer.

Still, I'm surprised that the club should buy him in 2005, when he was not too far away from his 35th birthday. Certainly you wouldn't be anxious to fork out £2 million for an outfielder of that age, and even though goalkeepers are in a different category, it seems a lot of money.

I just hope he will fit the bill. Whatever else, he needs to do better than recent signings in that position.

PARK JI-SUNG

OTHER HONOURS:
38 SOUTH KOREA CAPS

OTHER CLUBS:
KYOTO PURPLE SANGA, JAPAN 2002-03;
PSV EINDHOVEN 03/04-04/05.

BORN	SOUTH KOREA 25TH FEBRUARY 1981
POSITION	MIDFIELDER
JOINED UNITED	JUNE 2005 FROM PSV EINDHOVEN - £4M

Park, who was had just received his work-permit as the book went to press, comes with a decent track record, having helped South Korea reach the semi-finals of the 2002 World Cup and aided PSV's progress to the last four of the Champions League three years later. At 24, he's a good age, and he's highly energetic so the Premiership should suit him. Let's hope it does.

ADDENDA - AUGUST 2005

Nicky Butt - loaned from Newcastle Utd to Birmingham City
Phillip Neville - sold to Everton for £3.5m
Phil Mulryne - moved from Norwich City to Cardiff City
Keith Gillespie - moved from Leicester City to Sheffield Utd
David Jones - loaned to Preston NE
Luke Chadwick - loaned from West Ham Utd to Stoke City
Jose Kleberson - sold to Besiktas for £2.5m

MANAGERS

MATT BUSBY

ALSO MANAGED:
SCOTLAND

UNITED CAREER:
TEAM MANAGER 1945–1969,
GENERAL MANAGER 1969–1971,
DIRECTOR 1971–1982,
PRESIDENT 1980–1994

			MATT BUSBY			
COMP.	P	W	D	L	F	A
LEAGUE	972	480	231	261	1942	1361
FAC	100	58	20	22	215	118
LC	4	1	1	2	7	9
EUROPE	56	34	11	11	142	61
OTHERS	9	3	3	3	18	17
TOTAL	1141	576	266	299	2324	1566

BORN	ORBISTON, LANARKSHIRE 26TH MAY 1909
DIED	MANCHESTER 20TH JANUARY 1994
JOINED UNITED	OCTOBER 1945
FIRST GAME IN CHARGE	ACCRINGTON STANLEY (A) FAC - 05/01/1946
UNITED HONOURS	EUROPEAN CUP 1967/8 LEAGUE CHAMPIONS 1951/2, 1955/6. 1956/7, 1964/5, 1966/7 FA CUP 1947/8, 1962/3 CHARITY SHIELD 1952, 1956, 1957, 1965 (SHARED), 1967 (SHARED)
LAST GAME IN CHARGE	MANCHESTER CITY (A) DIV. 1 - 05/05/1971

I first met Matt Busby in 1949, which seems a long, long time ago now, but he is one man whom it is impossible to forget. He had a certain presence about him which I have never encountered in anyone else, an aura of quiet dignity and authority, and he always seemed to be in command of every situation.

Always immaculately dressed, invariably with his pipe in his mouth, he would dominate every room he entered, without apparent effort. I could never get over the way he remembered everybody's name, even the most casual of acquaintances, which typified his phenomenal attention to detail.

Yet for all that, Matt was never a great tactician, didn't talk deeply about the game, didn't tell us how to play. I think he took the view that we were Manchester United footballers, so we should know what to do.

This is borne out by the experience of Noel Cantwell, whom I met for a beer shortly after he arrived at Old Trafford from West Ham in 1960. Noel, an inveterate thinker about football, was plainly puzzled.

'John', he said, 'I don't know what to make of the Boss. Before a game he doesn't give us any instructions, just wishes us all the best, tells us to keep playing our football and to enjoy ourselves.'

I wasn't surprised, and replied: 'I suppose at West Ham you had people telling you what to do, how to play, how to cope with every situation', and he admitted that was the case. I reminded him that he had joined Manchester United, and the

'What a marvellous combination – a pipe-smoking Scot with the air of a nobleman and a cigarette-gasping Welsh dragon who would have your guts for garters. As for Bert [Whalley], the third member of the triumvirate, he was a lay preacher and one of the nicest fellows to walk God's earth.'

Boss's credo was that if he had to tell his players how to play, then he wouldn't have signed them in the first place. Noel couldn't believe that I was serious, but I was. Matt Busby's attitude to the game was so simple it was frightening.

But it's impossible to consider Matt and Jimmy Murphy in isolation, because they were one unit; two wonderful men, each with an enormous talent which complemented the other's perfectly, and with total respect for each other. Basically Matt looked after the first team, while Jimmy and the coach, Bert Whalley, looked after everything else.

When I was a teenager at United, Matt and Jimmy still played in the Tuesday morning practice games. They didn't have any pace, but Murphy could still kick you and Busby could still pass a ball. They built up a football club based on the ability to trap the ball and pass the ball.

They didn't want ale-house football, they wanted people who could play, especially in the midfield and up front, but also at the back. For instance, the two full-backs in the great post-war team were Johnny Carey and John Aston, both former inside-forwards.

Matt always came over as calm and gentle while Jimmy, whose job was to teach the kids, was fearsomely aggressive when he had to be. What a marvellous combination – a pipe-smoking Scot with the air of a nobleman and a cigarette-gasping Welsh dragon who would have your guts for garters. As for Bert, the third member of the triumvirate, he was a lay preacher and one of the nicest fellows to walk God's earth.

For all his apparent serenity, Matt was never a soft touch. Behind that ostensibly gentle exterior was a former miner, who had been brought up in a hard school and been introduced to family responsibility at an early age after his father had been killed by a sniper at Arras in the First World War.

He had seen people die in the pits, he had encountered genuine hardship and he understood that football was a privileged way to earn a living. As a result he made absolutely sure that the youngsters in his charge realised exactly how lucky they were.

So Matt Busby was a strong man, a hard man at need, because he'd had to be in his early life, and he had to be again as manager of Manchester United. I have never known a weakling be successful in any field, and he was no exception.

But was he fair? I would consider that I'd insulted him if I said he wasn't. I don't think he ever set out to be unjust, though I'm sure he must have been at times. You can't manage a football club for a quarter of a century, and have all those players go through your hands, without being unfair to somebody.

Certainly he had his differences with a lot of footballers

down the years and not once, to my knowledge, did he come out second best.

Matt and Jimmy had met in Italy towards the end of the war. The Boss happened to hear his future lieutenant working with a bunch of players, and was impressed by the sense he talked and the passion with which he put his views across.

So when Matt was asked to take over the destiny of Manchester United, a club which had not won a top honour for decades, he made Jimmy his first signing, and he never made a more inspired move.

Some critics say they had a ready-made side at Old Trafford, but they think differently to me. Go through the 1948 FA Cup winners: Jack Crompton was just stepping up from Goslings, the junior side; John Carey was an inside-forward, so was John Aston; John Anderson was a junior, Allenby Chilton had made one appearance pre-war, Henry Cockburn was another from Goslings; Jimmy Delaney was signed from Celtic, Johnny Morris had played no more than a handful of games during the war, and Charlie Mitten was another junior.

Only Jack Rowley and Stan Pearson could be called pre-war players, so where was this ready-made team? Okay, they were all on the books apart from Delaney, but they had to be moulded, and other clubs were in the same situation.

We talk now about the incredible intake of Scholes, Giggs, the Nevilles and company, but it was Busby and Murphy who blazed the trail for that policy at the club. For example, of the youth side I played in, every one of us made it to the first team, which is a staggering rate of success.

United's refreshing approach is exemplified by the experiences of Dennis Viollet and myself, both Manchester City supporters when we were boys, and therefore both disposed to look favourably towards Maine Road. But Billy Walsh, a former City player and my coach at college, told me: 'They're not interested in kids at City. Don't sign for them.' Then the United scout Louis Rocca got in touch and I went to see Jimmy Murphy, who said: 'We'll make you a player, son.'

Meanwhile Dennis had been told by

no less than the City manager, Les McDowall, that his club didn't mess about with kids. Despite the overwhelming logic that the future lay in youth, clubs just didn't bother with it in those days.

So Matt and Jimmy were carrying out a revolution, although it should be remembered that Major Frank Buckley had attempted something similar at Wolverhampton. What Matt took from that I don't know, but he knew that he didn't have unlimited funds and that if United were ever going to be a great club, then they would have to produce their own players. I think he followed it through rather well!

No one should begin to under-estimate the scale of what Matt Busby went though at Munich, or his achievement in building three fabulous teams. First came the 48-ers, who had to be broken up because of their age, and then the Babes, who were decimated by an accident which would have been enough to stifle the ambition out of anybody.

But, helped immeasurably by Jimmy, he found the will to carry on and put together yet another lovely side in the 1960s, winning plenty more and climaxing with the ultimate, the European Cup in 1968.

Like a lot of others, I had my differences with Matt Busby, and maybe I could have strangled him on occasions. But in the final analysis, he was a great man, and I loved him dearly.

THE MASTER'S VOICE: Matt Busby didn't say an awful lot about tactics, but when he did make a point then his players tended to listen. All ears, left to right, are Henry Cockburn, John Carey, Johnny Morris and Charlie Mitten, four members of Matt's first breathtakingly beautiful Manchester United team.

JIMMY MURPHY

ALSO MANAGED:

WALES

UNITED CAREER:

COACH 1945–1955,
ASSISTANT MANAGER 1955–1971,
ACTING MANAGER FEBRUARY – AUGUST 1958.

BORN	TON PENTRE, WALES AUGUST 1908	
DIED	MANCHESTER 15TH NOVEMBER 1989	
JOINED UNITED	OCTOBER 1945	
FIRST GAME IN CHARGE	SHEFFIELD WED. (H) FAC - 19/02/1958	
LAST GAME IN CHARGE	AC MILAN (A) EC - 14/05/1958	

JIMMY MURPHY						
COMP.	P	W	D	L	F	A
LEAGUE	14	1	5	8	12	28
FAC	6	3	2	1	13	9
EUROPE	2	1	0	1	2	5
TOTAL	22	5	7	10	27	42

When we were kids, it was Jimmy Murphy who kicked us into shape. If you were in a practice match at The Cliff and you came into contact with Jimmy, there was more chance of him kicking you than anything else.

I'm sure there must have been players whom he told to put their foot in on one or two opponents, but he never said that to me because that wasn't my style. I'm sure he never asked Bobby Charlton, either.

You couldn't put a price on what Jimmy did for United. Matt was the first-team supremo, the personality, the one who was always interviewed. Jimmy was always the quiet assassin in the background, picking up the pieces, shooting 'em down, building 'em up, teaching the lads how the game should be played.

The media thought it was revolutionary when they found out that the Brazilians played shadow football, but when I was a kid at Old Trafford we were playing it when nobody else knew what it was.

We would strip and change into full kit, then play against nobody, always passing and moving, getting it back and laying it off and moving again. We always had to end with a shot on goal and then we'd start again.

When anyone asked why we did it – and plenty did – Jimmy would explain that if we passed and moved enough it would become second nature, we'd all know where our mates were going to be without thinking. Today the coaches would probably scoff, but nobody could laugh at it then. We had only to point to our record. Certainly we players took it seriously; we had no choice or we were in big trouble.

I suppose there were similarities to Jock Stein's Celtic, to whom League matches were like practice matches as they piled up title after title. But when they met top teams in Europe, they carried on in the same vein and won the European Cup before any other British side.

Here's another example of the Murphy method. We'd won a reserve game 9-0 at Blackpool and, though self-praise is no recommendation at all, I have to say that I was brilliant that day. Having played on the Wednesday I thought we were having a day off on Thursday, but as I was getting off the coach in Manchester to get the bus home – what a contrast to modern

'It would be impossible for me to overstate the influence of Jimmy Murphy on the Busby Babes. If any of us had a problem as a young lad, it would be Jimmy we went to. He was always approachable – he might give you a good bollocking, but you could talk to him about anything.'

conditions – Jimmy told me to be in at 9.30 am the next day.

So I duly went in, was told to train as normal and then to report to him before going home. I did so, and was told to get some lunch, then return at two o'clock. After that I was told by the trainer, dear old Tom Curry, to change into full strip and eventually I met Jimmy on the pitch.

He had me on the edge of the box, passing balls out to both wings, then chasing to get them, and I still didn't have a clue what was going on. Neither did George Follows, a journalist with the old *Daily Herald*, who asked what was happening. Was I in trouble?

Jimmy's reply was that I had been magnificent against Blackpool, but late in the game I'd had the chance of an easy pass to the wing-half, yet I had hit a glory-ball to the outside-left. 'I'll f****** teach him never to do that again,' he told the astonished George. There's no way a coach could do that today. No modern player would take it. But it was a different time and a different world. We loved the game, loved Old Trafford, loved everything about our lives, and whatever Jimmy said was good enough for any of us.

Despite what he put me through that afternoon, I always had a terrific personal relationship with the man, and my regard for him had not lessened later, when I had been invalided

THE TEAM BEHIND THE TEAM: Matt Busby and Jimmy Murphy confer during the 1958 FA Cup Final.

out of the game and he was offered the chance to manage Arsenal. He asked me if I would go with him as his number-two, which was a tremendous compliment, but in the end nothing happened because he could not bring himself to be disloyal to Matt.

The approach from Highbury offered telling evidence of his stature in the game, as did overtures from Juventus and the Brazilian national team. Each time, though, his answer was the same. He could have made a fortune but his heart was at Old Trafford.

It would be impossible for me to overstate the influence of Jimmy Murphy on the Busby Babes. If any of us had a problem as a young lad, it would be Jimmy we went to. He was always approachable – he might give you a good bollocking, but you could talk to him about anything. Murphy's theory was that some players needed cuddling, some needed the hard word. He was prepared to administer both, depending on who it was, using his judgement of character, which was impeccable.

An example of Jimmy's clever psychology was his treatment of Albert Scanlon after our left-winger had endured a nightmare first half at Preston. At half-time Jimmy said: 'Well played, Albert,' and when I caught him on his own I asked him what the hell he was talking about. But in the second half, Albert was a different player, suddenly full of confidence, and it came home to me that Jimmy had handled him perfectly. People have got different temperaments and all play a different way, so you can't treat them all the same.

Jimmy Murphy was ahead of his time in so many ways, and he goes down as one of the key architects of the massive worldwide institution that Manchester United were destined to become.

Three others played crucially important behind-the-scenes roles at Old Trafford while I was growing up there. I have already mentioned coach Bert Whalley, as he played for the club on either side of the Second World War, and all I'll add here is that I'll hold him forever in the highest esteem and affection.

Then there were the two trainers, Tom Curry, who was responsible for the first team, and Bill Inglis, who saw to the reserves. They were both wonderful characters, kind and wise men who loved football and who were brilliant with the kids, always available to help us, always on our side.

As a wing-half in the outstanding Newcastle side of the 1920s, Tom had been good enough to appear for the Football League, and knew the game inside out.

A pipe-smoking, church-going Geordie, he wasn't a drinker and lived to a very orderly routine, to the extent that he always knew what he was going to have for tea on any given night.

Bill, a former full-back with United, offered a marked contrast, being a pint-drinking Scot who could seem quite intimidating at first meeting, as I discovered after playing for Manchester Boys against Hebburn Boys at Old Trafford before I had joined the club.

He was working with our team that day, and before the match I went to him with stomach ache. He asked me what I'd had for breakfast and I told him I'd had a bowl of porridge.

Bill's response was colourful: 'Porridge? Before you play football? F****** hell, you've got no chance!' A little later I started at United and when I walked in he asked where we had met before. I mentioned the porridge incident and he retorted: 'F****** hell, don't tell me they've signed you!' But all the bluster covered a heart of gold. We became great friends afterwards and I treasure my memories of him.

Tom and Bill were a fantastic pair, as different to one another as famous comedians of the day Jimmy Jewell and Ben Warriss, but both with the good of the lads at heart. They stood no nonsense but they'd never let us down, covering up if we came in late for training or hadn't performed some routine duty. They would always put themselves out for us, see that everything was in our favour.

I don't believe there are any like Tom Curry and Bill Inglis knocking about in today's game. It's all young professionals, looking to make names for themselves. I can't blame them because the world has moved on, but I can't believe the scene is not poorer for the lack of such lovely men as our two trainers.

I considered myself one of the luckiest people in the world to do a job with bosses such as Matt Busby, Jimmy Murphy, Bert Whalley, Tom Curry and Bill Inglis. Our wage-packets were immeasurably lighter than those of our modern counterparts, but I can't believe their lives are half as rich as ours.

TWO LOVELY CHARACTERS:
United trainers Bill Inglis
(left) and Tom Curry.
I consider myself privileged to
have worked alongside such
men.

WILF McGUINNESS

UNITED MANAGERIAL CAREER:

CHIEF COACH APRIL 1969 – JUNE 1970,
MANAGER JUNE 1970 – DECEMBER 1970

LATER MANAGED:

ARIS SALONIKA, PANARAKI PATRAS, YORK CITY, BURY (CARETAKER)

BORN	MANCHESTER 25TH OCTOBER 1937
JOINED UNITED (AS PLAYER)	JANUARY 1953
FIRST GAME IN CHARGE	CRYSTAL PALACE (A) DIV. 1 - 09/08/1969
LAST GAME IN CHARGE	DERBY COUNTY (A) DIV. 1 - 26/12/1970

WILF McGUINNESS						
COMP.	P	W	D	L	F	A
LEAGUE	64	19	25	20	90	95
FAC	8	4	3	1	15	5
LC	14	8	4	2	20	11
TOTAL	86	31	32	23	125	111

I don't think it would be overstating the case to say the football world was stunned when 31-year-old Wilf McGuinness was asked to follow in the footsteps of Sir Matt Busby in the spring of 1969.

He had been a player at Old Trafford back in the 1950s, after which he had coached at the club and been a part of Alf Ramsey's England set-up, but there was no obvious qualification for the mammoth task with which he was entrusted.

Some might have thought he was a lucky fellow, and it's true that he was handed an opportunity which many an experienced manager would have given the moon and the stars to receive, but the odds were always stacked against him.

Wilf's biggest problem was that he had to take charge of his own contemporaries, some of whom he had grown up alongside, and that proved immensely difficult.

He found himself issuing orders to three of the greatest players in the world – Bobby Charlton, Denis Law and George Best – and they wouldn't have been human if they hadn't wondered if he was the right man for such an onerous responsibility.

It should be remembered, too, that the side Wilf inherited, though not short of talent, was fundamentally over the hill. It was never going to produce the required results unless there was

'It should be remembered that the side Wilf inherited, though not short of talent, was fundamentally over the hill. It was never going to produce the required results unless there was a significant intrduction of top players, and obviously the new man wasn't afforded that luxury.'

a significant introduction of top players, and obviously the new man wasn't afforded that luxury.

It can't have been easy, either, with the immeasurably powerful presence of Sir Matt looming over his shoulder – influencing the big decisions, doubtlessly still making some of them himself – but that was a part of the arrangement over which he had no control.

Still, Wilf was a brash individual with no shortage of belief in his own ability and a glance at the record books will reveal that Manchester United did not exactly fall out of the sky during his 18 months in office.

In fact, his achievement of leading them to three major semi-finals would have been hailed as success by many clubs but the bar is rather higher at Old Trafford, as others were soon to discover to their cost.

Whatever else, Wilf McGuinness cared deeply about the club, and when the job was taken away from him, it hurt him cruelly, so much so that it made him ill and he lost his hair.

To his eternal credit, he fought back to manage York City, then he developed further in Greece and spent many years as a trainer/physiotherapist with Bury before carving a niche for himself as an after-dinner speaker.

BORN	CORK, ROI 9TH OCTOBER 1927
JOINED UNITED	JUNE 1971 FROM LEICESTER CITY
FIRST GAME IN CHARGE	DERBY COUNTY (A) DIV. 1 - 14/08/1971
LAST GAME IN CHARGE	CRYSTAL PALACE (A) DIV. 1 - 16/12/1972

FRANK O'FARRELL					
COMP.	P	W	D	L	F	A
LEAGUE	64	24	16	24	89	95
FAC	7	3	3	1	12	5
LC	10	3	5	2	14	11
TOTAL	81	30	24	27	115	111

FRANK O'FARRELL

UNITED MANAGERIAL CAREER:
MANAGER JUNE 1971 – DECEMBER 1972

PREVIOUSLY MANAGED:
TORQUAY UNITED, LEICESTER CITY

LATER MANAGED:
CARDIFF CITY, IRAN, TORQUAY UNITED

As Denis Law put it so aptly, Frank O'Farrell came to Old Trafford a stranger and he left a stranger. He had been recruited from Leicester with quite a decent pedigree, but he was part of the West Ham school of coaching, which never found great favour with me, and, for good or ill, he was the first modern manager of Manchester United to have no previous connection with the club.

Frank faced a major rebuilding task, but at least he had plenty of money at his disposal. He brought in Martin Buchan, who proved to be a magnificent signing, and he was horribly unlucky to lose another expensive buy, Ian Storey-Moore, to injury. But other important purchases, such as Ted Macdougall and Wyn Davies, did not meet with universal acclaim and he made an ill-advised attempt to turn the striker, Alan Gowling,

> *'I thought that the job proved far too big for Frank, that his judgement was found to be sorely wanting and that he and the club had nothing in common.'*

into a wing-half when the team's desperate need was for a top-quality specialist in that key position.

I thought that the job proved far too big for Frank, that his judgement was found to be sorely wanting and that he and the club had nothing in common.

Perhaps he was in awe of the status of people like George Best, Denis Law and Bobby Charlton. Certainly he wasn't popular with anybody, which might not have mattered had he been successful, but he wasn't.

True, the George Best situation must have been a nightmare, but if you're the manager you've got to find a way of dealing with it. To be fair, neither Matt nor Wilf had been able to resolve it, and it had deteriorated by the time it got to Frank.

Probably, and it's easy to say with hindsight, the first thing Frank should have done when he walked into Old Trafford was to put George on the list. It would have been awesomely difficult, but it would have shown who was boss. Perhaps he wasn't big enough to do it, perhaps he wasn't allowed to.

He presided over a wonderful start to 1971/72 when United went top in the autumn, but Best was carrying the team on his own, as Bobby Charlton admitted later. If Frank had gone out and bought the right players when that purple patch was happening, it could have been a different story.

When you're at a club that's won top prizes, and most of the players who helped to win them have gone, you can't twiddle your thumbs and talk about what might have happened if there had been no problems. You have to do something about it, and he didn't. Whether that was his fault, or the board's, I don't know. But somebody had to take the blame, and I think it resides with Frank O'Farrell. They tell me he was a very religious, good-living man. Perhaps he was in the wrong game. Certainly, he could never handle life at Old Trafford.

PUT IT THERE: Matt Busby welcomes Frank O'Farrell as the new boss of Manchester United. Club chairman Louis Edwards (centre) looks on.

BORN	PERSHAW, GLASGOW 24TH AUGUST 1928
JOINED UNITED	DECEMBER 1972 FROM SCOTLAND
FIRST GAME IN CHARGE	LEEDS UNITED (H) DIV.1 - 23/12/1972
HONOURS	FA CUP 1976/77 SECOND DIVISION CHAMPIONS 1974/75
LAST GAME IN CHARGE	LIVERPOOL (WEMBLEY) FAC - 21/05/1977

TOMMY DOCHERTY

COMP.	P	W	D	L	F	A
LEAGUE	188	84	49	55	267	208
FAC	19	12	3	4	28	18
LC	17	9	4	4	35	22
EUROPE	4	2	2	2	3	4
TOTAL	228	107	58	65	333	252

'In 1973/74 United were absolutely awful, as bad as I've ever known them, but the board retained faith in Docherty and he repaid them by winning the Second Division championship at the first attempt.'

TOMMY DOCHERTY

UNITED MANAGERIAL CAREER:

MANAGER DECEMBER 1972 – JULY 1977

PREVIOUSLY MANAGED:

CHELSEA, ROTHERHAM UNITED, QUEEN'S PARK RANGERS, ASTON VILLA, OPORTO, SCOTLAND

LATER MANAGED:

DERBY COUNTY, QUEEN'S PARK RANGERS, SYDNEY OLYMPIC (TWICE), PRESTON NORTH END, SOUTH MELBOURNE, WOLVERHAMPTON WANDERERS

Tommy Docherty appeared to have plenty going for him when he arrived at Old Trafford, having enjoyed a degree of success in charge of Scotland, with both Willie Morgan and Denis Law in his side.

Initial impressions were favourable as, against all the odds, he kept United up in 1972/73 after taking over a club at the bottom of the table in mid-season. But then, just when we thought he'd done the hard part, and that now he'd get the team sorted out, he led them to relegation in the next campaign.

In 1973/74 United were absolutely awful, as bad as I've ever known them, but the board retained faith in Docherty and he repaid them by winning the Second Division championship at the first attempt. In fairness, that remoulded team wasn't bad. It was hard-working, it always tried to attack, and it contained one or two people who could play, like Stuart Pearson and Steve Coppell. Once promoted, there was even a stage during the following season when it looked like United had a genuine chance of winning the title.

But when you look back at some of the people he signed, and how he fiddled about with players, they never had a price, certainly not in the long term. Here's a man who talked about George Graham being the new Gunter Netzer, then George turned out to be so much the new Gunter Netzer that pretty soon he was released in exchange for Ron Davies, who never got a first-team start. Some of Docherty's deals were strange, you might say bizarre, by any standards. It was impossible to comprehend what he was doing half the time.

A lot of people disapproved of the way he got rid of Denis Law, Tony Dunne and David Sadler, all less than honourably. It seemed that he fell out with almost everybody at one time or another, and there weren't many people with nice things to say about him by the time he left.

His situation worsened when he got involved in a law suit with Willie Morgan, which did nothing to help his image.

There were rumblings of other unsavoury disagreements behind the scenes, and he put the lid on things by embarking on a love affair with the wife of physiotherapist Laurie Brown.

His eventual sacking was a very difficult decision. If he'd run off with the wife of someone who wasn't a member of staff, then it wouldn't have cost him his job. But to run off with Laurie's wife made you wonder where it might end. If he could do that and get away with it, he could have had an affair with one of the player's wives, or anyone else he wanted. It seemed he had no respect for the people around him.

So I think United were absolutely correct to get rid of him. In a football club, people are living in each other's pockets, they're travelling together all the time, they're supposed to be part of a team working towards the same end.

Clearly the manager has to have a harmonious relationship with the physiotherapist, so that players' injuries can be evaluated, but how could Laurie talk dispassionately to the man who had just stolen his wife? You couldn't possibly get rid of Laurie Brown, because you'd be persecuting the poor man twice over, so Docherty had to go.

Football-wise, he will always be remembered as the man who took Manchester United into the Second Division, and although his team won the FA Cup shortly before his dismissal, I don't think it was anything like outstanding by Old Trafford standards.

BEFORE THE FALL: Tommy Docherty, with Jimmy Nicholl in close attendance, celebrates the FA Cup Final victory over Liverpool at Wembley in 1977. Soon afterwards the controversial Scot was sacked by the club over his love affair with the physiotherapist's wife.

BORN	ISLINGTON, LONDON 6TH APRIL 1930
JOINED UNITED	JULY 1977 FROM QUEEN'S PARK RANGERS
FIRST GAME IN CHARGE	LIVERPOOL (WEMBLEY) CS - 13/08/1977
HONOURS	CHARITY SHIELD 1977 (SHARED)
LAST GAME IN CHARGE	NORIWCH CITY (H) DIV. 1 - 25/04/1981

DAVE SEXTON						
COMP.	P	W	D	L	F	A
LEAGUE	168	70	53	45	243	197
FAC	18	7	7	4	27	19
LC	8	2	0	6	11	16
EUROPE	6	2	3	1	9	8
OTHERS	1	0	1	0	0	0
TOTAL	201	81	63	56	290	240

DAVE SEXTON

UNITED MANAGERIAL CAREER:
MANAGER JULY 1977 – APRIL 1981

PREVIOUSLY MANAGED:
LEYTON ORIENT, CHELSEA, QUEEN'S PARK RANGERS

LATER MANAGED:
COVENTRY CITY

Dave Sexton was another from the West Ham academy of soccer which produced Frank O'Farrell, but I don't hold that against him, and pass my opinion on him purely on his merits as manager of Manchester United.

Dave is known widely as a quiet, religious sort of person, a man of integrity who thinks deeply about the game, and whenever I met him he did nothing to dispel that image. I found him to be a very nice fellow, and it was easy to understand why there are plenty of players from his various clubs who won't hear a word against him.

Yet my brief encounters with Dave deepened my surprise that he retained the brash and opinionated Tommy Cavanagh, Tommy Docherty's number-two at Old Trafford, as his own assistant. Sexton had done well as a coach at Arsenal, then as manager with Chelsea and Queen's Park Rangers, and Cavanagh, to put it frankly, wasn't in the same league. In fact, the two men seemed to have nothing whatsoever in common and I simply couldn't imagine them ever being able to work together.

I regret to say that I could never understand Dave Sexton's stewardship of the club from first to last. His choice of players and his footballing philosophy appeared to be so totally un-United.

For example, I was dismayed by his rejection of Gordon Hill, who was not everyone's cup of tea but who had performed brilliantly for several seasons as a goal-scoring outside-left. It turned out that Gordon didn't suit Dave because he didn't tackle back, which typified the new manager's ultra-cautious methods and the timidity of his selections.

I don't think I'll ever forgive him for getting rid of Andy Ritchie, I thought Joe Jordan was wrong for the club . . . I could go on and on, but it's too painful.

If you come to Manchester United, you've got to have a smile on your face, but Dave never managed that, mirroring

'Dave Sexton's teams were dull, boring and uninteresting . . . apart from that, they were brilliant!'

the similarly dismal O'Farrell approach of several years earlier.

In fairness to Docherty, although I couldn't agree with much of what he did, at least he cracked a smile, and eventually his team played with a smile on its face, too.

Dave Sexton's teams were dull, boring, uninteresting . . . apart from that, they were brilliant!

RON ATKINSON

UNITED MANAGERIAL CAREER:
MANAGER JULY 1981 – NOVEMBER 1986

PREVIOUSLY MANAGED:
CAMBRIDGE UNITED, WEST BROMWICH ALBION

LATER MANAGED:
WEST BROMWICH ALBION, ATLETICO MADRID, SHEFFIELD WEDNESDAY, ASTON VILLA, COVENTRY CITY, NOTTINGHAM FOREST

BORN	LIVERPOOL 18TH MARCH 1939
JOINED UNITED	JUNE 1981 FROM WEST BROMWICH ALBION
FIRST GAME IN CHARGE	COVENTRY CITY (A) DIV. 1 - 29/08/1981
UNITED HONOURS	FA CUP 1982/3, 1984/5 CHARITY SHIELD 1983
LAST GAME IN CHARGE	SOUTHAMPTON (A) LC - 4/11/1986

RON ATKINSON						
COMP.	P	W	D	L	F	A
LEAGUE	223	108	63	52	349	207
FAC	21	14	4	3	36	15
LC	28	16	5	7	49	24
EUROPE	18	7	7	4	25	18
OTHERS	2	1	0	1	2	2
TOTAL	292	146	79	67	461	266

Big Ron Atkinson could not have offered a more complete contrast to the dour days of Dave Sexton. He wasn't first choice, but at least the supporters could thank their lucky stars that they didn't end up with Lawrie McMenemy, who was reportedly approached. He had no idea at all, and I think he would have been disastrous for the club.

I first met Ron when he was manager of West Bromwich Albion and I handled Peter Barnes' transfer to the Hawthorns. I've been reasonably friendly with him ever since and I've got a fair bit of time for him, but that doesn't mean I agreed with everything he did. Far from it.

At the finish, I'm not sure that Ron really knew what he was doing at United. I think he might have misjudged the feeling, perhaps over-done the flamboyance. Although it was a big club, and they wanted a smile, also they wanted the manager to be serious about his work.

'I had great expectatations of Ron, because after dismal Dave we needed a boss to put smiles on people's faces, and there's no doubt that the big fella encouraged people to play and to express themselves.'

Yet to be fair, despite all the Champagne Charlie nonsense, there was no doubt that Ron knew his business. For instance, he was responsible for bringing in Eric Harrison, who eventually did such a marvellous job in developing the Scholes generation, and he signed Bryan Robson, one of United's most influential players of all time.

I had great expectatations of Ron, because after dismal Dave we needed a boss to put smiles on people's faces, and there's no doubt that the big fella encouraged people to play and to express themselves.

He can point to two FA Cup triumphs, his team never finished a season outside the First Division's top four, and there were two occasions when there was a genuine feeling that he was about to end the agonising wait for the League title.

In the middle of March 1984 United were top of the League on merit before subsiding disappointingly after accumulating a few injuries towards the death. Then there was 1985/86, when they won the first ten games and remained unbeaten until the 16th before it all blew up again.

Had he finished either of those seasons with the big prize, then Alex Ferguson would never have arrived at Old Trafford and Ron might even still be the manager in 2005. After all, when Fergie came, who would have thought he'd have been here for the best part of 20 years?

In the end, though, the lights went out so quickly for Atkinson it was hard to comprehend. Later the same thing happened to him at Aston Villa and Coventry, both when it was least expected. Does this indicate that he's not cut out for the long haul, for seeing things through? I don't know.

One of the most damning accusations levelled at Ron as United boss was that he never paid attention to the reserves or the juniors, that he neglected the youth system, concentrating all his energies on the seniors. Also, while he signed some footballers of the highest quality, some of his transfer-market dabblings were peculiar in the extreme.

Against all that, his saving graces were that his sides always tried to play nice football, that he collected one or two pieces of silverware and that there was always an upbeat feel to the club, a sense of optimism, when he was in charge.

Whatever anyone says about Ron Atkinson, I'm absolutely certain of one truth: he never was, or is, anti the coloured boys. In his West Brom days he had the likes of Cyrille Regis and Laurie Cunningham playing for him, and you don't become as well-liked as Ron if you are a racist.

The unfortunate business about Marcel Desailly was a slip of the tongue, an example of lazy language. To some degree, however, that episode epitomises Ron in that he always wants to be the clown, the Jack the Lad. He even made a record one

Christmas which proved only one point – that he was tone deaf!

Maybe one of his problems is that he always wanted to be somebody as a player, but he never reached the top level. During his managerial days, when he joined in five-a-sides in training, he would always try to do his party pieces, he never lost his enthusisasm for that, and if they didn't come off, people would have a smile at him. Disarmingly, it must be admitted, he was ready to laugh along with them.

I suppose there's always been a lot of the little boy in the big man. The one sure thing about Ron is that he'll never grow up.

ALEX FERGUSON

UNITED MANAGERIAL CAREER:
MANAGER NOVEMBER 1986 TO PRESENT

PREVIOUSLY MANAGED:
EAST STIRLINGSHIRE, ST MIRREN, ABERDEEN, SCOTLAND

ALEX FERGUSON						
COMP.	P	W	D	L	F	A
LEAGUE	731	411	188	132	1304	682
FAC	85	58	16	11	164	65
LC	68	42	8	18	114	71
EUROPE	136	70	39	27	242	129
OTHERS	17	5	5	7	19	21
TOTAL	1037	586	256	195	1843	968

BORN	GOVAN, GLASGOW 31ST DECEMBER 1941
JOINED UNITED	NOVEMBER 1986 FROM ABERDEEN
FIRST GAME IN CHARGE	OXFORD UNITED (A) DIV. 1 - 8/11/1986
UNITED HONOURS	EUROPEAN CUP 1998/9 ECWC 1990/1 PREMIERSHIP 1992/3, 1993/4, 1995/6, 1996/7, 1998/9, 1999/2000, 2000/1, 2002/3 FA CUP 1989/90, 1993/4, 1995/6, 1998/9, 2003/4 LEAGUE CUP 1991/2 INTER-CONTINENTAL CUP 1999 UEFA SUPER CUP 1991 FA CHARITY/COMMUNITY SHIELD 1990 (SHARED) 1993, 1994, 1996, 1997, 2003

However you look at it, Alex Ferguson has got to go down as one of the top football managers of all time. His record demands that level of recognition, and you wouldn't catch me arguing with it.

Alex deserves all the credit in the world for turning round the fortunes of our club, once the most successful in the land under Matt Busby before falling into a depressing sequence which saw it lurching from one disappointment to the next.

Manchester United had become mediocre, desperately so at times, and there seemed no end to it until Alex came along, though people tend to forget with the passing of years that he was not a worker of instant miracles.

The first four or so seasons of the Ferguson reign were not good. It wasn't just the results, though they were bad enough; it was the standard of the football, which was downright drab at times. I can even recall a number of long-standing camp-followers who swore they would never watch United again while Fergie was the manager. Mind, they all changed their views quickly enough as the corner was turned, and there are one or two of them who can't stay away from him now.

So how did Alex achieve what had eluded Wilf McGuinness, Tommy Docherty, Dave Sexton and Ron Atkinson before him? Well, I go along with the popular view that he instilled some much-needed professionalism and discipline into various areas of the club where it was conspicuously lacking, that his personal hunger to succeed was insatiable, and that he had the remarkable knack of extracting the same kind of commitment from a collection of very rich young men.

Much is made, too, of the man's self-belief, which I'm sure is immense and I'm certain has played a colossal part in his unprecedented success, as did the fact that, like Sir Matt, he hailed from a hard-working Scottish background which instilled in him a sound set of values. But there is another element which cannot be under-estimated when considering the rise and rise of Sir Alex. I am not denigrating his staggering achievements in the least when I venture the opinion that, as well as being the most successful manager in Manchester United's history, he has also been the luckiest since Sir Matt.

Now I know that statement could be seized upon and twisted by some malicious, unscrupulous tabloid headline-writer, but if it's examined in the proper context, I believe it is perfectly valid.

The most extravagant stroke of fortune was the signing of Eric Cantona, which was completely unplanned, and followed no more than a speculative inquiry when a Leeds director had called to ask about the availability of Denis Irwin. Would the glorious Old Trafford renaissance have come about without the Frenchman's inspiration? We'll never know for sure, but I have to doubt that it would.

Then there is the likelihood that Alex owed his continuing employment by the club in 1990 to Mark Robins' FA Cup winner at Nottingham Forest. I know Martin Edwards has said that the manag-

'I am firmly in agreement with the essential logic behind golfer Gary Player's assertion that the harder an individual works, the luckier he gets - and that has certainly been the case with Alex Ferguson.'

er's job wasn't in jeopardy, but with United near the bottom of the League at the time and fans growing ominously restive, it's difficult to see how he could have survived for much longer if they had gone out of the cup.

A little later that year Fergie's fortune continued when the Jim Leighton-Les Sealey FA Cup Final drama ended with a trophy when it could easily have gone the other way, and that provided the platform for further success. Then, after his first League title gave him a security which no other United boss since Busby had enjoyed, there came the staggering bonus of 'the class of '92', that magical group of talented young men who formed the basis of another new team. That's never been repeated and it's not likely to be in the foreseeable future.

Of course, Alex deserves enormous credit for presiding over the revitalisation of the club's renowned youth policy, which had fallen into sad decline, but there has to be a certain amount of luck involved. If it was an exact science you'd be producing half a dozen decent new players every year, whereas I'm sure that any manager would be delighted with one uncut gem each season. Having said all that, I am firmly in agreement with the essential logic behind golfer Gary Player's assertion that the harder an individual works, the luckier he gets - and that has certainly been the case with Alex Ferguson.

As the League titles and FA Cups continued to mount up, Fergie's position became ever stronger, and finally his celebrity was cemented for all time by the treble, culminating with that breathtaking injury-time victory over Bayern Munich. I don't think anyone would deny that United enjoyed the bounce of the ball that night in Barcelona, and if things had worked out differently, then who knows?

That left Alex virtually impregnable and, in most subsequent campaigns, he has continued to bring home the bacon. Reasonably enough, he has spent heavily to do it, though while there have been fabulous signings such as Ruud van Nistelrooy and Jaap Stam (till he fell out of favour), the transfer record has not been all sweetness and light, as the purchases of Messrs Veron, Forlan, Blomqvist, Taibi and Fortune would indicate.

For all that, I must stress my untold admiration for his fantastic efforts in achieving more for the club than could be imagined in any fan's wildest dreams. Long may it continue, Boss.

JOHN'S SQUAD
(PLAYERS LISTED ALPHABETICALLY)

Picking my dream Manchester United team would have been an impossible task; even selecting this mouth-watering squad of 30 has caused untold mortification over the handful of truly magnificent performers whom I have been obliged to leave out if I was to keep within reasonable numbers. I know that, essentially, this type of activity is meaningless, but also it is immensely pleasurable, and I am convinced of one thing. Armed with the collection of players named below, their lucky manager would be equipped to take on any opponents who have ever walked on God's good earth.

GOALKEEPERS

REG ALLEN
HARRY GREGG
PETER SCHMEICHEL
ALEX STEPNEY

FULL-BACKS

ARTHUR ALBISTON
JOHN ASTON
ROGER BYRNE
JOHN CAREY
TONY DUNNE
DENIS IRWIN

CENTRE-HALVES

STEVE BRUCE
PAUL MCGRATH
GARY PALLISTER
JAAP STAM

MIDFIELDERS

BOBBY CHARLTON
EDDIE COLMAN
PADDY CRERAND
DUNCAN EDWARDS
ROY KEANE
BRYAN ROBSON
PAUL SCHOLES
NOBBY STILES

ATTACKERS

GEORGE BEST
ERIC CANTONA
RYAN GIGGS
DENIS LAW
CHARLIE MITTEN
TOMMY TAYLOR
RUUD VAN NISTELROOY
DENNIS VIOLLET

And now I'm going to cheat, just a little. After spoiling myself by making the above choice, I realised that there was one crucial name missing. So I'm going to indulge myself even further by adding it to the list without dropping one of the greats to make way. He's only been around for a very short period, but I don't think anyone will argue with his inclusion.

His name? WAYNE ROONEY.

ARSENAL v MANCHESTER UNITED
BY BEN, JOHN'S GRANDSON, AGED 11

Bust-ups, scuffles
Goals and cards
Passes and penalties
Arsenal v United
What a game

Vieira, Keane
Cards all round
Rooney, Campbell
Goals suspected
60,000 fans roaring aloud

Ronaldo, Cole
Watch for the step-overs
Henry, Ferdinand
Titanic clash
Ljungberg, Heinze
The new Argie's game

Fans roaring 'United!'
The Gooners screaming
'Vieira . . . whooa!'
Full time is here
And United have won!

Bottom Right:
MEET THE DOHERTYS:
lining up behind my wife,
Barbara, and myself are, left
to right, grandson Ben, son
Paul with grandson Jacob on
board, Barbara (Paul's wife),
grandson James, son Mark,
daughter Tracy and grandson
Caine.

Below:
A BOY AND HIS HERO:
Ben, my grandson and the
author of the poem on the
right, meets Ole Gunnar
Solskjaer, who could not have
been more kind and gave the
youngster a memory to
treasure all his life.

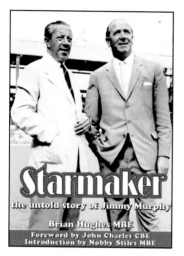

STARMAKER

THE UNTOLD STORY OF JIMMY MURPHY
BY BRIAN HUGHES MBE
£16.95 - 268 PP - HARDBACK

'My first signing and my most important'
SIR MATT BUSBY

The 'greatest coach in the world' trained the likes of George Best, Duncan Edwards, Bobby Charlton and Dennis Viollet and saved the club in the the wake of the Munich air disaster.

VIOLLET

LIFE OF A LEGENDARY GOALSCORER
BY BRIAN HUGHES
£10.95 - 334PP - PAPERBACK

A legendary goalscorer and Busby Babe, Dennis Viollet's career took in tragedy and triumph in equal measure. As a player he thrilled thousands as an outstanding teenage footballer with Manchester United's all-conquering Babes. Later, having survived the Munich air disaster, Viollet broke Manchester United's record for goals in a season - a mark he still holds.

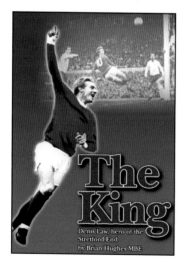

THE KING

DENIS LAW, HERO OF THE STRETFORD END
BY BRIAN HUGHES MBE
£18.95 - 403PP - HARDBACK

Denis Law was hero and villain all rolled into one: a player capable of incredible feats of skill and power, all carried off with the knowing smile and villainous touch that put some in mind of a Piccadilly pickpocket. To Mancunians, this son of an Aberdonian trawlerman became part of the fabric of the city; first as a dynamic frontman for the Sky Blues and later as an all-action hero at Matt Busby's United.

BACK FROM THE BRINK

by Justin Blundell

£10.95 - 480pp - paperback

To be published:

October 2005

The Manchester United
Crisis 1919-1932
by Justin Blundell

The twenty-odd years that separated the First World War from the Second World War have often been referred to as the long weekend. This book follows the fortunes of Manchester United from Friday night to Sunday afternoon. It is the story of how a pre-war giant fell asleep and very nearly did not wake up again. It is the story of record highs and record lows, of protests, punch-ups and revolts, of heroes, villains, wizards and saviours, of great escapes and even greater cock-ups, of joy and pain, tragedy and despair. Amazingly, it is a story that has never properly been told before. Hopefully, it has been now.

Back from the Brink chronicles the departure of the father of Manchester United, John Henry Davies and the arrival of its saviour and inspiration James Gibson. The debt modern United fans owe these two men cannot be underestimated. Had it not been for Davies there would be no Manchester United - when Newton Heath were bankrupted in 1902 he changed the name of the club found them a new stadium and, for the first time, injected the style and panache now known throughout the football world.

As for Gibson, he took a floundering club playing before dwindling support and introduced such notions as corporate hospitality, the tracksuit manager and a youth system as early as 1931. Thus Gibson paved the way for Busby and Ferguson - yet this tale concentrates on an era before glory and Manchester United became inextricably linked.

As United fans approach another era of uncertainty regarding their club, Back from the Brink is the first proper examination of a period during which the club won nothing but laid the groundwork for the club's post-war success.

The Birth of the Babes
Manchester United Youth Policy 1950-1957
Tony Whelan
Foreword by Sir Alex Ferguson

BIRTH OF THE BABES

by Tony Whelan

Foreword by Sir Alex Ferguson

£12.95 - 125pp - Landscape A4 paperback

Contains over 100 historic images

In *The Birth of the Babes*, current Manchester United Academy coach Tony Whelan examines not only the roots of Matt Busby's socialism, his approach to the care of his players, but illustrates the system of scouts, coaches and trainers that made Manchester United a prototype for the youth systems of today. Beautifully illustrated with photographs and memorabilia culled from the private collections of many of the youth players of the time, *The Birth of the Babes* is essential reading for anyone interested in the pre-Munich era when United took English football by storm.

COMPLETIST'S DELIGHT
The Full Empire Back List

ISBN	Title	Author	Price
1901746003	SF Barnes: His Life and Times	A Searle	£14.95
1901746011	Chasing Glory	R Grillo	£7.95
190174602X	Three Curries and a Shish Kebab	R Bott	£7.99
1901746038	Seasons to Remember	D Kirkley`	£6.95
1901746046	Cups For Cock-Ups+	A Shaw	£8.99
1901746054	Glory Denied	R Grillo	£8.95
1901746062	Standing the Test of Time	B Alley	£16.95
1901746070	The Encyclopaedia of Scottish Cricket	D Potter	£9.99
1901746089	The Silent Cry	J MacPhee	£7.99
1901746097	The Amazing Sports Quiz Book	F Brockett	£6.99
1901746100	I'm Not God, I'm Just a Referee	R Entwistle	£7.99
1901746119	The League Cricket Annual Review 2000	ed. S. Fish	£6.99
1901746143	Roger Byrne - Captain of the Busby Babes	I McCartney	£16.95
1901746151	The IT Manager's Handbook	D Miller	£24.99
190174616X	Blue Tomorrow	M Meehan	£9.99
1901746178	Atkinson for England	G James	£5.99
1901746186	Think Cricket	C Bazalgette	£6.00
1901746194	The League Cricket Annual Review 2001	ed. S. Fish	£7.99
1901746208	Jock McAvoy - Fighting Legend *	B Hughes	£9.95
1901746216	The Tommy Taylor Story*	B Hughes	£8.99
1901746224	Willie Pep*+	B Hughes	£9.95
1901746232	For King & Country*+	B Hughes	£8.95
1901746240	Three In A Row	P Windridge	£7.99
1901746259	Viollet - Life of a legendary goalscorer+PB	R Cavanagh	£16.95
1901746267	Starmaker	B Hughes	£16.95
1901746283	Morrissey's Manchester	P Gatenby	£5.99
1901746305	The IT Manager's Handbook (e-book)	D Miller	£17.99
1901746313	Sir Alex, United & Me	A Pacino	£8.99
1901746321	Bobby Murdoch, Different Class	D Potter	£10.99
190174633X	Goodison Maestros	D Hayes	£5.99
1901746348	Anfield Maestros	D Hayes	£5.99
1901746364	Out of the Void	B Yates	£9.99
1901746356	The King - Denis Law, hero of the...	B Hughes	£17.95
1901746372	The Two Faces of Lee Harvey Oswald	G B Fleming	£8.99
1901746380	My Blue Heaven	D Friend	£10.99
1901746399	Viollet - life of a legendary goalscorer	B Hughes	£11.99
1901746402	Quiz Setting Made Easy	J Dawson	£7.99
1901746437	Catch a Falling Star	N Young	£17.95
1901746453	Birth of the Babes	T Whelan	£12.95
190174647X	Back from the Brink	J Blundell	£10.95

* Originally published by Collyhurst & Moston Lads Club
+ Out of print   PB Superceded by Paperback edition

To order any of these books email: enquiries@empire-uk.com or call 0161 872 3319.